Democratic Theory and Post-Communist Change

ROBERT D. GREY
Editor

Grinnell College

Prentice Hall
Upper Saddle River, New Jersey 07458

Library of Congress Cataloging-in-Publication Data

Democratic theory and post-communist change / [edited by] Robert D. Grey.—1st ed.
p. cm.
Includes bibliographical references and index.
ISBN 0-13-190448-5
1. Democracy. 2. Post-communism. 3. Post-communism—Europe, Eastern. 4. Post-communism—Former Soviet republics. 5. Democracy—Europe, Eastern. 6. Democracy—Former Soviet republics. 7. Europe, Eastern—Politics and government—1989– 8. Former Soviet republics—Politics and government. I. Grey, Robert D.
JC423.D4428 1997
321.8—dc20 95–26818
CIP

Editor in chief: Nancy Roberts
Acquisitions editor: Michael Bickerstaff
Editorial/production supervision: Marianne Hutchinson (Pine Tree Composition, Inc.)
Cover art: Gerald Bustamente/Stock Illustration Source
Editorial assistant: Anita Castro
Buyer: Mary Ann Gloriande

This book was set in 10/12 Times Roman by Pine Tree Composition, Inc., and was printed and bound by Courier Companies, Inc. The cover was printed by Phoenix Color Corp.

Simon & Schuster/A Viacom Company
Upper Saddle River, New Jersey 07458

Printed in the United States of America
10 9 8 7 6 5 4 3 2 1

ISBN 0-13-190448-5

PRENTICE-HALL INTERNATIONAL (UK) LIMITED, *London*
PRENTICE-HALL OF AUSTRALIA PTY. LIMITED, *Sydney*
PRENTICE-HALL CANADA INC., *Toronto*
PRENTICE-HALL HISPANOAMERICANA, S.A., *Mexico*
PRENTICE-HALL OF INDIA PRIVATE LIMITED, *New Delhi*
PRENTICE-HALL OF JAPAN, INC., *Tokyo*
SIMON & SCHUSTER ASIA PTE. LTD., *Singapore*
EDITORA PRENTICE-HALL DO BRASIL, LTDA., *Rio de Janeiro*

CONTENTS

PREFACE *vii*

CONTRIBUTORS *xi*

1 INTRODUCTION: HOW TO UNDERSTAND THE PROBABLE POLITICAL FUTURE OF THE FORMERLY COMMUNIST STATES, ***Robert D. Grey*** *1*

The Rise of Communism and Its Transformation into Stalinism 2
Communist Rule: Its Strengths and Weaknesses 6
The Decline and Fall of Communism 9
Democracy in the Post-Communist World 11
Democratic Theory and Post-Communist Change 15
Conclusion 18
Notes 19
References 20

2 CHOICES FACING THE BUILDERS OF A LIBERAL DEMOCRACY, ***William M. Reisinger*** *24*

The Path to Modern Democratic Ideals 25
Democratic Processes 29
Conditions within a Democracy 38
Democracy and the Post-Communist Countries 43
Appendix 2.1: Selected Definitions of Democracy 44
Notes 46
References 48

3 **ESTABLISHING AND STRENGTHENING DEMOCRACY,** ***William M. Reisinger*** ***52***

Democratization 53
Theoretical Cluster 1: Societal Modernization as a Precondition for Democratization 54
Theoretical Cluster 2: Comparative Historical Approaches 58
Theoretical Cluster 3: Intra-Elite Bargaining and Transitions to Democracy 67
Theoretical Cluster 4: Constitutional Design and the Stability of Democracy 70
Conclusion 72
Notes 73
References 74

4 **THE ROLE OF MASS VALUES,** ***Kristen Hill Maher*** ***79***

Do "The People" Matter to Democracy? 80
Orientations Supportive of Democracy 86
Political Orientations in Post-Communist Societies 93
What Can We Expect? 99
Notes 101
References 105

5 **CONSTITUTIONALISM AND THE RULE OF LAW: THEORETICAL PERSPECTIVES,** ***John Reitz*** ***111***

Meaning of "Rule of Law" and "Constitutionalism" and Communist Attitudes toward These Terms 112
The Rule of Law and Its Relationship to Democracy and Free Markets 121
Transition to the Rule of Law 130
Conclusion 135
Notes 136
References 140

6 **PROGRESS IN BUILDING INSTITUTIONS FOR THE RULE OF LAW,** ***John Reitz*** ***144***

Strengthening the Independence of the Legal Profession 146
Development of Forms of Judicial Review 159
Conclusion 174
Notes 177
References 184

Constitutions and Statutes 184
Secondary Literature 185

7 **POLITICAL INSTITUTIONS AND DEMOCRATIC GOVERNANCE IN DIVIDED SOCIETIES,** ***Vicki L. Hesli*** ***190***

Theories of Ethnic Conflict 192
National Separatism and the Demise of the Soviet State 198
The Ethnic Factor in Political Development 201
Strategies for Accommodating Ethnicity through Democratic Structures and Procedures 206
Conclusion 213
Notes 213
References 214

8 **ECONOMIC POLICY AND DEMOCRATIZATION IN THE FORMER COMMUNIST STATES,** ***John H. Mutti*** ***217***

The Ambiguities of Economic and Political Transitions 217
Stabilization Policy 223
Structural Adjustment and Economic Policy in the Longer Run 233
Conclusion 243
Notes 245
References 245

9 **THE IMPACT OF EXTERNAL FACTORS ON THE FUTURE OF DEMOCRACY IN THE FSU AND EASTERN EUROPE,** ***Robert D. Grey*** ***248***

International Powers and the Promotion of Democracy during the Cold War 249
International Powers and the Promotion of Democracy after the Cold War 252
Modes of Assistance: Support for a Market Economy 256
Noneconomic Modes of External Assistance 257
The International Context and Democratization 258
Conclusion 262
Notes 263
References 264

INDEX ***267***

Preface

A major political transformation swept much of the world during the 1970s and early 1980s. In southern Europe fascist dictatorships collapsed or were overthrown to be replaced by fledgling democracies. The military dictatorships that had dominated Latin American politics also began to turn over power to civilians. Political parties were legalized, elections held, and democracy returned to the continent.

In response to these developments, the scholarly community returned to questions that had long animated it. Under what circumstances will authoritarian government give way to democratic governance? Will the resulting democracies endure? In the late 1980s and early 1990s a theoretically rich literature began to emerge. Such authors as Robert Dahl (*Democracy and Its Critics*), Samuel P. Huntington (*The Third Wave*), Giuseppe Di Palma (*To Craft Democracies*), and Adam Przeworski (*Democracy and the Market*) engaged in vigorous scholarly debate. However, their debate was rapidly overtaken by events.

In 1989 communism collapsed in Eastern and Central Europe. In 1991 it suffered a similar fate in the Soviet Union simultaneously with the dissolution of that multi-ethnic state into fifteen separate new states. The political future of the twenty-seven new political systems is highly uncertain. For the authors of this volume these events provided two stimuli. The first was to join the scholarly debate by testing competing theories against the twenty-seven new cases. The second was to use those theories to make some sense out of what was happening in these countries.

There was a serendipitous conjunction of these political and intellectual developments: growing intellectual cooperation by scholars at two Iowa academic institutions and a Ford Foundation grant to promote just such cross-fertilization. This volume emerged from a joint seminar of faculty and students, funded by the Bridging Project on International Studies, a joint initiative of Grinnell College and the University of Iowa. A Ford Foundation grant to both institutions made it possible for an interdisciplinary team to study "Democratization in Eastern Europe and the Former Soviet Republics." Our group included faculty trained in political science, sociology, law, and economics as well as two Iowa graduate students in political science and two Grinnell undergraduates majoring in political science and history. In addition to the contributing authors, Donald Smith, Professor of Journalism and Mass Communication of the University of Iowa, was a regular participant, as were Monty Marshall, a Ph.D. candidate in political science at Iowa, and Jill Cetina and Scott Wittstruck, from Grinnell.

During academic year 1991–92 the group participated in a study group consisting of six day-long meetings. In the summer of 1992, we gathered for an intensive three-week seminar. We read and discussed appropriate theoretical material and recent empirical work. In addition, several distinguished outside scholars—Valerie Bunce of Cornell University, Gerhard Loewenberg of the University of Iowa, and Joel Moses of Iowa State University—presented their recent work and led discussions. This cross-institutional and cross-disciplinary interaction provided us all with new insights. To prepare ourselves and our students both to grasp relevant theoretical material and to make some sense out of what was happening in the former Soviet bloc, narrow specialization did not suffice.

For the summer, seminar participants prepared for group discussion papers synthesizing a particular set of theories and relevant current developments. We wrote these papers with an intended audience of undergraduate college students. Our participating undergraduate students were charged with providing feedback to the paper authors about clarity, organization, and overall utility as a learning resource.

At the end of the seminar, in early June, we concluded that the papers indeed merited continuing work on our part. Each author agreed to spend time revising to incorporate the suggestions of the seminar participants. Subsequently we met twice in the fall of 1992 and again in the spring of 1994 to discuss the revised versions of the papers. We believe that the resulting volume nicely synthesizes a history/analysis of developments in the former communist states and the recent outpouring of theoretical literature on the conditions for and processes of democratization.

The authors wish to express their gratitude to several institutions and individuals whose support was crucial to our project. The Ford Foundation should be praised for its encouragement of intellectual and pedagogical collaboration between two very different types of educational institutions. Administration and faculty at Grinnell College and the University of Iowa consider the Ford Foundation funded Bridging Project a major contributor to the growing collaboration between them. It has greatly enriched both international studies and interdisciplinary studies.

The Project is currently co-directed by Helen Scott, Associate Dean of Grinnell, and Virginia Dominguez, Director of the University of Iowa Center for International and Comparative Studies (CICS). The grant is administered by Kathryn Touré, Assistant Director of CICS, who supervised arrangements for group meetings when we met in Iowa City. Alice Breemer, Administrative Assistant to the Dean, oversaw our arrangements when we met at Grinnell.

The editor wishes to express his thanks to Charles Duke, Dean of the College, Grinnell College, for financial support for this project continuing over several years, and to Karen Groves and Fawn Black, faculty secretaries, who helped at numerous stages in the process. He also expresses his gratitude to Glasgow University and to Stephen White, Chair of the Politics Department at Glasgow, for his appointment as Honorary Senior Research Fellow at Glasgow for the winter and spring terms of 1995. That appointment provided him with the time and facilities necessary to complete this project. Finally, he wishes to thank his wife Mary for contributing emotional support, as well as vital editorial skills.

Contributors

Robert D. Grey is a professor of political science at Grinnell College. He received his B.A. from Wesleyan University and his doctorate from Yale University. Early in his career, he worked on African politics and African foreign policy, but subsequently moved into Soviet foreign policy in Africa and into Soviet/Russian domestic politics. He has published on these subjects in *Coexistence,* the *Journal of Modern African Studies,* and *Slavic Review.*

Vicki L. Hesli is an assistant professor in the department of political science at the University of Iowa. She received her doctorate from the University of Minnesota and is co-author of two books on South Korea (with John Turner), co-editor of *Public Opinion and Regime Change* (with Arthur Miller and William Reisinger), and co-author of articles on Russia, Ukraine, and Lithuania appearing in the *American Political Science Review, Europe-Asia Studies*, and *Slavic Review.*

Kristen Hill Maher is a Ph.D. candidate in Comparative Politics and Social Theory at the University of California, Irvine. She is a co-author of a recent article in the *British Journal of Political Science.* Her current research addresses issues of trust and identity in the emerging nations.

John H. Mutti is the Sidney Meyer Professor of International Economics at Grinnell College. He received his B.A. from Earlham College and his Ph.D. from the University of Wisconsin. He served as a Peace Corps Volunteer working with agricultural cooperatives in Colombia. He has analyzed international trade, investment, and taxation issues in numerous academic publications and in government positions at the U.S. Treasury Department and the Council of Economic Advisors. Mutti has been a consultant on aspects of tax and trade policy reform in Colombia, Guatemala, and Indonesia.

WILLIAM M. REISINGER is Associate Professor of Political Science at the University of Iowa. Reisinger received his Ph.D. from the University of Michigan. His research has concerned Soviet-East European relations, Soviet elite politics, and post-Soviet public values, political behavior, and foreign policy preferences. He is the author of *Energy and the Soviet Bloc* as well as articles in the *American Political Science Review, British Journal of Political Science, International Organization, International Studies Quarterly, Slavic Review,* and other scholarly journals.

JOHN REITZ is a professor at the University of Iowa College of Law and a specialist in the comparative study of legal systems. Reitz attended Harvard College (B.A.) and the University of Michigan Law School (J.D.). His teaching and research interests include the relationship between legal, political, and economic systems; comparative contract law; comparative economic regulation; and the law of the European Community (now Union). During 1989–1990, he held scholarships from Fulbright and the German Marshall Fund of the United States to conduct research at the University of Muenster, Germany, where he also guest-taught during the summer of 1994.

CHAPTER
1

Introduction: How to Understand the Probable Political Future of the Formerly Communist States

ROBERT D. GREY

In 1989 communism collapsed in eastern and central Europe. In 1991, it suffered a similar fate in the Soviet Union, simultaneously with the dissolution of that multi-ethnic state into fifteen separate new states. The political future of the twenty-seven new political systems[1] is highly uncertain. Although the political leaders of all of these states professed a commitment to democracy, the genuineness of that commitment was open to question.

Many, but not all, of the new leaders had spent most of their adult careers as leaders of their countries' communist parties. Even the few leaders[2] who had had "careers" as leading dissidents had spent their whole adult lives as citizens of communist states. In neither case were there strong reasons to accept leadership understanding of democracy as equivalent to the comparable understanding of leaders of the long stable democracies of the west.

Even if one were to accept the new leaders as genuine democrats in some conventional sense(s), it is not clear that conditions are appropriate for the introduction and consolidation of democracy. The historical record is not promising. The new states emerging from the former Soviet Union (FSU) have had no experience of full or successful democracy.[3] After World War I, many of the new states of eastern and central Europe, created out of parts of the former Austro-Hungarian Empire, the former Ottoman Empire and the former Russian Empire, had adopted democratic constitutions. Full democracy, however, survived only in Czechoslovakia.[4]

Moreover, the new democracies face daunting problems. In the economic sphere, the communist bloc had achieved, at very high cost, significant economic successes, outstripping most third world states, albeit not approaching the wealth of the industrialized countries of the West and Japan. They had achieved industrial economies and moderately high standards of living for their populations. Moreover, as communist systems, they had promised to their citizens, and to a great extent delivered, very low unemployment, and subsidized food, housing, transportation, education, and medical care. However, by the late 1980s, these economies were in serious difficulties, with declining or negative growth rates, extremely low productivity, and large and growing external debt. In the short term, the effort to transform communist economies into market ones threatens to exacerbate these tendencies, as well as add to them factory bankruptcies, growing unemployment, inflation rates approaching hyperinflation, and a generally declining standard of living.

A further obstacle to successful democratization is the ethnic heterogeneity of many of these states. This problem was manifested most immediately and forcefully in the post-communist collapse of three multi-ethnic states, the USSR, Czechoslovakia, and Yugoslavia. This heterogeneity raises the specter of international wars, such as that between "Yugoslavia" (or Serbia) and Croatia, and further threatens the domestic peace of Bosnia, Romania, Bulgaria, Slovakia, and others. Democracy can hardly thrive under such conditions.

It is not only their present circumstances that affect the likelihood of successful democratization in these countries. The character of their communist systems had been affected by such factors as their size, geographical location, the friendliness and military power of their neighbors, their state of industrialization, the character of their dominant religion, and numerous other factors. Perhaps the most important of those was the character of their pre-communist history.

Similarly post-communist states do not arise out of nowhere. They have a communist history, of substantial duration and of traumatic character. The legacies of the communist period drive their politics in certain directions, while foreclosing other directions. While I cannot do justice to this complex and varied history in a few pages, it seems necessary to provide at least the basic background.

THE RISE OF COMMUNISM AND ITS TRANSFORMATION INTO STALINISM

In February 1917, the Tsarist regime that had ruled Russia for centuries toppled. After less than a year of rule, its successor, a "provisional" or transitional government, was overthrown by a communist coup. While the Tsarist regime had begun the industrial development of Russia, the communists inherited a country still largely rural and agricultural. While in the twelve years preceding the revolution the Tsarist autocracy had moved, in a very limited way, toward constitutionalism and democracy, the political tradition the communists inherited was overwhelmingly authoritarian.

The communists who came to power in October 1917 regarded themselves as followers of the ideas of Karl Marx. Marx had devoted most of his intellectual energies to an analysis of the character of capitalist economies, arguing that their dynamic was such that they would inevitably be overthrown, and replaced by socialist economies and democratic political systems.[5] However, Marx had spent little time outlining either desirable structures for such systems, or policies they should pursue. Moreover, he had assumed that socialist revolutions would occur only in economies that had achieved a highly developed capitalist industrialization. In such economies, the problem of industrializing the country would have been solved by capitalism, and socialism could turn its attention to other problems.

When they came to power, then, the communists confronted two intellectual problems: (1) they had taken power in a context other than that Marx had predicted, a context in which problems that capitalism was supposed to solve were still on their agenda, and (2) Marx had provided them with little guidance as to what they were supposed to do with that power. Intellectual problems, however, were far from their most pressing problems.

Russia, after all, was still in, and losing, a world war. Economic problems that had led to the fall of the autocracy and the overthrow of the provisional government continued. Moreover, the communists, although they had substantial support from the workers of St. Petersburg, Moscow, and a few other cities, as well as from soldiers at the front, had significant urban opposition and almost no support in the countryside, a major drawback in a country that remained overwhelmingly rural in character.

Early communist policies were, in substantial part, a response not to the dictates of Marxist thought, or even more narrowly, to the revisions of that thought that their leader, V.I. Lenin, had introduced, but to these crises they faced. At a substantial sacrifice of Russian territory, they concluded a peace treaty with Germany. Confronted by an increasingly militant opposition, which in 1918 took up a civil war against them, the communists adopted a harshly repressive style of rule. A secret police comparable to that of the Tsar's was recreated, as was a new "red" army. Opposition parties were banned, and trade unions lost their autonomy as they were subject to communist rule. Censorship was reintroduced, although initially it applied only to explicitly oppositional political writings and was supposed to be temporary. In the face of food shortages, the communists adopted a policy—war communism—in which they sent out teams of workers from the cities to forcibly requisition grain from peasants. Although these harsh and dictatorial policies were initially adopted in response to the severe pressures of the first years of the revolution, they were never explicitly repudiated.

The political system the communists established after the Russian civil war of 1918–1921 was in no sense a democracy. Established by a coup, communist rule was preserved by banning or controlling all potential opposition. Despite its dictatorial character, the political system was not, during its first decade, a highly repressive one. There were few political prisoners, and little censorship, for example.

While Marxist thought was not highly influential in the political sphere, it did shape early social and economic policies (Chase 1987; Farber, 1990; Hatch 1991; Siegelbaum 1992). Major industries were nationalized, and the small capitalist class of pre-revolutionary Russia was destroyed. Wage differentials were kept low. Efforts were made to realize the egalitarian thrust of socialism by promoting women's interests.[6] Despite the socialist character of some of these policies, radical restructuring of Soviet economic and social life was limited both by the communists' own sense of objective limitations in the way of their promoting any utopian visions and by the reality of objective limitations.

Thus, for example, they needed an educated class to run the government and to manage the economy, but the educated, from social classes economically privileged before the revolution, did not accept communist rule as legitimate. While there was greater, if limited, support among the mass population, most of them lacked the education to assume high positions. During the 1920s, then, the communists continued to employ in their government bureaucracies people out of sympathy with the new regime.

In the economic sphere, while major industries were nationalized, retail trade remained in private hands. In the countryside, the harsh policies of war communism were replaced by a return to a marketized private agricultural system. While a totally planned economy was articulated as a desirable goal, little planning in fact took place. Thus, while maintaining an authoritarian political system, the communists operated what might be called a very limited, or market, socialism, under the label of the New Economic Policy or NEP.

All of this changed when, at the end of the 1920s, Josif Stalin took full control of the Soviet political system, and introduced what some have called the second, or Stalinist, revolution. (Fitzpatrick 1986; Gill 1990; Reiman 1987) In the political sphere, what had been a dictatorial, but only mildly repressive, political system became a totalitarian one. Among its characteristics were the promotion of worship of Stalin, the leader. Mild repression was transformed into a massive program of government violence against its population.[7] There was an expansion of what had been a very limited system of political prisons into an extremely extensive system—the gulag—in which millions of Soviets were imprisoned during Stalin's years in power. In addition, vast numbers died, some opposing the major economic changes I will shortly describe, others in the famine that followed these changes, yet others while en route to or in the camps of the gulag, and, finally, large numbers were executed by what had become a Soviet police state. Censorship was expanded to cover all fields of Soviet life: politics, history, the arts, science. What had been, even during the twenties, a relatively free society, became a highly regimented one.

These political changes were accompanied by massive economic ones. During the market socialism of NEP, the agricultural sphere consisted of independent farmers, operating largely in response to market forces. For a number of complicated reasons, Stalin found both the independence of the farmers and their behavior as autonomous economic actors intolerable, and pushed what was labeled the collectivization of agriculture. This policy eliminated private ownership and control of land, agricultural machinery, and livestock, replacing them by large collective farms, to be managed by Communist Party officials. Rights of control of land, machinery, and livestock were transferred to the collectives and individual farmers became merely employees of these farms. When many farmers resisted these policies, large numbers were killed, and even larger numbers were arrested and sent to the camps.

In the industrial sphere there were also major changes. During the NEP period, only large industries were state owned and managed. The Stalin Revolution subjected virtually all economic activity to the same state ownership and control. Small industries, wholesale and retail trade, and services all became state activities. The Stalinist state ran the Soviet economy. To do this, that state embraced total planning, eliminating market considerations from the official economy, although at times an illegal black market flourished. What was produced, who produced it, where it was distributed, and for what price were all determined by the state. Where workers would work, what they would be paid, and what their work conditions and fringe benefits would be again were decisions of state agencies, reflecting not a market-oriented cost-benefit analysis, but the priorities of state decision makers. This "command economy," then, is a legacy of the Stalin revolution.

Another thrust of the Stalinist economic program was an extreme emphasis on rapid industrialization. While, in part, this emphasis reflected a Marxist commitment to the centrality of the industrialization process—and the fact that the Russian revolution had taken place before the capitalists had finished their historical role there—it also reflected Stalin's awareness that the Soviet Union was surrounded by hostile, potentially threatening, and very powerful capitalist countries. During the Russian Civil War, the British, French, Americans, and Japanese had assisted the Bolsheviks' opponents, and remained antagonistic to the USSR.[8] In addition, Germany was recovering from its war losses. Since all these states were more heavily industrialized than the Soviet Union, and thus had a greater war potential, rapid Soviet industrialization easily assumed the character of a central national interest. Such a priority to industrialization and the building up of military production precluded much spending on consumer goods, or mass welfare, and these took a back seat during the Stalin years.

These, then, were the essential characteristics of the Stalinist political and economic system, a system that, with only minor modifications, lasted until Stalin's death in 1953. Many would argue that, with somewhat more major modifications, the Stalinist system continued in the USSR until several years after Gorbachev came to power in 1985 (Friedgut 1979; Hahn 1988; Oliver 1968; Schultz and Adams 1981; White 1985).

Moreover, it was the system that the Soviet Union imposed on the countries of Eastern Europe after World War II. At the end of the war, the Red Army, which had swept west in its pursuit of the retreating German army, formally occupied East Germany, Romania, and those Eastern European countries that had been allied with Germany during the war: Hungary and Czechoslovakia—there had been a nominally independent Slovak state allied with Germany. In addition, Soviet troops were stationed in Bulgaria and Poland, ostensibly to protect Soviet supply lines to the occupied states. In part as a result of this Soviet military presence and the West's reluctance to challenge it, and in part as a result of complicated domestic politics, from 1945–1948, communists took power in all of these countries. They also came to power as a result of domestic revolutions in Albania and Yugoslavia.

Many of these newly powerful Communists had spent the war years in the USSR and had been impressed by its industrialization and success in the war. They had come to regard the Stalinist model as appropriate to their countries. Other Eastern European communist leaders, who challenged either the Stalinist model, or the overwhelming Soviet influence which characterized the first ten to fifteen years of communist rule, were removed from power at Soviet insistence. Thus the Stalinist model came to characterize the politics and economics of Eastern European communism, as it did in the People's Republic of China in the 1950s.

There were, of course, some variations in the institutions and practices of communism among the eight states of Eastern Europe and the Soviet Union. Thus, for instance, Poland after a limited experiment with agricultural collectivization, totally repudiated it. In Poland, too, given the immense popular support accorded the Catholic Church, the regime was forced to tolerate not only a degree of religious freedom unusual in communist countries, but a degree of censorship unusually low for such countries.

Over the years, the magnitude of variation among the communist states increased. Yugoslavia, expelled from the Soviet bloc in 1948, experimented with forms of market socialism, low levels of repression, and substantial devolution of power away from the center to subnational units. In the middle fifties, Hungary and Poland introduced political and economic innovations so substantial that the Soviets felt it necessary to threaten invasion of Poland and to actually invade Hungary in 1956. Even more substantial innovation led to a Soviet-led invasion by five Warsaw pact members of Czechoslovakia in 1968. Soviet perception of the need for these invasions was the most extreme evidence of the decline in day-to-day Soviet influence in these countries. At the same time, adoption of such an extreme strategy provided proof of the continuing Soviet commitment to guarantee the preservation of most elements of the Stalinist system in these countries.

Prior to the ascension of Gorbachev to power in 1985, then, communism had lasted sixty-eight years in the USSR. The Stalinist version, the one inherited by Eastern European states, had lasted fifty-eight years. Communism, in that Stalinist version, had endured for some thirty-seven years in the states of Eastern Europe. How did it survive for so long? What brought it down? Most importantly, what do these dynamics tell us about the likelihood that democracy will emerge or endure in these countries?

COMMUNIST RULE: ITS STRENGTHS AND WEAKNESSES

The most obvious explanation for the longevity of communist rule in the USSR and Eastern Europe was the extremely repressive character of the communist party state (Knight 1988). In all of the communist countries, dictatorship prevailed. The party totally dominated politics. What they called elections were noncompetitive, with slates nominated by the party unanimously elected. Potential sources of opposition were either illegal (other political parties) or tightly controlled by the party (e.g., trade unions). The media were tightly censored to control the perceptions of the population. Any opposition that arose, despite these safeguards, was subject to rapid and harsh punishment. The secret police in all of these countries were active and fairly effective. Political prisons were widespread and full. Since the state controlled all employment, it could use the threat of firing people for lesser offenses. Supporting the coercive capabilities of Eastern European communism was the implicit threat of Soviet invasion, should domestic opposition get out of hand. In 1956 in Hungary and in 1968 in Czechoslovakia, that threat was carried out.

The coercive mechanisms of the communist state were powerful and a crucially important part of the explanation for communist longevity. Perhaps a combination of such mechanisms and nationalist support generated by a limited defiance of the Soviet Union can account for the political passivity of the Albanian and Romanian peoples. However, it would be distorting reality to ignore other elements of life in the other communist countries. It is wildly inaccurate to portray the populations of these countries as sullenly obeying the rules of governments they regarded as harsh and illegitimate oppressors. During the decades of communist rule in Europe, governments supplemented, and, in the last decades, largely replaced, coercion with more positive mechanisms for generating popular support for or, at least, acquiescence in, communist rule.[9]

Political Socialization

One such mechanism was a massive effort to inculcate popular support for the nation, the communist political/economic system, and the leaders of that system (Avis 1987; Brown 1985; Hahn 1991; White 1985). In that effort, the schools played a central role. Through the use of patriotic ritual, the explicit content of school texts, and the emphasis on working and learning collectively, the schools promoted the legitimacy of the system.

Supplementing the schools was a network of patriotic youth organizations. In the Soviet Union, young people joined the Octobrists, moved to the Young Pioneers, and then the Young Communist League, or Komsomol, where membership was a precursor to membership in the communist party. Comparable organizations existed in all of the other communist systems. All of these organizations spent much time and effort on developing among their members politically desired attitudes.

I have already mentioned that the content of the media was totally subject to censorship (Remington 1988). The media, however, were also required to play a positive role. They, like the schools, were expected to "sell" the political system. Thus, the media trumpeted the achievements of the communist political and economic system and ignored not only its failures, but also the weaknesses it shared with all social systems: crime, accidents, and such negative social phenomena as alcoholism.

Without relevant research it is difficult to know how effective all of these efforts were (see White 1980). There is evidence of great skepticism, in part linked to anti-Russian nationalism in Eastern Europe from an early period and growing cynicism, from the 1970s on, in the Soviet Union itself (White 1979).

The Social Contract

As I indicated previously, the initial emphasis of the Stalinist economic program was on industrialization and the military buildup this made possible. The Eastern European states, as they became communist, adopted the same priorities. As a result, the standard of living of the populations of these countries remained quite low.

One of the dramatic changes that followed the death of Stalin was a certain reshuffling of priorities. Under the leadership of Soviet Premier Malenkov, Stalin's first successor, a modest effort was made to increase the Soviet supply of housing, a policy desperately needed in the face of both the increasing urbanization of the USSR and of the destruction wrought on Soviet housing by World War II. He and his successor, Khrushchev, also worked to increase food supplies available to the population. Increased capital resources poured into agriculture to finance new machinery and fertilizers. During the three decades from Stalin's death until Gorbachev's ascension, the average Soviet citizen ate increasingly well.

During that same period, increasing resources were also allocated to light industry, with the result that more and more consumer durables became available to the population. Ownership of radios, then televisions, refrigerators, and cars, became quite widespread, particularly in the cities.

Furthermore, many of the necessities of life were heavily subsidized. Food was sold far below cost. Rents were unbelievably low, as were utilities. Health and education costs were kept to a minimum. Public transportation and entertainment, too, were state subsidized. The right to a job was constitutionally guaranteed, and, although there appears to have been some unemployment, by western standards it was quite low.

Thus, the peoples of the communist world had grounds for perceiving that their economic systems had created for them substantially higher standards of living than they had had in the past. These peoples had no way of determining whether a different kind of economic system might have done even better, and no way of knowing at what costs their systems had achieved these goals.

Moreover, those in the communist countries were, until recently, unaware of the far higher standards of living in the industrialized west. Information about the outside world was limited, although it began to increase substantially in the late 1960s, and has continued to grow, decade by decade since (White 1979). Most could not leave the communist world as travel was quite restricted. Until the last years of communism, relatively few travelers from outside entered "the Soviet bloc." Radio broadcasts from the West were jammed until 1973, and print media and films unavailable. Media in the USSR and in the communist states of eastern and central Europe tended to emphasize, in their coverage of the noncommunist world, the harshest features of life there. Thus, citizens had little sense that their own standard of living was not impressive by world standards.

Citizens of the communist countries, then, had made what some scholars have called a social contract (Cook 1993). In exchange for a rising standard of living, they supported, or at least acquiesced in, continuing communist rule.

THE DECLINE AND FALL OF COMMUNISM

However, by the early 1980s, many of these supports for communist rule had begun to erode. Although the communist states remained police states, repression had become both less common and less effective. In virtually all of the communist states, dissident movements had arisen to challenge various policies of their governments. Although such challenges remained risky, and the numbers of dissidents were never large, it became clear that police repression was no longer a fully effective deterrent to political action (Rothberg 1972).

Socialization mechanisms, too, seemed to lose their effectiveness. Membership in such organizations as the Komsomol declined, and it became apparent that even the remaining members were increasingly cynical. The effectiveness of the media was reduced as Soviets and Eastern Europeans acquired access to competing versions of reality from such western sources as the British Broadcasting Corporation (B.B.C.), Voice of America, and Radio Free Europe.

Finally, the social contract had depended on the very high rate of economic growth in the communist countries during the 1950s and 1960s. But that growth had been in large part a consequence of early industrialism, and depended upon increasing inputs of labor (drawn from the large numbers of peasants) and raw materials. By the 1970s, further large increases in the labor supply were impossible, and valuable raw materials were getting scarce. A number of the eastern European countries supplemented these during the 1970s with capital borrowed from western sources, but these sources expected repayment, with interest.

The inherent inefficiencies of a command economy, and the economic irrationality (whatever the moral or political attractiveness) of heavily subsidizing food, housing, and other amenities began to be manifest by the end of the 1970s. Moreover, particularly for the Soviet Union, the economy was further strained by strenuous efforts to compete with the West in general and the United States in particular in the arms race. Given these stresses, the social contract could no longer continue. Improvements in living standards slowed down, and, in some cases there were actual declines.

Moreover, the successes of the communist states in building industry had required the transformation of communist societies from rural to urban, and the conversion of peasants to workers. Populations that at the beginning of the communist era had been largely illiterate were, at its end, overwhelmingly literate and even well educated. Well-educated urban workers, however, are not likely to be tolerant of declining living standards, or, for that matter, of political repression.

This was the context in which Mikhail Gorbachev came to power in 1985. During the six years of his leadership, the Soviet Union underwent massive transformation (Balzer 1991; Joyce, Ticktin, and White 1989; McCauley 1990; Lewin 1988; Dallin and Lapidus 1991; Sedaitis and Butterfield 1991; Lane 1990; White 1993). What had been relatively minor revisions of the Stalinist political and economic systems between 1953 and 1985 became, at least rhetorically, the total rejection of that system by 1991. Although Gorbachev himself at times indicated nostalgia for the communism of NEP, even that form of communism was, in the end, rejected.

Among the aspects of the system that largely disappeared (in the order of their disappearance) during those years were (1) any significant political repression, (2) censorship (with the introduction and expansion of "glasnost"), and (3) dictatorial monopoly of political power, with first the introduction of competition for party and state elections, then the unofficial legitimating of competing parties, the strengthening of state institutions at the expense of the communist party, the elimination of the constitutional provision mandating a special, monopolistic role for the communist party, and finally, formal multipartyism.

These changes were all in the political sphere. Many scholars have argued, however, that the primary goal of the Gorbachev reforms was, in fact, economic restructuring, or "perestroika." During the seventies and early eighties, the Soviet economy had manifested a declining performance. The economic growth rate was falling. By 1990, it had "achieved" negative growth. The USSR found it difficult to simultaneously innovate technologically, maintain a rising Soviet standard of living, and compete with the Americans in the arms race necessitated by the cold war. While at the time of Gorbachev's accession to power there did not appear to be an immediate economic crisis, the future looked bleak.

During Gorbachev's first two years in office, he introduced a number of limited initiatives to deal with these problems: increased work discipline and an anti-alcoholism campaign, among others. None of these challenged basic features of the Stalinist, or command economy. When it became clear that these measures had had little impact, Gorbachev began to consider more basic departures from the command economy: decentralization of decision making from government ministries to individual factories, and the limited introduction of market mechanisms into the economy. Almost immediately, it became obvious that very powerful party and state elites were hostile to such changes.

Although during his first two years in office Gorbachev had been able to remove from high party and state office most of the holdovers from the past, it was clearly more difficult to remove the people he had installed as their successors. Unfortunately, these new elites, too, opposed his increasingly radical reforms.

It was in this context that Gorbachev introduced first glasnost and then democratization. They were intended, argue many scholars, to provide processes where the Soviet public, mobilized by Gorbachev, could either bring pressure to bear on the powerful or, in the extreme, remove them. Thus, the political reforms were seen not as intrinsically desirable, but as useful means to promote economic reform. I want to emphasize this point, in part because it helps to clarify the dynamics of the Gorbachev era, but also because its distinctions help to clarify the complexities of the post-communist era in Russia.

Mikhail Gorbachev not only accepted and even encouraged substantial economic and domestic political reform, he also transformed Soviet foreign policy. Under his direction, the "new thinking" in Soviet foreign policy included improved U.S.-Soviet relations, a withdrawal of Soviet troops from Afghanistan, and Soviet cooperation in ending regional conflicts in Angola, Ethiopia, and Nicaragua. Most important, from our perspective, the new thinking rejected Soviet use of large-scale military force as a means for settling conflicts with other countries. This represented a significant change from previous Soviet policy, since the Soviet army had marched into Hungary in 1956, Czechoslovakia in 1968, and Afghanistan in 1979 in order to preserve what the Soviet Union regarded as acceptable forms of communist rule. In the late sixties, the principle that the Soviet Union had a right to intervene in fellow communist countries to preserve communism (the Brezhnev doctrine) was articulated. The new Gorbachev foreign policy, however, not only repudiated that doctrine, it permitted and encouraged the reform of Eastern European communism away from the Stalinist model.

It is probable that, in his naïveté, Gorbachev had assumed that the reform process in Eastern Europe would stop short of the destruction of communism itself. His renunciation of the Brezhnev doctrine, however, while only one of the factors driving the reform process in Eastern Europe, virtually guaranteed the demise of communism. When, in 1989–1990, the communists were swept from power everywhere in Eastern Europe, the Soviet army, as promised, stayed out of the process. The end of communism in Eastern Europe was followed, two years later, by its demise in the Soviet Union itself. In August 1991, a failed coup by opponents of Gorbachev's radical reforms led to the end of the Soviet Union and the disappearance of formal communist rule itself in the fifteen new countries that emerged from the collapse of the USSR.

DEMOCRACY IN THE POST-COMMUNIST WORLD

Russia and Democracy

Boris Yeltsin came to power in 1990 as Chairman of the Russian Supreme Soviet, or leader of the Russian Republic, merely one of fifteen Soviet republics. In June 1991, he was elected by the Russian people to the newly created position of President of that Republic. After the collapse of the Soviet Union in late 1991, he became President of the newly independent Russian Federation.[10] He advocated a radical yet peaceful revolution toward a market economy, as well as toward democracy. However, radical economic reform quickly ran into the opposition of the Russian parliament, originally elected during the Gorbachev era, and significantly less committed to reform than Yeltsin himself. Distressed by a political standoff that had lasted into 1993, Yeltsin sponsored a referendum in which the Russian people had the opportunity to express their support both for him and for his economic program. Hopes that the support so expressed in this April 1993 referendum would resolve the conflict vanished when parliament proposed legislation in the late summer of 1993 that would have stripped Yeltsin of many of his presidential powers and would have hindered the executive branch's attempts to bring inflation under control and to move privatization forward.

Continued parliamentary frustration of his reforms led Yeltsin to first dissolve the legislature and then, when it refused to disperse, to bomb it in October 1993. In December, he held new parliamentary elections. At the same time he put to the Russian people in a referendum a proposed new constitution, which they approved. The extra-constitutional character of these actions raises grave doubts about the genuineness of the Yeltsin commitment to democracy, if not to the transformation of the Russian economy. The new parliamentary elections, moreover, returned to office deputies equally resistant to a program of radical economic reform and equally determined to thwart it.

Was Russia, at the end of 1994, a democracy? The answer to that question depends, of course, on how that concept is defined, and in Chapter 2, William Reisinger explores in depth the complexities of the question. However, a preliminary evaluation seems appropriate here. There were certainly elements of democracy present. The chief executive, President Yeltsin, had been directly elected by the Russian people in a competitive election, although that election took place in the Russian Republic of the communist Soviet Union. The parliament in place in Russia at the collapse of the USSR had been elected in a quasi-competitive election, and it has since been replaced, in December 1993, by a legislative body elected in a fully competitive contest. Relations between the executive and legislature have a conflictual character similar to that of the President and Congress in the United States. Thus, the dictatorial concentration of power characteristic of the communist era has largely disappeared.

Subordination of politics to the dictates of law, a topic explored in depth by John Reitz in Chapters 5 and 6, took place to a limited extent. The Soviet constitution, written by the communists and amended numerous times during the Gorbachev era, became the founding constitution of the Russian Federation. Despite its dubious lineage, it continued to structure much of the rhetorical debate surrounding the executive-legislative conflict of 1992–1993. Much political energy was expended, first on amending that constitution, and then on writing and passing a new one. While much of this activity was merely rhetorical, the rhetoric suggested growing respect for the force of law.

There were other developments that could provide support for those who saw Russia as democratic. In the last years of the Gorbachev era, political parties had begun to develop, and they continued to exist and operate, albeit in embryonic form, in the Russian Federation. Parliamentarians divided themselves into blocs, to which they gave the name parties. At elections the same groups contested for office, although the extra-parliamentary organization of these groups was rudimentary. The ideological range of the parties was substantial, from supporters of a weak state and a market-oriented economy to those who clung to communism, and others whose orientation to politics was largely nationalist in character. Although the Yeltsin government had initially banned the communists, they soon returned to politics under other guises. In 1993, the party was again made legal. There seemed to be virtually no state-imposed obstacles to the free operation of parties, a dramatically different situation than had existed under communism.

The rich associational life characteristic of democracies (labeled by some scholars "civil society" or "political society") also began to flourish in Russia. Trade unions grew active and strikes were common. Business associations also developed as the economy privatized. A rich array of other groups also flourished: ecologists, feminists, numerous religious movements, and others.

Censorship of the media under communism had largely disappeared under Gorbachev's glasnost. In 1990 in the Soviet Union and in 1991 in Russia, laws were passed banning censorship. It is true that, during the Gorbachev era, the media had been constrained in various ways. The print media frequently found that overly antagonistic treatment of the government led to "shortages" of paper or newsprint. Representatives of the electronic media, government owned, were on occasion chastised or even fired. In the Yeltsin era, the government has fewer controls, and the media are correspondingly more free of government control. They are under the severe financial constraints of having to operate in a market economy, but the limitations this imposes are substantially different in character and degree from communist censorship.

The analysis so far suggests a positive response to the question of whether Russia is a democracy. But there is another side to the question. After Russia became independent, there developed a major conflict, as I have said, between Yeltsin and the Parliament. Although the rhetoric of that dispute focused on the constitutionality of each side's actions, impartial analysis would suggest that neither side paid much attention to their constitution and that the struggle between them was more a pure power struggle, unregulated by democratic rules. This interpretation is clearly strengthened by Yeltsin's unconstitutional dissolution of parliament, parliament's refusal to leave its building, and Yeltsin's use of the army to drive them from the building! The Russian Federation's first elected parliament and the new Russian Constitution are metaphorically splattered with blood.

Moreover, the new Russia is constitutionally a federation, that is, a political system with a central government with certain powers, and subnational units with both other powers and a certain, perhaps high, degree of autonomy from the central government. Despite this federal character, Yeltsin attempted to dissolve subnational governments and to send in central government representatives to rule in local areas. Moreover, in the face of an assertion of independence by the Chechen Autonomous Republic, he sent in Russian troops in late 1994. These attacks on federalism further qualify the democratic character of Russia.

In this brief overview of Russian democracy, I should make one final point. Many analysts of democracy have emphasized the crucial importance of mass participation in democracy. Some have suggested that the "richer" the participation, the more democratic the politics (see Reisinger, Chapter 2 and Maher, Chapter 4). In any case, almost all students of democracy have considered mass involvement in voting as a desirable democratic trait. Initial competitive elections in the Soviet Union under communism elicited quite high levels of voter participation, as voters took advantage of this new and apparently potent power they had been given. In Russia, as citizens have become more skeptical/realistic about the power of the polls, there has been a decline in the percentage of those voting. In the 1989 elections for the Supreme Soviet, 89.8 percent of the eligible electorate voted (White 1993, 51). By the time of the Russian presidential elections of June 1991, turnout had declined to 75 percent. It further dropped to 65 percent in the referendum of March 1993 on confidence in President Yeltsin, and finally, in the parliamentary elections of December 1993, to 54.8 percent (Wyman, Miller, White, and Heywood 1994, 259).

Thus, there remain serious questions as to whether Russia is democratic and as to just how democratic it is. However democratic it is now seen to be, the future state of its democracy is also open to question. What about the other post-communist states?

Democracy in Central Europe, Eastern Europe, and the FSU

By 1995, excluding Russia, there were twenty-six states in central Europe, eastern Europe, and the former Soviet Union that had once been formally communist and were no longer so. Their political fates were widely varied (Ekiert 1991; Mestrovic 1993; Pridham and Vanhanen 1994; Berglund and Dellenbrant 1994; Roeder 1994). Some—like Bosnia, Georgia and Tajikistan—were so torn by internal warfare that to consider them coherent or effective states was to indulge in myth making. For such "states," concern about the character of their political systems was misplaced (Huntington 1968, 1–92). Their leaders did not govern; there were no governments. Until effective governance could be established, democracy was far beyond their capabilities. Other states, also beset by ethnic, religious, or regional conflict, clung precariously to civil order.

In another subset, the demise of communism was more apparent than real. In such states as Serbia/Yugoslavia, the Ukraine, and Kazakstan, former communists retained both power and most of the characteristics of a communist political and economic system. Roeder (1994) argues that communism in the former Soviet Union has been replaced by one variant or another of authoritarianism.

Finally, there were those states that had genuinely cast off the communist system and were trying, with greater or lesser success, to introduce both democracy and a market economy. Among these were the Czech Republic, Hungary, Poland, and the Baltic states. In these states new constitutions had been written and adopted. These states were led, at least initially, by anti-communists whose democratic credentials were fairly convincing. There have been several competitive elections, and in many of them the initially victorious post-communist leaders have already faced the electorate and lost.

The character of their political systems varied, with some having a presidential/parliamentary system on the French Fifth Republic model and others having a purer parliamentary form.[11] Whatever their system, their politics were characterized by lively debate and conflict. Parties were free to organize and were active, as were business associations, trade unions, and other elements of "civil society." Although there were various economic and political constraints on them, the media remained free and vigorous. They seemed genuinely democratic. It is important to note that such states, while providing some evidence that it is possible to move, at least in the short run, from communism to democracy, constitute a minority of the post-communist states. Moreover, even for these states, as for Russia, it is appropriate to ask if democracy will survive.

DEMOCRATIC THEORY AND POST-COMMUNIST CHANGE

Theoretical efforts to understand the factors that shape the emergence and consolidation of democracy go back a long way. In his *Politics*, Aristotle treats democracy as one of the basic forms of governance a polity might adopt, and argues that it is only appropriate for and only likely to last under certain special conditions. A number of contemporary scholars continue the Aristotelian tradition in their efforts to understand the recent third wave (Huntington 1991) of democracy (Dahl 1989; Lipset 1960, 1990, 1994; Di Palma 1990; Vanhanen 1990, 1992; Przeworski 1986, 1991). These efforts, however, largely predate the collapse of communism, and as a result, are unable either to enrich their understanding of the processes of democratization by utilizing the experiences of these twenty-seven "cases," or to bring their theoretical understanding to bear to help understand what is likely to happen in the former communist states. The authors of this volume have concentrated on these tasks.

The most inspiring and fascinating aspect of recent landmark changes in the former Soviet Union and Eastern Europe is that the downfall of communism occurred, without exception, in the name of democracy. Communists in power in the former Soviet Union and in the former Soviet bloc in Eastern Europe were replaced by "democrats," that is, by people who declared their commitment to democratic political systems. Such verbal commitments were made concrete by the introduction of some of the "institutions" of democracy: competitive elections, multiple political parties, an independent judiciary, the legalization of such associations as independent trade unions, an end to political censorship, and so on.

Does the introduction of these institutions mean that democracy has come to this part of the world? In Chapter 2, William Reisinger makes clear how complex a problem it is to define democracy, and the difficulties implicit in using a purely institutional definition. In Chapters 5 and 6, John Reitz enriches this discussion by analyzing the character of "law-based" (democratic?) states. Adding to the intellectual complexities of defining democracy are what one might call the "political difficulties." Some analysts would argue that a supposedly neutral institutional definition in fact conceals a conservative political bias, that it "privileges" political rule by narrow elites, usually conterminous with the economically privileged (see Chapter 2 and Kristen Maher's analysis in Chapter 4).

Even if the conclusion from this analysis is that, at the moment, many of these states are now democratic, a further and more difficult question is, will they remain so? Only a relatively small, if growing, number of the countries in the world have democratic political systems. Moreover, many of these formerly communist states introduced democratic institutions in the interwar period, only to see them overturned and replaced by authoritarian rule. These facts suggest that it may be very difficult not only to introduce democracy, but to sustain it. In Chapter 3, Reisinger compares various political science perspectives on the conditions and processes of successful democratization.

Here I would briefly argue that the survival of nascent democracies depends on two basic elements: (1) whether powerful political forces support and will continue to support democracy, and (2) whether subsequent political/economic processes at work in these countries will sustain that support. Di Palma (1990) argues that new democracies will be secure if all powerful elites "sign on" to democracy. In the post-communist world, the powerful elites are a fragmented group. Among them are:

1. Former dissidents, turned into—in at least some states—new rulers
2. Former communist leaders, reformed and not so reformed, in power or seeking power
3. Former communist party or state bureaucratic elites, seeking to cling to their high bureaucratic positions and to ensure that those positions continue to carry with them power, status, and wealth
4. The new entrepreneurs, taking advantage of the conversion of command economies into market ones to enrich themselves
5. The new Mafia—hard to distinguish from the new entrepreneurs—seeking wealth in ways perhaps more clearly unethical if not illegal
6. Secret police and military leaders, whose command of information and guns give them potent political resources.

Members of the first two groups compete for the highest elected positions. They, and others who play the party-political game, strengthen democracy by their electoral competition and the implicit message such competition carries. "Play by democratic rules. If you are dissatisfied with those who govern the society, vote for their opposition. If none of their opponents satisfy you, organize your own party." So long as no party competing in the electoral arena advocates a transformation of the system in an undemocratic fashion, or, in Sartori's language, is an anti-system party (Sartori 1976, 132–3), democracy is strengthened. Up to the end of 1994, no such party had won mass support in Russia or in eastern or central Europe. It might be argued, however, that the fundamentalist Islamic parties operating in some of the new central Asian states represent a serious threat to the future of democracy there.

To the extent that bureaucratic holdovers from the communist era maximize their own power, they undermine to a degree the effective power of elected officials. In so doing, they qualify, perhaps to a great degree, the meaningfulness of apparently democratic institutions and lessen the degree of democracy in a society.

However, they do not threaten the nominally democratic character of a political system.

Those whose primary goal is the accumulation of wealth, whether legal entrepreneurs or illegal Mafia members, like the bureaucrats might seek to limit or to corrupt democracy, but not to overthrow it. However, should they find democratic instabilities threaten their ability to enrich themselves, they might well support an overthrow of democracy carried out either by an anti-system party, or by the police or military.

Finally, the secret police and/or military have both resources and incentives to overthrow democratic governments. As the institutions that monopolize the use of force, they have the capacity, if united, to easily remove democratically elected governments. During the twentieth century, military coups have been by far the most common way to overthrow democratic governments (Huntington 1968; First 1970; Decalo 1976; Lowenthal 1976). Efforts to identify the causes for military intervention in politics suggest that it takes very little to motivate the military. Certainly one cause is the sense that the nation they have sworn to defend is being put at risk by democratic government. The collapse of several of the post-communist states and the overwhelming of others by civil war might well suggest to the military the need for their intervention.

So far my analysis has focused on post-communist political elites. Do the masses[12] support democracy? Do their opinions matter politically?[13] There are five possible scenarios: If the military or police are determined to bring democracy down, it is likely to fall, despite mass support; if an anti-system party seeks, but does not receive, mass support, democracy will survive; if, on the other hand, the masses are antagonistic to democracy, but all segments of the political elite support it, it is likely to survive. Mass opposition, in the presence of an anti-system party—the Nazi scenario—however, is likely to be fatal. Finally, to complicate the analysis, mass opposition may well lead to the creation of an anti-system party, and thus to the overthrow of democracy. While I would thus emphasize that the survival of democracy is dependent on a complex elite/mass interaction, I would further argue that while (at least some segments of) the elites can themselves destroy democracy, the masses alone cannot do so.

The emergence of democracies is no guarantee of their longevity, but it is not clear that deep pessimism about their future is warranted, either. Processes at work may serve to consolidate democracy, or they may erode elite or mass support for that form of governance. Two processes seem especially relevant. The former communist states have not only sought to become politically democratic, they have also sought to convert their economies from command economies to market ones. Successful conversion, resulting in increasingly prosperous citizenries, is likely to generate increasing elite and mass attachment to political democracy, however unreasonable it may be to make the linkage between democracy and economic prosperity. That makes the economic conversion vital to the fate of democracy. In Chapter 8, Jack Mutti examines the problems of conversion and some strategies that might be fruitfully adopted.

Growing ethnic and/or religious conflict might also erode support for democracy. Such conflict has already destroyed three post-communist states, the USSR, Yugoslavia, and Czechoslovakia. It appears that it has destroyed Bosnia as well. Less virulent conflict might leave in place the existing states, but promote elite overthrow of democracy to preserve "law and order." A comparable dynamic lay behind, or at least justified, the overthrow of democracy in much of Africa during the 1960s and 1970s. In Chapter 7, Vicki Hesli analyzes this threat, and the measures that might be adopted to counter it.

Finally, while I propose that the fate of democracy largely lies in the hands of the elites and masses of these new democracies, these countries do not exist in a vacuum, and outside actors and forces may impinge on their political system. In Chapter 9, I analyze the various ways the external world might affect the likelihood of continuing democracy in the former communist states.

CONCLUSION

It is not our task, in this volume, to predict the future of democracy in the former communist states. If pushed, the authors would, I suspect, disagree. My own remarks in this introduction convey a degree of pessimism about prospects for democracy in most of these states. I think both democratic theory and the histories of these countries justify such pessimism. However, there are some grounds for optimism, as well. The achievement of democratic ideals is an elusive goal everywhere. In recent years, Spain, Portugal, Greece, Turkey, and numerous Latin American countries have built democratic structures and are attempting to instill democratic values in spite of numerous challenges and adversities. We have no reason to assume that the peoples of the post-communist states are any less well equipped to face this challenge than are other peoples throughout the world.

There are additional factors at work, moreover, to justify a limited optimism. The positive "demonstration effect" of successful efforts elsewhere should serve to raise hopes and foster a commitment to democratic principles in post-communist polities. Also, if social and economic development is related to the emergence and/or consolidation of democracy, as much of the theoretical literature suggests, then the relatively high levels of industrialization, urbanization, and literacy of the formerly communist states are promising. So, too, are the findings of numerous studies that have demonstrated higher levels of support for such democratic orientations as tolerance and political efficacy among better-educated sectors. The educational levels achieved by communist states remain impressive by international standards. These societies are also receiving some material and technical assistance from "established democracies." Although the level of assistance might ideally be higher, the constant exchanges in economic, cultural, and scientific spheres has to support democracy, if only marginally.

The open discussions and self-criticism of the Gorbachev era have carried over to the Yeltsin era in Russia and characterize politics in the more successfully democratic states of eastern and central Europe. The possibility of a return to the old days seems remote. Also progress has been made, although maybe not as rapidly as might have been hoped, in the process of conversion to a market economy. As the concept of private ownership takes hold again, the economic incentive structure of the society will shift. Freedom and new opportunities in the economic sphere may extend into the political sphere. So perhaps a qualified optimism is in order.

NOTES

1. Counting them is rather difficult. To the fifteen states arising from the disappearance of the USSR we might have added initially Albania, Bulgaria, Czechoslovakia, East Germany, Hungary, Poland, and Romania. Whether it is, or was, appropriate to count Yugoslavia, not a member of the Soviet bloc after 1948, and with a very different political and economic system, is not clear. If it is counted, then eight eastern and central European states are added to the Soviet fifteen. However, East Germany soon rejoined West Germany, Czechoslovakia split into the Czech Republic and Slovakia, and Yugoslavia fragmented into Bosnia, Croatia, Macedonia, Slovenia, and the rump Yugoslavia (Serbia and Montenegro).
2. Most prominent, of course, were the former playwright, Vaclav Havel in Czechoslovakia, and the former leader of the once illegal Polish trade union Solidarity, Lech Walesa.
3. It could be argued that the Russian Constitution of 1905 introduced into the Empire many elements of democracy. Some scholars have argued that, save for Russian involvement in World War I, that system would have evolved into a constitutional, parliamentary democracy. Others, challenging this thesis, have offered the few months' experience of the provisional government, from February 1917 to October of that year, as a proto-democratic experience. Neither experience merits the adjectives full and complete.
4. There, of course, it was destroyed by Nazi invasion and occupation in 1938–39.
5. While never fully articulated, Marx's conception of democracy seemed to be very different from that utilized in these pages. It emphasized very heavily economic and political equality, and de-emphasized particular political institutions (parliaments, for example) and practices, such as mass participation in voting or associational activity.
6. The provisional government had previously introduced measures to promote women's rights that were in advance of anything yet done in Western Europe.
7. There continues to be an intense scholarly debate about both the scope of the terror and its motivations. See Conquest 1990 and Getty and Manning 1993 for recent contributions.

8. It is the case that Soviet foreign policy, and that of its "agent," the Comintern, or Communist International, gave these states good grounds for such hostility.
9. I recognize that the concepts of "support for" and "acquiesence in" communist rule are very different in tone. While either or both may account for a lack of active popular opposition to the regime, it would be highly desirable to know the mix of these two in popular opinion. Unfortunately, there seems to be no plausible method for establishing that mix.
10. It is far too soon for definitive assessments of the Yeltsin regime, which remains in place. For very useful interim analyses, see McFaul 1993; McFaul and Markov 1993; Sergeyev 1993; Sakwa 1993; and Steele 1994.
11. See Reisinger's Chapter 3, this volume, for a clarification of this distinction.
12. Obviously mass opinions will vary. When I say that the masses support (or, for that matter, oppose) democracy, I mean that substantial numbers of the politically active citizens support, or oppose.
13. Kristen Maher focuses on these questions in Chapter 4.

REFERENCES

AVIS, GEORGE, ed. 1987. *The Making of the Soviet Citizen: Character Formation and Civic Training in Soviet Education.* New York: Croom Helm.

BERGLUND, STEN, and JAN AKE DELLENBRANT. 1994. *The New Democracies in Eastern Europe: Party Systems and Political Cleavages.* Brookfield, Vt.: E. Elgar.

BALZER, HARLEY D., ed. 1991. *Five Years That Shook the World: Gorbachev's Unfinished Revolution.* Boulder, Colo.: Westview Press.

BROWN, ARCHIE, ed. 1985. *Political Culture and Communist Studies.* Armonk, N.Y.: M.E. Sharpe.

CHASE, WILLIAM J. 1987. *Workers, Society, and the Soviet State: Labor and Life in Moscow, 1918–1929.* Urbana: University of Illinois Press.

CONQUEST, ROBERT. 1990. *The Great Terror: A Reassessment.* New York: Oxford University Press.

COOK, LINDA J. 1993. *The Soviet Social Contract and Why It Failed: Welfare Policy and Workers' Politics from Brezhnev to Yeltsin.* Cambridge: Harvard University Press.

DAHL, ROBERT. 1989. *Democracy and Its Critics.* New Haven: Yale University Press.

DALLIN, ALEXANDER, and GAIL W. LAPIDUS, eds. 1991. *The Soviet System in Crisis: A Reader in Western and Soviet Views.* Boulder, Colo.: Westview Press.

DECALO, SAMUEL. 1976. *Coups and Army Rule in Africa: Studies in Military Style.* New Haven: Yale University Press.

DI PALMA, GIUSEPPE. 1990. *To Craft Democracies: An Essay on Democratic Transitions.* Berkeley: University of California Press.

EKIERT, GZREGORZ. 1991. "Democratization Processes in East Central Europe: A Theoretical Reconsideration." *British Journal of Political Science* 21:285–313.

FARBER, SAMUEL. 1990. *Before Stalinism: The Rise and Fall of Soviet Democracy.* New York: Verso.

FIRST, RUTH. 1970. *The Barrel of a Gun: Political Power in Africa and the Coup d'État.* London: Allen Lane.

FITZPATRICK, SHEILA. 1986. "New Perspectives on Stalinism." *The Russian Review* 45:357–73.

FRIEDGUT, THEODORE H., 1979. *Political Participation in the USSR.* Princeton: Princeton University Press.

GETTY, J. ARCH, and ROBERTA MANNING. 1993. *Stalinist Terror: New Perspectives.* New York: Cambridge University Press.

GILL, GRAEME. 1990. *Stalinism.* Atlantic Highlands, N.J.: Humanities Press International.

HAHN, JEFFREY W. 1988. *Soviet Grassroots: Citizen Participation in Local Soviet Government.* Princeton: Princeton University Press.

———. 1991. "Continuity and Change in Russian Political Culture." *British Journal of Political Science* 21:393–421.

HATCH, JOHN B. 1991. "Labor Conflict in Moscow, 1921–1925." In Sheila Fitzpatrick, Alexander Rabinowitch, and Richard Stites, eds., *Russia in the Era of NEP.* Bloomington: Indiana University Press, 58–71.

HUNTINGTON, SAMUEL P. 1968. *Political Order in Changing Societies.* New Haven: Yale University Press.

———. 1991. *The Third Wave: Democratization in the Late Twentieth Century.* Norman: University of Oklahoma Press.

JOYCE, WALTER, HILLEL TICKTIN, and STEPHEN WHITE. 1989. *Gorbachev and Gorbachevism.* Totowa, N.J.: F. Cass.

KNIGHT, AMY. 1988. *The KGB, Police and Politics in the Soviet Union.* Boston: Allen & Unwin.

LANE, DAVID. 1990. *Soviet Society Under Perestroika.* Boston: Unwin Hyman.

LEWIN, MOSHE. 1988. *The Gorbachev Phenomenon: A Historical Interpretation.* Berkeley: University of California Press.

LIPSET, SEYMOUR MARTIN. 1960. *Political Man: The Social Bases of Politics.* Baltimore: Johns Hopkins University Press.

———. 1990. "The Centrality of Political Culture." *Journal of Democracy* 1(4, Fall):80–83.

———. 1994. "The Social Requisites of Democracy Revisited." *American Sociological Review* 59 (February):1–22.

LOWENTHAL, ABRAHAM F., 1976. *Armies and Politics in Latin America.* New York: Holmes & Meier.

MCCAULEY, MARTIN. 1990. *Gorbachev and Perestroika.* New York: St. Martin's Press.

MCFAUL, MICHAEL. 1993. *Post-communist Politics: Democratic Prospects in Russia and Eastern Europe.* Washington, D.C.: Center for Strategic and International Studies.

——— and SERGEI MARKOV. 1993. *The Troubled Birth of Russian Democracy: Parties, Personalities and Programs.* Stanford, Calif.: Hoover Institution Press.

MESTROVIC, STJEPAN. 1993. *The Road from Paradise: Prospects for Democracy in Eastern Europe.* Lexington, Ky.: University Press of Kentucky.

OLIVER, JAMES. 1968. "Citizen Demands in the Soviet Political System." *American Political Science Review* 63:465–75.

PRIDHAM, GEOFFREY, and TATU VANHANEN. 1994. *Democratization in Eastern Europe: Domestic and International Perspectives.* New York: Routledge.

PRZEWORSKI, ADAM. 1986. "Some Problems in the Study of the Transition to Democracy." In Guillermo O'Donnell, Phillipe C. Schmitter, and Laurence Whitehead, eds., *Transitions from Authoritarian Rule: Prospects for Democracy,* Part III. Baltimore: Johns Hopkins University Press, 47–63.

———. 1991. *Democracy and the Market.* New York: Cambridge University Press.

REIMAN, MICHAL. 1987. *The Birth of Stalinism: The USSR on the Eve of the "Second Revolution."* Bloomington: Indiana University Press.

REMINGTON, THOMAS. 1988. *Truth of Authority: Ideology and Communication in the Soviet Union.* Pittsburgh: University of Pittsburgh Press.

ROEDER, PHILIP. 1994. "Varieties of Post-Soviet Authoritarian Regimes." *Post-Soviet Studies* 10(1):61–101.

ROTHBERG, ABRAHAM. 1972. *The Heirs of Stalin: Dissidence and the Soviet Regime, 1953–1970.* Ithaca, N.Y.: Cornell University Press.

SAKWA, RICHARD. 1993. *Russian Politics and Society.* New York: Routledge.

SARTORI, GIOVANNI. 1976. *Parties and Party Systems: A Framework for Analysis.* New York: Cambridge University Press.

SCHULTZ, DONALD, and JAN S. ADAMS, eds. 1981. *Political Participation in Communist Systems.* Elmsford, N.Y.: Pergamon Press.

SEDAITIS, JUDITH B., and JIM BUTTERFIELD, eds. 1991. *Perestroika From Below: Social Movements in the Soviet Union.* Boulder, Colo.: Westview Press.

SERGEYEV, VICTOR. 1993. *Russia's Road to Democracy: Parliament, Communism, and Traditional Culture.* Brookfield, Vt.: E. Elgar.

SIEGELBAUM, LEWIS H. 1992. *Soviet State and Society Between Revolutions. 1918–1929.* New York: Cambridge University Press.

STEELE, JONATHAN. 1994. *Eternal Russia: Yeltsin, Gorbachev, and the Mirage of Democracy.* Cambridge: Harvard University Press.

VANHANEN, TATU. 1990. *The Process of Democratization: A Comparative Study of 147 States, 1980–88.* New York: Crane Russak.

———, ed. 1992. *Strategies of Democratization.* Washington, D.C.: Crane Russak.

WHITE, STEPHEN. 1979. *Political Culture and Soviet Politics.* London: The Macmillan Press Limited.

———. 1980. "The Effectiveness of Political Propaganda in the USSR." *Soviet Studies* 32(3, July):323–48.

———. 1985. "Soviet Political Culture Reassessed." In Archie Brown, ed., *Political Culture and Communist Studies.* Armonk, N.Y.: M.E. Sharpe, 62–99.

———. 1993. *After Gorbachev.* Cambridge: Cambridge University Press.

WYMAN, MATTHEW, BILL MILLER, STEPHEN WHITE and PAUL HEYWOOD. 1994. "The Russian Elections of December 1993." *Electoral Studies* 13(3):254–71.

CHAPTER
2

Choices Facing the Builders of a Liberal Democracy

WILLIAM R. REISINGER

> *For some time, the word democracy has been circulating as a debased currency in the political marketplace. Politicians with a wide range of convictions and practices strove to appropriate the label and attach it to their ac[illegible]ns. Scholars, conversely, hesitated to use it—without adding qualifying adjectives—because of the ambiguity that surrounds it. . . . But, for better or worse, we are "stuck" with democracy as the catchword of contemporary political discourse. It is the word that resonates in people's minds and springs from their lips as they struggle for freedom and a better way of life; it is the word whose meaning we must discern if it is to be of any use in guiding political analysis and practice.*
>
> —Schmitter and Karl 1991, 75.

Most world leaders claim that their political systems are democratic. Only a few states, such as the princely states of the Islamic middle east, reject that claim. Until the virtual collapse of world communism, its leaders described themselves as having more genuinely democratic polities than those of the western world, which they characterized as merely "bourgeois democracies." They themselves had "people's democracies," not dominated, as they argued capitalist countries were, by rich ruling classes.

The world has been watching with fascination the political changes occurring in these formerly communist societies. Many are curious to know the likelihood that democracy, as we understand it, will result. Such assessments require an understanding of the term "democracy." Unfortunately, as Schmitter and Karl note, the term is so ambiguous that different understandings of democracy may be unavoidable. (Appendix 2.1 presents a few of the many definitions of democracy one can find.) In this chapter, I will attempt to reduce that ambiguity, to produce criteria for knowing democracy when we see it. Since Western governments and private actors are actively pushing these countries to adopt democracy, we need to be conscious about what we expect from these societies.

In this chapter, I begin by reviewing differing perspectives on the meaning of western, or liberal democracy. These stem from the understandings of democracy and the debates about democracy that have gained preeminence among Western policy makers and thinkers over roughly the last three centuries. The issues in those debates have risen anew in the newly independent or newly post-communist countries of Eastern European and the successor states to the USSR.

THE PATH TO MODERN DEMOCRATIC IDEALS

Democracy comes into English from the Greek phrase meaning "rule by the people." Both the idea of "ruling" and that of "the people" are ambiguous. The former implies that democracy as a *form of governance or rule* is not incompatible with clear and even forceful authority relationships. Some systems of authority, however, are quite clearly preferable to others. Proponents of democracy argue that, of the authority systems currently existing, those labeled "democratic" exhibit clear-cut advantages over the remainder.[1] Whether or not contemporary democracy represents the final stage of history's ideological evolution (Fukuyama 1992), the dramatic events of 1989–1991 make clear that proponents of liberal democracy can be found in large numbers throughout the world, including the former Soviet bloc.

Though democracy can be discussed as a system of authority within the workplace or other social contexts, I restrict my use of the term to a form of governance or rule over a territorially defined political unit. Most commonly, of course, democracy is analyzed with regard to the territorially defined political units known as countries or, in international law, states. (Terms such as "political system," "system of governance," and "polity" are synonyms for the entirety of aspects of governing such a territorial unit.) It is worth stressing that a democratic state must succeed as a state, not just as a democracy. In addition to overcoming the many challenges of democratic governance discussed below, a successful democracy must adequately defend its territory from outside attack, preserve internal order, and promote economic prosperity.[2]

The concept of "the people" is also somewhat abstract. First, whom do we mean by "the people"? Answering this question requires answering two subsidiary questions: Which individuals can participate in politics and what are the boundaries of the polity? The proportion of society possessing rights of political participation must presumably be large enough so that we cannot term the polity an oligarchy, or government by a small elite. At the same time, it cannot include absolutely everyone, since minors, the mentally incapable, and others are reasonably excluded from voting and certain other political rights in even the most democratic state. In Athens, "democracy" meant rule by the *demos*, which was not a reference to rule by all but to rule by the lower class of citizens. To Plato, Aristotle, and many other philosophers, democracy therefore meant rule by those with skills and assets and stakes in politics different from those economic or military elites that frequently governed. Many who advocate government only by those highly qualified to govern have regarded democracy as rule by the unqualified. Even today, some argue that people should have to qualify for the right to vote, for example, by having a college degree. Nevertheless, the trend in modern large-scale democracies has been to give almost all adults the right to vote.

Whereas American and British democracies of the eighteenth century granted suffrage only to land-owning males, the nineteenth and twentieth centuries saw the landless, former slaves, and women gain voting and other civil rights. At present, the practice of democratic countries together with such normative documents as the Universal Declaration of Human Rights (Articles 2 and 21) provide an answer to the question of which members of a community are entitled to participate politically. With increasingly fewer exceptions worldwide, this right is extended to all those who meet formally established general qualifications for citizenship and have reached the age of adulthood (usually eighteen to twenty-one years old) without regard—in the words of the Universal Declaration—to "race, color, sex, language, religion, political and other opinion, national or social origin, property, birth, or other status." The only permissible exception involves those who have legally been declared to be incompetent to formulate their views and participate.

The question of boundaries is a second difficulty that besets the idea of "the people." It, unfortunately, has no commonly accepted answer. How does one draw the lines on a map to make a single political system? If the people within those lines regard themselves not as a single "people" (nation or ethnic group) but as two or more such peoples, and, worse yet, are hostile to each other, how will they be able to adopt a common set of governing rules binding on all those resident in the territory? The situation of any group other than the largest is conceivably that of a permanent and subordinate minority living under a political system that gives power to the majority. Resolving such an issue in practice is almost always extremely difficult, as is shown by the recent collapse of the Soviet Union, Yugoslavia, and Czechoslovakia. The nationalist fervor of the post-communist era threatens to create still smaller and more ethnically homogeneous states. While such a development might reduce the dilemmas of multinational democratic states, small states have inherent drawbacks, military and economic, in the modern world. In Chapter 7, Hesli looks at alternative solutions to these problems.

Another significant issue for democratic theory concerns the size of political systems, and the relationship between size and effective and democratic governance. Large political systems seem, as I said above, to have inherent advantages. In ancient Athens, however, democracy was seen as appropriate only to city-states with a small citizenry—thousands, not millions. By the twentieth century, there were few such systems still in existence. They had been replaced everywhere by vast political systems. If political systems were to be democratic, democracy would have to change in character. Large-state, or representative, democracy has proven itself a successful method of governing both large and small nation-states, with no inherent limit on the size of the population being governed. Such a system is not democratic in any sense the ancient Greeks would accept, but there has been a gradual reinterpretation of democracy since the Greeks (Dunn 1992).

During this philosophic evolution, governance became linked to the concept of "sovereignty," that is, the idea that within certain territorial boundaries, one person or body has the final word. The sovereign can make authoritative decisions about the allocation of goods, services, and duties within the territory. While the term sovereignty arose as a justification for monarchy (*a* sovereign), theorists were able to expand its meaning to treat the citizenry as *collectively* sovereign. The concept that first emerged as the alternative to monarchy or other autocratic rule was a *republic* (Ceaser 1990, 6–11). What distinguishes a republic from a monarchy is the existence of clearly stated rules that provide rights to members of different social groups (e.g., royalty, nobility, and commoners) and that set limits on each group's power. Such rules make up a constitution, whether written or not. The Roman Republic was the most prominent model for later anti-monarchical reformers. An important but unstable predemocratic form of republican rule emerged in the twelfth century in several northern Italian city-states, such as Milan, Florence, and Venice (Skinner 1992). Another experiment in republican governance that deserves note is the Polish-Lithuanian state during the sixteenth to eighteenth centuries. The Polish gentry won the right to create a legislative body, the *Sejm,* which had, among other powers, the power to elect the Polish king. Although this republic later proved unable to safeguard the Polish state from powerful neighboring empires, it provided in later centuries a potent symbol of Poland's participation in the Western political tradition.

As the republican tradition developed, it had two strains. The earliest version, aristocratic republicanism, provided for a division of power among the monarch, the aristocracy, and the masses. Its most important thrust was to limit the power of the monarch vis-à-vis the aristocracy. Although mass involvement was an important means of doing this, its proponents saw potential dangers arising from popular involvement in politics and stressed the need to limit it. The city-state of Florence and Britain prior to the twentieth century were such republics.

Democratic republicanism, by contrast, stressed the danger of allowing power to reside in the hands of the few and sought both to limit the power of the state over individual members of the society and to increase the political power of the masses. The behavior of the masses in society had a critical role to play in providing a check on the power of the government. This tradition sought to provide good governance by means of checks and balances among institutions with different types of links to the populace.

Modern democracy predominantly reflects this democratic republicanism. It is not a child solely of the tradition known as *liberalism*, stemming primarily from Locke, which stresses individual natural-law rights directed primarily against the attempts by governments to restrict those rights. People, in the classical liberal view, are "born equal," and the state ought to be constructed to accomplish little beyond maintaining this "natural equality." By contrast, within the democratic republican tradition, ". . . the fundamental challenge of human life is not to lose oneself in Lockean pursuit of life, liberty and property but to join with fellow citizens in the ongoing project of political self-government" (Pocock, quoted in Ackerman 1991, 28).

The synthesis of democracy and republicanism by theorists produced an intertwining of democratic and republican elements in the practices of contemporary democracies. "Liberal democracy is more than a combination of liberal and republican elements; it is a compound or a new synthetic whole, and as such it has its own distinct needs and properties" (Ceaser 1990, 18). For example, although liberty and representation motivated those who fought in the American revolution, the U.S. constitution primarily reflected its authors' concern with building a strong but limited republic. The constitution did not enumerate in its body the basic liberties to be protected in the new order, yet heavy political pressure caused the Bill of Rights to be added as a set of amendments. (The depiction of the United States as a democratic republic is the source of the names of both major U.S. political parties.)

Along with the intellectual conditions that spawned modern forms of democracy, military and economic developments deserve note as well. If, as I argued earlier, democracies must succeed as states, then the emergence of democracy as a way to govern states had to be linked to the military realities that states faced in defending their territory. For example, one factor leading to the democratic regime in ancient Athens was the military importance of the infantry soldier fighting with a spear in close formation (*hoplites*). This gave relatively large numbers of individual men greater bargaining power in matters of the state (Hornblower 1992, 4).

In general, however, the prevalence of war tends to lead to concentrated power (see Chapter 9). A hierarchical, nondemocratic form of political organization makes it possible to extract militarily necessary economic and manpower resources from the society. Medieval and renaissance Europe experienced frequent warfare, and most forms of political organization were monarchies or empires with few or no restrictions on the sovereign's power. Downing (1992) has shown that only those countries able to meet their defensive needs without *forcibly* mobilizing domestic resources developed constitutional restraints on their monarchs that prevailed into modern times.

Modern democracy arose in Britain and the United States at a time when the industrial revolution was transforming their economies and societies, creating the political economy known as capitalism. As Moore (1966) has argued, the British and American cases involved commercial forces coming to the fore and transforming the agricultural sector to support them. With the ascendancy of merchants over the landed gentry (and, in the British case, the crown) came a strong impetus for public officials to be elected, for checks and balances, for the rule of law, and other restraints on government. Yet stressing market capitalism as the building block of democracy can go too far.[3]

Although the United States and Great Britain did establish their democratic structures during the ascendancy of *laissez-faire* capitalism, our current understanding of democracy owes even more to developments since the late nineteenth century. The extension of suffrage to a majority of the population (that is, to former slaves, non–land-owning males and women) became formally complete in the U.S. and Britain only in the 1920s and 1930s. A spread of democratic governance to the European continent and Scandinavia—with innovations in institutional form, electoral systems, and other attributes—occurred from the 1880s to the 1920s. If one focuses on full adult suffrage, as does Lijphart (1984, 37), then "not a single democratic government can be found in the nineteenth century." So, the high point of what Huntington (1991) calls the "first wave" of democratization took place a century or more after American independence. This was also a period when the excesses of unchecked capitalism were under attack. The classical liberalism of the eighteenth century, with its emphasis on economic and political *laissez-faire*, was being replaced by progressive liberalism that envisioned a larger role for the state in making freedoms accessible to the populace (Van Dyke 1992, Chs. 19–20). In reality, what we now understand to be basic components of democracy depended as much on checking capitalism as on its operation (see Dahl 1989, Chs. 20–21; Ackerman 1992).

Political entities in the modern era tend to be much larger than the Greek and Italian city-states that pioneered democratic and republican forms of rule. Modern democracy thus required correspondingly dramatic changes in the institutions and practices of democracy. The primary solution for the dilemma of how to make "rule by the people" work on a large scale was to introduce institutions of representative government. While individual participation tends to be limited in large representative systems, these institutions permit a greater degree of collective popular rule than would be possible if direct participation in decision making were required of people in these very large modern states. It introduces, however, a tension between decision-making efficiency and responsiveness to the citizenry. Politicians, even elected ones, are elites who will differ in outlook and behavior from the mass public. Unless the rules and norms of a specific representative democracy are carefully crafted, incompetent governance and/or tyranny can emerge despite elections. I now review a selection of the many dilemmas of properly crafting a democratic polity.

DEMOCRATIC PROCESSES

Some definitions posit one or more ideal qualities constituting "democracy" and judge to what degree a country is "democratic" by how closely its political system approximates that ideal. Other definitions put forth a set of institutional or procedural features which, if present, indicate that the country is "*a* democracy," allowing one to evaluate the presence or absence of those features. Sometimes, theorists opt to provide *both* types of definitions (see the definitions by Pennock 1979 and Sartori 1987 in Appendix 2.1). This distinction can be referred to as a distinction between definitions that stress conditions and those that stress processes. The separation into conditions and processes when discussing a democracy has been overdrawn; it blurs the fact that certain conditions (the existence of individual rights, for instance) flow precisely from the procedural safeguards in a democracy: "The right to the democratic process is not 'merely formal,' because in order to exercise this right all the resources and institutions necessary to it must exist; to the extent that these are absent, the democratic process itself does not exist" (Dahl 1989, 175).

Nevertheless, if we seek to understand what the formerly communist societies are undergoing and the criteria by which to judge their progress, this distinction marks a notable difference in perspective. The most common approach, particularly in contemporary American scholarship, is to focus on the operation of certain formal procedures. When such scholars talk about securing "democracy" or a country becoming "democratic" or "democratizing," they mean it is developing the institutions and practices that characterize the currently most democratic states. This approach has the value of allowing one to relatively easily determine whether a country has become democratic. For reformist politicians seeking to dismantle an authoritarian communist-party regime, focusing on procedures and institutions provides a reachable goal, a set of tasks that, while difficult to carry off, are comprehensible and achievable. What, then, are "democratic" processes and institutions, and what challenges does their establishment pose?

Popular Participation

To have a system of rule by "the people" (defined inclusively, as noted above) requires as a matter of definition that more than just a narrow stratum of society take part in the political struggles. A democracy must rest on influential actions on the part of the citizens. But what kinds of actions are mandated, how often must they occur, and how many citizens must so act in order to give life to popular rule? With the rise of representative democracy in modern times, democratic theory maintained the Athenian stress on informed and active citizens. Such citizens were deemed crucial for keeping tabs on their representatives. This so-called "classical liberal theory of democracy" was called into question beginning in the 1940s for resting on assumptions about human behavior that were false.

The first serious studies of American voter behavior showed that citizen attitudes and behaviors did not match the image of active and informed citizens found in classical liberal theory (Dalton 1988, Chs. 3–4). These surveys found the "attentive public," that is, politically knowledgeable and active citizens, to be a rather small proportion of society. There has even been debate about whether most people really *have* political opinions, that is, abiding preferences or views apart from how they formulate answers to specific survey questions (Converse 1964, Dalton 1988, Ch. 2). In addition, only a minority of citizens undertakes any politically relevant behaviors other than voting. Few practice such socially approved activities as campaigning on behalf of a candidate for office or such "unconventional" activities as demonstrating or going on strike. Those who do tend to have a better education and more money to spend, and thus are better equipped to follow politics and to attempt to influence it. This pattern holds within most contemporary democracies even though the overall level of popular involvement in politics varies widely among them.

This "truth" about contemporary democracy has led political scientists to divide into two camps. One group, whom I might call "procedural democrats," regard mass political passivity and elite political domination as inevitable, and, perhaps, desirable. This group adopted the view that democracy rests more on contestation among elites than on mass participation. In this view, democracy requires no more than regularly occurring opportunities for masses to pass review on the actions of the elites (and to replace government leaders if elite actions were found wanting). In the eyes of those who urge this conception of democracy, elections without undue restrictions suffice to define the existence of democracy.

Other recent theorists, whom I might label "participatory democrats," regard this state of affairs as both reprehensible and correctable (Pateman 1970; Barber 1984; Slaton 1992). They argue that participation is central to democracy and that strengthening contemporary democracies requires efforts to broaden and improve participation even between elections—by encouraging, for example, such activities as initiating petition drives, writing letters to politicians, or working for local political party organizations. Not only does an active citizenry provide a basis for controlling elites (and thereby vitalizing the legal and electoral controls), but it is involved in the actual processes that make democracy what it is; the members of society must "*do* democracy." These theorists call attention to the importance of public education. They argue that a large flow of information through the mass media is critical if citizens are to formulate preferences and use their participation to pursue those preferences. Some call for a program of extensive measures to involve the public in the task of governance.

The Importance of Competition

To the extent that a political system restricts or forbids competition among groups representing differing political ideas (for example, by permitting only a single political party to exist), this lack of political competition subverts the link between popular participation and rule by the people. Certainly, the communist regimes worked hard to produce public behavior that would uniformly show support for the regime. Voter turnout rates approached 100 percent, and participation in parades and other demonstrations were high. Such participation, of course, did not make these political systems democratic. What they lacked was competition among organized political groups holding different views about public policy. Hence, one must focus on elite competition in democracies as well as on mass participation. (For influential arguments along these lines, see Schumpeter 1942; Schattschneider 1942 and 1960).

For some, democracy involves competition by elites for people's votes. In between elections, the role of ordinary citizens is and must be quite limited. A low level of citizen activity, moreover, does not undercut the principle of democracy. Voters go to the voting booth primarily to select among competing potential governments, not to express themselves on issues or to "re-present" themselves within the legislature. Democracy is served by creating an elite that is good at governing (and thus, most likely, an *un*representative sample of the citizenry by virtue of their governing talent). Pressure is kept on the elites to govern well by the possibility of being replaced at reasonable intervals. (Because of differences in electoral procedures, this view fits the British and, to a lesser extent, American cases better than others.)

To offset the lower status of mass participation, theorists in this school place greater emphasis on factors that promote free-wheeling contestation among the elites. For example, the "pluralist" approach to the functioning of democracy (Truman 1951; Dahl and Lindblom 1953; Dahl 1961) stresses the existence of competition between and possibilities for influence over policy of a vast array of interest groups.[4] Pluralists stress Madison's famous argument that the very multiplicity of organizations would ensure that there would be no tyranny of a majority. The pluralist view of democratic political processes sees them as roughly analogous to an economic market, with government the marketplace, an arena within which politics is played out. Interest groups, like firms, should compete on the basis of their differing interests and capabilities and the outcomes will be the most desirable ones for society because of the operation of the political competition (the "free market").

This focus on elite competition gained renewed attention in the 1980s by those studying newly democratized regimes in Southern Europe and the third world (O'Donnell and Schmitter 1986; Przeworski 1986; Burton, Gunther, and Higley 1992). Out of this work came a frequently cited definition of democracy as "a form of institutionalization of continual conflicts . . . [and] of uncertainty, of subjecting all interests to uncertainty" (Przeworski 1986, 58–9). Przeworski's notion of "institutionalized uncertainty" has gained prominence, yet the term uncertainty must be understood rather carefully. The uncertainty must refer to uncertainty about the nature of political outcomes, of the choices that will receive formalization as policies. What cannot be subject to uncertainty, however, are the rules of competition. Democratic politics must permit each social force or grouping to compete without fear of being eliminated from the process. Maintaining certainty about this outcome thus generally requires that certain political developments be forbidden. In democratic polities, constitutional provisions normally provide the necessary guarantees. For this reason, many of those who promote a procedural definition of democracy, emphasizing competition, nevertheless stress "consensual unity"—when all important elite groups and factions share a consensus about rules and codes of political conduct and the worth of political institutions (Burton, Gunther, and Higley 1992, 4)—rather than competition among elites as the vital component of democracy.[5]

These recent theorists depart from earlier pluralist theorists by placing elections in a distinctly subsidiary position. They also disagree with participatory democrats by rejecting the importance of both voting and nonelectoral modes of mass participation. Przeworski (1991, 10) makes this explicit: "Most definitions of democracy, including Dahl's own, treat participation on a par with contestation. . . . Yet from the analytic point of view, the possibility of contestation by conflicting interests is sufficient to explain the dynamics of democracy. Once political rights are sufficiently extensive to admit of conflicting interests, everything else follows." Bobbio (1987, 116) states the case most strongly:

> [C]ollective decisions are a fruit of negotiation and agreements between groups which represent social forces (unions) and political forces (parties) rather than an assembly where voting operates. These votes take place, in fact, so as to adhere to the constitutional principle of the modern representative state, which says that individuals and not groups are politically relevant . . . ; but they end up possessing the purely formal value of ratifying decisions reached in other places by the process of negotiation.

Given its de-emphasis of the importance both of elections and of mass political participation this image of democracy seems to resemble the one that political scientists have traditionally had of authoritarian regimes. This image of democracy and our usual understanding of politics in authoritarian regimes do not seem very different. For this reason, relatively few theorists are willing to go this far in downplaying the role of mass publics. For example, Schmitter and Karl's recent formulation (see Appendix 2.1) seeks a middle ground between the Przeworski emphasis on competition and those who stress participation.

Voting and Rule by the Majority

Whatever the level of popular participation in a given democracy, the public must elect governing elites. This requirement raises several fundamental issues. First, what decision rule shall operate in the voting? Second, what institutional form should a democratic government in a given country take, and which posts in it should be popularly elected? Third, what rules shall relate votes cast to elite offices held? Fourth, what decisions, if any, should be *outside* the control of democratically elected elites?

The basic rule of conducting democratic elections is one person, one vote (or one fraction of a vote). Yet this immediately creates a profound dilemma. Unless one is willing to put up with the inefficiency of consensus decision making, there is no entirely satisfactory method of deciding who has won a vote. Some form of *majority rule* generally is the method of choice (the alternative receiving the majority of votes if there are only two alternatives, or a plurality, or more than any other alternative, if there are three or more alternatives, wins). But, how can this be a form of "equality"? It leaves as many as 49 percent of the citizens in the minority. Those who consistently belong to an electoral minority may, in effect, seem to be disenfranchised and therefore subject to a tyranny of the majority. Prior to the U.S. Civil War, such figures as John Calhoun argued the southern states faced such a tyranny (see Roper 1989, 56–65). At present, many societies find this a particularly daunting challenge because they have what Coleman (1992) calls "permanently divided systems." Dahl (1989, Chs. 10–11), however, poses the argument that a tyranny of the majority is not necessarily worse than a tyranny of the minority, by which he means a minority that can block the wishes of a majority consistently. Moreover, a polity can mediate the danger that a majority will tyrannize a minority: having a federal structure that places certain decisions in the hands of regional leaders, providing for judicial review of legislative acts to protect basic rights for members of the minority, or making use of referendums. (Chapter 7 by Hesli discusses these matters in more detail.)

Methods of Representation

A key dimension of constitutional design is selecting the nature of the electoral system. The rules for how voting will occur shape the number of political parties, the way those parties operate, relations among top institutions and politicians, and the general tenor of political life. Although there are many hybrids, two basic modes of voting predominate worldwide. One involves the system familiar in the United States, generally termed majoritarian or plurality voting. Each elected post has a unique electoral district associated with it (a single-member district). Whichever candidate receives the most votes is selected from that district. (Rules vary as to whether a winner can be declared with only a plurality of votes. In some cases, a plurality suffices. In others, a runoff is held. In some, a new election must be held.)

Other countries, though, have rules for voting known as proportional representation (PR), that is, there is some mechanism for relating the number of seats in the legislature that a party receives to its proportion of the total vote. Typically, this is achieved by having a smaller number of multi-member electoral districts. For instance, voters in a given district might be responsible for electing ten members of parliament. Each voter would vote for a particular party, which would have provided a list of the ten candidates it was supporting. A party that received 40 percent of the votes in the district would receive four of the ten seats, and the top four names on that party's list would get the nod. Under this electoral method, a political party that receives, say, 13 percent of the popular vote nationwide is more likely to receive roughly 13 percent of the seats in the legislature. In a majoritarian system such as the United States, Democrats could hold every single seat in Congress while only receiving 51 percent of the votes cast nationwide if each Democratic candidate received 51 percent of the votes in his or her district.

The proposition that countries with a certain type of electoral procedure are likely to have a two-party system while others have a multi-party system has achieved the status of a social science "law"—Duverger's Law.[6] According to Duverger's law, when an electoral system has single-candidate, winner-takes-all districts, the country will likely have a two-party system. Third parties (and independent challengers) find their task so daunting that they rarely remain active over several elections. The logic is that, in a country with such voting rules, voting for a third party is unlikely to increase that party's influence since only the majority party controls the legislature. Moreover, voting for a third party actually takes a vote away from whichever of the two largest parties the voter finds less repellent. Thus, in the United States, voting socialist increases the chance that *Republicans* will be setting U.S. policy, not Democrats. In a system with proportional voting, by contrast, each vote for a given party helps to increase the number of seats it controls in the legislature and thereby to increase its influence over policy. Voting for a minor party might allow one a voice in the legislature and thus might make sense. Polities with three or more active and competitive political parties are mostly found in countries with PR electoral rules.

Not only is the number of political parties affected by the electoral rules, but also their platforms and activities. In a two-party majoritarian system, both parties will generally need to appeal to the broad middle of the ideological spectrum as well as those ranged along one extreme (Downs 1957). Thus, in the United States, for example, moderate Democrats may hold policy views closer to those of moderate Republicans than those of extremist Democrats. In a PR system, each party must stake out a particular policy position that will define it in the eyes of voters so that voters can decide which of the several parties best matches their views. Some will be centrist, some will be extremist, but the range of the ideological spectrum a viable party encompasses can be smaller than that of a party in a two-party system.

In many parts of the former Soviet Union, electoral rules remain as they were in the late 1980s. These rules are "majoritarian" since one candidate becomes the legislator out of each district, and there are as many districts as there are seats in the parliament. In most of these post-Soviet states, however, political parties remain poorly organized and weak in influence, so it is too early to assess whether Duverger's law will hold true here as well. By contrast, a number of Eastern European states adopted proportional representation voting after 1989. In these states, a multitude of party organizations quickly emerged to field candidates for election. In several cases, the number of parties acquiring a seat in the legislature grew too large to be manageable. Rules setting a minimum vote percentage necessary for any representation in the legislature were then introduced to reduce the number of viable parties. More recently Russia created a mixed majoritarian and PR system, with one-half of the seats to the lower house of the legislature elected by proportional representation in December 1993. Thirteen parties acquired seats in the parliament, with seven gaining more than 5 percent of the seats.

Institutional Variants

Popular rule on the large scale of modern countries requires that, out of the populace at large, a group of elite office-holders be chosen who are empowered to make and enforce decisions for the collectivity. But this is not the end of the story. Imagine if the country's political order were only to specify the electing of representatives, who would comprise an assembly. The assembled representatives would face the dilemmas of voting procedures discussed above. The decision they reach would influence future policy making. Moreover, this assembly would very quickly create a division of labor to facilitate its work. This division of labor implies the setting of procedural rules (such as when parliaments stipulate that bills must be passed by a committee before the entire body considers it). Such rules must perforce influence the types of policies eventually adopted. Furthermore, this division of labor would no doubt involve designating a single individual or small group to monitor the public's obedience to the assembly's policies. This executive officer or agency would have an advantage over fellow representatives in organizational resources and the power that derives from prominence.

Clearly, few societies would be willing to leave the setting of such influential rules to those individuals who happen to be elected to the first session of the legislature. Those establishing a democracy will consciously seek to structure the institutional division of labor at the elite level to achieve certain ends. Generally, this structuring takes place in the context of writing and ratifying a constitution. The drafters of the U.S. constitution were much concerned about separating and making interdependent three particular types of governing functions: the making of laws, the administering of laws, and the interpretation of laws. Thus, they created a separate and interdependent Congress, presidency, and judiciary. They also were concerned about the relationship between individual citizens' power and the power of the constituent states (the former colonies). Their response was to divide the legislature into two houses that differ in size, certain powers, and the manner in which their members are selected. In other countries, the constitution writers were concerned with other issues and created different institutions.

Contemporary democracies vary institutionally along a number of dimensions and a wide-ranging literature examines the causes and consequences of the variety (e.g., Powell 1982; Lijphart 1984; Taagepera and Shugart 1989). In Chapter 3, I discuss the debate over how to design institutions so as to strengthen a new democracy. Also, questions of institutional structures and democracy are covered in Chapters 5, 6, and 7. In this chapter, therefore, I will merely point to what is commonly the defining feature of a particular "type" of democracy—the legislative-executive relationship. Three such types cover most existing democracies. The "parliamentary" model confers executive power on that legislator who commands the predominant support in the legislature. Great Britain was the forerunner of this type of democracy. In the second category are the United States and others that have followed in its footsteps. Countries in this category have what is known as a "presidential" system because the chief executive officer, the President, is elected independently of the legislature. The third category follows the model of the quasi-presidential French system. In this arrangement, there is a President elected separately from the members of the legislature, but this official's duties are defined differently than in the pure presidential model. The President of France, for instance, is head of state yet not the head of government. The head of government is the official responsible for the cabinet and the executive bureaucracies that cabinet members head, and, in the French case, this is the Prime Minister. He or she is appointed by the President, subject to legislative ratification, and can be dismissed by the President. These three arrangements plus the many hybrids that exist provide new democracies with a menu of institutional structures from which to choose. The choice that is made in a particular case will, for good or ill, provide certain incentives and place certain constraints on the policy-making process.

Given the institutional similarities imposed on former Communist societies by Soviet domination, it is not surprising that their institutional structures even now share much in common. Few have ratified entirely new constitutions with resulting new institutions. Only Hungary created a parliamentary system on the model of numerous continental west European democracies. In the rest of the former Soviet bloc, the Soviet pattern of state institutions shapes current executive-legislative relations. In particular, the Soviet (and Soviet-influenced East European) practice was for a Prime Minister to head a government (a "cabinet" known as the Council of Ministers whose members managed numerous ministries and other executive agencies). The Prime Minister was not simultaneously an elected member of parliament. Formally, this Prime Minister was subordinate to the legislative body. No separate executive existed until Soviet leader Gorbachev introduced the post of President for himself in 1990, thus creating a system that resembled the French model. Armenia, Azerbaijan, Kazakhstan, Kirghizia, Moldova, Russia, Tajikistan, Turkmenistan, Ukraine, and Uzbekistan followed suit in 1990 or 1991. Most of these now independent states maintain this structure. Also, as the Eastern European states redesigned their institutions following 1989, Bulgaria, the Czech Republic, Poland, Romania, and Slovakia adopted comparable systems with a President and a Prime Minister.

Interestingly, not every Soviet republic followed Gorbachev's path of separating the Presidency from the legislature. Belarus, Estonia, Latvia, and Lithuania kept executive power with the head of the legislature. Georgia had a French-style presidential system until the elected President, Zviad Gamsakhurdia, was ousted by a military junta in early 1992. That fall, elections were held to the new executive post, head of the legislature, which former Soviet Foreign Minister Eduard Shevardnadze won. This pattern of a head of state located in the legislature and a head of government separate from but subordinate to the legislature falls outside any of the three major institutional patterns.

Constitutional Constraints on Policy

Most democracies place a number of constraints on the sovereignty of the people, embodied in the choices of majorities. Often, a written constitution enshrines these limits. On certain matters, if the current government wants to overturn constitutional provisions, it must vote these changes by a larger majority than it needs for passage of ordinary legislation. The American founding fathers adopted complex procedures for passing constitutional amendments to so constrain both the American people and its government.

Because a "higher law" can be used to overturn a decision by the legislature, "constitutionalism" is closely associated with, though not limited to, judicial review (see Chapter 5 by Reitz). Judicial review is the placing of ultimate decisions about the constitutionality of a given law in the hands of a judicial branch. It therefore restricts the powers of the majority (or the coalition of power democratically arrived at).

This raises the issue of why the current generation of voters and its elected representatives should be bound by the decisions of a previous generation. If taken too far, giving preeminence to long-ago decisions can be undemocratic and can create undesirable rigidity. Yet doing so can also support and protect democracy. For one thing, constitutional provisions are often set down during an extraordinary, or even a revolutionary, period. In these cases, the constitution represents a broader societal consensus than that resulting from the normal policy-making process (Ackerman 1992). Further, constitutions generally serve to protect individual rights, and they form an obstacle to certain political changes that would have been carried out had a temporary majority had its perhaps short-sighted way (Elster 1988). In other words, by protecting individual rights against a majority, a constitution guards against arbitrariness by an executive interested in administering policy without constraint, and by forming an obstacle to changes backed by a slim and short-term majority, even when rights are not being violated, a constitution provides a check on the making of bad decisions during a time of passion.

Constitutionalism, then, fights a two-front war: against the executive and against the legislative branches of government. Any government wants to receive its mandate in a general form that allows for efficient use of discretionary judgment, whereas any assembly wants to specify as much as possible how the mandate is to be carried out (Elster 1988, 7).

Constitutionalism therefore also maintains a helpful degree of stability in society. The uncertainty about outcomes that Przeworski (1986) and others view as the essence of democracy cannot extend to uncertainty about the rules of the political game. These rules must be clear and resistant to change.

CONDITIONS WITHIN A DEMOCRACY

Those who depict the nature of contemporary political democracy by delineating its institutional features or rules believe that the resulting processes produce better government than is otherwise possible. Certainly, a comparison of the track record of institutionally democratic states to those of authoritarian regimes provides support for this claim. Yet this may be deceptive. If democracy is held to a rather low standard, it may fall well short of its own potential. While institutions and rules are relatively easy to establish, they may please only those whom they immediately benefit. As a result, the new democracy may develop little popular support. Unless democratic political procedures are accompanied by democratic conditions within the country the democratic regime may be rejected or toppled. Many democracies have indeed had a brief existence. Promoting both democratic institutions and procedures and the societal conditions that inspired the founders of a democracy is no easy task, but its success may be essential to the survival of democracy.

Popular Empowerment

One perspective sometimes blurred in efforts to move beyond a purely institutional conception of democracy is the original sense of the term democracy as referring to rule by the people. In other words, discussions of rights or goals need to keep in view that a political system can be democratic in the strict sense only to the extent that it *empowers* its members politically. Such a perspective highlights the dimensions of depth and breadth of popular empowerment within a country. How small is the circle of individuals who exercise some degree of influence over important national decisions? If non-elites do have channels to influence national decisions, how accessible are such channels across different social groups or regions? As one moves from national to regional to local policies, does the degree of influence by nonelites increase correspondingly? Recall that many of the practical and moral arguments in favor of democracy rest on the way in which it can strengthen the political power of citizens. Empowering a polity's citizens helps prevent tyranny by a narrow minority and strengthens the moral development of individuals. "If freedom, self-development, and the advancement of shared interests are good ends, and if persons are intrinsically equal in their moral worth, then opportunities for attaining these goods should be distributed equally to all persons. Considered from this perspective, the democratic process becomes nothing less than a requirement of distributive justice" (Dahl 1989, 311–2).

By power here I refer to influence over the outcome of events that concern one. This requires that I distinguish matters of direct and immediate personal concern from those decisions that affect much larger numbers of people. Because democracy is an authority structure, relatively few will be authorized to make the widest-ranging policy decisions. Most citizens will have quite limited influence over the outcomes of national policies (scholars even debate why a reasonable person would bother to vote when the odds of affecting the outcome of an election are so slight). For most, any significant influence over the course of events will occur within the family, the neighborhood, the school district, or the workplace. This positive correlation between the degree of one's influence and the proximity of the setting to oneself seems natural and to be expected.

Yet achieving this relationship might be more of an accomplishment than it would appear at first glance. The images of totalitarianism presented so vividly by Orwell or Arendt convey a society in which citizens are equally powerless over personal matters and matters of state. Although the former Communist societies had not matched these images for some while, if at all, the regimes had thwarted many channels for individuals to be influential within a variety of settings. A central theme of Eastern European and Soviet intellectuals during the 1980s and 1990s has been how to re-create a vital "civil society," that is, a society in which citizens have a multiplicity of nonstate ties, and belong to a number of nonstate organizations that provide them with channels of some influence (Miller 1992).

So, one important dimension of popular empowerment is to establish the capacity for all to have significant and direct influence over outcomes that occur within the closest social proximity. (Held [1987] uses the term "autonomy" in a similar manner). A second dimension is to provide any citizen who desires a fair opportunity to become one of the few with influence over more wide-ranging outcomes. This is so intrinsic to the procedures and rationales of democracy that I will not elaborate further except to say that opportunities to pursue higher levels of influence are rarely distributed entirely fairly. A focus on popular empowerment requires that the accomplishment be measured, not just the aspiration stated.

Finally, both equality and liberty empower citizens. Liberty can be thought of as empowering a citizen *against* the state, while equality empowers a citizen *within* the state. Focusing on empowerment, then, might prove a useful way to combine—or at least to evaluate the balance between—the goals of liberty and equality. Liberties that give rise to gross inequities in economic power or access to information (Dahl 1989, Ch. 23) would be *disempowering* liberties. An equality that hedged individuals' freedom to pursue self-development and common goals would similarly be a *disempowering* equality.

Liberty, Equality, and the Tension between Them

The two central values that underpin democracy are liberty and equality.[7] Liberty and its synonym freedom were first understood as referring to a sphere of human activity outside the control of the state. For proponents of liberty ("liberals" in the sense in which the term was understood from the seventeenth through nineteenth centuries), the need for liberty flows from both a moral and a practical reason. The moral reason was the understanding, then gaining acceptance, that human dignity requires moral autonomy and an opportunity for self-development. The greater the individual freedom allowed within a polity, the more each person will be able to (and have to) make moral choices. Thus, a sphere of liberty allows individualists to flourish. It thereby provides a potential check against the tendency of democracies to produce social pressure for conformity and mediocrity. Thus, the greater the self-betterment that will result. The practical reason is that the provision of liberty to citizens—that is, the setting of boundaries on state power—makes it more feasible for citizens to guard against possible harm from bad government.

In the nineteenth and twentieth centuries, this conception of liberty as freedom from government has battled with arguments that freedom must also have a positive rather than negative sense. Citizens who lack the capacity to take advantage of their liberty cannot attain the benefits that freedom is supposed to produce. This implies that freedom requires a certain role for the state in providing educational opportunity, social security, and other measures meant to make liberty meaningful. At present, the term "liberal" is typically applied to those who favor a role for the state in actualizing liberty. Those who most strongly condemn an active state are now known as libertarians.

The development of the concept of positive liberty indicates how liberty has become intertwined with the other central democratic value, equality. The meaning of equality is, if anything, even less agreed upon than the concept of liberty. Does it mean that all should be equal in their actual material wealth or status? Or, should all citizens be equal only in the opportunity to pursue that wealth or status? As a third possibility, perhaps equality ought to mean equality of treatment by the state.

The first understanding of equality is the least accepted in democratic theory because it is not possible in practice and is inconsistent with the capitalist economic systems that prevail in modern democracies. Yet one can plausibly argue that economic wealth provides one with political power. Thus, economic inequality undercuts full political equality. Moreover, most democracies now accept that the state must provide a floor below which no one can fall so that citizenship can be reasonably pursued. This floor generally includes access to free or low-cost education, health-care opportunities, especially for children, and laws on humane working conditions.

These latter policies are usually defended in terms of the second meaning of equality: providing equality of opportunity. The idea is to reduce discrimination or inequities for which society or the state is responsible so that each individual can use his or her innate talents to the fullest. This understanding of equality still provides a much larger sphere of liberty—and thus a highly unequal range of outcomes—than does a stress on equalizing wealth or status. Even so, efforts to provide equality of opportunity can require actions by the state that apply differently to different citizens. In the United States, affirmative action policies raise this dilemma quite sharply. These policies are meant to offset the discriminatory effects of past state actions that gave preferential treatment to white males at the expense of African American citizens, other ethnic minorities, and women. Achieving this requires policies that provide explicit advantages or incentives to these formerly mistreated social categories. Thus, in some cases, producing equality of opportunity has been seen as necessitating *unequal* treatment by the state.

A third way to define equality is equality of treatment by the state, or *impartiality*. Equality in this sense would require such things as equality of protection by the state from external attack, equality of protection against internal attack (i.e., safety on the street and in one's home), equal treatment by the legal system, and equality of provision by the state of those things the state normally provides or regulates in order to facilitate economic possibilities, such as access to education and information. It does not, however, require the state to enhance any citizen's access to these, merely not to deny such access.

Both liberty and equality have achieved an unshakable acceptance as positive values in democratic theory. Ironically, perhaps the most difficult normative dilemma that democracies must resolve (and whose resolution must be constantly reworked) is the tension between equality and liberty. Like beams in an A-frame structure, each supports the other while exerting continual pressure on it. Different societies in practice have struck different balances between the two, but neither can be entirely ignored. The Marxist-Leninist ideology of the communist regimes stressed equality over political liberty. Though full commitment to reducing distinctions among the status and wealth of citizens was dropped in the USSR by the early 1930s, Soviet notions of equality fell much closer to the ideal of equality of status and wealth. This has been seen by many as an obstacle to marketization of the economy (see Chapter 8). Such notions also could be an obstacle to democratization if they do not allow room for individual liberty and, more broadly, for a civil society.

The Protection of the Rights of Individuals

As the occurrence of the word "rights" throughout this chapter attests, much of the promise of political democracy stems from its promise to uphold certain individual rights. Verba, Nie, and Kim (1978) summarize this relationship as follows:

"Democracies have evolved in two ways: by expanding the number of political rights and the number of people who have the rights."

Current debates about what rights a citizen actually has and how to protect that citizen's rights are the product of the evolution of understandings about what kind of *rights* each individual is entitled to. Cicero, Aquinas, and others argued that there is something called "natural law" that is *knowable* by humans but *derives from* God or the nature of things, thus superseding human-made law. Natural law applies by definition to all human beings equally. It implies that this law extends certain natural rights to all people equally. This is the underpinning of the phrase in the U.S. Declaration of Independence: "We hold these truths to be self-evident, that man is endowed by his creator with certain *inalienable rights*." Different thinkers focus on different inherent rights: property (Epstein 1985), equality (Dworkin 1977), and others. Each approach that focuses on a given set of rights, though, argues that protecting these rights must supersede any political decisions, democratically reached or otherwise, including constitutional provisions. They worry that a democratically elected government could enact all kinds of oppressive or repressive acts. The Supreme Court and other institutions, then, are in place to protect the primacy of one or more rights against encroachment by politicians.

Civil rights, by contrast, place the emphasis on conditions within a country and how the state treats individuals. Within the United States, for instance, a person would be entitled to a different set of civil rights—interpreted differently—than in Britain. "Human rights," a largely twentieth-century formulation, returns to the concept of assigning rights to all human beings regardless of their citizenship (or any other attribute).[8] The set of human rights, moreover, includes numerous rights that previously had been seen as civil rights, owed to some because of their citizenship but not to all. The pursuit of human rights represents an updating of the concept of natural rights, though without the same religious underpinning. It has become common in the twentieth century to judge polities by the degree to which human rights are provided. For a democracy to be a "good" polity, therefore, it must provide rights beyond the minimal rights required for democracy to operate. It must also, in this view, produce a wide range of individual rights at least at a level exceeding that of nondemocratic states.

Peaceful Conflict Resolution

While the provision of rights has perhaps been the most common focus of what a democratic polity should give rise to, an equally attractive perspective is to argue that democracy ought to prevent violent social conflict among its citizens. A polity that does not provide means to articulate and peacefully resolve conflicts is unlikely to satisfy other criteria. (It is difficult, after all, to maintain the "right to life, liberty, and the pursuit of happiness" in a war zone.) Many consider that democracy has great advantages over autocratic regimes of various stripes in satisfying this criterion. Democracies are likely to provide more numerous channels of redress for those with a grievance. Political institutions, parties, the legal system, media outlets, religious institutions, and other social networks can all play such roles when the democratic procedures discussed earlier are working well. Having a variety of nonviolent paths should lead to a reduction in violent conflict (Eckstein 1980, 150). However, it must be noted that two of the most politically violent polities on earth, India and the United States, are both procedurally democratic (Powell, 1982).

It is particularly important that whatever institutions and procedures apply to policy making in a particular country provide adequate channels for nonviolent conflict resolution among policy makers. The processes by which elites struggle over policy outcomes should encourage the expression of many viewpoints, promoting compromises and tradeoffs, and generosity toward the losers of a particular political struggle. The authors of the U.S. Constitution created institutional "checks and balances" to increase the occasions on which elites from different sides of an issue would have to reach a compromise. Furthermore, within institutions—most particularly the legislature—the rules can encourage compromise and bargaining among opposing groups. The groups in question can be political parties or any of the various types of interest groups that have received sustained attention by the pluralist school. As discussed above, institutional configurations in existing democracies vary quite widely. Depending on a country's electoral rules, types of parties and other institutions, politicians (and hence the social groups they speak for) may make crucial deals during a party convention, when two or more parties agree to form a coalition government, during the course of gaining a legislative majority behind a bill, or in some other venue.[9] Whatever the forum in a given country, the critical issue is whether contending elites are encouraged, when the issue permits, to reach mutually acceptable outcomes and, for other issues, to decide who wins in such a way that the losers remain in the game.

A point made by Rustow (1970, 354) seems strikingly relevant to the formerly communist countries: "a country is likely to attain democracy not by copying the constitutional laws or parliamentary practices of some previous democracy but rather by honestly facing up to its particular conflicts and by devising or adapting effective procedures for their accommodation." The Russian politician Gennadii Burbulis (1992, 15) has expressed a similar sentiment:

> I have often repeated that being a democrat is not an occupation and not a life-achievement award but an outlook and means of conduct. . . . We are not threatened by copying western democracy since there is no such pure model. And, as far as democratic governance, this is the most complicated and delicate type of power, which rests on mutual effort by the highest organs and the mass public.

DEMOCRACY AND THE POST-COMMUNIST COUNTRIES

With few exceptions, all of the post-communist countries claim to be committed to democracy. Scholars who define democracy by its institutions and procedures would likely place these new regimes in the democratic camp, while acknowledging how fragile those democratic institutions remain. Those who focus on substantive conditions would point out that these polities remain much farther from providing democratic conditions for their citizens than most established democracies. Few citizens have been empowered. The continuance of state ownership of almost the entire economy in many post-communist countries restricts citizens' liberties. Equality, even equality of opportunity, remains an elusive goal. The economic crisis attendant on the effort to marketize these economies has made it impossible to provide adequate education, health care, or environmental protection and difficult for independent media to establish themselves. Also, the existence of bloody and seemingly irreconcilable conflicts in some areas sharply restricts the relevance of fledgling democratic institutions.

Despite all this, the continuing respect for democratic governance as a principle remains a tribute to these many peoples. We do not know which societies will succeed in building democratic institutions and practices sufficiently effective and resilient to last. (In Chapter 3, I review some prominent theories about which societies have the best prospects). Many key choices and struggles lie in front of them. We can watch as the leaders and publics of the former communist states grapple with fundamental political issues that elsewhere are settled and little remarked upon.

APPENDIX 2.1: SELECTED DEFINITIONS OF DEMOCRACY

Definitions of democracy come in all shapes and sizes. Here are a variety of others' definitions for your perusal:

> Democracy is "government by the people; that form of government in which the sovereign power resides in the people as a whole, and is exercised either directly by them . . . or by officers elected by them."
>
> (*Oxford English Dictionary,* 1933)

> "Democracy [is] not majority rule: democracy [is] diffusion of power, representation of interests, recognition of minorities."
>
> (John Calhoun, as paraphrased by Roper 1989, 63)

> "Democracy is the form of state within which the distribution of power in the state is determined *exclusively* by the social factors of power, but is not shifted in favor of any one class through the application of material means of coercion."
>
> (Otto Bauer, quoted in Meyer 1957 [1986], 65)

> "Democracy is a competitive political system in which competing leaders and organizations define the alternatives of public policy in such a way that the public can participate in the decision-making process."
>
> (Schattschneider 1960, 141)

"[A] social decision function $F(D_1, D_2, \ldots, D_n)$ is called a *democracy*, if the function can be expressed only by voting operators—without any resort to negations and constants—and the function is nondictatorial, where nondictatorial is defined as follows: . . . 'A social decision function $F(D_1, D_2, \ldots, D_n)$ is called *nondictatorial*, if there is no individual whose preference is always adopted by the society."

(Murakami 1968, 28–29)

A democratic regime is one ". . . in which *the peaceful rivalry for the exercise of power exists constitutionally*." (italics in original) The phrase "exercise of power" implies temporary control.

(Aron 1969, 41)

A definition of the ideal:

"Government by the people, where liberty, equality and fraternity are secured to the greatest possible degree and in which human capacities are developed to the utmost, by means including free and full discussion of common problems and interests."

(Pennock 1979, 7)

And of the practice:

"Rule by the people where 'the people' includes all adult citizens not excluded by some generally agreed upon and reasonable disqualifying factor. . . . 'Rule' means that public policies are determined either directly by vote of the electorate or indirectly by officials freely elected at reasonably frequent intervals and by a process in which each voter who chooses to vote counts equally. . . and in which a plurality is determinative."

(Pennock 1979, 9)

"The competitive electoral context, with several political parties organizing the alternatives that face the voters, is the identifying property of the contemporary democratic process. . . . [D]emocratic systems [are] . . . characterized by competitive elections in which most citizens are eligible to participate."

(Powell 1982, 3)

"[D]emocracy is a form of institutionalization of continual conflicts . . . [and] of uncertainty, of subjecting all interests to uncertainty. . . ."

(Przeworski 1986, 58)

A *democratic regime* is "first and foremost a set of procedural rules for arriving at collective decisions in a way which accommodates and facilitates the fullest possible participation of interested parties."

(Bobbio 1987, 19)

"Democracy is a system in which parties lose elections. There are parties: divisions of interest, values and opinions. There is competition, organized by rules. And there are periodic winners and losers."

(Przeworski 1991, 10)

"Modern political democracy is a system of governance in which rulers are held accountable for their actions in the public realm by citizens, acting indirectly through the competition and cooperation of their elected representatives."

(Schmitter and Karl 1991, 76)

NOTES

1. Most political theorists accept this proposition but not all. Some would deny that a society can attain democracy's lofty goals when the society's authority relations are hierarchical ones backed by violence or the threat of its use. Anarchists are an example: "The defining feature of anarchism is its opposition to the states and the accompanying institutions of government and law." (Heywood 1992, 196) The phrase "the state" (as opposed to "a state") is usually used in the Weberian sense to refer to the institutions that exert the decisive control over matters within a territorially defined political unit (Evans, Rueschemeyer, and Skocpol 1985). The state is separate from and counterbalanced by non-state organizations, groups, or communities, known collectively as "civil society" (Gramsci 1929–1935 [1971]; Keane 1988). Also the Marxist perspective has generally held that democracy is not present so long as one class dominates the others within a society. Thus, achieving democracy requires and is tantamount to ending class domination: achieving communism. Under communism, the state would wither away.
2. Some would dispute that a successful state must view its requirements as the pursuit of economic prosperity for the country. Classical liberals, for example, would stress that the best state is one that remains uninvolved in its citizens' affairs as much as possible. Yet whether a country's government pursues prosperity through activism or through avoidance of regulation of the economy, the goals of external defense and internal order become difficult to pursue without a certain degree of economic strength. Thus, economic prosperity must concern officials of the state. Further, in many societies during this century, the public has come to place responsibility for economic improvement at the feet of the government. Times of economic hardship generally weaken support for the government in place and severe economic difficulties can potentially threaten the popular legitimacy of state institutions.
3. Whether and in what fashion democratic governance requires market capital-

ism of the western type is a hotly debated question. For a recent symposium of representative views on the topic, see *Journal of Democracy* 3:3 (July, 1992).

4. Allman and Anderson (1974, 198–200) criticize this pluralist group approach as an "invisible ideology" because it begs the question of whether contemporary American politics is democratic. It defines democracy in a way that makes it identical to the American practice. Thus, behavioralists can be both "scientific" and patriotic. They go on to argue that the behavioral paradigm has stressed fitting people to the system rather than vice versa.
5. Marxists argue that because class conflict underlies all societal cleavages, a society could not have the kind of consensus about fundamentals deemed necessary for democracy until class conflict had been eradicated. At this point, though, the state itself is no longer necessary and will wither away. See Meyer (1957 [1986], 58–59).
6. For empirical findings regarding this and other political consequences of electoral laws, see Rae (1967); Lijphart and Grofman (1984); Grofman and Lijphart (1986); Taagepera and Shugart (1989); Lijphart (1990); and Kim and Ohn (1992). For formal modeling of the problem, see Cox (1990). Recent research (Lijphart 1990; Kim and Ohn 1992) suggests that this "law" may have less utility than some have claimed for predicting the number of parties in an electoral system, but the overall relationship remains clear.
7. The famous cry of the French revolutionaries was "Liberty, equality, fraternity." The latter, indicating the goal of true community among the members of a society, adds an important element to the other two central values. It has not received the same attention from theorists of liberal democracy as liberty and equality. This might in part be because, as I am about to discuss, the fight over the primacy of liberty or equality has dominated efforts to analyze as well as to craft democracies. It might also be because it relates less directly (though no less importantly) to issues of the organization of the state and its relationship to the public. The value of fraternity, or community, remains an important part of theories of democracy in two ways. It underlies one strand of the analyses of "civil society" (as discussed in Chapter 3). Concern with it has also given rise to "communitarianism" as an outlook meant to be distinguished from both libertarianism and egalitarianism (for a defense of this outlook by one of its leading exponents, see Etzioni, 1993; for a critique, see Phillips 1993).
8. The key list of human rights is recorded in the Universal Declaration of Human Rights, first signed in 1948 and accepted by almost every state worldwide. Two United Nations covenants passed in 1966 extended these rights and provided some limited means of monitoring the signatories' observation of their provisions. The covenants, with their stronger terms, have been signed by many of the world's states, but represent less of a consensus than the Declaration.
9. Useful studies of how different countries' varying institutional configurations influence the effectiveness of governance include Powell (1982) and Weaver and Rockman (1993).

REFERENCES

ACKERMAN, BRUCE. 1991. *We the People: I. Foundations.* Cambridge: Harvard University Press.

———. 1992. *The Future of Liberal Revolution.* New Haven: Yale University Press.

ALLMAN, JOE, and WALT ANDERSON. 1974. *Evaluating Democracy: An Introduction to Political Science.* Pacific Palisades, Calif.: Goodyear Publishing.

ARON, RAYMOND. 1969. *Democracy and Totalitarianism.* New York: Praeger.

BARBER, BENJAMIN. 1984. *Strong Democracy: Participatory Politics for a New Age.* Berkeley: University of California Press.

BOBBIO, NORBERTO. 1987. *The Future of Democracy: A Defence of the Rules of the Game.* New York: Polity.

BURBULIS, GENNADII. 1992. "*Ne Chustvami, a Razumom* [Not by emotions but by reason]," *Delovoi Mir.* March 26, 14–5.

BURTON, MICHAEL, RICHARD GUNTHER, and JOHN HIGLEY. 1992. "Introduction: Elite Transformations and Democratic Regimes." In Higley and Gunther, eds., *Elites and Democratic Consolidation in Latin America and Southern Europe.* New York: Cambridge University Press, 1–37.

CEASER, JAMES W. 1990. *Liberal Democracy and Political Science.* Baltimore: Johns Hopkins University Press.

COLEMAN, JAMES S. 1992. "Democracy in Permanently Divided Systems." *American Behavioral Scientist* 35(4/5, March/June):363–74.

CONVERSE, PHILIP E. 1964. "The Nature of Belief Systems in Mass Publics." In David Apter, ed., *Ideology and Discontent.* New York: Free Press of Glencoe, 206–61.

COX, GARY W. 1990. "Centripetal and Centrifugal Incentives in Electoral Systems." *American Journal of Political Science* 34(4, November):903–35.

DAHL, ROBERT A. 1961. *Who Governs?* New Haven: Yale University Press.

———. 1989. *Democracy and Its Critics.* New Haven: Yale University Press.

———, and CHARLES E. LINDBLOM. 1953. *Politics, Economics and Welfare.* Chicago: University of Chicago Press.

DALTON, RUSSELL J. 1988. *Citizen Politics in Western Democracies: Public Opinion and Parties in the United States, Great Britain, West Germany and France.* Chatham, N.J.: Chatham House.

DOWNING, BRIAN M. 1992. *The Military Revolution and Political Change.* Princeton: Princeton University Press.

DOWNS, ANTHONY. 1957. *An Economic Theory of Democracy.* New York: Harper and Row.

DUNN, JOHN, ed. 1992. *Democracy: The Unfinished Journey, 508 BC to AD 1993.* New York: Oxford University Press.

DWORKIN, R. M. 1977. *Taking Rights Seriously.* Cambridge: Harvard University Press.

ECKSTEIN, HARRY. 1980. "Theoretical Approaches to Explaining Collective Political Violence." In Ted Robert Gurr, ed., *Handbook of Political Conflict: Theory and Research.* New York: Free Press, 135–66.

ELSTER, JON. 1988. "Introduction." In Jon Elster and Rune Slagstad, eds., *Constitutionalism and Democracy.* Cambridge: Cambridge University Press, 1–17.

EPSTEIN, RICHARD ALLEN. 1985. *Takings: Private Property and the Power of Eminent Domain.* Cambridge: Harvard University Press.

ETZIONI, AMITAI. 1993. *The Spirit of Community: Rights, Responsibilities and the Communitarian Agenda.* New York: Crown Publishers.

EVANS, PETER B., DIETRICH RUESCHEMEYER, and THEDA SKOCPOL, eds. 1985. *Bringing the State Back In.* New York: Cambridge University Press.

FUKUYAMA, FRANCIS. 1992. *The End of History and the Last Man.* New York: Free Press.

GRAMSCI, ANTONIO. 1929–1935 [1971]. *Selections from the Prison Notebooks of Antonio Gramsci.* Quintin Hoare and Geoffrey Nowell Smith, eds. New York: International Publishers.

GROFMAN, BERNARD, and AREND LIJPHART, eds. 1986. *Electoral Laws and Their Political Consequences.* New York: Agathon Press.

HELD, DAVID. 1987. *Models of Democracy.* Stanford: Stanford University Press.

HEYWOOD, ANDREW. 1992. *Political Ideologies: An Introduction.* New York: St. Martin's Press.

HORNBLOWER, SIMON. 1992. "Creation and Development of Democratic Institutions in Ancient Greece." In John Dunn, ed., *Democracy: The Unfinished Journey, 508 BC to AD 1993.* New York: Oxford University Press, 1–16.

HUNTINGTON, SAMUEL P. 1991. *The Third Wave: Democratization in the Late Twentieth Century.* Norman: University of Oklahoma Press.

KEANE, JOHN. 1988. *Democracy and Civil Society.* London: Verso.

KIM, JAE-ON, and MAHN-GEUM OHN. 1992. "A Theory of Minor-Party Persistence: Election Rules, Social Cleavage, and the Number of Political Parties." *Social Forces* 70(3, March):575–99.

LIJPHART, AREND. 1984. *Democracies: Patterns of Majoritarian and Consensus Government in Twenty One Countries.* New Haven: Yale University Press.

———. 1990. "The Political Consequences of Electoral Laws: 1945–85." *American Political Science Review* 84(2, June):481–96.

———, and BERNARD GROFMAN, eds. 1984. *Choosing an Electoral System: Issues and Alternatives.* New York: Praeger.

MEYER, ALFRED G. 1957 [1986]. *Leninism.* Boulder, Colo.: Westview.

MILLER, ROBERT F., ed., 1992. *The Development of Civil Society in Communist Systems.* Boston: Allen and Unwin.

MOORE, BARRINGTON JR. 1966. *Social Origins of Dictatorship and Democracy: Lord and Peasant in the Making of the Modern World.* Boston: Beacon Press.

MURAKAMI, Y. 1968. *Logic and Social Choice.* New York: Dover Publications.

O'DONNELL, GUILLERMO, and PHILIPPE C. SCHMITTER. 1986. "Tentative Conclusions About Uncertain Democracies." In O'Donnell, Schmitter, and Laurence Whitehead, eds., *Transitions from Authoritarian Rule: Prospects for Democracy, Part IV.* Baltimore: Johns Hopkins University Press, 1–72.

PATEMAN, CAROL. 1970. *Participation and Democratic Theory.* New York: Cambridge University Press.

PENNOCK, J. ROLAND. 1979. *Democratic Political Theory.* Princeton: Princeton University Press.

PHILLIPS, DEREK L. 1993. *Looking Backward: A Critical Appraisal of Communitarian Thought.* Princeton: Princeton University Press.

POWELL, G. BINGHAM. 1982. *Contemporary Democracies: Participation, Stability and Violence.* Cambridge: Harvard University Press.

PRZEWORSKI, ADAM. 1986. "Some Problems in the Study of the Transition to Democracy." In Guillermo O'Donnell, Philippe C. Schmitter, and Laurence Whitehead, eds., *Transitions from Authoritarian Rule: Prospects for Democracy,* Part III. Baltimore: Johns Hopkins University Press, 47–63.

———. 1991. *Democracy and the Market: Political and Economic Reforms in Eastern Europe and Latin America.* New York: Cambridge University Press.

RAE, DOUGLAS W. 1967. *The Political Consequences of Electoral Laws.* New Haven: Yale University Press.

ROPER, JON. 1989. *Democracy and Its Critics: Anglo-American Democratic Thought in the Nineteenth Century.* Boston: Unwin Hyman.

RUSTOW, DANKWART A. 1970. "Transitions to Democracy: Toward a Dynamic Model," *Comparative Politics* 2(3, April):337–63.

SARTORI, GIOVANNI. 1987. *The Theory of Democracy Revisited.* Chatham, N.J.: Chatham House.

SCHATTSCHNEIDER, E. E. 1942. *Party Government.* New York: Holt, Rinehart and Winston.

———. 1960. *The Semisovereign People.* New York: Holt, Rinehart and Winston.

SCHMITTER, PHILIPPE C., and TERRY LYNN KARL. 1991. "What Democracy Is . . . and Is Not," *Journal of Democracy* 2(3, Summer):75–88.

SCHUMPETER, JOSEPH. 1942. *Capitalism, Socialism and Democracy,* Second Edition. New York: Harper and Bros.

SKINNER, QUENTIN. 1992. "The Italian City-Republics." In John Dunn, ed., *Democracy: The Unfinished Journey, 508 BC to AD 1993.* New York: Oxford University Press, 57–69.

SLATON, CHRISTA DARYL. 1992. *Televote: Expanding Citizen Participation in the Quantum Age.* New York: Praeger.

TAAGEPERA, REIN, and MATTHEW SOBERG SHUGART. 1989. *Seats and Votes: The Effects and Determinants of Electoral Systems.* New Haven: Yale University Press.

TRUMAN, DAVID. 1951. *The Governmental Process: Political Interests and Public Opinion.* New York: Knopf.

VAN DYKE, VERNON. 1992. *Introduction of Politics,* Second Edition. Chicago: Nelson-Hall.

VERBA, SYDNEY, NORMAN H. NIE, and JAE-ON KIM. 1978. *Participation and Political Equality: A Seven-Nation Comparison.* New York: Cambridge University Press.

WEAVER, R. KENT, and BERT A. ROCKMAN. 1993. *Do Institutions Matter? Government Capabilities in the United States and Abroad.* Washington, D.C.: Brookings Institution.

CHAPTER
3

Establishing and Strengthening Democracy

WILLIAM R. REISINGER

According to the annual Freedom House ratings (Karatnycky 1994), seventy-two states, or not quite 40 percent of the world's 190 recognized states at the end of 1993, were "free" in the sense of having democratic institutions and actually providing political and civil liberties to their citizens. An even smaller percentage of countries have had long periods of uninterrupted democratic governance. Mainwaring (1993), for example, counts thirty-one countries—16 percent—which have had at least twenty-five years of uninterrupted democracy. Moreover, the countries with lengthy democratic traditions are almost all western industrialized market societies. This fact has prompted a large scholarly literature seeking to understand why one well-defined subset of the world's regimes are (and seem likely to remain) democratic whereas most other states have experienced great difficulty establishing and maintaining democratic rule. By comparing the democracies, the intermittent democracies, and the nondemocracies, scholars have come up with competing lists of conditions or actions that seem most likely to facilitate democratization.[1] The generalizations derived from the study of democratization in other regions may or may not apply to developments in a given post-communist country. Yet they need keeping in mind as guideposts, at least, in assessing whether the formal commitments to democracy can be translated into genuine and long-lasting democratic governance.

Because the question of the sources of democratization has fascinated so many, I cannot review all the many arguments available. Moreover, several approaches are taken up and examined in detail in later chapters. I have therefore selected four prominent clusters of democratization theories. The first cluster consists of those scholars who examine one or another aspect of the society in question—the level of economic development or public attitudes, for instance—as a requisite condition for the development of democracy. The second cluster uses historical case studies to identify the factors influencing the sequencing of political change. The third cluster consists of those focusing on the choices and strategies of key political elites during (short-term) struggles over the shape of political life in a given country. The final cluster examines the nature of the democratic institutions established in order to judge how likely it is that those institutions will survive the challenges they will inevitably face. Each of the four has been developed by numerous scholars and includes as much diversity as it does unity. In addition, each approach draws our attention to quite different influences, including socioeconomic development, political values, class structure, regime structure, and bargaining among elites. Familiarity with these four viewpoints will help orient the reader to the rich variety of propositions available for studying democratization.

DEMOCRATIZATION

In Chapter 2, I reviewed the different pieces of the puzzle of how a stable liberal democracy functions. A democracy must create a workable whole out of such things as the mechanisms for public participation in politics, competition among organized political interests, the election of representatives to conduct the government in the name of the people, and checks on the range of decisions that these elected representatives can take. The study of democra*tization* is actually the study of two potentially distinct questions: What facilitates the replacement of one or another form of authoritarian rule with democratic institutions, norms, and procedures? And, what facilitates the *consolidation* of democracy? Once democracy is consolidated, in Juan Linz's (1990c, 158) words, "none of the major political actors, parties or organized interests, forces or institutions consider that there is any alternative to democratic processes to gain power, and . . . no political institution or group has a claim to veto the action of democratically elected decision makers." Phillipe Schmitter (1992, 424) provides a related formulation:

> Consolidation could be defined as the process of transforming the accidental arrangements, prudential norms, and contingent solutions that have emerged during the transition into relations of cooperation and competition that are reliably known, regularly practiced, and voluntarily accepted by those persons or collectivities (i.e., politicians and citizens) that participate in democratic governance.

As noted, democratic consolidation, according to these authors, requires not only that the institution and procedures of democracy be introduced but that democratic conditions must be created by the procedures to a degree sufficient for the public to feel that democratic institutions have some significant payoff to them. Furthermore, the Linz and Schmitter definitions of consolidation imply the importance of the democratic institutions proving themselves efficient in the pursuit of state goals. Democratic regimes most often fail following a state crisis in the security or economic realms.

So democratization refers to the processes of political change involved in efforts to create, broaden, or solidify democratic modes of governance. In some countries, democratization has resulted in a consolidated democracy. In others, the creation (perhaps more accurately, the announcement) of democratic institutions fails to produce patterns of governance that are both democratic and sufficiently capable to survive.

The study of democratization has produced two distinct modes of argument. Some scholars focus on long-term societal changes as the source of democracy. These "structural" theories draw our focus to societal features that change only slowly and imply that some of these societies are likely candidates to become democracies while others are not. Structural approaches regard strategies and choices made by individual actors as affecting things only at the margin and for a short time only. They tend to ignore the distinction between the establishment and the consolidation of democracy. By contrast, other scholars pay more attention to short-term choices and strategies as determinants of whether a democracy emerges and lasts. They look at a society's structural conditions as the "soil" of democracy. Skillful political actors can harvest democracy out of relatively barren soil, or events can transpire to trample the fruits of rich soil. These "contextualists" are more likely to distinguish the breaking down of an authoritarian regime (that is, "liberalizing") from the process of introducing democratic patterns of rule. I review four general approaches to the study of democratization below:

1. modernization theories
2. comparative historical studies
3. elite contestation theories
4. institutional configuration theories

The first two are structural and the final two contextual. The structural and contextual approaches are not incompatible; their relationship to each other is, potentially, analogous to the relationship between macro- and microeconomics. Yet no commonly accepted synthesis of structural and contextual approaches has been found. The careful application of all of these types of theory to developments in post-communist countries, which is now underway, may well permit new progress toward linking structural and contextual understanding.

THEORETICAL CLUSTER 1: SOCIETAL MODERNIZATION AS A PRECONDITION FOR DEMOCRATIZATION

Although the democratic ideal has long enjoyed widespread acceptance, the spread of democratic governance has proceeded in fits and starts. Outside a core of West European and Anglo-American countries with highly developed capitalist economies, there have been few democratic regimes and these have had short half-lives. With this in mind, scholars, not surprisingly, surmised that perhaps some societies were not as ready for democracy as others. They argued that democracy had been adopted earlier and with more success in the Western capitalist countries because their societies had earlier undergone a long-term process of socioeconomic change sometimes dubbed "modernization." Some theorists believe that scientific and technical innovations provide the driving force behind modernization, while others focus on changes in the patterns of the global economy.[2] Whatever the origin, modernization theorists argue that democratic institutions are far more likely to be established in a society with the socioeconomic requisites. If a society that is not yet ready nevertheless puts democratic institutions in place, they are more likely to fail, producing a return to authoritarian rule.

Seymour Martin Lipset, in his influential volume *Political Man* (1960, Chs. 2–3), pointed to the tendency for countries that scored high on measures of societal modernization, in particular those that had a highly developed (market) economy, to be governed democratically. He demonstrated this tendency by separating numerous countries into democratic and nondemocratic categories and then determining what the democracies had that the others lacked. Lipset found that the democracies were characterized by higher degrees of societal wealth, industrialization, urbanization, and provision of higher education.

Lipset's methodology quickly came under attack. Lipset provided an analysis of differences across countries at a single time in order to make a point about process. He assumed a linearity in development and political change unlikely to be found in actual cases. He did not provide a multivariate analysis that would permit him to assess the significance of a given explanatory variable while holding other factors constant. In addition, the exceptions to the empirical pattern itself raised doubts. European nondemocracies in Lipset's own data tended to have higher levels of economic development than the democracies in Latin America (Diamond 1992). O'Donnell (1973) argues that, among states outside Western Europe and North America, a technocratic elite intent on promoting development is likely to ally itself with the military to introduce an authoritarian modernizing regime. Democracy will therefore be found, O'Donnell argued, in partly developed states whereas those at the low and high ends of the scale will be authoritarian. On the other hand, Lipset's basic argument received support from later, more methodologically sophisticated empirical studies (Bollen 1979; Muller 1988). The relationship to which Lipset pointed therefore deserves note as a fact about the pattern of democratization to date (cf. Lipset 1994).

Why should this pattern exist? Lipset, Robert Dahl (1989, 251–4), Samuel Huntington (1991, Ch. 2), and others argue that economic development creates a more complex and diverse society that is more difficult for an authoritarian regime to control.[3] An important component of this is that the furthering of economic development requires that the populace be removed from abject poverty, be kept healthy and sheltered, and be granted a formal education, including higher education for many. Development also requires the creation of channels of communication and transportation. A developed economy, by doing these things, disperses power away from a single center. As economic power is disseminated throughout a society whose members have better education and more effective communications, a larger portion of the populace will seek political influence. This trend creates pressures for democracy. Note that these arguments stress the role that a developing market economy plays in fostering *liberty*, which, as was discussed in Chapter 2, is a crucial component of modern democratic governance.

Whether a developing market economy fosters *equality*, however, is a more difficult question. Economic development in capitalist economies has an inherently anti-egalitarian tendency. By increasing the inequality in wealth (that is, in economic power), economic growth likewise creates inequality in political power, and such inequities are not easily overcome without violating norms of liberty. Lipset and other modernization theorists argue that economic development will promote a partial shift toward income equality that is conducive to democratization. That is, they view economic growth as a process that, while making some extremely rich, simultaneously increases the size of the middle class. The middle class, composed of skilled workers and professionals, then forms a bridge between the haves and have-nots in society. If the middle class is large, sharp polarization between two sectors of society becomes less likely; tolerance, moderation, hard work, and other virtues ensue.

In line with these propositions, a vast amount of research has investigated the link between democracy and the public's attitudes or values. In Dahl's (1989, 30) words, "It is obvious . . . that the emergence and persistence of a democratic government among a group of people depends in some way on their *beliefs*." Each society will have a particular distribution of individual outlooks on politics. That distribution is usually dubbed the society's "political culture." Some political cultures will be conducive to the establishment and consolidation of democracy while others will not. The source of mass support for democratization comes largely from the society's own past developments, and certain mass orientations must be present *prior to* democracy taking root.

Various attitudes or values have been put forth as vital to democracy. Maher reviews these in greater depth in Chapter 4. I will just mention here Almond and Verba's (1963) pioneering investigation of the link between political culture and democracy. They stressed a pattern they called the "civic culture," which contains three elements: (1) a mix of those predisposed to participate actively in politics and those not inclined to, (2) a high level of trust among fellow citizens, and (3) a general (or "diffuse") support for democratic institutions and practices, as opposed to support for a particular set of leaders. As discussed in Chapter 2, the optimum level of public participation is disputed; Almond and Verba stressed that both too much public participation and too little can harm a democracy. Trust among members of a society is seen as necessary in order for participants to follow the rules of the game: to see opponents as loyal opponents who will not kill or imprison them if they lose. Also, people need to trust others for them to be able to form and participate in "secondary associations" such as clubs, movements, and interest groups. Such associations support and extend the capabilities of democratic institutions, thus enabling democracies to function better than they could on their own. Diffuse support allows a democratic regime to survive periodic crises of confidence. Even when a particular set of rulers or policies has failed miserably, an authoritarian group is less likely to seize power if the populace values the democratic institutions themselves.

The economic and attitudinal strands of modernization theory are compatible and fit together well for many scholars. Inglehart (1990) has recently made a case for combining both aspects of societal modernization. He argues that, as a society begins the long-term process of industrialization and economic development, new patterns of economic life change people's expectations and increase their willingness to press demands on the elites, a process he terms "social mobilization." He then points out that social mobilization can result either in the establishment of democratic institutions or in the establishment of a fascist or communist regime.[4] Later, as economic development continues, more and more citizens undergo "cognitive mobilization," the process of acquiring the desire and skills to influence the government in ways that are more direct and more effective than just voting every so often. Inglehart declares that the long-term expansion of cognitive mobilization in the most developed countries has reduced the effectiveness of centralized power. Cognitive mobilization, together with an increase in what Inglehart calls "post-materialist" values (Inglehart 1977), creates pressure on elites to establish formal democratic institutions, institutions that may later stabilize and become consolidated.

Can the "modernization" arguments be applied to the societies of Eastern Europe and the former USSR? Many see the development-democracy relationship as directly pertinent to the second world. Robert Dahl (1971, 78) argued over two decades ago that "as countries with hegemonic systems move to high levels of economic development (for example, the USSR and the Eastern European countries) a centrally dominated social order is increasingly difficult to maintain." Hough (1988) and Lewin (1988 [1991]) maintain that industrialization of the economy, collectivization of agriculture, the resulting migration to the cities, as well as increased literacy and access to higher education all changed the societies in the USSR in a manner that made them more "modern" and therefore more supportive of democratic and market reforms. (Even though, ironically, the Soviet and East European economies actually were collapsing when the move to democracy began.) Others challenge the presumption that modernization in the same sense took place at all under communist regimes (White 1979, 57–8; Jowitt 1992). Most crucially, in the economic sphere, communist industrialization did not create a market economy based on private property, a common feature of the countries studied by Lipset and others. Therefore, "anti-modernizationists" argue that economic transformation could not and did not influence the communist societies in the manner that economic development shaped the Western democracies that Lipset studied.

> To put it bluntly: the Leninist legacy, understood as the impact of Party organization, practice, and ethos, *and* the initial charismatic ethical opposition to it favor an authoritarian, not a liberal democratic capitalist, way of life; the obstacles to

> which are not simply how to privatize and marketize the economy, or organize an electoral campaign, but rather how to institutionalize public virtues. (Jowitt 1992, 293)

What does the course of events to date suggest about modernization under communism? With regard to political changes, modernization arguments provide the following hypothesis: The most economically developed Eastern European and post-Soviet societies should have been the first to experience public pressure for democratization and should possess the best prospects for consolidating their democratic systems. This hypothesis is supported by the relatively early establishment of democratic movements in Poland, Hungary, and the Baltic countries as well as the relatively late appearance of democratic pressure in the Balkan and Central Asian regions. Yet democratic movements in Armenia and Georgia got underway before those in more industrialized and better educated Russia, Ukraine, and Byelarus. So, there is only a weak relationship between economic development levels within the bloc and the timing of the onset of pressure for democratization.

If the level of economic development is related to the establishment of democracy to a certain extent, how well will it serve as a guide to the consolidation of democracy? It is too early to provide a definitive answer, but here, too, economic development seems a useful though partial guide. Civil disturbances or outright warfare in some of the least economically developed regions (Central Asia, the Caucasus, the Balkans) certainly make democratic consolidation a distant goal for those societies. Yet even among the more economically developed and more Westernized post-communist societies, the enthusiasm and optimism that Eastern Europe's miraculous revolutions created in 1989 have now given way to the reality of party factionalization and ineffective governance (Poland), separatism (the 1992 split of Czechoslovakia into the Czech republic and Slovakia), and disillusionment (the eastern portion of Germany). Similar problems characterized other recently established democracies, included the Federal Republic of Germany, Spain, and others. If the periods of disorientation and disillusionment are short-lived, their existence does not contradict modernization theory. If, however, democracy is actually floundering in the north-central European societies, which, among communist states, had the highest per capita gross national products, modernization theory suggests that the chance of democracy taking root elsewhere is slim.

THEORETICAL CLUSTER 2: COMPARATIVE HISTORICAL APPROACHES

I will now introduce a perspective that incorporates several quite distinct approaches to studying political change, including democratization. These approaches consist of various Marxist and neo-Marxist theories, as well as diverse non-Marxist scholarship by sociologists and anthropologists. By discussing them together, I do not want to imply even the minimal commonalty found among discussions of societal modernization. Yet the works I will refer to do have in common the use of certain key concepts as well as an emphasis on explicating and defending their arguments through studies of historical change in one or more societies. Also, they tend to share a deep suspicion of the cross-national generalizations profered by modernization theories. For these theorists, only a particular confluence of factors *and the sequence in which they occur* in a given society can explain the success or failure of democratization.

Concepts

The key concepts that run through studies of this sort are (1) the state, (2) civil society, (3) socioeconomic classes, and (4) the nature of the international situation, including changes in the global economy. The concepts that theories in this cluster share are central ones in the social sciences, yet are generally given less attention by theorists in the other three clusters. We certainly need to examine their pertinence to post-communist democratization.

Social scientists' use of the term the "state" adds to American understanding of "government" the organs of coercion—the police, the tax collectors, the military, the courts, and other institutions that can enforce the decisions of political leaders. Most commonly, scholars adopt Weber's (1946 [1958], 78) definition: "[A] state is a human community that (successfully) claims the *monopoly of the legitimate use of physical force* within a given territory." Skocpol (1985, 7) adds that "Administrative, legal, extractive, and coercive organizations are the core of any state. Even when these organizations are embedded in a constitutional system of parliamentary decision making and electoral contests for key executive and legislative posts, there still is a 'state.'" Note the terminological distinction between *a* state—a given human community—and *the* state—the administrative, legal, extractive, and coercive organizations that Skocpol calls the core of any state.

The importance of the state for democratic consolidation is twofold: The state must be strong and effective in carrying out such tasks as protection from outside attack and the maintenance of internal order, yet it must not become so dominant that it chokes off liberty, popular participation, and other elements of a democratic order. Modern state institutions concentrate so much potential power in the hands of top officials that corruption and other abuses of power become very tempting. Machine politics and repression of the populace become real possibilities. If no force offsets the concentration of power in state institutions, democratic competition would not be possible.

The organizations, groups, and communities outside the state that can serve to counterbalance it are known collectively as "civil society." In Keane's (1988, 14) definition, civil society is: "an aggregate of institutions whose members are engaged primarily in a complex of non-state activities—economic and cultural production, household life and voluntary associations—and who in this way preserve and transform their identity by exercising all sorts of pressures or controls upon state institutions. . . ." A country's civil society has what might be thought of as two distinct components. The first is what is sometimes called "the private sector": nongovernmental economic activities in which firms and individuals compete against each other for economic gain (and, hopefully, enrich the society and the state in the process). Those who point out the need for this aspect of civil society stress the autonomy, privacy, and liberty of citizens. The second component consists of all the various activities that people undertake and associations they form with their fellow members of society without being directed to do so by the state. This second component of civil society is celebrated not as a source of freedom and competition (the "rat race") but as the source of community for individuals. The stress falls on citizens' identity, societal traditions, and bonds among people, on the formation of a "social fabric." "[Civil society] points, in its different articulations, to those elements of both community and individualism that have served to define political thought for the past two hundred years. For civil society is, at the same time, that realm of 'natural affections and sociability' recognized by Adam Smith, as well as that arena where man 'acts as a private individual, regards other men as means, degrades himself into a means and becomes a plaything of alien powers,' in Marx's famous characterization of market relations" (Seligman 1992, 3). These two dimensions can work at cross purposes but need not do so.

Both dimensions of civil society can serve democracy by checking and counterbalancing state institutions that might otherwise take on authoritarian or totalitarian traits. The private economic sphere generates a nonstate means of acquiring status and influence over the state, which limits the ability of state elites to exclude certain groups, ideas, or policies from the political process, thereby limiting popular rule (Ware 1987, 7–16). To the extent there is a civil society in the communitarian sense, even a dominating state will be unable to manipulate society as it wishes. Each member of society will be linked to and supported by his or her friends, colleagues, fellow church members, and so on.

Even as it restrains the state, however, the civil society can strengthen it. The influential Italian Marxist Gramsci (1929–1935 [1971]) focused on the communitarian dimension in arguing that civil society serves as the "battlements" surrounding the capitalist state and protecting it against attack from socialist revolutionaries. If the private economic sphere is operating properly, it supports the state by generating wealth. Also, many argue that civil society in both senses is crucial for the country to respond well to challenges and adapt to changing conditions. Note that the argument that democracy requires a strong civil society is similar to the argument made by modernization scholars such as Lipset who stress the importance of a middle class, of education, of a market economy, and of the secondary associations that arise in a society with such attributes. Overall, then, democratic consolidation will depend on finding a workable balance between the competitive and communitarian dimensions of civil society as well as between civil society and the state.

Several theorists have argued that civil society should be distinguished from *political society* (Stepan 1978, 1985, 1988; Weintraub 1993). Political society refers to "that arena in which the polity specifically arranges itself for political contestation to gain control over public power and the state apparatus." Its components include political parties, elections, electoral rules, political leadership, intra-party alliances, and legislatures. By means of these components, civil society is able to constitute itself politically and monitor democratic government. There are several reasons for making this distinction. One is that it allows the distinguishing between countries in which the state dominates the political society but allows civil society to operate with fewer fetters (an authoritarian regime) and countries in which the state dominates not just the political sphere but the economy and social structures as well (a totalitarian regime). In Brazil, Stepan (1988, 6) argues, the various organizations of civil society sought the opportunity during the 1970s and 1980s to speak out and act yet did not seek to modify political society, which was controlled by the military in Brasilia. Thus, civil society was supporting *liberalization* but not *democratization*. Similarly, one could argue that Soviet leader Gorbachev sought to liberalize the USSR with his policies of glasnost and perestroika, but was unwilling to democratize in the sense of allowing political competition outside the control of the Communist Party (until he was forced into doing so).

So, in examining political change in a country, or comparing such change across several countries, theorists in this cluster would want to identify the nature of the state, of civil and perhaps political society, and of the relationship between state and society. However, to understand a given society and the state-society relationship adequately, one needs to examine key differences within the society. Theorists have long understood that people in a society will behave differently and have different values depending on their economic status and the culture and traditions associated with their economic status. A group of people sharing economic status and the associated culture is typically referred to as a (socioeconomic) class. The use of class as a central analytic tool is most closely associated with the work of Karl Marx and the many scholars and activists influenced by him. Marx's emphasis on the importance of an individual's place in the economy—that individual's "relationship to the means of production"—sheds light on a crucial source of any society's internal conflict. Marx's understanding of what defines a class is not, of course, universally shared. Some stress the socioeconomic status and opportunities that come from one's family background (Rueschemeyer, Stephens, and Stephens 1992, 47–8). In addition, the classes that receive scrutiny vary quite a bit. Marx focused on the industrial working class and the capital-owning class as the central "players" in the class struggle of capitalist societies, yet he incorporated discussions of landowners, peasants, and petty bourgeoisie (what would now be called "small businesspeople"). Each of these classes could be subdivided, and classes not anticipated by Marx are frequently discussed: managers, for example, who run the major corporations but do not own them.

Because members of different classes are likely to be affected in different ways by a state's institutions and policies, political battle lines can fall along class lines. In other words, many theories of political change start from, or incorporate, the notion of class *conflict*. Conflict among two or more socioeconomic classes plays itself out primarily through clashes between organizations representing them. The class that a political party represents is, generally speaking, quite evident.

Often, it is enshrined in the party's name: the Labor Party or the Freeholders Party, for example. (Whether one should include here the Polish Beer Drinker's Party, the success story of the 1991 Polish elections, is left to the reader.) Interest groups and other associations can also be linked primarily to one class or another. Finally, in the eyes of many theorists, the state is both an instrument of class struggle and the object of such struggle.

The final concept common to comparative historical case studies is that societies are influenced by trends and economic developments outside their borders. Following Lenin's internationalization of Marxist class analysis in his *Imperialism* (1917 [1975]), Marxist analyses of political change have placed great emphasis on the ways in which global economics can influence states, societies, and classes in virtually every country. In particular, much analysis has traced how the disadvantageous economic positions of developing countries—their "dependence" on the more economically developed capitalist states—has hindered positive social and political changes and even promoted harmful developments. Many non-Marxists come to similar conclusions about the centrality of international economic developments. Who could now doubt the centrality to almost every country of global financial and trade transactions, as well as of the rapid transmission of information and culture across borders? In the noneconomic sphere, it is obvious that warfare in neighboring locales influences domestic politics, either by involving the country directly or through such indirect sources as gun-running, refugees, and militarization to deter an attack. Thus, the influence of "extrasocietal" influences on democratization and other political change must be acknowledged (See Chapter 9 by Grey).

Employing the Concepts

So, comparative historical studies of political change—whatever the theoretical arguments being assumed—place before the investigator certain questions about the case(s) at hand. What institutions control state power? What capabilities does the state possess and how extensively throughout society? To what degree is there a civil society providing a nonstate space for popular behavior? How is this civil society organized? How do the state and the society interact? What is the balance of power or division of labor between them? (Optionally, one might also ask: How is political society organized and how does it interact with both the state and the civil society?) Of what major socioeconomic classes does the society consist? What role does each class play in the state as well as in civil society (and thus what is the balance of power among these classes)? What is the nature of the economic change underway during the period under study? How are changing regional and global economic patterns altering the answers to the previous questions? What is the security situation the country faces? As noted, the range of theoretical propositions to which questions like these give rise is staggering, and even to review them is beyond the scope of this chapter. However, brief descriptions of two comparative historical investigations of democratization will help illustrate how the concepts can be deployed.

Barrington Moore, Jr.'s *Social Origins of Dictatorship and Democracy* (1966) focused on the landed nobility and the peasantry in several countries, though he discussed these classes' interaction with the Crown, merchants, and other social strata as well. Moore concluded that there are three main routes to the "modern world." These three can be described as (1) capitalist revolution from below, (2) capitalist revolution from above, and (3) peasant revolution. In the first route, a bourgeois revolution led to an industrial revolution. Moore had in mind the English Civil War, the French Revolution, and the U.S. Civil War. "A key feature in such revolutions is the development of a group in society with an independent economic base. . . ." (*xv*). If the landed nobles were part of this movement, they prospered. If not, they were swept aside in a violent way. If the peasantry were not part of the rise of capitalism, they were crushed by it. (The United States was a new country without a peasantry.) In countries taking the second route, the bourgeois or merchant sectors of society were relatively weak. The landed nobles were able to remain in power and control industrialization. This route resulted in industrialization, but under fascist control (à la Germany and Japan). Countries taking the third route ended up with communism (USSR, China). Even more than in Germany and Japan, Russian and Chinese agricultural bureaucracies prevented a reduction in the size of the agrarian sector and the peasant population. As the peasantry was squeezed, Moore argues, it became a potent revolutionary force. This force led to communist regimes, which, ironically, treated the peasantry yet worse.[5]

A recent effort to transform Moore's approach and apply it to contemporary cases is Rueschemeyer, Stephens, and Stephens, *Capitalist Development and Democracy* (1992). Their analyses are sophisticated and cover a wide range of countries. Their conclusions therefore deserve note. The puzzle that generated their research was the contradictory analyses being generated by the two structural approaches covered in this chapter: the upbeat assessment of the prospects for democratization provided by those in the modernization school and the more gloomy predictions provided by comparative historical studies. Rueschemeyer, Stephens, and Stephens set out a conceptual framework resting on three groups of circumstances in a country: the balance of power among different social classes, the nature of state-society relations, and transnational influences. They argue that democratization is pushed by the subordinate classes in a society as a means to increase their power relative to the dominant class or classes. When conditions such as capitalist economic development provide a formerly nonexistent or politically uninvolved class with growing social power, that class will struggle to advance democratic forms of governance since those reduce, though by no means eliminate, the political power held by the upper classes. This trend will be modified in any country by the character and strength of state institutions, as well as by transnational developments such as war, economic interdependence, and cultural transmission.

Using this framework, Rueschemeyer, Stephens, and Stephens carry out case studies of democratization in western Europe and Latin America. They find that an organized working class was important to the development of full democracy (that is, democratic institutions with inclusive suffrage) almost everywhere. The research of Moore and others had generally found industrial workers to be opposed to democratization or not important to the process. The Rueschemeyer, Stephens, and Stephens argument is supported by the prominent role played by miners and shipbuilders in Poland's mass organization, Solidarity, as well as the importance of miners' strikes in the Soviet Union from 1989 on. Rueschemeyer, Stephens, and Stephens also find that landlords, particularly those who depended on a large supply of cheap labor, were consistent *opponents* of democracy. (This parallels Moore's arguments.) Civil society generally did support democracy by counterbalancing the power of state institutions, but in cases such as Germany, Austria, and Brazil, the organizations of civil society helped transmit an antidemocratic ideology from the dominant classes downward. Political parties emerged as crucial mediating institutions among classes in the cases that Rueschemeyer, Stephens, and Stephens studied. Given these findings, Rueschemeyer, Stephens, and Stephens reject the assumption of modernization approaches that a single set of causal factors is at work for democratization worldwide. They do find regional similarities in the experiences of the countries, but stress how important are the paths followed previously in each country.

Evaluation

What are the strengths and weaknesses of comparative historical case studies for analyzing democratization? Among the weaknesses of work in this cluster would be a tendency to reify the concepts, to speak, for example, not of "a state" but of "The State" (Tilly 1984, 20–6). If one's theory requires that many different people be treated in the aggregate as a single "actor," one must be extremely careful in specifying why doing so reflects a social reality. A second weakness is the difficulty of generalizing from one study to a new set of conditions (Skocpol and Somers 1980, 195). This is acknowledged by Rueschemeyer, Stephens, and Stephens (1992, 75–6) and other proponents of this approach. Still, in the quest to reflect the complexity of actual historical change, it is possible to make one's theory so complex that generalization is virtually impossible. The stress that "each case is unique" comes close at times to genetic determinism (Skocpol and Somers 1980, 192–3). Finally, the key terms share no generally agreed upon definitions. "There are enough different theoretical approaches to the concept of 'civil society' and enough varying historical contents of the notion to turn every work dealing with this subject into a philosophical and/or historical treatise devoted to conceptual variations and subtleties." (Frentzel-Zagorska 1992, 40)

Among the strengths of work in this cluster is that it tends to be more sophisticated theoretically than other approaches. Authors approaching democratization from this perspective acknowledge the complexities of a process of political change such as democratization and try to incorporate those complexities, not put them aside as many theories do. Models that examine state-society relations have an advantage over elite-only or mass-only models by positing that society is more than a mass of individuals and that those individuals are tied together in a complex variety of ways as well as being tied to the state in a variety of ways. Further, the focus on tracing the path followed in a particular country is a big advantage given that the subject of study is a type of change.

The formerly communist countries provide a particularly intriguing site for employing the concepts and arguments of comparative historical studies because some common features of state-society relations existed in all of them. State-society relations in communist systems have been depicted as being totalitarian. Theorists of totalitarianism highlighted the "atomization" of society that communist regimes undertook in the course of mobilizing the populations for large-scale ideological, economic, and demographic transformations (Arendt 1951). By atomization, they referred to the breaking of various social ties among people, tearing the fabric of society, such that each individual is like a separate atom not joined into any larger molecules. The terror caused by mass arrests, informants, show trials, and executions made people too frightened to trust others and therefore too distrusting to form groupings that might challenge the state. Migranyan (1987) was one of the first Soviet scholars to employ the state-civil society approach to analyze Soviet history. He argued that during the industrialization and collectivization period, when the state should have been working to build up civil society (as part of building socialism so that the state could wither away), it instead reduced civil society practically to zero.

For many students of communist politics, civil society did not reappear even after de-Stalinization. Instead, post-Stalinist leaders, while putting a stop to the most totalitarian elements of rule, still prevented a vibrant civil society from emerging. Ekiert (1991) argues, for instance, that Stalinism destroyed political society and assaulted civil or domestic society. But, in de-Stalinization, the state and the domestic society came to a *modus vivendi* that allowed civil society only a minor role. The weakness of civil society had the unintended consequence of harming the state because it led to corruption and the emergence of nonofficial mechanisms of interest mediation and representation. Rather than state bureaucracies applying state policy downward on domestic society, there grew up networks of clientelism that favored some groups. Also, a second, illegal economy blossomed. The resulting disrespect for law and the demoralization of society soon pervaded the ruling communist parties themselves. The breakdown of the communist regimes began with their opponents' attempt to reconstitute political society by reinvigorating traditional political and cultural values.

More optimistic interpretations of the situation existed as well, however. For example, several observers argue that the development of a genuine civil society in the USSR was complete or well on its way by the Gorbachev years. As evidence, they pointed to the burgeoning unofficial organizations, youth groups, and other "informals." Interestingly, these authors argue that civil society emerged because of demographic trends—industrialization, urbanization, and education—that all the communist societies underwent. A fascinating use of state-society relations as a prism for understanding communist politics was that of scholars and activists in Poland, Czechoslovakia, and Hungary, who, by the late 1970s, were increasingly arguing that they could construct a viable civil society from within a communist country (Goldfarb 1992). Their conviction proved important in the organizing success of anti-communist movements such as Solidarity in Poland. (Poland was the most successful example at that early date because of some favorable conditions, including the role of the Catholic church in that society.)

As a result, one of the most widely shared understandings of what must be done to ensure the survival of democracy has been that civil society must be further developed and strengthened. A critical component of developing a civil society capable of defending democratic institutions is to create a sufficiently large market sector of the economy for nonstate economic power to grow. Proponents of rapid and radical marketization in the region argue that market economics will produce societal changes that will rule out a "return to the past." As noted above, though, market relations stress competition among citizens, not common action. Although the Eastern European activists who sought to build civil society began by stressing the sharing of ideas and assistance against the state, the fall of the regimes eliminated the common enemy that bound them together. Moreover, these countries do not have the dense networks of political and social organizations present in Western societies that offset the competitive realm of market economics. So, while successful marketization of some degree will be crucial to democratization, marketization alone will not lead to a civil society supportive of democracy. Equally crucial will be the establishment of political parties, interest groups, and social organizations and, through their operation, the creation of centripetal, not centrifugal, social forces.

Furthermore, an irony common to many post-communist countries is that strengthening the state may be just as important as strengthening civil society. Remember that these were considered "totalitarian" or at least highly authoritarian regimes in which state authorities could decide a range of matters considered private in other countries. Surely a strong state is something the successor regimes began with. Yet several aspects of the fall of communist power tore down old state structures and placed restrengthening at the top of the agenda. Most directly, of course, is that newly independent countries emerged from the former state boundaries. Fifteen countries took the place of the USSR, while two replaced Czechoslovakia. (Granted, the disappearance of East Germany reduced the number by one.) Boundary issues have become extremely volatile as a result. A second reason for the weakness of current state structures is that "the state" under communism included institutions of the Communist Parties. The administrative, legal, extractive, and coercive bodies in these countries were all tightly linked to the ruling parties. With the outlawing of those parties, the formal state institutions must take over functions previously held by party organs, in some cases while facing *sub rosa* challenges from former party officials. So, the development of autonomous and effective states must accompany the building of civil society in many of the post-communist countries.

THEORETICAL CLUSTER 3: INTRA-ELITE BARGAINING AND TRANSITIONS TO DEMOCRACY

A currently prominent approach to understanding the establishment of democracy—its timing, its ease, its longevity—focuses on short-term political *dynamics*. Its proponents are reacting against the various approaches that focus on correlates of democratization. The first work in this tradition and the benchmark for those that followed was Rustow (1970), who saw democratization as a series of stages: the *preparatory*, *decision*, and *habituation* phases. (It is typical of this approach to separate changes into three stages, now generally referred to as breakdown, transition, and consolidation.)

Those examining short-term dynamics place the bulk of the responsibility for successful or failed democratization on the shoulders of key individuals. In this approach, one explains democratization (successful or failed) by examining choices, bargains, power plays, and most importantly, the interrelationship and sequencing of such acts. In this perspective, what is crucial for democratization, and what analysts should look for, is agreement among a sufficient number of powerful people (and the groups they represent) on the need for clearly defined, open, and democratic rules of competition. A winning coalition, so to speak, must emerge from elites who have decided that they are better off competing with their opponents in the regulated ways that democratic institutions make necessary. Such a winning coalition must generally incorporate more than just a bare majority. Some authors even speak of achieving elite "consensus" in favor of democratic procedures (Burton, Gunther, and Higley 1992, 13–30).

The winning coalition can emerge either through settlement (a compromise) or convergence (intra-elite differences grow smaller). The process of reaching settlements or pacts, known as *pactadura*, has received particular attention with regard to Latin America. As Przeworski (1986, 59–60) points out, the elite compromise involved in a democratic transition cannot be a compromise about substance. A democracy by definition cannot guarantee policy outcomes ahead of time, even if all the elites involved in the discussions agree on how to resolve an issue.[6] "What is possible are institutional agreements, that is, compromises about the institutions that shape prior probabilities of the realization of group-specific interests. If a peaceful transition to democracy is to be possible, the first problem to be solved is how to institutionalize uncertainty without threatening the interests of those who can still reverse this process. The solution to the democratic compromise consists of institutions."

This raises a critical question. In an authoritarian regime, by definition, one group or coalition of elites dominates the political scene sufficiently to eliminate the need to compete against other groups for power. Why should those in a position of authoritarian power ever agree to a new institutional arrangement that places them in a competitive situation, as democratic procedures must? One answer, of course, is that events may cause their authoritarian hold to slip: a defeat in battle, enduring economic stagnation, vanishing popular legitimacy, a domestic guerrilla force, and the like. Under contemporary circumstances, putting democratic institutions in place may be a prerequisite for gaining foreign aid that can help alleviate such problems. In addition, democratic institutions offer authoritarian leaders under attack the benefit of rules guaranteeing political competition, which can increase the possibility of rebounding later. In other words, if the alternatives are to lose an election or to lose one's life to a new junta, the former can seem relatively attractive. Finally, and this is crucial to *pactadura*, members of the authoritarian regime can often work things so that they do just fine in the new order.

One advantage of this approach to the study of democratization is its focus on individuals with definable interests competing with each other to maximize their winnings in the face of definable constraints. In other words, it fits well in the research tradition known as rational-choice modeling, or positive political theory. Researchers can represent their hypotheses in formal mathematical form, derive expected outcomes, and thereby shed light on strategic interactions that might not be obvious otherwise. Work of this kind is already underway (for example, Caspar and Taylor 1993a and 1993b).

Another important benefit produced so far by research in this school is the accumulation of propositions about short-term political change. Whereas structural approaches stress political change that occurs over decades or generations, we now know more about why a seemingly entrenched authoritarian regime will be pushed aside in favor of democratic institutions in the course of a few years. Yet contextual studies do not claim merely to represent a finer-grained enlargement of the long-term picture painted by structuralists. They deny the inevitability implied (or stated) by structural theorists. Given certain intra-elite dynamics, a country could develop and maintain democratic forms of governance before it should be "ready." (Costa Rica tends to be mentioned as an example.) In addition, countries that may be highly developed economically can retain highly authoritarian regimes (South Korea, for example).

Theories of intra-elite bargaining thus make a genuine contribution by combating a sense of determinacy. Yet that can leave even this approach's proponents with critical questions unanswered. Few studies have clearly discussed the ways in which particular outcomes were shaped by the society in which they occurred. Scholars acknowledge the need to investigate the links between larger structural features of a society and short-term elite strategies, what Karl (1991) calls "structured contingency." Karl (1991, 180–1, Table 8.3) has suggested that a country's structural situation will result in either elites or masses primarily advancing the transition, and the transition coming about through either force or compromise. This pair of dichotomies produce four possible "modes" of transition from authoritarian rule. Each mode results in one of four types of regime that she labels conservative democracy, corporatist democracy, competitive democracy, and one-party dominant regime. She finds that democracies that came about through elite-directed compromise (that is, through some form of a "pact") have tended to be the most stable. In a similar effort to differentiate transitions, Huntington (1991, Ch. 3) presents three categories: transformations, replacements, and "transplacements." A transformation is directed by the elites in power, a replacement occurs when opposition groups play the primary role, and a transplacement involves joint action by those within and outside the regime.

This school tends to focus the bulk of its attention on bargaining and choices made by fairly well defined political elites (such as leaders of political parties, trade unions, or the military). Though the discussion of elite factions and alliances will often mention broader structural, that is, class, affiliations, these discussions tend to revolve around the policy position of an organization or the individual heading it, not around the social base of the organization or group. Thus, even though one finds concepts such as the state and civil society in this approach, they are placed in the background.[7] In addition, by taking the existence of these organizations as a given, this approach neglects the possibility that such ties will themselves be in flux during a democratization process. Certainly, post-communist societies have very unstable sets of parties, trade unions, interest groups, and other organizations. Developments in this area seems likely to influence intra-elite dynamics as well as to reflect them.

Even so, the patterns of inter-elite bargaining discerned in previous transitions to democracy may provide insights into the downfall of the communist regimes. Bova (1991), for instance, has applied the concepts and basic arguments of democratic transition to Gorbachev's reforms in the USSR. Bova notes that typically a split in the ruling elite leads to a process of liberalization (referred to as *decompressao* or *apertura* in Latin America and glasnost in the Soviet Union). Then, one side of the elite split will seek support outside the elite. Bova points to Gorbachev's calls for support from the public against the entrenched bureaucrats. Bova then discusses the interplay of four categories of actors: (1) hard-liners who oppose all but the most cosmetic changes, (2) opponents of the regime who want a complete and immediate break with the past, (3) centrists who want only liberalized authoritarianism, and (4) centrists who want more complete movement toward democratization. The centrist groups can keep regime opponents at bay at times by threatening that all liberalization will be lost unless the most radical demands are kept at bay (cf. O'Donnell and Schmitter 1986, 24). Moreover, liberalization strengthens the centrists vis-à-vis the hard-liners. The second stage after liberalization, according to Bova, is the collapse of the center. Liberalization can lead to increasingly radical demands from the public. This in turn energizes previously quiet hard-liners in the elite. Such trends can bring down reformist leaders who try to stick to the center too long. Certainly, Gorbachev's efforts to hold onto the middle ground became increasingly futile from 1989 on. Therefore, Bova's use of the elite-bargaining literature in the Soviet context is suggestive.

With regard to the third stage of democratization, democratic *consolidation*, the ability to import insights from Latin America and southern Europe to the post-communist societies may be more limited. A crucial difference is that the events of 1989 and 1991 were not changes of political leadership and procedures only, with the political institutions and economic system left largely intact. In Latin America, transitions from authoritarianism to democracy and back again have often been surprisingly smooth. With the fall of the communist-party systems, these countries must rebuild all aspects of politics and economics (and significant portions of their societal relations as well).

Another difference worth noting, one that is favorable for democratic consolidation, is that the Eastern European and Soviet militaries do not have an extensive tradition of interference in politics (with the primary exception of Poland, which had military leaders during this century in Generals Pilsudski and Jaruzelski). So far, the prospect of military intervention in the ongoing political struggles has not been as prominent as it was during Latin American crises. An exception to this generalization is Georgia, which saw a military junta seize power in 1992 from its elected President, Zviad Gamsakhurdia. Also, the Russian military's role in the October 1993 storming of the Russian legislature under orders from President Yeltsin has raised concern among many that the military's influence of the civilian politicians may be too strong.

THEORETICAL CLUSTER 4: CONSTITUTIONAL DESIGN AND THE STABILITY OF DEMOCRACY

What offices shall be created to rule in the name of the people? The debate over how to answer this question has been rekindled in recent years as constitutional design became a priority item in new democracies worldwide. I reviewed in Chapter 2 the basic institutional choices that new democracies have open to them. In this chapter, I address a literature that argues that the successful consolidation of democracy rests on finding a constitutional design—a set of democratic political institutions and the rules governing their interrelations—that properly matches the country's circumstances.[8] In Lijphart's (1992a, 207) words, "Among the most—and, arguably, *the* most important—of all constitutional choices that have to be made in democracies is the choice of electoral system . . . and the choice of relationship between the executive and the legislature. . . ."

In any country, the nature of the governing institutions and their interrelationship influence the flow of political life and the effectiveness of the government. For this reason, those designing democratic institutions must do so with an eye on two key issues. They must attend carefully to whether the arrangement they arrive at will stabilize politics, channel and reconcile competing interests and demands, permit a workable balance between flexible and decisive government action, and accrue sufficient obedience and respect from the citizenry that the institutional arrangement cannot easily be toppled. (The latter is another way of saying democratic consolidation.) At the same time, however, they must attend to the impact different constitutional designs will have on their own future political fortunes and the fortunes of the party or group or ideology with which they identify (Bawn 1993).

This latter strategic motivation underlying constitutional design complicates the process of constitution writing and gives it its political dynamics. It means that constitutional design is intimately connected to the intra-elite bargaining dynamics described above. The long-term goal of building an effective, stable, and democratic political order can serve as a public good that most of the competing elites hope will result from their bargaining. Unfortunately, many politicians may decide to push for the institutional rules that best benefit their party's individual interests even if such rules will harm the country as a whole. Competing elites may also refuse to support a new constitutional arrangement because some provisions are unfavorable to them. Moreover, elites may agree on a new constitutional order that serves their interests quite well, and may even fit well with general principles of democratic institutions, but which is a poor match for the political, economic and social realities of the country as a whole.

For this reason, scholars have examined the fit between institutional arrangements and societal conditions. Three primary institutional choices have received attention: (1) the executive-legislative arrangement ("presidential" versus "parliamentary" government), (2) the nature of the electoral system (proportional representation versus majority or plurality voting), and (3) having a federal or unitary state. Theoretical arguments from Montesquieu and Madison onward suggest likely ramifications of different choices. This is also an area in which it is possible to examine the historical record of democracies with different institutional structures and reach conclusions about how the success or failure of those institutions relates to constitutional design.

For example, Powell (1982) examined the "performance" of democracies along several dimensions to produce some tentative arguments about the links between how a democracy is structured and how well it performs. He found a slight tendency for the consensual institutional structures to have greater political order: fewer riots and political deaths. Lijphart (1984) reinforced Powell's conclusion through an empirical look at twenty-one democracies. He combined electoral rules, degree of federalism, presidential versus parliamentary, and other dimensions of constitutional design into two ideal types of democracy: majoritarian and consensual. Then, dividing the twenty-one democracies into one category or the other, he concludes that consensual institutional structures (proportional representation, etc.) are most commonly found in—and, he concludes, must have therefore proven themselves preferable for—countries with significant ethnic/cultural cleavages.

> In plural societies, therefore, majority rules spells majority dictatorship and civil strife rather than democracy. What these societies need is a democratic regime that emphasizes consensus instead of opposition, that includes rather than excludes, and that tries to maximize the size of the ruling majority rather than being satisfied with a bare majority: consensus democracy. (Lijphart 1984, 23)

The fact that Lijphart is examining only developed Western capitalist democracies reduces the generalizability of this argument, however. Though the evidence is extremely tentative, the possibility that consensual institutions facilitate interethnic accord should be taken seriously by constitution writers in post-Soviet societies (cf. Ordeshook and Shvetsova 1994). Also, it is worth pondering that, as described in Chapter 2, Russia has largely majoritarian institutions—the kind associated with a homogenous society—in a pluralist, highly divided society. The introduction of proportional representation voting for a portion of the legislature marks a move toward combining the two types of electoral systems. (For more discussion of these issues, see Chapter 7 by Hesli.) A point that several authors make (Diamond 1990; Shugart and Carey 1992, 7; Gladdish 1993; Huber and Powell 1994) is that the different electoral systems produce a different compromise between producing an elite that *represents* the populace and producing one that better *governs* the populace. The latter refers to the ability of the populace to choose from among a small number (at the extreme, just two) of competing governing groups and, through their voting, "send a signal" that they are satisfied or dissatisfied with the performance of the one in power. Both principles cannot be maximized simultaneously. Neither can be left entirely unprovided for. Depending on such things as social cleavages, popular political attitudes, regional divisions, and the type of economic problems facing a country, a new democracy's constitutional arrangement should give greater weight to one or the other. Linz (1990a) argues that, because the presidency, the most important post in a presidential system, can be won by only a single individual representing a single party or social movement, parliamentary systems should be preferred when political order is fragile. Yet Shugart and Carey (1992, 13) argue that having a presidential system provides an expanded ability to produce a workable compromise between the principles of representativeness and governability since the legislature can be representative while the presidential elections allow a clearer choice between alternative governing plans. This, they believe, helps explain the attractiveness of presidential systems in most new democracies, even those whose cleavage pattern might suggest that a presidential system would be dangerous.

In some of the Eastern European and former Soviet states, politicians and scholars are struggling over how to design new political institutions. In other countries, new arrangements are in place, and citizens are in the first stages of experiencing the consequences of their choices. For both groups, the issues of institutional design remain salient. Political ambitions and conflicts cannot be avoided (cf. Lijphart 1992a). In the long run, however, the key is whether the institutions that emerge can channel and respond to deeper societal cleavages.

CONCLUSION

The diversity of work on democratization in Western Europe, Latin America, and elsewhere provides a wealth of concepts, arguments, and insights for those seeking to understand the fall of the communist regimes and the course of political change thereafter. Each of the four clusters of research that I review can be used to scrutinize post-communist change. None seems likely to satisfy an observer entirely. The modernization theories leave too much detail about political struggle unexamined.

Moreover, they provide no guidelines for the policymakers responsible for making and sustaining the democratic transition. Theories devised through historical case studies provide multifaceted pictures of the process of change but require one to start from scratch and analyze the equivalent processes in each country; generalizations are rare. Studies of intra-elite bargaining have produced several generalizations with much comparative utility but because they are not yet carefully linked to non-elite dynamics and to the structural circumstances of a country, they tell only a portion of the story. Arguments about the impact on democratic consolidation of different institutional arrangements remain at a rudimentary stage. More research is needed into the relationship between societal cleavages or traditions and the effectiveness of different constitutional designs.

In addition, no theory developed with reference to other democratic transitions could adequately explain post-communist democratizations. They present numerous elements not found in other democratic transitions. The insecure and ill-defined nature of statehood, the attempt to transform centrally planned economies into market-directed economies, the need to redefine the perception and role of law, the uncertainty of these new regimes' place in regional alliances and in world affairs more generally—these and other circumstances combine to give post-communist democratization its own flavor. Yet this is the good news, not the bad news. Analysts' theories will be immeasurably enriched by the opportunity to observe the outcomes in the region. The following chapters take up these issues in more detail to present a fuller picture of the unfolding drama of democratization in Eastern Europe and the former Soviet Union.

NOTES

1. By common convention, the object of study is referred to as the study of democratization even though theorists derive their efforts from *failures* to democratize as well as from the successes.
2. One extreme version of modernization theory that is currently much discussed is Fukuyama's (1992) argument that, even if the process is not a smooth one, long-term historical trends are pushing all societies to resemble one another, establishing some form of democratic political institutions.
3. These arguments stress economic development, promoting dispersion of economic resources, as the key factor, not a high national income per se. Great wealth that is extremely concentrated in a small segment of society (the oil wealth accumulated in some OPEC member-countries, for example) will not transform a society in the manner that their model expects.
4. One shortcoming in the chart of the process Inglehart depicts is that he does not indicate why some countries democratize while others experience an authoritarian regime, nor how a country that has gone the fascist/communist route gets back on track toward the inevitable democratization.

5. Note that Moore saw the three routes not as separate items on a country's historical menu but as ". . . successive historical stages. As such, they display a limited determinate relation to each other. The methods of modernization chosen in one country change the dimensions of the problem for the next countries who take the step. The historical preconditions of each major political species differ sharply from the others." (Moore 1966, 414) This quotation suggests that Moore would not want his analyses applied to current transformations without substantial revision.
6. In practice, as Chapter 2 notes, many democracies do take certain matters of substance off the negotiating table in the form of constitutional stipulations.
7. As Kitschelt (1992, 1032) notes, elite-bargaining approaches argue against the modernization approach but do not deal with other structural approaches. See also Levine's (1988) critique of O'Donnell and Schmitter (1986) for mentioning but not analyzing the role of civil society in individual countries. Two pioneers in the analysis of intra-elite bargaining and democratization, Juan Linz and Alfred Stepan, recently (1992) pointed to the relative neglect of statehood issues in the literature.
8. A closely related but not directly germane set of debates revolves around which choices are generally preferable without regard to country specifics. See the debate among Linz (1990a, 1990b), Horowitz (1990), Lipset (1990), Stepan and Skach (1993) concerning presidential versus parliamentary forms, as well as the debate among Lijphart (1991a, 1991b, 1992b), Lardeyret (1991), and Quade (1991) concerning electoral systems. For a critique of debating the merits of institutional design without reference to concrete circumstances, see Gladdish (1993).

REFERENCES

ALMOND, GABRIEL A., and SYDNEY VERBA. 1963. *The Civic Culture: Political Attitudes and Democracy in Five Nations*. Princeton: Princeton University Press.

ARENDT, HANNAH. 1951. *The Origins of Totalitarianism*, Second Edition. New York: Harcourt, Brace.

BAWN, KATHLEEN. 1993. "The Logic of Institutional Preferences: German Electoral Law as a Social Choice Outcome." *American Journal of Political Science* 37(4, November):965–89.

BOLLEN, KENNETH A. 1979. "Political Democracy and the Timing of Development." *American Sociological Review* 44:572–87

BOVA, RUSSELL. 1991. "Political Dynamics of the Post-Communist Transition: A Comparative Perspective." *World Politics* 44(1, October):113–38.

BURTON, MICHAEL, RICHARD GUNTHER, and JOHN HIGLEY. 1992. "Introduction: Elite Transformations and Democratic Regimes." In Higley and Gunther, eds.,

Elites and Democratic Consolidation in Latin America and Southern Europe. New York: Cambridge University Press, 1–37.

CASPAR, GRETCHEN, and MICHELLE TAYLOR. 1993a. "Why Competitors Cooperate." Paper presented at the 1993 Annual Meetings of the Midwest Political Science Association, Chicago, April 8–11.

———.1993b. "A Game-Theoretic Analysis of Elite Cooperation and the Prospects for Democratic Consolidation." Paper presented at the 1993 Annual Meetings of the American Political Science Association, Washington DC, September 2–5.

DAHL, ROBERT A. 1971. *Polyarchy: Participation and Opposition.* New Haven: Yale University Press.

———. 1989. *Democracy and Its Critics.* New Haven: Yale University Press.

DIAMOND, LARRY. 1990. "Three Paradoxes of Democracy." *Journal of Democracy* 1(3, Summer):48–60.

———. 1992. "Economic Development and Democracy Reconsidered." *American Behavioral Scientist* 35(4/5, March/June):450–99.

EKIERT, GRZEGORZ. 1991. "Democratic Processes in East Central Europe, A Theoretical Reconsideration." *British Journal of Political Science* 21(3):285–313.

FRENTZEL-ZAGORSKA, JANIAN. 1992. "Patterns of Transition from a One-Party State to Democracy in Poland and Hungary." In Robert F. Miller, ed., *The Developments of Civil Society in Communist Systems.* Boston: Allen and Unwin, 40–64.

FUKUYAMA, FRANCIS. 1992. *The End of History and the Last Man.* New York: Free Press.

GLADDISH, KEN. 1993. "The Primacy of the Particular." *Journal of Democracy* 4(1, January): 53–65.

GOLDFARB, JEFFREY. 1992. *After the Fall: The Pursuit of Democracy in Central Europe.* New York: Basic Books.

GRAMSCI, ANTONIO. 1929–1935 [1971]. *Selections from the Prison Notebooks of Antonio Gramsci*, Quintin Hoare and Geoffrey Nowell Smith, eds. New York: International Publishers.

HOROWITZ, DONALD L. 1990. "Comparing Democratic Systems." *Journal of Democracy* 1(4, Fall):73–9.

HOUGH, JERRY F. 1988. *Opening Up the Soviet Economy.* Washington: Brookings Institution.

HUBER, JOHN D., and G. BINGHAM POWELL. 1994. "Congruence between Citizens and Policymakers in Two Visions of Liberal Democracy." *World Politics* 46(3, April):291–326.

HUNTINGTON, SAMUEL P. 1991. *The Third Wave: Democratization in the Late Twentieth Century.* Norman: University of Oklahoma Press.

INGLEHART, RONALD. 1977. *The Silent Revolution: Changing Values and Political Styles Among Western Publics.* Princeton: Princeton University Press.

———. 1990. *Culture Shift in Advanced Industrial Society.* Princeton: Princeton University Press.

JOWITT, KENNETH. 1992. "Soviet Neotraditionalism: The Political Corruption of a Leninist Regime." In *New World Disorder: The Leninist Extinction.* Berkeley: University of California Press, 121–58.

KARATNYCKY, ADRIAN. 1994. "Freedom in Retreat." *Freedom Review* 25(1, February):4–9.

KARL, TERRY LYNN. 1991. "Dilemmas of Democratization in Latin America." In Dankwart A. Rustow and Kenneth Paul Erickson, eds., *Comparative Political Dynamics: Global Research Perspectives.* New York: Harper Collins, 163–91.

KEANE, JOHN. 1988. *Democracy and Civil Society.* London: Verso.

KITSCHELT, HERBERT. 1992. "Political Regime Change: Structure and Process-Driven Explanations?" *American Political Science Review* 86(4, December):1028–34.

LARDEYRET, GUY. 1991. "The Problem with PR." *Journal of Democracy* 2(3, Summer):30–5.

LENIN, VLADIMIR I. 1917 [1975]. "Imperialism, the Highest Stage of Capitalism." In Robert C. Tucker, ed., *The Lenin Anthology.* New York: Norton, 204–74.

LEVINE, DANIEL H. 1988. "Paradigm Lost: Dependence to Democracy." *World Politics* 40(3, April):377–94.

LEWIN, MOSHE 1988. [1991]. *The Gorbachev Phenomenon: A Historical Interpretation,* Second Edition. Berkeley: University of California Press.

LIJPHART, AREND. 1984. *Democracies: Patterns of Majoritarian and Consensus Government in Twenty-One Countries.* New Haven: Yale University Press.

———. 1991a. "Constitutional Choices for New Democracies." *Journal of Democracy* 2(1, Winter):72–84.

———. 1991b. "Double-Checking the Evidence." *Journal of Democracy* 2(3, Summer):42–8.

———. 1992a. "Democratization and Constitutional Choices in Czechoslovakia, Hungary and Poland, 1989–1991." *Journal of Theoretical Politics* 4(2): 207–23.

———, ed. 1992b. *Parliamentary versus Presidential Government.* New York: Oxford University Press.

LINZ, JUAN J. 1990a. "The Perils of Presidentialism." *Journal of Democracy* 1(1, January):51–69.

———. 1990b. "The Virtues of Parliamentarism." *Journal of Democracy* 1(4 Fall):84–91.

———. 1990c. "Transitions to Democracy." *The Washington Quarterly* 13(3):143–64.

LINZ, JUAN J. and ALFRED STEPAN. 1992. "Political Identities and Electoral Sequences: Spain, the Soviet Union and Yugoslavia." *Daedalus: Journal of the American Academy of Arts and Sciences* 121(2, Spring):123–39.

LIPSET, SEYMOUR MARTIN. 1960. *Political Man: The Social Bases of Politics*. Baltimore: Johns Hopkins University Press.

———. 1990. "The Centrality of Political Culture." *Journal of Democracy,* 1(4, Fall):80–3.

———. 1994. "The Social Requisites of Democracy Revisited." *American Sociological Review* 59(February):1–22.

MAINWARING, SCOTT. 1993. "Presidentialism, Multipartism and Democracy: The Difficult Combination." *Comparative Political Studies* 26(2, July):198–228.

MIGRANYAN, ANDRANIK. 1987. "*Vzaimnootnosheniya Individa, Obshchestva i Gosudarstva v Politicheskoi Teorii Marksizma i Problemy Demokratizatsii Sotsialisticheskogo Obshchestvo* [The Interrelationship of the Individual, Society and the State in the Political Theory of Marxism and Problems of Democratization of Socialist Society]," *Voprosy Filosofii* 8(August):75–91.

MOORE, BARRINGTON, JR. 1966. *Social Origins of Dictatorship and Democracy: Lord and Peasant in the Making of the Modern World.* Boston: Beacon Press.

MULLER, EDWARD N. 1988. Democracy, Economic Development and Income Inequality." *American Sociological Review* 53:50–68

O'DONNELL, GUILLERMO. 1973. *Modernization and Bureaucratic- Authoritarianism: Studies in South American Politics*. Berkeley: Institute of International Studies, University of California.

——— and PHILLIPE C. SCHMITTER. 1986. "Tentative Conclusions About Uncertain Democracies." In O'Donnell, Schmitter, and Laurence Whitehead, eds., *Transitions from Authoritarian Rule: Prospects for Democracy*, Part IV. Baltimore: Johns Hopkins University Press, 1–72.

ORDESHOOK, PETER C., and OLGA V. SHVETSOVA. 1994. "Ethnic Heterogeneity, District Magnitude and the Number of Parties." *American Journal of Political Science* 38(1, February):100–23.

POWELL, G. BINGHAM. 1982. *Contemporary Democracies: Participation, Stability and Violence*. Cambridge: Harvard University Press.

PRZEWORSKI, ADAM. 1986. "Some Problems in the Study of the Transition to Democracy." In Guillermo O'Donnell, Phillipe C. Schmitter, and Laurence Whitehead, eds., *Transitions from Authoritarian Rule: Prospects for Democracy*, Part III. Baltimore: Johns Hopkins University Press, 47–63.

QUADE, QUENTIN L. 1991. "PR and Democratic Statecraft," *Journal of Democracy* 2(3, Summer):36–41.

RUESCHEMEYER, DIETRICH, EVELYNE HUBER STEPHENS, and JOHN D. STEPHENS. 1992. *Capitalist Development and Democracy*. Chicago: University of Chicago Press.

RUSTOW, DANKWART A. 1970. "Transitions to Democracy: Toward a Dynamic Model." *Comparative Politics* 2(3, April):337–63.

SCHMITTER, PHILLIPPE C. 1992. "The Consolidation of Democracy and Representation of Social Groups." *American Behavioral Scientist* 35(4–5, March/June): 422–49.

SELIGMAN, ADAM B. 1992. *The Idea of Civil Society.* New York: Free Press.

SHUGART, MATTHEW SOBERG, and JOHN M. CAREY. 1992. *Presidents and Assemblies: Constitutional Design and Electoral Dynamics.* New York: Cambridge University Press.

SKOCPOL, THEDA. 1985. "Bringing the State Back In: Strategies of Analysis in Current Research." In Peter B. Evans, Dietrich Rueschemeyer, and Theda Skocpol, eds., *Bringing the State Back In.* New York: Cambridge University Press, 3–37.

——— and MARGARET SOMERS. 1980. "The Uses of Comparative History in Macrosocial Inquiry." *Comparative Studies in Society and History* 22(2, April): 174–97.

STEPAN, ALFRED. 1978. *The State and Society: Peru in Comparative Perspective.* Princeton: Princeton University Press.

———. 1985. "State Power and the Strength of Civil Society in the Southern Cone of Latin America." In Peter B. Evans, Dietrich Rueschemeyer, and Theda Skocpol, eds., *Bringing the State Back In.* New York: Cambridge University Press, 317–43.

———. 1988. *Rethinking Military Politics: Brazil and the Southern Cone.* Princeton: Princeton University Press.

——— and CINDY SKACH. 1993. "Constitutional Frameworks and Democratic Consolidation: Parliamentarism vs. Presidentialism." *World Politics* 46(1, October): 1–22.

TILLY, CHARLES. 1984. *Big Structures, Large Processes, Huge Comparisons.* New York: Russell Sage Foundation.

WARE, ALAN. 1987. *Citizens, Parties and the State.* Cambridge, Mass.: Polity Press.

WEBER, MAX. 1946 [1958]. "Politics as a Vocation." In H. H. Gerth and C. Wright Mills, eds., *From Max Weber: Essays in Sociology.* New York: Oxford University Press [originally published in 1946].

WEINTRAUB, JEFF. 1993. "Democracy and the Market: A Marriage of Inconvenience." In Margaret Latus Nugent, ed., *From Leninism to Freedom: The Challenges of Democratization.* Boulder, Colo.: Westview, 47–66.

WHITE, STEPHEN. 1979. *Political Culture and Soviet Politics.* London: Macmillan.

CHAPTER
4

THE ROLE OF MASS VALUES

KRISTEN HILL MAHER

Mass publics[1] play a minor role in the political engineering of new institutions in most new democracies. Although popular unrest and mobilization may accompany or precipitate democratic reform, elites and not masses are ultimately responsible for instituting democratic governance. Hence, many of the recent studies of democratization focus on the "crafting" or pact-making that takes place among elites to institutionalize democratic procedures and rules of decision making (see Chapter 3 by Reisinger). An emphasis on elites is not inappropriate in discussions of immediate institutional change. In the long run, however, successful democracies must do more than establish new sets of rules. They must also establish enough legitimacy for these rules that people are willing to abide by them. New democratic institutions in many states in the past fifty years have lived very short lives because they lacked popular support and legitimacy. Stability is the minimum requirement for democratic institutional success.

In addition, I will argue that successfully democratic political systems must also maximize those social conditions that distinguish them from purely nominal democratic systems, as well as autocratic ones. As Reisinger points out in Chapter 2, although a state that adopts democratic institutions may be considered "*a* democracy," it will not be a fully democratic society unless it also provides democratic conditions like liberty, equality, and popular empowerment. Like new institutions, these conditions require popular support.

Classical democratic theory centers around "rule by the people." This chapter attempts to add "the people" to a literature that has been generally elite-oriented, exploring the ways in which the political orientations[2] of common citizens can support the institutions, procedures, and conditions of democracy. I will first address the most general question underlying the role of mass values in democratic societies: Does it matter what ordinary citizens think? In brief, it does matter. I will then elaborate which orientations would best facilitate a successful democratic society. Finally, although this chapter is primarily theoretical, the theory developed in the first sections will provide the basis for a discussion of mass values and prospects for democracy in post-communist societies.

DO "THE PEOPLE" MATTER TO DEMOCRACY?

At first glance, this question may strike the reader as ridiculous. The democratic ideals of civics textbooks and Abraham Lincoln[3] leave little room for doubt. However, this ideal does not often resemble democracy in practice. Even in long-standing democracies such as the United States or Britain, political elites make policy, and popular input is generally indirect and intermittent. It is not entirely misguided to question the relevance of mass publics to the continuing success of these democracies.

In the post-communist states of Eastern Europe and Central Eurasia, the role of mass orientations may be more immediately critical. Many of these states have adopted democratic institutions such as regular elections, referenda, and constitutions, but the impetus for reform has in great measure come from elites. Will these new institutions work if they are not able to garner considerable popular support? To what extent might democratic commitments develop among people whose political experience has been almost exclusively authoritarian?[4] These kinds of questions raise considerable debate among contemporary scholars, centering on the issue of whether the values of ordinary people matter to democratic success.

Our evaluation of whether they do matter rests upon two considerations. First, how do we conceptualize the relationship between mass values and the governing institutions and elites? Are democratic values a prerequisite or a product of democratic government? Second, how do we conceptualize the actual influence of citizens in a democratic society? Both considerations merit some discussion.

The Relationship between Mass Values and Democratic Institutions

There are (at least) two ways to think about the relationship between mass values and democratic institutions. On one hand, we might expect that a government would need to "fit" a particular culture like well-tailored clothing. If a democratic government is to work, the fundamental predispositions, beliefs, and values of its citizens must also be democratic. I will call this the "culturalist" approach. On the other hand, we might expect that governments can mold or shape the citizens who live under them. In this case, any group of people could learn democratic orientations once the proper institutions were in place. This might be called the "institutionalist" approach. Both expectations are well-founded, although we would have more interest in the orientations of mass publics if we thought that new governments needed to be tailored to fit particular cultural contexts.

One of the first empirical studies based on the culturalist approach was *The Civic Culture* by Gabriel Almond and Sidney Verba (1963). Almond and Verba conducted interviews among the citizens of five nations in an attempt to explain why democracy flourished in some nations (the United States and Britain) better than others (Germany, Italy, Mexico). Their questions were designed to measure these nations' political cultures, which they defined as "the particular distribution of patterns of orientation toward political objects among the members of the nation" (15). On the basis of this study, Almond and Verba distinguished between three types of political culture—parochial, subject, and participant—that form the basis for three forms of government: traditional, authoritarian, and democratic governmental structures, respectively (21). They argued that each kind of institutional arrangement (traditional, authoritarian, or democratic) has *one form* of culture that is congruent with it, and that incongruence between political institutions and political culture would lead to institutional instability.

Although *The Civic Culture* does suffer from some methodological flaws, this study laid the foundation for a large and growing body of academic literature on national "cultures" and their relationships to political institutions. Subsequent studies also used surveys to identify the dynamics of attitudes and beliefs in given nations, and to understand their propensity toward a particular form of government.[5] Many of these later studies have focused exclusively on the extent to which "democratic" characteristics or orientations exist in a given population, in order to estimate their prospects for stable democratic governance.[6]

Studies based on a culturalist approach assume that people's social and political orientations are a product of socialization, or early learning during childhood. Such an assumption implies that political orientations will not change much over an individual's lifetime (nor sometimes over the centuries in the course of the society's "lifetime"). The expected continuity comes from what Eckstein (1988) calls the "postulate of cumulative socialization," which proposes that although a person continues learning throughout his or her lifetime, the earliest learning during his or her formative years is hardest to undo. In other words, once people reach adulthood, their habits and beliefs about the world are fairly permanent (you can't teach an old dog new tricks).

The culturalist approach, therefore, suggests that people who have been socialized under the Soviet system will retain and reproduce this learning even after this system has disintegrated. It suggests that mass orientations will change only gradually as new generations replace the old ones. Culturalists considering the prospects for democracy in post-communist states hence tend to focus on the kind of learning that went on under Soviet rule and whether the citizens' learned orientations will support or hinder a democratic system.

One of the most serious challenges to the culturalist approach to mass orientations and democracy is posed by Brian Barry (1970): Are these orientations prerequisites or the products of democracy? Institutionalists suspect the latter. Schmitter and Karl (1991, 83) argue that democratic governments can be successfully instituted without congruent democratic orientations. The rules and procedures of democracy (particularly electoral competition) can take place even if the parties involved are "antagonistic and mutually suspicious." Over time, law-abiding, civil interactions may provide a basis for some of the more civic values of a democratic society, which are merely a byproduct of the institutions.

Institutionalists make a fair point. In fact, we have seen some evidence that democratic institutions—even when imposed on a society by outside forces, such as in the case of Germany and Japan after WWII—do seem to encourage the development of democratic orientations over time. There is evidence of a considerable shift in political orientations in these two countries since the time that they came under democratic rule. This shift indicates that "orthodox" culturalists do not tell the whole story about where mass orientations come from. It also suggests that the current values of citizens in post-communist states might not significantly affect whether these states eventually succeed as democracies.

At the same time, there are empirical exceptions to the institutionalist story, as well. Very similar political institutions have experienced disparate fates in different cultural contexts. Perhaps the most striking example of this is presented in Robert Putnam's (1993) study of regional governments in Italy. Putnam observed fifteen identical regional governments that were initiated in 1970. Over the course of twenty years, these governments came to differ widely in their performance, and Putnam finds that the critical factor determining their success or failure is the degree to which the citizens in the region are "civic-minded." Regions in which citizens trust each other, collaborate in associations, and share a great deal of equality and reciprocity have developed far more effective governments than regions without a civic community. In this case, democratic institutions did not reliably produce democratic mass values, nor did they succeed equally well despite differences in citizen orientations.

The truth of the relationship between values and democratic institutions is probably somewhere in between these two approaches: There is an interaction between culture and government. People's political orientations are influenced by their early learning and their cultural context; however, these orientations are not so permanent by adulthood that they cannot change gradually in response to a new (democratic) institutional context.

It is therefore appropriate to consider the mass values in post-communist societies as one of the factors relevant to their prospects for becoming successful democracies. At the same time, if the orientations among citizens in these states are not strongly supportive of democracy, there is some possibility that they will shift over time in response to their experience under democratic institutions. The most critical issue for these states is not whether they have a long history of the "cultural soil" most fertile for democracy, but whether citizens can and will support and help build a democratic society in the long run.

What Influence Do Ordinary People Have in Democratic Societies?

Even if citizens *will* support democratic institutions and conditions, the question remains whether they *can*. It might be argued that what ordinary citizens think and do is greatly irrelevant to the practice and success of democratic government. As I mentioned earlier, elites run most of the day-to-day business of governing and make some policy decisions quite independently of constituent input.[7]

The extent to which we think ordinary people are relevant to democracy depends in great part on what kind of democracy we envision. In Chapter 2, Reisinger presents two approaches to defining democracy. The first—procedural democracy—focuses on democratic institutions and procedures based upon sets of rules to protect citizens against tyranny or arbitrary state power. These include, for instance, the competitive election of elites to political office and the rule of law. The second approach—which I will call "substantive" democracy—centers on democratic conditions, or substantive goals for democratic societies, like liberty, equality, and popular empowerment. Both democratic approaches require popular support in differing forms and degrees.

Since procedural democracy is the more common approach and is covered most thoroughly in earlier chapters, I will explain it only briefly here. Joseph Schumpeter (1942) provided what has become the most widely cited definition of a procedural democracy: "the democratic method is that institutional arrangement for arriving at decisions in which individuals acquire the power to decide by means of a competitive struggle for the people's vote."[8] Scholars who adopt this procedural, or elitist, version of democracy tend to be concerned primarily with the stability of the system. Once the rules are in place, is the system able to maintain itself without experiencing outbursts of violence or becoming oligarchical? Rule of law and constitutionalism help regulate both government and citizen activity to limit abuses of power and keep the system running.

Neither law nor political processes can function without widespread trust and legitimacy. Although the nature of the elites would be most relevant to the success and stability of democratic procedures, the masses also provide critical support for long-term stability. The likelihood of mass compliance to governmental policy, even when these policies are not to their individual advantage (such as in the case of taxes or mandatory military service), depends upon popular acceptance of the "rules" and general satisfaction with the system.[9] The chances for long-term stability of democratic procedures and institutions, then, are enhanced when ordinary citizens trust representative government and the rule of law as legitimate decision-making systems and are satisfied with the level of apparent responsiveness. The "short list" of mass orientations that would support these democratic procedures includes: support for multiparty competition and nonviolent conflict resolution, external efficacy, and support for the rule of law and constitutionalism. I will elaborate upon (and add to) these in a moment.

Stable governing procedures of some sort are essential to democracy. However, regular elections and a constitution do not alone ensure that many of the social conditions that are often expected to accompany democracy will come about. For instance, some critics of procedural democracy argue that it does not promote citizen participation or popular empowerment (Pateman 1970, 1985; MacPherson 1977; Barber 1984; Isaac 1994; Boyte 1990). Although procedural democracy does require mass support for institutional stability, it depends upon a primarily *reactive* rather than active public. Stability can be achieved with a complacent citizenry as well as through one actively committed to democratic forms.

Procedural democracy's lack of an emphasis on citizen participation is not merely an oversight. In fact, some theorists have argued that a government that protects a society against abuses of power (by elites or by the masses) will ultimately be safer and more stable than one which includes a great deal of citizen participation (Kornhauser 1959; Schumpeter 1942; Dahl 1956; Sartori 1962).[10] This argument is based in part upon a distrust of the *demos*, the common people, to provide competent political input.

This distrust has several identifiable origins. First, the seeming mass acquiescence and support for Hitler and Stalin in the 1930s and 1940s led some to conclude that ordinary people are vulnerable to the sway of totalitarian demagogues and are not to be trusted to think independently (Kornhauser 1959). This interpretation of events was supported by early social psychology, which theorized that crowds (or, more abstractly, "the masses") are subject to persuasion by charismatic leaders and to outbursts of violence and irrationality. Elites, on the other hand, gather in smaller groups to engage in more reasoned discourse, and hence are more trustworthy as decision makers.[11] Second, early political attitude surveys like *The American Voter* (Campbell et al. 1960) found that most Americans did not even closely resemble the citizen ideal; they were ignorant of many issues, frequently inconsistent in their beliefs, and generally politically apathetic. This finding caught many social scientists by surprise and led some to question the competence of ordinary citizens to have any significant responsibility in public life. Although the basic premises of both sources of distrust have been largely discredited,[12] there is still a lingering tendency to assume that those who are best "fit" to govern should make decisions for the rest. It does make sense for a state to take advantage of elite political, economic, and legal expertise when necessary, but not to the extent that the mass public is essentially disempowered as decision makers.

Another critique of procedural democracy is that it does not provide adequate social, economic, or political equalities. The rule of law does (in theory) offer equal consideration before the law and certain equal rights. However, the social and economic inequalities that remain strongly inhibit many people's ability to genuinely enjoy these rights (MacPherson 1966, 1977). In other words, to be a free and equal citizen "means not only to enjoy equality before the law, important though this unquestionably is, but also to have the capacities (the material and cultural resources) to be able to pursue different courses of action" (Held 1987, 254). For instance, all adult citizens (who meet certain age and residency requirements) have the equal right to seek political office. However, those without the financial resources have a hard time getting enough publicity to have a reasonable chance of success. Similarly, female or nonwhite candidates face the considerable obstacle of not "looking like" legitimate authority figures. While the trend in the United States and some state Congresses looks somewhat hopeful in this last regard, the example points to the complexity of some of the factors that subtly inhibit genuine equality in daily life.

Increasing democratic conditions such as equality or popular empowerment implies the need for some sort of institutional, procedural, or cultural reform even in most liberal democracies, although there is little agreement about how we should go about it. Marxists and socialists argue that there can be no political equality under unfettered free market competition, both because of the exploitative nature of capital, and because any kind of competition favors the strong over the weak. Participatory democrats tend to argue that individual empowerment and development require people to be directly involved in their own governance in some way. They posit that, while abolishing the state-level system of representation might be unrealistic in large and complex societies, "democratizing" the local and the civil realms would provide substantially greater self-determination (Pateman 1970; MacPherson 1977; Held 1987; Isaac 1994; Sorensen 1994). Some feminists would argue that cultural change is central, including the representations of "others" ("other"-than-white-men) in public domains such as media, advertising, literature, and art.[13] Changing such representations would be a first step in combating the negative stereotypes, violence, and voicelessness that stand as obstacles to genuine freedom and equality.

Although these critiques come from many different sources, they collectively suggest that we miss significant pieces of the picture by focusing only on democratic procedures, maintaining stability, and preventing abuses of power. In addition, a definition of democracy needs to incorporate positive goals in terms of human dignity and overall quality of life. Let me offer a working definition: A fully democratic society essentially requires the opportunity for substantial and equal self-determination by all adult citizens, and a realm of individual autonomy from government, sometimes even against duly enacted expressions of the majority's will. Following this definition, democracy should provide the following five conditions.

1. Negative freedoms, which Reisinger calls "rights against the state" (Chapter 2). These refer to the realm of *autonomy* citizens maintain outside of governmental influence. Authority is diffuse rather than centralized in democratic societies; state power is greatly constrained from interfering in the citizens' private realm. For instance, in the United States, the state may not interfere with or prevent public assembly, free speech, or the private ownership of weapons (to use some examples from the Bill of Rights).
2. Positive freedoms, or "rights within the state." These refer to the obligations or responsibilities of government toward citizens. These differ from one country to another, but may include such things as defense, public services, education, health care, and a minimum standard of living.[14]

3. Equality, in the sense of equal distribution of and access to positive and negative freedoms. Particularly as these freedoms relate to a standard of living, the "democratic condition" of equality implies an economic order in which there is a fairly equitable distribution of wealth and productive resources.
4. Maximized inclusion, or widespread eligibility for citizen rights.
5. Popular empowerment, or maximized control over those outcomes most relevant to one's own life. The domain of "relevant" political decisions goes beyond that of the central government of large nation-states, upon which individuals have minimal impact. A person can be most effective on a local level, where one's input is proportionately more important (e.g., when the relative "weight" of an individual's input into a collective decision amounts to one-tenth or one-hundredth rather than one-millionth). Relevant decision-making contexts thus include local governments, workplaces, schools, and families, as well as state-level policy making.

Because these conditions are abstract political ideals rather than institutions, we cannot effectively use them to divide the world into democratic and nondemocratic states. Instead, they can serve as the standard by which we can judge the extent to which democracy exists in a given society. Including certain conditions as being necessary to democracy introduces the possibility of considering democracy as a continuum (of "more" to "less") rather than a dichotomy (either it is or it isn't). No actual society could be considered fully democratic by these standards, although some certainly come closer to achieving democratic ideals than others.

None of these standards for democracy could be effectively achieved without broad-based support among the people. Democratic institutions formally promote many of these conditions, but widespread supportive political orientations and the common practice of everyday life are ultimately more critical for ensuring and maximizing them in society at large. Let me, then, add the following to the earlier "short list" of mass orientations that would support a democratic society: political tolerance; a value of individual liberty, or a "rights orientation"; interpersonal trust and cooperative social relations; and a participatory orientation and efficacy. In the following section, I will elaborate upon each of these orientations, explaining its relevance and logical connection to democracy. I will begin with those supportive of democratic procedures and institutions, and follow with those supportive of the conditions of substantive democracy.

ORIENTATIONS SUPPORTIVE OF DEMOCRACY

Support for Multiparty Competition and Nonviolent Conflict Resolution

Central to procedural definitions of democracy is the free and fair competition among political parties for the power to make public decisions (Dahl 1971; Sartori 1962). This regular competition for power keeps conflictual groups from engaging in violence, much like individuals in conflict might "settle it" through a coin toss or an arm-wrestling match rather than in a fist fight. Hence, in a procedural democracy, conflicts are legitimate and not adverse to public interest (Dalton 1994), as long as they are contained within the rules of competition and decision making.

Some scholars (e.g., DiPalma 1990) argue that only elites in competition need to accept the rules in order to ensure fair outcomes. However, these elites often represent factional interest groups among society at large—groups that might engage in violent conflict if they did not also accept the arbitration of democratic methods of decision making. This point becomes increasingly clear as religious and ethnic groups in places like Northern Ireland and India continue to engage in bloody conflict, even when they live in formally "democratic" societies in which elites have negotiated at least temporary settlements. Common agreement to abide by the rules of competition requires that all groups in conflict will be willing to accept any outcome produced democratically, and in the meantime, live in uncertainty.

External Efficacy

Although efficacy is also mentioned in the following section, it deserves a quick mention here. Efficacy is the sense that one can or will have effective input into a common decision, and external efficacy more specifically refers to the faith that political elites or institutions will be responsive to one's needs and requests. Much like the above two orientations, external efficacy is critical to the widespread legitimacy of democratic institutions. Representative government is intended to give large numbers of people a voice in a relatively small decision-making body. Citizens select a delegate who they think will best re-present (literally, to "present again") their ideas to the legislature, but need to feel as if the delegate was listening to their ideas the first time. This sense of responsiveness is critical for maintaining the legitimacy of a system that would otherwise resemble nondemocratic governments in which elites make decisions for the masses.

Support for the Rule of Law and Democratic Constitutionalism

In Chapters 5 and 6, John Reitz explains how rule of law—under which both private and public power are limited by law—can support democracy. By limiting state power, rule of law protects individual rights. By regulating all private and public power according to laws enacted by an elected legislative body, rule of law can also empower the legislature. And because the legislative members are elected and accountable to the electorate, rule of law indirectly empowers the citizens themselves.

Rule of law is particularly important to the stability of a democracy in which many of the citizens do not trust the outcomes of normal policy processes, particularly that of majority rule. Majority rule decision making produces "good policy" through the process of competition and voting, without limits to the realm of potential outcomes.[15] It would thus be feasible under procedural, majority-rule democracy, to legalize discrimination or the persecution of minority groups.[16] In societies containing minority groups that fear discrimination or persecution, rule of law could place limits on policy outcomes to the extent that they must "treat all like cases alike" (See Reitz, Chapter 5).[17] Because law is (in principle) general, whereas political processes are often specific, rule of law helps ensure the equal treatment of all citizens.

Reitz adds, however, that law has no means of commanding obedience. Its power lies not in coercion, but in how deeply its norms permeate society. The institutions themselves would be powerless if no one believed they produce fair or just decisions. Hence, the courts need the support of a "legal culture" that grants them legitimacy as a decision-making body. In addition, a polity that takes the rules of law seriously can actually expand the realm over which law arbitrates. The electorate may come to expect more and more decision making to be justified by reference to generally applicable rules making bare assertions of personal or group interest or special favoritism or discrimination politically unacceptable.

Similarly, constitutionalism requires normative support and congruent, or appropriate, citizen orientations. Constitutions, among other things, delineate the division of power among those who make and interpret law. Many contemporary scholars focus on constitution making as a means to engineer new forms of social and political relations. If a nation wants to democratize, it needs to start by establishing norms for a "democratic" division of power. However, new constitutions cannot construct political norms from scratch. In order to function effectively, they must reflect some continuity with the political orientations and traditions already within a society.

We could compare constitutional engineering to the design of paved walkways between buildings on a college campus. If university architects try to build sidewalks according to some abstract or aesthetic principle rather than the preferences of students, they will likely find that students take the most efficient routes, even if they are not paved. Successfully keeping students from trampling the grass requires that sidewalk architects pay some attention to the everyday practices of students going from one class to the next. Similarly, constitutions can bend but not shape citizen or elite behavior and political relations; to some extent, existing traditions and norms limit the range of constitutional designs that can successfully regulate power relations in a society. In fact, in some cases like Britain and Israel, which have "constitutional" governments but no written constitutions, these traditions and norms actually function as the constitution.

Political Tolerance

In order to maintain a system in which people are permitted to participate freely, there must be broad-based tolerance even of disliked groups. Because authority is more dispersed in democratic societies than in autocratic ones, people with vastly different preferences and values find themselves needing to coexist without denying others their opportunity to participate or be heard, and without breaking out into violent conflict.

Opportunities for participation can be limited by individuals and groups, as well as through governmental policy. It would be a dysfunctional democracy indeed if people were not willing to allow their "enemies" or opponents a voice in public matters. In measuring social tolerance, Sullivan, Shamir, Walsh, and Roberts (1985)[18] let survey respondents select their own "most disliked" groups, and then measure tolerance according to how willing the respondents are to allow the groups they dislike the most to participate in public life (e.g., teaching in schools, holding public office, giving public speeches). Even groups that are not particularly "disliked" sometimes find their political participation limited by discriminatory customs governing social relations. In the United States, for example, women and ethnic minority groups like African-Americans continue to struggle for substantive political equality and participation, long after they gained formal legal suffrage. Widespread tolerance is necessary in order to maximize inclusion, provide popular empowerment, and promote equal access to positive freedoms.

Issues of inclusion can become particularly problematic in nations with deep cleavages between national groups, especially when national identity and the identity of a dominant ethnic group become synonymous. For instance, if an individual living in Latvia must be Latvian by nationality in order to be considered a legitimate participant in political processes, then nearly one-half of all those living in Latvia today would be excluded from political life.[19] Tolerance of ethnic minorities has become a particularly loaded issue in some of the former republics of the Soviet Union, because the primary ethnic minority in most republics (Russians) still carry the stigma of having recently been part of a nationally oppressive or dominant group. Issues of tolerance and inclusion in these places may play out most visibly in language policies and practices, as local languages again gain precedence over Russian in all forms of public interactions (see Chapter 7 by Vicki Hesli on ethnic cleavages in post-communist societies).

Value of Individual Liberty/Rights Orientation

The autonomy that people hold from the state allows them to disagree with governmental policy and to express their views in public ways. Collectively, the expression of this disagreement can cause considerable disruption in daily life and a "messiness" that more authoritarian states generally do not allow. But a society in which the value of order takes precedence over respect for autonomy could not long maintain the high levels of liberty necessary to democracy.

Gibson, Duch and Tedin (1993) argue that citizens themselves are responsible for guarding freedom and liberty for everyone. They refer to rights consciousness as the "degree to which citizens are willing to assert rights for themselves" (343). Citizen vigilance in protection of rights is critical in order to give rights that may be formally extended by a constitution substantive meaning. If people do not individually demand liberty, even democratic institutions are not likely to provide it. Individuals themselves are the only ones equipped to determine which freedoms or rights they require and which policies or restrictions are unacceptable to them.

Closely related to the value of individual liberty is valuing minority rights, which requires a compromise of majority rule. Robert Dahl argues that majority rule maximizes self-determination: "if a law is adopted by less than a majority, then the number who have chosen that law will necessarily be smaller than the number of citizens who would have chosen the alternative" (1989, 138). At the same time, equal political power in a majoritarian system can only be achieved if there are no permanent minorities, or minority groups that have no chance of having their political views matter. If all citizens are to have positive freedom, or equal rights within the state, then members of the majority must be willing to allow permanent minorities some authority over themselves and within society.

Interpersonal Trust and Cooperative Social Relations

Trust is essentially the faith one must put in others or in systems under conditions of incomplete information and risk (Luhmann 1979, 1988; Giddens 1990). Interpersonal trust is a necessary corollary of trust in the "system" or in the rule of law. Even if a person believes that the law, properly executed, will produce fair outcomes, one must also trust that other participants in the system are informed and honest enough to ensure the proper working of democratic rules. Inglehart (1988) describes how trust between opposing political groups is crucial to the peaceful operation of democratic conflict resolution. In order for any group to be willing to even temporarily allow their opponents the upper hand, they must trust that their opponents will not abuse their advantage. They must trust that participants will play by the rules, and that if they surrender political power now, they will later have fair opportunities to succeed in their objectives. In addition, in order to accept that it is appropriate for ordinary people to collectively make group decisions, there must be a diffuse trust in people's competence and virtue. Popular empowerment requires "populist" orientations as opposed to "elitist" ones, or too much emphasis on expertise.

Citizens who trust others will also be more likely to join secondary associations and create an active civil society, which is the primary source of citizen autonomy against the state. For this reason, totalitarian regimes, which attempt total state domination over a society, have actively discouraged citizen associations of any kind—including trusting interpersonal relationships. Such relationships compete with the state for an individual's loyalty (Coser 1974), and provide a context for honest and often "subversive" communication (Scott 1990; Arendt 1973). One of the primary mechanisms totalitarian regimes have used to eliminate civil society is discouraging interpersonal trust, since a certain degree of trust is necessary in order to establish effective communication in any social context.[20] In a democratic society, where state power must remain weak and diffuse, interpersonal trust and the civil associations that grow out of it constitute the social fabric that ensures citizen autonomy and, hence, liberty.

Trusting, cooperative social relations and active associational life have been identified as some of the most critical elements to successful democracies by theorists as early as Alexis de Tocqueville in 1835, and as recently as Robert Putnam in

1993. De Tocqueville, as a Frenchman observing the United States, found that Americans were "joiners" more than Europeans:

> The Americans make associations to give entertainments, to found seminaries, to build inns, to construct churches, to diffuse books, to send missionaries to the antipodes . . . Wherever at the head of some new undertaking you see the government in France, or a man of rank in England, in the United States you will be sure to find an association (1961, 106).

People who pursue common interests together, Tocqueville concluded, construct mutual dependence and affection, and tend to feel more duty to the community and to public matters. Robert Putnam's (1993) study in Italy reinforces that an active associational life and a civic or communitarian ethic does in fact translate into successful representative government. Putnam concludes that "social capital" is the key to making democracy work (185).[21]

We might expect "social capital" or trust to be scarce in newly democratic states, particularly after long periods of authoritarian rule and rampant corruption. People estimate whether to trust others based on their previous experience; those in Eastern Europe and the former Soviet republics might be distrustful if they lack positive civic experience.

Participatory Orientation and Efficacy

Popular empowerment and dispersed authority in a democratic society require an active, participatory mass public, but it is not clear to what extent a mass public can or should directly rule itself through political participation. As mentioned earlier, the arguments against allowing the masses any active voice in politics (but rather a *reactive* role as an electorate) are based on the conclusion that common people are not equipped to make good political decisions. Clearly, it would be better for a nation to have informed citizens rather than ignorant ones making national decisions. However, citizens do not need to understand every law or issue in order to be informed about those issues that touch them directly. In addition, those who promote more substantive, direct participation in order to disseminate power more equally among a polity argue that people will rise to the level of responsibility they are given—that greater decision-making responsibility and experience makes people more competent participants (Pateman 1970).

However, even citizens competent in decision making who are offered the opportunity to participate might decline, because participation has costs. Not only must people spend time and energy participating, but they must also share responsibility for the outcomes. When collectively derived outcomes do not turn out as a particular citizen would have them, it would be much easier for that person to pin the loss on a scapegoat—a representative, or congress, or the president—than to have advocated a particular policy and lost. Contributing to collective decisions is empowering, but is also a burden. Regardless of how participatory the democratic ideal is, it makes sense that a citizenry that is informed, assertive, and "participatory" in orientation would provide critical support for a political system in which power is diffuse and common citizens as well as elites contribute to political decision making.

An attitude that is important to this participatory orientation is internal efficacy—the counterpart to external efficacy, mentioned earlier. Whereas *external efficacy* is the expectation that one can have some real effect on political outcomes because elites and institutions will be responsive, *internal efficacy* refers to the confidence in one's own ability to be politically effective. Many empirical studies have shown that people who feel that they can or will be effective are much more likely to participate in politics than those who do not feel efficacious (Verba, Nie, and Kim 1978; Almond and Verba 1963; Pateman 1970).

Finally, it has been argued that participation and the accompanying responsibility requires a communitarian orientation (MacIntyre 1984, 1988; Etzioni 1993; Putnam 1993), or at least limited individualism. Active, participatory citizens, rather than imagining themselves as discrete political beings with isolated interests, see themselves as having interests in common with the polity as a whole. This does not mean that they lose their identity as individuals, sacrifice their individual autonomy, or become altruistic. Rather, they interpret their own self-interest in terms of what is good for the entire polity. As U.S. President Bill Clinton urged in an address before Congress, they stop thinking in terms of "what is in it for me" and start thinking in terms of "what is in it for us" (1993). Citizens who have this kind of communitarian orientation would be more willing to bear the costs of participation and the responsibility of sharing authority.

Theoretical Summary

One of the reasons that it has been so appealing for scholars to refer to democracy in terms of institutions rather than conditions is that many of the normative goals of democracy are related to one another in complicated and sometimes contradictory ways. Democracy has been aptly described as a government of "balanced disparities" (Eckstein 1992, 207). William Reisinger describes in Chapter 2 the tension between liberty and equality. Each supports the other at the same time as it exerts pressure on it. This tension, he says, needs to be constantly reworked in any democracy. None of the conditions for democracy are independent of all the others, and each one should exist in a democratic society *not* as an absolute, but rather should be maximized *in relation to all the others*. Some societies might choose to emphasize one democratic condition over another, and the theorist's challenge, then, is to decide which combinations of democratic elements produce the most effective democracy.

Similarly, the orientations that would support democratic conditions and democratic institutions are frequently in tension with one another. For example, democratic citizens should be skeptical of governmental or institutional authority (in order to limit state power), yet also believe in the legitimacy of the system and the rule of law. Democratic citizens should jealously guard their individual rights, but they also need to be tolerant and respectful of others' rights, and perhaps have a nonindividualistic (communitarian) orientation. And, finally, democratic citizens should cherish their autonomy from the state, yet they need to sacrifice some of this autonomy insofar as citizens in a participatory system need to spend some of their free time "doing" democracy. It is necessary for the citizens of democratic societies to find a balance between some of these values and needs, and to maintain this balance through a continuing process of revision and negotiation. Ultimately, a fully democratic society must find a point of equilibrium between some of these elements in order to maximize popular empowerment (equality and individual self-determination), liberty (autonomy), and stability (institutional longevity/nonviolent conflict resolution).

POLITICAL ORIENTATIONS IN POST-COMMUNIST SOCIETIES

In the previous sections, I have tried to demonstrate two things. First, the political orientations of common people do matter to the success of democratic institutions and procedures and to the prevalence of democratic conditions. Second, there are specific orientations that—if widespread in a given society—increase the likelihood of substantive and stable democracy developing. To recap briefly, these orientations include:

1. Support for multiparty competition and nonviolent conflict resolution
2. External efficacy
3. Support for the rule of law and democratic constitutionalism
4. Political tolerance
5. A value of individual liberty, or a "rights orientation"
6. Interpersonal trust and cooperative social relations
7. A participatory orientation and internal efficacy

Identifying such orientations and their theoretical connection to democracy is admittedly the easy part. Establishing the extent to which these orientations exist in post-communist societies is much less straightforward. And even when we do identify a number of democratic orientations in a society, it is nearly impossible to say whether they will be *enough* to ensure a successful democracy in the long run. In part, this uncertainty is a product of the need to balance sometimes contradictory orientations; the relationship between these values and democracy is not a simple function of "the more, the better." In addition, we cannot know for certain how these values will change over time.

That said, there have been a number of studies—both before and after glasnost—that have addressed the nature and extent of these kinds of political orientations in post-communist societies. Their findings offer a general (albeit preliminary) picture of what the mass publics in Eastern Europe and the former Soviet republics are thinking.[22] This picture then provides a basis for us to discuss what to expect in terms of mass support in these newly democratic states. I will focus on those regions for which the most data are available—predominantly Russia, but also some of the other former Soviet republics and some Eastern European states.

Pre-Glasnost Studies

Our earliest clues about the mass orientations in communist societies came from historical, anthropological, and sociological sources. Until about 1989 in Eastern Europe and 1990 in the Soviet Union under Gorbachev's policies of glasnost, the possibilities for research on mass orientations were severely limited for western researchers (as well as for Eastern European or Soviet ones). Since they were not allowed free access to the people living under communist rule, historians inferred contemporary orientations from those of prerevolutionary Russia, from Soviet structures and institutions, and from literature.[23] Political scientists and sociologists utilized surveys of those who had emigrated from the Soviet Union, despite the problem that emigre responses might not be representative of the Soviet population in general.[24]

The picture these researchers presented of the political orientations of Soviets, and of Russians in particular, was bleak in terms of democratic possibilities. They emphasized the "authoritarian" aspects of the Russian tradition, many of which predate the Soviet regime. One such aspect is a preference for strong leadership, with its roots in the absolutist rule of the tsars, but which also was evident in emigre surveys (Pipes 1974; White 1979, 29–30; Inkeles and Bauer 1959, 246-247; and Grey, Jennisch, and Tyler, 1990). Other "nondemocratic" orientations that researchers found to be predominant were a love of order (White 1979), low levels of political efficacy (Smith 1991, 13–4), and a general proclivity to be "autocratic" (Brzezinski 1989). These kinds of conclusions made it seem unlikely that Soviet—and now formerly Soviet—citizens could accommodate a political system in which authority is dispersed and citizens have greater opportunities and responsibilities to express themselves politically. Democratic societies are frequently far from orderly.

Post-Glasnost Studies[25]

In the late 1980s and early 1990s, there have been much greater opportunities to actually interview, and have respond openly, citizens who have been living in formerly communist bloc nations. There has been a consequent rush by western social scientists to conduct survey research there. The results of these surveys suggest that earlier research done in these areas had missed some important political dynamics. In fact, there is some evidence of popular orientations that would support a democracy. But these survey results are mixed at best. They also reflect a rapid rate of change in institutions, practices, and popular attitudes towards both, and leave quite open the question of what will happen next.

Orientations Supportive of Democratic Institutions and Procedures

Several surveys have found relatively strong support for democratic institutions in some of the post-communist states. For example, a survey of citizens in the Moscow *oblast* found that "by any comparative or absolute standard, support for competitive elections in March 1990 is adequate to maintain the institution at the mass level" (Gibson, Duch, and Tedin 1992, 351). Two years later, a survey in Russia, Ukraine, and Lithuania found slightly lower levels of support for electoral competition: Only 47 (in Lithuania) to 56 (in Ukraine) percent of all respondents said they would "agree" or "strongly agree" that party competition makes the political system stronger (Reisinger, Miller, Hesli, and Maher 1994). Similar results were found in the Russian city of Yaroslavl' in 1990 (Hahn 1991).

Support for democratic institutions and processes appears to be more shaky in east-central Europe, where there is considerable evidence of a growing alienation from politics and disillusionment with new democratic regimes. Surveys in Hungary have found that Hungarians' estimation of the openness and responsiveness of the system (external efficacy) has actually decreased since 1985. In 1985, between 34 and 40 percent of respondents agreed that "you can never trust politicians completely," "simple people are always excluded from power," and "politicians are happy if people are not involved in dealing with the country's matters." By 1991—*after* the democratic revolution—agreement with these statements had climbed to between 72 and 79 percent (Simon 1993, 232). Similarly, a 1992 survey in Czechoslovakia found that 68 percent of all respondents (and 79 percent in Slovakia) were either dissatisfied or very dissatisfied with the political developments since 1989. Even in 1993, after this state divided into two republics, only about half of the respondents expressed support for the republic governments and legislatures (Wolchik 1993, 428).[26] What might explain this discontent?

One possibility is that these respondents are just pessimists, and would be dissatisfied with any regime. Rose and Mishler (1994) discount this hypothesis by examining the correlations between support for the present regime and support for the previous communist regime in five Eastern European nations. Although there were some "skeptics" who expressed distaste for both the old and the new regimes—up to 17 percent in Poland and Romania—many of those who do not like the current regime are much more positive about the old one.[27] Rose and Mishler credit the relative lack of support for current regimes as the product of economic difficulties rather than fundamental anti-democratic orientations. The transition from centrally planned economies to market economies has made the daily lives for many people much more difficult and uncertain. However, these authors are inclined to be hopeful about future regime legitimacy, as respondents who estimated that the economy would improve in the next five years also estimated that they would be much more supportive of the regime at that time (179).

Elizabeth Kiss (1992) argues that the current discontent with new regimes in east-central Europe is also a product of the dominant expectations about democracy in this region. Dissidents in Poland, Czechoslovakia, and Hungary tended to emphasize the need for a rich civil society that would provide common citizens opportunities to influence public life. This emphasis was their basis for criticizing communism as well as criticizing the western tendency to equate democracy with free elections. While their focus was certainly democratic in intent, it was not well balanced with a respect for traditional democratic institutions. Whereas multiparty competition provides a means to peacefully resolve conflicts, east-central European dissidents tended to downplay internal conflicts. Rather than engaging in "power politics," they emphasized consensus, nonconfrontation, and the toleration of a plurality of opinions (Kiss, 229). This philosophical foundation proved to be effective for dissident movements, but became problematic once those former dissidents came into office. Kiss argues that the emphasis on consensus kept new regimes such as those of Vaclav Havel in Czechoslovakia and Lech Walesa in Poland from making effective policy, and generated conflicts that tended to come to the fore as personal animosity rather than political difference. The lack of support for new regimes in this region, therefore, might stem from ineffective government as well as the failed ideal after the democratic transition.

Even surveys that demonstrate relatively strong support for democratic processes in some of the former Soviet republics reveal low levels of legitimacy for particular governments and elites during this period of transition (Miller, Hesli, and Reisinger 1992). In a more established democracy, a lack of support for political elites would not threaten the survival of the whole system, since citizens could better differentiate between particular regimes and institutional structures. When citizens in more established democracies do not like how things are going—especially during times of economic crisis—they vote out of office the incumbents whom they hold responsible. But when new elites and new institutions come to power together, citizens are more likely to reject the whole package. Hence, we see considerable support among the citizens of post-communist states for total institutional overhaul, most frequently for a return to aspects of a past system. A lack of support for the current regime could translate into a lack of support for democratic institutions and processes altogether.

Orientations Supportive of Democratic Conditions

Recent surveys have found a fairly wide distribution of those orientations supportive of democratic conditions in some of the post-communist states. More than one survey has found that many former Soviet citizens value individual liberty and rights strongly. In Lithuania in 1992, three-quarters of all respondents demonstrated rights consciousness,[28] and 70 percent agreed or fully agreed that "anyone can oppose or resist any governmental initiative" (Reisinger et al. 1994). Such responses indicate that the Lithuanians may be willing to defend their individual authority and their autonomy from the state, as citizens in a democracy need to do.

Gibson, Duch, and Tedin found even higher levels of rights consciousness among Muscovites in 1990, and conclude that these respondents "look uncannily like their Western neighbors in terms of their willingness to assert basic citizenship rights" (1992, 345). These authors hypothesize that rights consciousness should be strongest in those places where people have at one time lived under arbitrary authoritarian rule. Liberty should be most precious to those who have had it denied. And, in fact, they do find that among citizens of European and Eurasian nations, the percentages of those who defend a wide range of individual rights are highest not only in Moscow, but also in some of the other newest democracies in Western Europe (Spain, Portugal, and Greece) (347). However, the considerable extent of rights-consciousness in these places could backfire. Again, lacking experience under democratic rule, expectations of the rights and benefits democracy will bring tend to be unrealistically high. Among policy makers, such expectations can lead to deadlock; among the citizens, it can lead to disillusionment.

Studies in east-central Europe have found that the citizen emphasis on rights in this region tends to emphasize positive freedoms over negative ones. While there is some evidence that liberal rights like the freedom of speech or the right of assembly are becoming more widely valued, respondents to surveys in both Hungary (1991) and Czechoslovakia (1992) gave economic rights primary importance. Their priorities included the right to work, to health care, to social security, and "to live without worries" (Simon 1993; Wolchik 1993). A Hungarian factory worker expresses his ambivalence about freedom in this new democracy quite succinctly: "I was freed from four decades of communism as well as from my job. Now I am so free that I don't even know what to do" (Simon 1993, 227).

There has also been some evidence of an emerging participatory society in newly liberalized states. Cynthia Kaplan found, for instance, that although a relatively low percentage of citizens in Estonia participated in elections or campaign activities prior to independence, many Estonians in 1990 considered themselves members of associations, particularly those oriented around national identity and sovereignty (Kaplan 1993). Similarly, although studies in Russia have found that their respondents were highly alienated from both state and local governments (Miller, Hesli, and Reisinger 1992; Hahn 1991), Hahn found a level of personal efficacy in Yaroslavl' in 1990 that was comparable in most respects to that in the United States (410). These studies suggest that even though there has not been a long history of opportunities for meaningful political participation in post-Soviet societies, the art of political association and collective political action has not been completely lost.

David Lempert (1993) tells an opposing, more pessimistic story. He points out that participatory orientations and opportunities are actually quite limited in the newly reformed Russian society. He argues that democratic reform in Russia has not been grassroots, but rather has involved the breakup of a centralized state into smaller loci of elite control, which still exclude ordinary citizens from having any degree of meaningful self-determination. Lempert conducted interviews and ran focus group discussions in Leningrad (now St. Petersburg) in 1990 that also demonstrated very little citizen efficacy (639). He found that rather than creating reform from the bottom up, Russians continue "looking up . . . to someone 'above' to save them" (643). Market economics is widely held as a liberating influence, Lempert says, although most ordinary citizens (up to 90 percent) have no real access to private ownership. This economic inequality may translate into a lack of access to political and social influence, as well (643).

There are some contradictory tendencies in east-central Europe concerning participation and political efficacy. On one hand, there have been active grassroots dissident movements in all three societies (Poland, Hungary, Czechoslovakia).[29] The ethic and drive of these movements strongly resembled the participatory democratic ideal—they were highly inclusive, nonhierarchical, and bottom-up. On the other hand, the initial euphoria surrounding the democratic transitions in these societies has been greatly replaced by alienation and disillusionment. These attitudes have tended to translate into orientations which are either apolitical or lacking efficacy. For instance, in 1990, only 18 percent of the Hungarian respondents to a survey said they could "do something about it" if the government made a decision which violated their interests. This figure compares to about 75 percent in the United States, 62 percent in Great Britain, or 28 percent in Italy.[30] The same survey in other Eastern European states reported similar or lower levels of efficacy on a national level. Even on a local level, only between 14 and 31 percent of the respondents in east-central Europe said they thought they could counteract council decisions (Simon 1993, 235).[31] Similarly, in early 1992, only 24 and 28 percent of Hungarian and Polish respondents, respectively, said they felt that voting gave citizens some say in decision making (Wolchik 1993, 423). These kinds of beliefs tend to translate into low voter turnout and minimal political interest or participation in general.

Recent studies have also found less widespread distributions of interpersonal trust and tolerance. In 1992, from 21 percent (in Ukraine) to 33 percent (in Russia) of the respondents from Ukraine, Lithuania, and Russia said that they believed most people can be trusted (Reisinger et al. 1994). Although these are not nearly as high as the levels of trust in Scandinavia, which generally top 50 percent, they are comparable to those of some other Western European democracies, like Belgium, France, and Italy.[32]

Gibson, Duch, and Tedin found very little tolerance in 1990 among Muscovites for the political and social groups they dislike the most. Large majorities (from 63 to 84 percent) said that the groups they dislike should be outlawed, banned from running for public office, and disallowed free speech or the right to hold public rallies (1992, 341).[33] At the same time, a majority of their respondents expressed support for minority rights and tolerance in the abstract (343). The gap between principle and practice looms large when people are faced with specific opponents and particular political problems.

This distance between principles and practices of tolerance may reflect tendencies to support democratic institutions and norms more in the abstract than in the concrete. For instance, surveys in Lithuania—the first Soviet republic to gain sovereignty—over the period from 1990 to 1992 suggest that the reality of self-rule has been somewhat disillusioning (Reisinger et al. 1994). In 1992, Lithuanians expressed a greater desire for order and less support for party competition than they had in 1990. Although these data are far from conclusive, it appears that in the years *before* political reform, there were actually higher levels of support for democratic ideals and institutions than there are now that these citizens have more practical experience with democracy. This is a pattern that we see replicated in Eastern Europe as well. While participation and interest in politics were widespread in the period immediately after the fall of communist rule, they declined as people "faced the need to come to terms with the meaning of the changes on their livelihoods and daily routines" (Wolchik 1993).

Certainly, democratic institutions have not been the political or economic panacea that many people had hoped. Along with political liberalization comes greater disorder, more clearly defined conflicts between groups in competition for power, and a loss of central authority and power. Whereas the centralized control of the former communist regimes severely limited individual liberties, the less-centralized successor states appear to many of their citizens to be directionless and floundering by comparison. This perception is only augmented by the economic difficulties these states are experiencing in their simultaneous transition to a market economy.

There is little doubt that failed ideals and practical hardships have tended to disillusion the masses with their new institutions in post-communist societies. People's high expectations for reform continue to go greatly unfulfilled. Their discontent—the sense that things should (and can) be better—may prove to undermine new democratic institutions. But this same discontent might also provide the impetus for grassroots reform, and the development of a more substantive democracy. Discontent of this sort is not necessarily an anti-democratic phenomenon (Sniderman 1993, 238).

WHAT CAN WE EXPECT?

Recent surveys of mass orientations in post-communist societies give us some basis for optimism regarding their prospects to develop into successful democracies. Although orientations supportive of democracy do not completely pervade these societies, there seems to be ground on which to build. The occasional optimism of these studies stands in some contrast to the expectations based on earlier historical-anthropological studies of the pre-glasnost era, which were downright pessimistic. Much of the difference in the expectations of these two bodies of research stems from their divergent assumptions about where individual orientations come from and how subject they are to change over time.

The historical-anthropological studies of communist and post-communist societies adopt fairly "orthodox" culturalist assumptions (as defined in the first section of this chapter). In other words, they expect the strongest influence on current orientations to come from individuals' past—and especially their early—experiences. In the case of post-communist societies, this would suggest that the orientations people learned during their formative years under communist rule would continue to influence their behavior even after the system has changed. And indeed, there does seem to be some evidence that values learned under communism still are salient for some of the citizens in post-communist societies, such as the priority of economic "rights" over liberal or legal ones.

In addition, pre-glasnost studies of culture in communist societies tended to adopt an assumption that might be called the "postulate of cumulative history": A particular culture's characteristics and traditions have deep historical roots and carry considerable momentum. For example, today we see gross intolerance and persecution of Bosnian Muslims by Orthodox Serbs in the Balkans—a conflict that some attribute to the forced conversions and persecution of Serbs by Bosnians (and Turks) under the rule of the Ottoman Empire in the 1400s. This postulate emphasizes the persistence of historical patterns, and—in expecting the ancient past to be the most critical determinant of the present—leaves very little hope for change or for new patterns to develop.[34]

Adopting either of these assumptions would lead us to conclude that the prospects for democracy in post-communist societies are dim. Most of these societies do not have strong democratic traditions to fall back on, and—according to many historical studies—the kinds of orientations that would support a successful democracy have been largely absent among their populations in the past. Expectations of continuity make successful democratic reforms seem unlikely.

The recent evidence from surveys that democratic orientations are not completely absent, on the other hand, suggests that some changes have occurred. There are a number of potential sources for change that postulates of cumulative history and socialization do not emphasize. One is the cultural change that tends to accompany modernization. Rapid urbanization and industrialization disrupt traditional social relations and create considerable mobility and discontinuity. In addition, mass communications and education both often expose people to a wider range of ideas and beliefs. Hypothetically, traditional sets of beliefs are challenged and debated more often in this kind of atmosphere, and people would thus be less likely to reproduce the same sets of beliefs over generations than they would in places where traditions maintain an unchallenged hegemony. The modernization that occurred under the Soviet regime may have created more fertile soil for institutional and social reform than many earlier scholars expected.[35]

Another potential source of change is the rapid economic and political upheaval in the past several years; there have been considerable discontinuities in the norms governing economic and political relations since the Soviet Union disintegrated. As I discussed earlier, institutions and elites may shape citizens' subjective orientations as much as popular orientations affect the nature and success of institutions. The leaders of a politically and economically centralized system, for example, would need to promote the kinds of popular beliefs and values that would ensure their legitimacy and authority. When the system changes, elites need to promote correlative value change. Whereas non-elected rulers may base their legitimacy upon displays of military power, a popularly elected president must gain legitimacy through demonstrations of responsiveness and competence. Because the justifications for new representative institutions rest on new sets of values and norms, these structural changes could significantly influence the orientations of common people.

At the same time as elites may affect mass orientations, they do not totally mold them. Some of the expectations the masses hold are based on their sense of the democratic ideal and how close the system comes to meeting it. Some of their expectations seem to be more practical and material. Hence, continued support for these regimes (insofar as they have support now) will depend in great part upon system outputs, in terms of the expected conditions of democracy and the overall quality of life.

Particularly during the initial trial period when new institutions lack the benefit of tradition or momentum, the burden of proof for popular support will still lie heavily upon effective and responsive policy. Citizens who participate politically but do not feel that their input is effective or has any possibility of becoming effective will not likely continue to participate, or else they might "participate" in extra-legal ways, such as through terrorism or mafia activities. This issue is timely, as the crime rate in Russia as well as in most other post-communist societies is skyrocketing.[36]

States in economic crisis may run into further problems: decentralized decision making concerning the distribution and use of resources still assumes that resources exist. When equality among citizens means they are equally powerless and poor, democratic ideals like tolerance or rules of conflict resolution may fall before more immediate needs for subsistence. There may be a certain level of economic security necessary before people can entrust political outcomes to the uncertainties of popular rule (Lipset 1960). Hence, economic scarcity may present one of the biggest obstacles to democratic success in many newly democratizing post-communist states in upcoming years. However, Duch (1994) has found support for democracy to be impervious to the economic difficulties of the population.

In those cases where the citizens of post-communist societies do not strongly demonstrate orientations supportive of democracy, what is the likelihood that such orientations will develop? It would be naive to expect that institutional changes can wipe the slate clean and reconstruct orientations from the ground up. At the same time, if political orientations can undergo rapid change in times of economic and political upheaval, issues of historical precedence or even socialization in former authoritarian states might not be determinative of a society's prospects for democracy. Instead, it will be most telling to continue to listen to what people caught up in these transitions make of their changing environment, what they think they have learned from their own history, and which principles have the greatest resonance for them.

NOTES

1. "Mass" here and throughout the text refers to the "general public."
2. By "orientations," I refer to a broad range of beliefs, values, and assumptions that people hold about social and political life. Such orientations may be cognitive, affective, or evaluative (see Eckstein 1988; Pye and Verba 1965). They are *general,* and as such may structure many more specific attitudes or opinions.
3. "A government of the people, by the people, and for the people."

4. I do not mean to suggest that democratic orientations are nonexistent in these places. We will return to the actual extent of such orientations in the third section of this chapter.
5. For examples, see Pye and Verba 1965; Inglehart 1977, 1988; Dalton 1994; Hahn 1991; and Reisinger, Miller, Hesli, and Maher 1994. These later studies generally incorporate more sophisticated data analysis in order to identify intra-national differences between demographic groups as well as differences between nations. There are also culturalist analyses that do not incorporate survey data; for example, see Huntington 1991 for general comparative analysis, or White 1979 for an analysis of Russian political culture.
6. The assumption that common people have anything at all to do with forms of government is less problematic in societies with democratic institutions than in those with authoritarian institutions. Democratic states include formal channels for citizen influence, and are by definition governments in which "the people" have some consequence. Making a similar assumption in societies with authoritarian institutions might unfairly pin the responsibility for despotic or oligarchic control on a population that is "passive," unable or unwilling to exert individual responsibility or initiative.
7. In recent years, there has also been more attention paid to the extent to which elites are able to create public support for their policy preferences through media (see, for example, Entman 1989). This political model stands in stark contrast to the expectation that elites should listen and respond to constituents' wishes.
8. For other works that adopt a procedural definition of democracy, see Rustow 1970; Przeworski 1986; di Palma 1990; and others cited in Chapter 2 in this volume.
9. We should not overlook the fact that even democratic states can enforce what might otherwise be unpopular policies such as tax collection or the military draft with the threat of punishment. But we cannot consider compliance to the law as a simple function of the degree of potential punishment; some people break laws in spite of potential punishment, while some others would comply even without a real risk of being punished. The difference between the two groups is the degree to which they accept the laws (and the policy-making bodies that created them) as legitimate and just.
10. Several of these theorists argued that it would be most realistic to redefine democracy in a way consistent with the reality in contemporary liberal democracies, rather than attempting an ideal that would be both hard to attain and "dangerous." Isaac (1994) argues that this procedurally based redefinition left too much of the meaning of democracy behind: "In the name of realism, the idea of rule by the people became wholly metaphorical, meaning nothing more than the right of citizens occasionally to select candidates who appeared to offer them some of what they wanted from government . . . this is clearly wanting from the perspective of the democratic ideal of self-government" (164–5).

11. Crowd psychology had its heyday in the early twentieth century and was championed primarily by Gustave LeBon. It was then adopted in some form by Gaetano Mosca and—most significantly to contemporary social science—by Robert Michels, who developed the "iron law" of elite rule (or oligarchy) on this basis (1962).

12. Although it is still generally acknowledged that most ordinary citizens are not "ideal" in terms of being active and informed, research in the 1980s and 1990s has offered alternative explanations for these survey results that do not suggest that the masses are essentially incompetent, irrational or apathetic as political actors. See, for example, Elkins 1993; Popkin 1991; Sniderman, Brody, and Tetlock 1991; and Page and Shapiro 1992.

13. See, for example, Wolf 1991 and de Lauretis 1987 for quite different analyses of representations of women in film and media.

14. By focusing on citizen rights, I do not mean to obscure the obligations of citizenship or the considerable "rights" and coercive powers of democratic states. State power and citizen duty are elements common to most forms of government.

15. Przeworski (1986) refers to democracy as "the institutionalization of uncertainty," meaning that the outcomes must never be certain (although the rules of decision making *must* be certain).

16. One of the most horrific examples of legalized persecution, of course, was under the rule of the National Socialists (Nazis) in Germany from 1932–1945, when Hitler came to power through popular elections. Because it had been legal in Germany to carry out the extermination of Jews and other "genetically inferior" groups at the time, international courts were later challenged to find grounds on which to convict Nazi administrators like Adolf Eichmann as war criminals (Arendt 1963). Some of these trials helped establish international standards of human rights.

17. In practice, this guideline can backfire for minority groups, however. For instance, King Henry VIII prohibited the Welsh language on the grounds that everyone should have an "equal right to use the king's language." And more recently, the law has allowed U.S. citizens in some states the equal right to be heterosexual.

18. See also Stouffer 1955; Sullivan, Piereson, and Marcus 1979, 1982; Barnum and Sullivan 1989; and, in the Russian context, Gibson and Duch 1993.

19. Citizenship laws in Latvia (or other former Soviet republics) only approximate this hypothetical situation. Currently, citizenship in Latvia is defined by those who were citizens in 1939 and their descendants, which effectively limits citizenship to Latvians, as most Russian residents did not move to Latvia until after its occupation by the USSR.

20. Interpersonal trust was discouraged during the Third Reich in Germany, for instance, through policies of mutual surveillance. People were rewarded for reporting any suspected lack of allegiance they witnessed among their friends, neighbors, and family. Because the costs of being found lacking in allegiance to the state were so high (imprisonment or death), many people found it safest to stop communicating with others except in perfunctory, state-supportive terms.

21. Putnam finds that a collaborative ethic, social trust, and solidarity are the restraints that—in game theory language—keep people from "defecting." People whose political action is based only on self-interest narrowly defined (that is, what will maximize one's personal utility) get caught in a cycle of defection, where lawlessness becomes expected and patron-client politics abound. Only when people define their self-interest in terms of common goals and build expectations of cooperation can decentralized representative government prosper. Although his emphasis on "civic virtue" is hardly new, the empirical evidence he brings in support of it is quite impressive—a novelty in the political culture literature.

22. In the following discussion I aim for breadth rather than depth; there will not be a comprehensive discussion of democratic orientations in any one state. In great part, this strategy reflects the available data, which is still somewhat piecemeal. However, in discussing general patterns, I do not mean to suggest that there are not significant differences across these regions.

23. For examples of the historical-anthropological interpretations of Russian culture, see Pipes 1974; Tucker 1960; White 1979, 1984; and Brzezinski 1989.

24. See Inkeles and Bauer 1959; Millar 1987; and Grey, Jennisch, and Tyler 1990.

25. The survey results cited in this section come from many different studies. Articles by Reisinger et al. (1994), and Miller, Hesli, and Reisinger (1992) are based on the Iowa New Soviet Citizen surveys of Lithuania, Ukraine, and Russia in 1990 through 1992. Articles by Gibson and Duch (1993), and Gibson, Duch and Tedin (1992) are based on their survey of residents of the Moscow oblast and the European USSR in 1990. Kaplan's (1993) article on Estonia draws its data from their survey of Estonian residents in 1991. Hahn (1991) conducted a study in the Russian city of Yaroslavl' as the basis for his work. Simon (1993) draws his data from his survey with L. Bruszt on ten Central and Eastern European countries over a period from 1985–1991. Rose and Mishler (1994) base their findings on their New Democracies Barometer (NDB) study that drew nationwide samples of citizens in Bulgaria, Czechoslovakia, Hungary, Poland, and Romania in 1991. Other sources of data are cited in the text and notes.

26. Data cited is from ASIA, "Vyzkum politckych postoju, 15–24 dubna 1992," Prague, May 1992; and the Public Opinion Research Institute, "Trust in State Institutions in the years 1990–1991–1992," June 1992.

27. Rose and Mishler did find slightly higher levels of support for the new regimes in 1991 than are reported by other surveys: from a low of 52 percent in Poland to a high of 69 percent in Romania.

28. This measure of rights consciousness was in an three-part index: freedom of speech, freedom of association, and religious liberty or freedom of conscience.

I have counted as "rights conscious" all those who said that all three always need to be observed, and those who said that two out of three always needed to be observed, and the third depending on the situation.

29. Poland had the most extensive grassroots movements, Hungary somewhat less, and Czechoslovakia the least of the three since its regime until 1989 was the most repressive. They did, however, share a common commitment to the idea of an autonomous "civil society" as the basis for opposing state power.
30. Simon draws the comparative data from Almond and Powell 1978.
31. Even then, there is some question about what respondents had in mind in terms of the action they might take. The open-ended part of the questionnaire asked respondents what they might do, and (particularly in Romania) received some answers such as "I have two fists" and "I would shove the table in his face" (236). These might fairly be discounted as predemocratic forms of efficacy.
32. The percentages for other European nations come from the 1980 World Values Survey (Inglehart 1988).
33. Similarly, Wolchik (1993) finds considerable intolerance among Czech and Slovak respondents who, she claims, are quite prejudiced towards gypsies and Jews. She notes also that women are systematically excluded from political leadership and are devalued at the workplace.
34. Although there is evidence of considerable similarities between the past and present cultures of many societies, it is problematic to assume that the past *determines* the present, in part because there is no mechanism for this kind of continuity besides socialization, which does involve some change with passing generations in response to circumstances and events. For an excellent critique of the assumptions of this kind of historical analysis, see McAuley 1984.
35. Hough 1988, Lewin 1988, and Starr 1989 all argue that the social changes accompanying modernization in the Soviet Union made the ground more fertile for democratic reform. Reisinger et al. 1994 affirm that there is a much more complex society in some of the former Soviet republics than culturalists would expect. These authors also attribute the intra-societal variation in great part to the effects of modernization, in general, and the expansion of education in particular.
36. See the Radio Free Europe / Radio Liberty Research Bulletin, vol. X, no. 11 (June 1, 1993), p. 4.

REFERENCES

ALMOND, GABRIEL, and G. BINGHAM POWELL. 1978. *Comparative Politics: System, Process, and Policy*, Second Edition. Boston: Little, Brown.

———, and SIDNEY VERBA. 1963. *The Civic Culture: Political Attitudes and Democracy in Five Nations*. Boston: Little, Brown.

ARENDT, HANNAH. 1963. *Eichmann in Jerusalem*. New York: Penguin Books.

———. 1973. *The Origins of Totalitarianism*. New York: Harcourt Brace Jovanovich.

BARNUM, DAVID G., and JOHN L. SULLIVAN. 1989. "Attitudinal Tolerance and Political Freedom in Britain." *British Journal of Political Science* 19:136–46.

BARBER, BENJAMIN. 1984. *Strong Democracy: Participatory Politics for a New Age*. Berkeley: University of California Press.

BARRY, BRIAN. 1970. *Sociology, Economics, and Democracy*. Chicago: University of Chicago Press.

BOYTE, HARRY. 1990. *Commonwealth*. New York: Free Press.

BRZEZINSKI, ZBIGNIEW. 1989. *The Grand Failure*. New York: Scribners.

CAMPBELL, ANGUS et al. 1960. *The American Voter*. New York: Wiley.

CLINTON, WILLIAM. 1993. Address to Congress, February 17.

COSER, LEWIS A. 1974. *Greedy Institutions: Patterns of Undivided Commitment*. New York: The Free Press.

DAHL, ROBERT A. 1956. *A Preface to Democratic Theory*. Chicago: University of Chicago Press.

———. 1971. *Polyarchy*. New Haven: Yale University Press.

———. 1989. *Democracy and Its Critics*. New Haven: Yale University Press.

DALTON, RUSSELL J. 1994. "Communists and Democrats: Attitudes Toward Democracy in the Two Germanies." *British Journal of Political Science* 24:469–93.

DE LAURETIS, TERESA. 1987. *Technologies of Gender: Essays on Theory, Film, and Fiction*. Bloomington: Indiana University Press.

DI PALMA, GIUSEPPE. 1990. *To Craft Democracies: An Essay on Democratic Transition*. Berkeley: University of California Press.

DUCH, RAYMOND M. 1994. "Institutions, Economic Chaos and Regime Instability." Paper presented at the Annual Meeting of the Midwest Political Science Association, Chicago, April 13–16.

ECKSTEIN, HARRY. 1988. "A Culturalist Theory of Political Change." *American Political Science Review* 82:789–804.

———. 1992. "A Theory of Stable Democracy." In Harry Eckstein, ed., *Regarding Politics: Essays on Political Theory, Stability, and Change*. Berkeley; Los Angeles: University of California Press, 179–226.

ELKINS, DAVID J. 1993. *Manipulation and Consent: How Voters and Leaders Manage Complexity*. Vancouver: University of British Columbia Press.

ENTMAN, ROBERT M. 1989. *Democracy Without Citizens: Media and the Decay of American Politics*. New York: Oxford University Press.

ETZIONI, AMITAI. 1993. *The Spirit of Community: Rights, Responsibilities, and the Communitarian Agenda*. New York: Crown Publishers.

GIBSON, JAMES, RAYMOND DUCH, and KENT TEDIN. 1992. "Democratic Values and the Transformation of the Soviet Union." *The Journal of Politics* 54(May): 329–71.

———, and RAYMOND DUCH. 1993. "Political Intolerance in the USSR: The Distribution and Etiology of Mass Opinion." *Comparative Political Studies* 26(3):286–329.

GIDDENS, ANTHONY. 1990. *The Consequences of Modernity*. Stanford: Stanford University Press.

GREY, ROBERT, LAURI JENNISCH, and ALANNA TYLER. 1990. "Soviet Public Opinion and the Gorbachev Reforms." *Slavic Review* 49(2):261–71.

HAHN, JEFFREY. 1991. "Continuity and Change in Russian Political Culture." *British Journal of Political Science* 21(4):393–421.

HELD, DAVID. 1987. *Models of Democracy*. Stanford: Stanford University Press.

HOUGH, JERRY F. 1988. *Russia and The West*. New York: Simon and Schuster.

HUNTINGTON, SAMUEL. 1991. *The Third Wave: Democratization in the Late Twentieth Century*. Norman: University of Oklahoma Press.

INGLEHART, RONALD. 1977. *The Silent Revolution: Changing Values and Political Styles Among Western Publics*. Princeton: Princeton University Press.

———. 1988. "The Renaissance of Political Culture." *American Political Science Review* 82(4):1203–30.

INKELES, ALEX, and RAYMOND BAUER. 1959. *The Soviet Citizen: Daily Life in a Totalitarian Society*. Cambridge: Harvard University Press.

ISAAC, JEFFREY C. 1994. "Oases in the Desert: Hannah Arendt on Democratic Politics." *American Political Science Review* 88(1):156–68.

KAPLAN, CYNTHIA S. 1993. "New Forms of Political Participation." In Arthur H. Miller, William M. Reisinger, and Vicki L. Hesli, eds., *Public Opinion and Regime Change: The New Politics of Post-Soviet Societies*. Boulder, Colo.: Westview, 153–67.

KISS, ELIZABETH. 1992. "Democracy Without Parties?: Civil Society in East-Central Europe." *Dissent* 39(2):226–31.

KORNHAUSER, WILLIAM. 1959. *The Politics of Mass Society*. Glencoe, Ill.: Free Press.

LEMPERT, DAVID. 1993. "Changing Russian Political Culture in the 1990s: Parasites, Paradigms, and Perestroika." *Comparative Studies in Society and History* 35(3):628–46.

LEWIN, MOSHE. 1988. *The Gorbachev Phenomenon: A Historical Interpretation*. Berkeley: University of California Press.

LIPSET, SEYMOUR MARTIN. 1960. *Political Man: The Social Bases of Politics*. Garden City, N.Y.: Doubleday.

LUHMANN, NIKLAS. 1979. *Trust and Power*. Chichester, U.K.: Wiley.

———. 1988. "Familiarity, Confidence, Trust: Problems and Alternatives." In

Diego Gambetta, ed., *Trust: Making and Breaking Cooperative Relations*. Oxford, U.K.: Blackwell.

McAuley, Mary. 1984. "Political Culture and Communist Politics: One Step Forward, Two Steps Back." In Archie Brown, ed., *Political Culture and Communist Studies*. New York: M.E. Sharpe, 13–39.

MacIntyre, Alasdair. 1984. *After Virtue*, Second Edition. Notre Dame: Notre Dame University Press.

———. 1988. *Whose Justice? Which Rationality?* Notre Dame: Notre Dame University Press.

MacPherson, C. B. 1966. *The Real World of Democracy*. Oxford: Oxford University Press.

———. 1977. *The Life and Times of Liberal Democracy*. Oxford: Oxford University Press.

Michels, Robert. 1962. *Political Parties: A Sociological Study of the Oligarchical Tendencies of Modern Democracy*. Eden and Cedar Paul, trans. New York: The Free Press.

Millar, James R., ed. 1987. *Politics, Work and Daily Life in the USSR: A Survey of Former Soviet Citizens*. New York: Cambridge University Press.

Miller, Arthur H., Vicki L. Hesli, and William R. Reisinger. 1992. "Regime Legitimacy and the Transition from Authoritarian Rule." Paper prepared for the Annual Meeting of the Midwest Political Science Association, Chicago, April 17–20.

Page, Benjamin I., and Robert Y. Shapiro. 1992. *The Rational Public: Fifty Years of Trends in Americans' Policy Preferences*. Chicago: University of Chicago Press.

Pateman, Carole. 1970. *Participation and Democratic Theory*. Cambridge: Cambridge University Press.

———. 1985. *The Problem of Political Obligation: A Critique of Liberal Theory*. Cambridge, Mass.: Polity Press.

Pipes, Richard. 1974. *Russia Under the Old Regime*. New York: Scribners.

Popkin, Samuel. 1991. *The Reasoning Voter*. Chicago: The University of Chicago Press.

Przeworski, Adam. 1986. "Some Problems in the Study of the Transition to Democracy." In Guillermo O'Donnell, Phillipe Schmitter, and Laurence Whitehead, eds., *Transitions from Authoritarian Rule: Prospects for Democracy*. Baltimore: Johns Hopkins Press, 47–63.

Putnam, Robert. 1993. *Making Democracy Work: Civic Traditions in Modern Italy*. Princeton: Princeton University Press.

Pye, Lucian W., and Sidney Verba, eds. 1965. *Political Culture and Political Development*. Princeton: Princeton University Press.

Reisinger, William M., Arthur H. Miller, Vicki L. Hesli, and Kristen Hill

MAHER. 1994. "Political Values in Russia, Ukraine and Lithuania: Sources and Implications for Democracy." *British Journal of Political Science* 24:183–223.

ROSE, RICHARD, and WILLIAM T. E. MISHLER. 1994. "Mass Reaction to Regime Change in Eastern Europe: Polarization or Leaders and Laggards?" *British Journal of Political Science* 24:159–82.

RUSTOW, DANKWART A. 1970. "Transitions to Democracy: Toward a Dynamic Model." *Comparative Politics* 2(3):337–63.

SARTORI, GIOVANNI. 1962. *Democratic Theory*. Detroit: Wayne State University Press.

SCHMITTER, PHILIPPE C., and TERRY LYNN KARL. 1991. "What Democracy Is . . . and Is Not." *Journal of Democracy* 2(3):75–88.

SCHUMPETER, JOSEPH A. 1942. *Capitalism, Socialism, and Democracy*. New York: Harper and Row.

SCOTT, JAMES C. 1990. *Domination and the Arts of Resistance: Hidden Transcripts*. New Haven: Yale University Press.

SIMON, JANOS. 1993. "Post-paternalist Political Culture in Hungary: Relationship Between Citizens and Politics During and After the 'Melancholic Revolution' (1989–1991)." *Communist and Post-Communist Studies* 26(2):226–38.

SMITH, GORDON B. 1991. *Soviet Politics: Struggling with Change*, Second Edition. New York: St. Martin's.

SNIDERMAN, PAUL M. 1993. "The New Look in Public Opinion Research." In Ada Finifter, ed., *Political Science: The State of the Discipline II*. Washington, D.C.: American Political Science Association.

———, RICHARD A. BRODY, and PHILIP E. TETLOCK. 1991. *Reasoning and Choice: Explorations in Political Psychology*. New York: Cambridge University Press.

SORENSON, EVA. 1994. "Democracy and Regulation in Public Institutions." Dissertation, Institute of Political Science, University of Copenhagen, Denmark.

STARR, FREDERICK. 1989. "A Usable Past: Russia's Democratic Roots." *New Republic* 200:20, 24.

STOUFFER, SAMUEL. 1955. *Communism, Conformity and Civil Liberties*. New York: Doubleday.

SULLIVAN, JOHN, JAMES E. PIERESON, and GEORGE E. MARCUS. 1979. "An Alternative Conceptualization of Political Tolerance: Illusory Increases 1950's–1970's." *American Political Science Review* 73:781–94.

———, JAMES E. PIERESON, and GEORGE E. MARCUS. 1982. *Political Tolerance and American Democracy*. Chicago: The University of Chicago Press.

———, MICHAL SHAMIR, PATRICK WALSH, and NIGEL S. ROBERTS. 1985. *Political Tolerance in Context: Support for Unpopular Minorities in Israel, New Zealand, and the United States*. Boulder, Colo.: Westview.

TOCQUEVILLE, ALEXIS DE. 1961. *Democracy in America.* Henry Reeve, Trans. First Shocken Edition. New York: Shocken Books.

TUCKER, ROBERT C. 1960. "The Image of Dual Russia." In Cyril Black, ed., *The Transformation of Russian Society.* Cambridge: Harvard University Press, 587–605.

VERBA, SIDNEY, NORMAN H. NIE, and JAE-ON KIM. 1978. *Participation and Political Equality: A Seven-Nation Comparison.* Cambridge, England; New York: Cambridge University Press.

WHITE, STEPHEN. 1979. *Political Culture and Soviet Politics.* London: Macmillan.

———. 1984. "Soviet Political Culture Reassessed." In Archie Brown, ed., *Political Culture and Communist Studies.* New York: M.E. Sharpe, 40–99.

WOLCHIK, SHARON. 1993. "The Repluralization of Politics in Czechoslovakia." *Communist and Post-Communist Studies* 26(4):412–31.

WOLF, NAOMI. 1991. *The Beauty Myth.* New York, London, Toronto: Anchor Books.

CHAPTER
5

CONSTITUTIONALISM AND THE RULE OF LAW: THEORETICAL PERSPECTIVES

JOHN REITZ [1]

The Soviet Union today faces the problems of developing a law-abiding state—the challenge of forming a state which is based on the rule of law and which will serve as an instrument of freedom as we move toward the creation of a democratic society. . . .

. . . In the West, the idea of the law-abiding state is customarily taken for granted; it is something which Americans have assimilated in their daily lives. In Soviet society, this idea was raised as a counter against the monopoly of the Communist Party, which actually substituted itself for all governmental institutions.

—Sobchak 1990, 211.

As the above quotation from the reform leader, then Chairman of the City Council, now Mayor of St. Petersburg indicates, many of those who are attempting to bring the countries of Eastern Europe and the former Soviet Union from communism to democracy place great emphasis on implementing the rule of law in order to achieve the transition. Chairman Sobchak's statement also shows that by "rule of law" these reformers have in mind the idea that, just like its citizens, the state should have to abide by the rules; that is, that no individual or unit of the state's government should be free to wield power except in accordance with law. This notion is closely related to the concept of constitutionalism, since constitutions generally set limits to the exercise of state power by each branch or unit of government.

This chapter explores key issues in the establishment of constitutionalism and the rule of law in the countries of Eastern Europe and the former Soviet Union. The first section discusses definitions of the terms "rule of law" and "constitutionalism" and describes the traditionally negative attitudes communists held concerning these ideas and the rehabilitation of these concepts during the Gorbachev era. The second section explores the relationship between constitutionalism and the rule of law on the one hand and both a democratic political order and a market economy on the other, including the special problem of judicial review. The final section discusses what we know and do not know about transitions to the rule of law and constitutionalism. The next chapter supplements this general and theoretical approach with an analysis of the progress post-communist societies have made in building key institutions necessary for the rule of law. While both chapters attempt to discuss matters that are generally relevant to legal developments in all of the post-communist countries, for the sake of concreteness the focus throughout both chapters is on Russia and, to a lesser extent, Poland.

MEANING OF "RULE OF LAW" AND "CONSTITUTIONALISM" AND COMMUNIST ATTITUDES TOWARD THESE TERMS

Definitions

The terms "rule of law" and "constitutionalism" are complex terms whose precise meanings vary at different times and places. Krygier (1990, 640), for example, calls the rule of law "a notoriously contested concept." The two terms share some core ideas but come with different baggage.

Definitions of the rule of law vary greatly in breadth. Some emphasize particular formal requirements of law or legal process, some also insist on specific content for the legal rules. Lon Fuller's (1969, 39) catalogue of the minimum formal requirements for law is, for example, often taken as a definition of the rule of law: law must be public (not secret), understandable and consistent, applied in a manner consistent with the published law, having the degree of reasonableness and stability that parties can comply with them, and not abusively retroactive. Krygier's (1990, 646) definition includes features of a legal system. The rule of law requires written laws that are "prospective, clear, open and accessible, [and] noncontradictory, . . . an independent and impartial judiciary, and independent legal profession, [and] honest and apolitical law enforcement." "[I]ndependence of the 'judicial department' may indeed be regarded as the very definition of the 'rule of law': It is certainly an important part of it" (Dahrendorf 1977, 9), and an independent bar is thought necessary to assure access to the courts.

Virtually all definitions of rule of law agree on the importance of law's function to set limits to the exercise of private and state power (e.g., Altman 1990; Dworkin 1986, 93; Hutchinson and Monahan 1987a, ix; Walker 1988, 23–42). Some go further, seeing the concept as necessarily setting certain types of limits to the state, such as those based on the basic civil and political rights (like the rights in the U.S. Bill of Rights). Walker (1988, 25–7), for example, stresses the importance of the principle of equality. The 1959 Declaration of Delhi by the International Commission of Jurists (ICJ), an organization of lawyers from many different countries, even ties the concept to broader social and welfare rights (like the right to adequate housing or medical care) by stating that

> the Rule of Law is a dynamic concept for the expansion and fulfilment of which jurists are primarily responsible and which should be employed not only to safeguard and advance the civil and political rights of the individual in a free society, but also to establish social, economic, educational and cultural conditions under which his legitimate aspirations and dignity may be realized . . . .

(quoted in Marsh 1959, 3). The more recent "Copenhagen Document," agreed to in 1990 by thirty-two nations of Europe, the Soviet Union, the United States, and Canada meeting together as the Conference on Security and Cooperation in Europe (CSCE), affirms that "democracy is an inherent element of the rule of law" (quoted in Buergenthal 1991, 356). The emphasis in both the ICJ and CSCE statements on the rule of law is, however, on the concept that fundamental human rights of a civil and political nature—like the principle of equality, the presumption of innocence in criminal cases, freedoms of speech and assembly, and the right to be tried before independent courts—should set limits to the exercise of power by either the legislature or the executive. I will therefore take as the hallmark of the rule of law the claim most commonly made for it, namely, that under the rule of law the exercise of all power, both private and public, is limited by law. A brief survey of the historical development of the concept will show that this focus is justified, especially the focus on the limitation of state power,[2] and will also illuminate the relationship to constitutionalism.

There are at least three distinct traditions that have contributed to our concepts of the rule of law. One important tradition developed in England out of the struggles between Parliament and the English king. Parliament's assertion of authority over the monarch was defended in part by reference to the natural law tradition, which taught that natural law (principles of justice derived from human reason and conscience) is superior to positive law, that is, the law created by the state. Out of this background came two important developments. The British developed the idea that the Monarchy, and the executive power that evolved from it, was subject to law. Thus the British came to give their courts the power to review executive and administrative[3] action to ensure that it was authorized by Parliament and consistent with the Common Law unless Parliament clearly had changed the Common Law (Wade and Bradley 1993, 99–100). The British also developed the notion that even Parliament was bound by the fundamental principles of justice found in the Common Law and other historical traditions of the English people. These natural law principles are collectively known as the "unwritten British constitution," but in the traditional British version, no court, only Parliament, has the power to determine whether its legislation comports with the unwritten constitution, a principle the British call "Parliamentary sovereignty" (Berman 1991, 2; Wade and Bradley 1993, 26).

The United States created a second model of the rule of law by adding to the British tradition a written constitution and by entrusting to the courts the power to refuse to apply statutes they deem to be unconstitutional, a process referred to as "judicial review of legislative action." Both the British version with unwritten constitution and absence of judicial review and the American version with written constitution and judicial review are referred to as "constitutionalism," which at its core means a system in which a body of constitutional rules are superior to all other laws created by any organ of the state.[4] One of the most important functions of such constitutional rules is to define certain areas of individual freedom upon which the state cannot infringe. These areas constitute the human rights that are guaranteed by the constitution. The term constitutionalism is often used with as broad a sense as the rule of law (e.g., LaPalombara 1974, 105), but I shall restrict the term to its core meaning as well.

The Russian term that is generally used to express the idea of the rule of law is *pravovoe gosudarstvo*, and it comes out of the third tradition, which developed on the European continent. The Russian term is a literal translation of the German term *Rechtsstaat*, which is often translated as "law-based state" or "state under the rule of law." The term *Rechtsstaat* developed in the early nineteenth century in France and in German-speaking lands. In France following the French Revolution, the doctrine made the law created by Parliament supreme. During periods of dictatorship or monarchy in France and in the absolutist German states, the doctrine made the law created by the dictator or monarch supreme. In either case, the *Rechtsstaat* was part of the tradition of positivist jurisprudence, in which the will of the lawmaker was the supreme source of law, and there was no source of law outside of the state's law-giving power. This use of the term, which dominated the Civil Law tradition of the European continent[5] until the end of World War II, thus originally excluded the idea that the supreme lawmaker—be it an absolute monarch, dictator, or democratically elected legislature—was in any way bound by a higher law. The state's power could be limited by law, but the lawmaker could change the laws as it saw fit (Berman 1991, 3; LaPolombara 1974, 106; Urabe 1990, 61–3). This narrower or weaker version of rule of law thus excluded constitutionalism.

The primary goal of the legal system in the weak version of the *Rechtsstaat* is to ensure that all state power, including that of the courts, is exercised as directed by the supreme lawgiver. Law is seen as an instrument to subjugate all persons and all other organs of government to the rules promulgated by the supreme lawmaker. Continental societies like France and the German states had developed large and powerful administrative bureaucracies. The *Rechtsstaat* tradition thus included the idea of court review to assure that all administrative action was in accordance with the law created by the sovereign or, in the case of democracies, the sovereign legislature. This kind of *Rechtsstaat,* then, was not rule *of* law, but rule *by* law. Moreover, this tradition had developed without any particular connection to democracy or fundamental human rights. The emphasis on the obedience of all state organs to the law promulgated by the highest law-making body permitted even Nazis and authoritarian Communist rulers to claim that their states were constructed according to the theory of the *Rechtsstaat* (Berman 1991, 3).

By comparison with the U.S. version of rule of law, which includes constitutionalism and judicial review, the traditional form of the *Rechtsstaat* is obviously a weaker or more limited form of rule of law. But the concept of the *Rechtsstaat* in Western Europe has continued to evolve. After World War II, Germany and many other European countries drafted new constitutions establishing various forms of judicial review. Some German writers today even use *Rechtsstaat* to include the notion of constitutional restraints on the legislature.[6] Thus the strong version of the term, implying constitutional limits on all branches of government, is the meaning most commonly used today, not only in Western Europe, the United States, and much of the Commonwealth, but also throughout the world, as reflected, for example, in the ICJ and CSCE documents.

Berman (1991, 3) and Shelley (1992, 68) warn, however, that the weak meaning of *Rechtsstaat* (rule *by* law) is what Gorbachev meant when he first began using *pravovoe gosudarstvo* as a reform slogan. As we will see, a strongly instrumental view that law is a tool to extend control over a society was characteristic of much of Soviet thinking about law. Even though—as this and the next chapter will show—much of the recent law reform in Eastern Europe and the former Soviet Union appears to have been animated by the strong form of the ideal, Sajó and Losonci (1993, 327) caution that the traditional meaning of *Rechtsstaat* still dominates the mass public's understanding of the rule of law in this part of the world. Confusion about the rule of law and its various possible equivalents in various languages is thus common.

One particular source of confusion is the similarity between the British version of the rule of law, which I have classified among the strong forms of the rule of law even though it traditionally excludes judicial review of legislative action,[7] and the weaker form of the traditional *Rechtsstaat*, which insists on the supremacy of the lawmaker, whether it be a democratically elected legislature or an authoritarian leader. To the extent that nineteenth-century *Rechtsstaat* theory applied to democracies, it spoke of parliamentary sovereignty in the same categorical way that the British traditionally have.[8] One therefore has to ask whether the traditional British view is not functionally the same as the weak form of the rule of law (rule *by* law).

It is commonly thought that there are two safeguards that ensure Parliamentary respect for the limits of the British constitution, their political and legal cultures and the stubborn independence of the Common Law courts that makes them to some extent critical opponents of the state. Neither of these factors is part of the traditional *Rechtsstaat* theory. In the first place, the British assert that their politicians really do respect the restrictive effect of the Constitution.[9] In the second place, since the Middle Ages, the British tradition has included Common Law courts independent of the executive and legislative branches. The power that independent courts have to serve as a restraint on the legislature should not be underestimated. Even if they do not have the formally recognized power to review the constitutionality of legislation, courts necessarily have the power to interpret legislation. The British courts are supposed to interpret legislation to be consistent with the Common Law, including its ancient constitutional principles (like due process), unless Parliament has made it clear that the legislation is intended to violate those principles. As Allan (1985, 119) says,

> The rule of law, as a juristic principle, thus embodies the liberal and individualistic bias of the common law in favour of the citizen. It transcends the principle of legality by authorizing, and demanding, an attitude of independence and scepticism on the part of the judges in the face of claims of governmental power.

But even a Parliament bent on abridging constitutional rights will often be reluctant to admit clearly to either domestic or international audiences that it is doing so. Thus, the courts' interpretative stance can serve as a substantial barrier, at least forcing Parliament to reenact unconstitutional legislation one or more times—each time more clearly than before—until the courts are forced to give it effect. The political cost of admitting the intent to abridge the Constitution will be too high, it is hoped, in many cases, and attempts at reenactment may be given up.

The British form of rule of law thus is thought to give meaningful effect to a strong form of the term even though it does not include judicial review of legislation. British rule of law is more than a simple insistence on legality, the characteristic of the weak form of the rule of law, which many authoritarian governments can claim to follow. If we accept the British system as an example of the strong version of the rule of law, then we cannot say that that form has to include judicial review of legislation though many—perhaps most—countries seeking to implement the strong version have adopted some form of judicial review. The arguments for and against judicial review are discussed elsewhere in this chapter. While there is considerable international agreement on most of the features of the strong version of the rule of law, many countries still harbor significant doubts about the wisdom of judicial review of legislative acts. Thus, that feature cannot be taken as a required element of the rule of law.

Our discussion of the British version also highlights one further feature of the strong version of the rule of law, which applies equally to those forms with or without judicial review. In the last analysis, the rule of law depends on culture—the culture of politicians, lawyers, judges, and the rest of the citizenry. As Krygier (1990, 646) says, the essence of the rule of law is "a widespread assumption within society that law *matters* and should matter." Walker (1988, 41) calls it "an attitude of legality" and "a 'spirit'" that law should command obedience. No set of legal institutions, processes, and substantive rules of public and private law will be effective to do the things claimed for the rule of law unless there is a legal culture—i.e., a combination of practices and attitudes concerning the law and legal system—that is supportive of the rule of law. The legal culture concerns the society as a whole, but the special role played by the "legal community"—who lead society in forming and maintaining a legal culture that law matters and should matter—will be discussed in the next section.

In sum, constitutionalism expresses the idea that there are constitutional rules that are binding on all organs of the state and superior to rules created by all other organs. Constitutional rules can be changed only in ways more difficult to enact than ordinary statutes. Constitutions generally seek to guarantee at least a catalog of the basic civil and political rights, such as equality before the law; freedoms of speech, assembly, and religion; due process, including open and unbiased courts and fair hearing; and criminal procedure protections, such as the presumption of innocence and freedom from unreasonable searches and seizures or forced confessions.

The weak form of the rule of law developed quite independently of democracy and emphasizes the notion of legality. It excludes the idea of constitutionalism. In this conception, law is binding on all private and public power, except that the supreme lawgiver has the power to change law. Western European countries have abandoned this form of the rule of law in favor of various forms of the strong version, but authoritarian states often claim to be instituting the weak version.

The strong version of the rule of law developed in close association with democratic forms of government. It includes constitutionalism to express the idea that the exercise of all power in a state, whether by persons acting in public or private capacity, is limited by law. In many countries, this ideal is implemented in part by judicial review of the constitutionality of legislative action. The rule of law does not necessarily require this type of judicial review, but it does require judicial review of the legality of executive and administrative action through constitutional and administrative law and the legality of private action through the private law, administrative law, and criminal law. The fair adjudication of these issues requires independent courts and independent lawyers to assist individuals to assert their rights in court. Finally, the strong version of the rule of law implies a legal culture, widespread among politicians as well as among the rest of society, that supports the rule of law through (1) an attitude that law should command obedience and (2) behavior consistent with that ideal.

Traditional Communist Rejection of the Rule of Law

Because Marxist thought seeks to explain social change on the basis of the material circumstances of life, nonmaterial aspects like law do not provide a foundation for their social theorizing (Collins 1982, 9). Their focus on material circumstances leads them to view law as necessarily reflecting the ideology of the dominant class (Collins 1982, 17–34). Moreover, Marxists view claims that law can operate as an autonomous restraint on public or private power as reprehensible attempts to camouflage the raw domination of the working class by the propertied class (Collins 1982, 137–38). In fact, Marxists doubt the importance of law as a form of social control (Collins 1982, 95), and Engels and Lenin predicted that law would wither away under communism (Collins 1982, 101).

Law did not, however, disappear completely from any communist states, but the liberal ideal of the rule of law was strongly repudiated in general by the communist world. Suppression of the rule of law ideal in Russia was especially easy because "neither the prerevolutionary state nor the citizenry ever developed a firm commitment to legal ideals" (Shelley 1992, 65). In fact, in 1864 Tsar Alexander II had made the first attempt in Russian history to establish an independent judiciary. He also introduced jury trials for serious crimes, but by the 1870s, he was already undermining the judges' independence, in part by freezing their salaries. In 1905–1906, Nicholas II issued a manifesto, which created a legislative Duma and granted civil liberties to the Russian people, but it essentially entrenched the Tsar's autocratic powers and amounted to at most "sham constitutionalism." (Lien 1994, 59–63). In the mid-nineteenth century, Herzen had cynically observed, "Whatever his station, the Russian evades or violates the law wherever he can do so with impunity; the government does exactly the same thing" (quoted in Huskey 1991, 68). Toward the end of that century, Kistiakovsky wrote, "Of all the cultural values [of the Russian intelligentsia], law was the most suppressed" (quoted in Huskey 1991, 68). So in 1917 what little rule of law culture existed was found only among a "small circle of Westernized *intelligenty*" (quoted in Huskey 1991, 68). The Bolshevik Revolution of 1917 eradicated this circle and substituted for the prerevolutionary legal system a system of administrative commands, enforced largely by the army and secret police (Huskey 1992, 25). The chaos and violence that accompanied the Revolution and civil war "obliterated respect for legal norms by the law enforcers as well as those subject to their authority" (Shelley 1992, 65).

With the cessation of the civil war, Lenin and the other leaders reversed their position on law to a limited extent as part of the New Economic Policy (NEP), which restored to urban areas important elements of the capitalist economy in an attempt to stave off utter economic disaster for the country. Consequently, the 1920s saw some revival of the legal structures. There was even some discussion of the rule of law, as well as an explosion of new legislation, including substantial codification of Soviet law (Huskey 1992, 25–7). It was during this period that the USSR Supreme Court exercised a limited form of judicial review by rendering advisory opinions at the request of certain governmental bodies on the conformity of law of the republics with the All-Union law and on the legality of adminstrative orders issued by the central agencies. The opinions, however, were not binding on the Soviet legislature (Solomon 1990b, 128–29). Despite these legal developments, there was no revival of even the meager prerevolutionary legal culture (Shelley 1992, 66).

The new respect for law and legal institutions came to an end in 1928, and from 1928 to 1932, according to Huskey (1992, 28) "a naked instrumentalism . . . informed Soviet legal policy." Stalin wielded law as a tool of state coercion and repression (Shelley 1992, 66–7). Moreover, the "Stalin" constitution of 1936 formally recognized the leading role of the Communist Party.[10] The Party hegemony clause was carried over into the "Brezhnev" constitution of 1977, which declared in Article 6 that "the leading and guiding force of Soviet society and the nucleus of its political system, of all state organizations and public organizations, is the Communist Party of the Soviet Union" (quoted in Hazard 1992, 6).[11]

Communist rule did not come to Eastern European countries until after World War II. Prior to that time, several had had the opportunity to develop legal cultures strongly influenced by Western European traditions. Poland had actually adopted the first written constitution in Europe in 1791, though it lasted only slightly more than a year before it was swept away by the second of the partitions that ultimately wiped that country off the map for over a century. The parts of Poland that fell to Prussia and to the Habsburg monarchy were exposed to the weak forms of the rule of law that were being developed in those countries under autocratic rule. Poland was reconstituted an independent country by the Treaty of Versailles ending the First World War. While strongman rule eventually undermined its democracy during the interwar period, it also had the major political and legal institutions needed for the rule of law, including a popularly elected legislature and an independent judiciary (Brzezinski 1991, 60–86). Hungary and the Czech and Slovak lands similarly were part of the Habsburg Empire and its weak version of the rule of law before they were made into two independent countries by the Treaty of Versailles. Czechoslovakia also enjoyed a reasonably well functioning democracy during the interwar period (Mathernova 1992, 474). The parts of Germany that became East Germany had, of course, fully participated in the development of the German legal culture of the *Rechtsstaat*, including the Nazi perversion, up until 1945.

Communist leaders after World War II in these countries therefore faced a much greater job to dismantle and suppress rule of law institutions and culture than was the case in Russia. While that process ran a different course in each of these countries, the Communist Parties in each secured constitutional status for the guiding role of their Communist Party. In Poland, however, the leading role of the Polish United Workers' Party (PUWP) (the Polish version of the Communist Party) was not enshrined in the constitution until 1976, little more than four years before the national labor movement known as Solidarity would give the lie to the notion that the PUWP was the main force guiding events there (Pomorski 1984).

In this way, the primacy of one political party and its political decisions was elevated to the status of a basic constitutional principle in all communist countries. These communist constitutions thus officially rejected the strong version of the rule of law. The "guiding role" of the Communist Party was actualized in each country by the Party's tendency to form a shadow government so that Party officials were in a position to dictate important decisions to government officials. As Anatoly Sobchak put it, "for many, many years most of the functions of the state in the Soviet Union were fulfilled by the Communist Party. . . . Until recently, . . . we had no division between the Party and the state, and the Communist Party held all of the real power in its hands" (Sobchak 1990, 211 [footnote omitted]).

One of the most notorious of the abuses resulting from the "guiding role" of the Party was so-called "telephone law." It has been widely reported that judges in the formerly socialist countries often received telephone calls instructing them how to decide politically sensitive cases (Markovits 1990, 229; Huskey 1991, 63; Frankowski 1991, 47). The practice was, of course, not in accordance with socialist theory, but it appears to have been widespread. Even though the judges were supposed to be independent, they were in fact highly susceptible to control through "telephone law" because Party officials controlled their election to office, as well as the allocation of virtually all benefits in society, including housing for the judges and fuel for heating the courtrooms (Solomon 1990a, 185–6).

Thus the communist period in the countries of Eastern Europe and the former Soviet Union left a legacy of what is often referred to as "legal nihilism." This attitude held that law is only one instrument of politics and should be completely subservient to other political processes, especially revolutionary ones; the party in political power could and should manipulate law to further its own ends. While the nihilist view predominated during the Bolshevik Revolution and has continued to exercise strong influence within the communist world since then, there have been a number of windows of law reform throughout the Soviet period (Huskey 1992, 30–3), during which more favorable views of law have predominated, including the view—which Huskey calls "legalism"—that law is a "universal value of human development" and consequently a system worth developing in a socialist political system as much as in a capitalist one (Huskey 1991, 56). However, there was no movement to institute the strong version of the rule of law before the Gorbachev era of reforms (Huskey 1992, 33).

Reform Communism: Toward the Rule of Law

As the next chapter will show, some modest legal reforms aimed at strengthening at least the weak version of the rule of law took hold in some communist countries as far back as the 1950s. Nevertheless, with the long-standing exception of Yugoslavia, which under Tito charted a unique socialist course, the bulk of significant legal reform did not start until the twilight of communist power that for the sake of simplicity we might mark by two events, one for Poland and one for Russia: the 1980 strike by Solidarity that fatally challenged Communist Party rule in Poland and the rise of Mikhail Gorbachev to the post of General Secretary of the Communist Party in the Soviet Union in 1985. The period of reform communism that these events inaugurated led to a veritable ferment of legal reform. Starting in 1980, communism in Poland was forced to consider reforms in order to deal with the threat posed by its noncommunist rival, Solidarity, but because of the threat of military intervention by the Soviet Union, reform communism itself could not officially hold power in any of the East Bloc countries outside Yugoslavia until reform communism took hold in the Soviet Union itself. Thus, Gorbachev's reform policies were the key events ushering in a general period of legal and political reform in Eastern Europe in the direction of the rule of law.

Gorbachev first sounded the rule of law theme in his address to the Nineteenth Party Conference in 1988. He stated that in order to achieve the "democratization of the life of the state and society" the USSR must "move along the path of the creation of a socialist state under the rule of law" (quoted in Quigley 1990, 205). While at first it may have seemed that the rule of law slogan was just concerned with modest reforms to the Soviet judicial system, by spring of 1990 Gorbachev and his colleagues had instituted such a sweeping program of reform that it seemed clear that they "were serious about shedding the old role of law as a mere instrument of power and about making law the basis of their rule" (Solomon 1990a, 184).

Gorbachev and his fellow legal reformers first appealed to the notion of rule of law explicitly in order to humanize communism. They were responding to the deepening crisis of confidence in the Soviet Union as the citizenry learned of such discrepancies between socialist practice and theory as "telephone law." The appeal to a truly law-based form of socialism was at first intended simply to relegitimize Communist Party leadership of the country (Hazard 1992, 9–10). As it became apparent that the Party could not be saved, Gorbachev appears to have regarded legal reform as a way of legitimating the central Soviet government and eventually as a necessary step in the transition to democracy. Most significant of all the legal reforms was the wave of constitutional amendments that swept this part of the world eliminating the notion that the Communist Party was above the law. For example, in March 1990, Article 6 of the Soviet Constitution was amended to eliminate the "leading role" of the Communist Party[12] (Hazard 1992, 6). Only after this was the way formally clear for introduction of the strong version of the rule of law. Only then was it possible, even as a theoretical matter, to maintain that the exercise of public and private power could be limited by law.

THE RULE OF LAW AND ITS RELATIONSHIP TO DEMOCRACY AND FREE MARKETS

This section will lay the theoretical basis for understanding legal reform in post-communist countries by examining views about the role that constitutionalism and the rule of law play in the establishment and maintenance of (1) democracy and (2) a market economy. The section will also discuss (3) the special problem of judicial review of legislative action.

The Rule of Law and the Democratic Order

The historical development of the strong version of the rule of law shows that it is intimately connected to democracy. Indeed, as evidenced by the CSCE Copenhagen Document mentioned earlier, there is widespread sentiment among world leaders that democracy is part of the rule of law. Nevertheless, this chapter has taken a narrower definition of rule of law that does not link it axiomatically to democracy. Liberal theory postulates a very strong, mutual relationship between the two, but skeptics argue that there is a strong tension between them. Some critics go so far as to claim that the rule of law is "a clear check on the flourishing of a rigorous democracy" (Hutchinson and Monahan 1987b, 99). Therefore, we have to examine the claim that imposing legal limits on all private and state power, protecting the basic civil and political rights normally included in a written constitution, supports a democratic order.

Since most of the liberal arguments that the rule of law supports democracy depend on the claim that law can constrain the exercise of power in a way different from other political processes, this section will first address that question. The second section then addresses the arguments that follow from that premise, as well as the converse argument that democracy supports the rule of law.

Law and Politics

I have said that the rule of law ideal requires that all public and private power be limited by law, but what does it mean for the exercise of power to be "limited by law"?[13] When a court decides a case, how is what it is doing distinguishable from other political processes? Legal process is a way in which power is exercised in society. In the broadest sense, therefore, legal processes are political processes. But if they are no different from the way a legislature acts or the way the President reaches a decision on a matter of public policy, then the claim that law can set limits to the exercise of power rings hollow. The critics of liberalism charge that what judges do is a type of political decision-making process indistinguishable in essence from partisan politics in the legislative arena and therefore that the rule of law is a sham (Hutchinson 1989; Kennedy 1973).

Maintaining a clear-cut distinction between law and other forms of politics may appear difficult in part because there is a large overlap in the types of argumentation that can be made in each type of process. Legal argumentation may include reference to the policies behind the relevant legal rules and so may sound at times like political discussion of a nonlegal variety. We may think of laws as normally being rules of general application—that is, rules expressed in terms that purport to make them applicable to all individuals who fall within the scope of the statute—rather than rules that apply only to named individuals.[14] Legal debate therefore usually concerns the application of general rules to specific cases. But other forms of political debate may also revolve around the application of generally stated principles. The claim of justification by reference to principled rules of general application and equal treatment of like cases is a powerful claim to justice in any debate, whether or not controlled by law.

But there is one salient difference between a legal decision and the normal political decision. Unlike the possible justifications for any other type of political decision, the justification of a legal decision must include, as a formal matter, reference to the rules recognized to have the force of law. Ordinary political decisions need not be formally justified by reference to legal rules. For example, a congressional representative may justify voting for a particular law on the grounds that it is a morally good rule. Judges are not free to apply a rule merely because they think it is moral; if the applicable law includes a rule different from the one the judge would choose on moral grounds, the judge must nevertheless apply the rule found in the applicable law.[15] For example, if state law allows the use of deadly force in some circumstances to protect one's dwelling, the judge is not free to apply the rule that deadly force can only be justified in defense of life, never in defense of mere property. Even if the judge believes the latter rule to be morally superior, he or she must decide cases before him or her on the basis of the rule of state law if there is one relevant to the issue.[16] Thus, the distinguishing feature of law is the notion that law limits legal argument and decision making in a way that does not apply to other forms of political discourse.

But does law limit decision making in more than the formalistic sense that the legal argument must start with relevant legal rules? There are a number of problems in responding to that question. The most important problem results from the fact that legal argumentation often does not lead to one and only one defensible solution to a legal problem. The reasons for law's indeterminacy include the inherent ambiguity of words, the complexity of law, which embraces conflicting rules and principles, and the discretion that legal rules sometimes openly give to the court. Because of this, it often happens that there is real uncertainty as to what a legal rule is or how a given legal rule is to apply to a specific case. If there is uncertainty about the "correct" legal result, then it can be argued that the law is not serving as a constraint and there is furthermore a danger that decisions that are presented as legal decisions are in fact driven by partisan politics or self-interest.

The conventional form of liberalism that prevails in the United States, however, insists on the distinction between law and other forms of politics, however difficult the distinction may be to draw in practice. Burton (1992, 140–57), for example, argues that even when indeterminate, law constrains decision in that it authorizes decision on certain grounds while excluding other possible grounds of decision. Burton (1992, 152) refers to the judges' authorization as an "authorization chain" because it is "more like a chain of command than like the chains that control a wild beast." Thus, he argues (1992, 153–4), that all power to make law or to make decisions applying law is conferred within a "complex web of authorizations." At the first stage, the legislator is authorized to pass statutes, but the laws that limit that power exclude some reasons for action. In a constitutional democracy like the United States, law at a minimum rules out decisions on the grounds of invidious racial discrimination or arbitrary whim.

The process of law making generally further narrows the field of permissible grounds for decision. For example, the aforementioned criminal law permitting the use of deadly force in certain circumstances to defend one's dwelling prevents the court from assigning guilt on the grounds that it is never permissible to use deadly force to defend mere property. If the law is embodied in a statute, the legislature has obviously considered that principle and rejected it, so the judge is not authorized to base a decision on it, though it is open to the judge to find that the use of deadly force was not warranted by the circumstances of the case before him or her if such a factual determination can be made consistent with the statute in good faith. Thus, Burton argues, the "Rule of Law in a constitutional democracy should be understood to require official action in accordance with the law, understood as a provider of legal reasons for action within a complex authorization chain" (Burton 1992, 154 [footnote omitted]).

Still, it must be admitted that this form of constraint appears quite mild because this account of it so far has postulated only the internal control of the judge's conscience. What prevents legal decision makers from violating their duty to decide in good faith according to the law and instead manipulating the law in outright bad faith—perhaps by using words in ways that do violence to accepted meanings of words? Judicial review provides only a partial answer. In no country is there effective court review of all decisions supposedly governed by law, but even if there were, we would still have to ask what prevents the judges of the highest appellate courts from judging in bad faith.

A plausible answer is the legal culture, that combination of attitudes and practices that concern law. A legal culture is supportive of the rule of law if these attitudes and practices reinforce in society the view that all legal decisions should be made in good faith within the authorization chain of the law. Because the law's restraint is merely formal, judges and other legal decision makers are constrained by law in the last analysis only if they take seriously their duty to decide according to law (Burton 1992, 162). A legal culture that is supportive of the rule of law will appear likely to reinforce this attitude among judges and other legal decision makers.

The key element for the development and maintenance of a supportive legal culture is the legal community. The legal profession (judges, attorneys, law professors, etc.) obviously forms the core of the legal community, but it also includes knowledgeable lay people such as journalists and teachers who also serve as opinion leaders with respect to legal issues. As the chief audience for the legal arguments given in justification of legal decisions, the legal community functions as a kind of Greek chorus for each legal argument asserted to justify a legal decision, critiquing the soundness of the logic and the fidelity to established meanings of language and policy of the rules. Political decisions masquerading as legal decisions will (we hope!) be unmasked. Judges or other legal decision makers who try to rationalize truly novel legal positions will find themselves harshly criticized unless through the force of their opinion writing they succeed in persuading a significant part of the legal community of the justice and fairness under the law of their arguments (Burton 1985, 204–14).

The force of the legal culture may be relatively ineffectual in restraining the rogue judge who is bent on disregarding the law, but it can have a powerful effect on the formation of attitudes, including most importantly the attitudes of future judges. A legal culture that strongly supports the rule of law is "a good environment for growing judges" (Burton 1992, 164). Nor will a few errant judges or administrators have much impact on the legal culture unless they succeed in persuading many people to abandon faith in the rule of law. Thus, a few unsound opinions—or even a few bad judges—will fail to subvert the rule of law as long as the legal culture as a whole continues to be actuated by the ideal and continues to hold all legal decisions to the standard that they be good faith decisions within the authorization chain of the applicable law.

Crucial to the conventional liberal understanding of the strong version of the rule of law is, therefore, the notion that there is a legal culture—led by the legal community—that serves to insist, however imperfectly, on the distinction between legal and other kinds of political decision making. To the extent that such a distinction can be maintained, it is possible to claim that public and private decision making is, at least in principle, limited by law.

How the Rule of Law and Democracy Support Each Other

On the premise that law can be distinguished from other forms of political decision and, therefore, can set limits to political decision making, liberalism raises the argument that the rule of law can enhance citizen trust in government and hence enhance participation in and support for the democratic order. As Krygier (1990, 642–3) argues, by forcing governments to act openly, with advance notice according to laws that are general and reasonably stable, the rule of law enhances the citizenry's "ability to coordinate their activities with each other and with the government, and it decreases the possibility or apprehension . . . of political arbitrariness." While one could make this argument for either the strong or weak version of the rule of law, the strong version's constitutional guarantee of equality, which forbids certain types of discrimination, offers a broader basis to encourage citizen trust. Under the strong version, it is not just rules of general applicability that have to be applied equally, but in fact all rules have to respect the constitutional prohibition on invidious discrimination. Such a legal system would appear more likely to increase trust, both vis-à-vis other citizens and, more importantly, vis-à-vis the government. As argued in Chapter 4, reasonable levels of trust—especially trust that the overall system will treat rivals, competitors, or opponents equally—may be an important factor in the consolidation and maintenance of democracy. The argument based on citizen trust thus appears to be stronger for the strong form of the rule of law than for the weak form of the rule of law.[17]

One critical challenge to the liberal argument is based on Marx's view that law is more of an effect than a cause and rather unimportant to the way society actually functions. According to Hutchinson and Monahan (1987b, 115), for example, "numerous opinion surveys confirm that the public has only marginal awareness of legal institutions and decisions." These skeptics, therefore, deny that the rule of law in fact has any power to enhance citizen trust. Law may simply be irrelevant to most democratic processes. But law's importance lies not in the unwarranted assumption that it generally controls behavior, but in its availability to be applied when one party wants to seek its protection.

Another challenge to the rule of law sees its effects as largely negative. For example, the liberal values underlying the rule of law tend to favor freedom at the expense of equality, thus skewing the balance between those two values that is at the heart of democracy, as discussed in Chapter 2. For example, by enforcing contract and property rights, the rule of law may tend to reinforce social and economic inequalities in society. As Chapter 2 indicates, significant socioeconomic disparities may limit participation in democratic processes. The liberal values of individualism at the heart of the rule of law are even charged with detracting from our understanding of community, and the limits imposed by the rule of law on political debate are charged with limiting the scope for popular participation in politics (Hutchinson and Monahan 1987b, 111). The latter charge is based chiefly on the "countermajoritarian" effect of judicial review, discussed below.

There is one vital liberal argument, however, that even the skeptics appear to accept. Liberalism argues that the crucial contribution to the maintenance of democracy is the effect the strong version of the rule of law has on safeguarding the democratic process. For example, by subjecting the federal Congress and all state legislatures to the Constitution, the rule of law in the United States seeks to prevent legislative majorities from effectively suppressing the political opposition. Basic political and civil rights protected by the Constitution—such as the right to a fair hearing; equality before the law regardless of race or religion; the right not to be deprived of one's life, liberty, or property without due process of law; the freedom of speech and religion; and the right to hold public meetings—set limits to the scope of political decision, thereby protecting a sphere of personal and political liberty for each individual. As a result, opposition to the governing majority can be exercised meaningfully within democratic processes, like open debate and contested elections, and individuals can act within the various types of organizations, including political parties, that constitute the kind of civil society identified in Chapter 3 as playing a vital role in the development and maintenance of a democracy.

As Hutchinson and Monahan (1987b, 122) state at the end of their critical review of the rule of law and democracy:

> A commitment to democracy does not mean that constraints on popular decision making must always and everywhere be condemned. It is important that the basic institutions and practices of democracy—free elections, debate and assembly—be guaranteed and extended. Further, democracy implies the necessity for general laws which do not single out particular groups or individuals for special treatment and which are applied in nondiscriminatory fashion across the whole community.

Thus, while one might oppose judicial review of legislation as sustaining an elitist form of politics (see the section entitled The Problem of Judicial Review), one can admit that the very nature of democracy requires at least the safeguards of the British form of the rule of law in order to be self-sustaining.

There is one additional important basis for an attack on the liberal theory of the rule of law: the substantial gap between the ideal and the reality of the rule of law. No country achieves the ideal at all times and places. In the United States, for example, judges have been known to take bribes, U.S. Supreme Court decisions are often criticized as being driven more by politics or ideology than by law, and the rich clearly have much greater access to the courts than do the poor. The fact that there is a gap between ideal and reality is an important criticism, but it is a criticism of the actual operation of the legal system, not necessarily a criticism of the ideal itself. Of course, the bitterest critics see the gap as evidence of the impracticality of the ideal, but it is not apparent what other ideal offers a more practical method of preventing abuse of power.

So far, we have been considering primarily the question of the influence of the rule of law on democracy. One important statement can also be made about the reverse relationship: Failure to develop democratic structures would appear to inhibit development of the strong version of the rule of law. For example, a strongly authoritarian executive power by definition will not permit meaningful judicial review of its actions. To the extent that a country is ruled by authoritarianism instead of by democracy, either the strong version of the rule of law cannot develop or, if already somewhat developed, it is so limited that it becomes unimportant.[18] This point will be further discussed in connection with the question of transition to the rule of law.

The Rule of Law and Free Markets

The relationship between the strong version of the rule of law and markets is more subtle than the relationship with democracy. Business people's most obvious interests concern the aspects of legality that characterize the weak version of the rule of law: the definition and enforcement of property rights so they can determine what is theirs at any given time; enforcement of contracts in order to encourage consensual, private agreeements to effectuate exchanges on the market; enforcement of criminal, tort, and property law in order to protect their profits; enforcement of criminal and administrative law to curb government corruption and ensure that government intervention in the market is in accordance with governing legislation. (For discussion of the uncertainty of obtaining similar guarantees from the bureaucracy in socialist states without the rule of law, see Kornai 1992, 451–3.) Even this argument may overstate the business need for law, however. Empirical studies have shown, for example, that contract law is but one of several factors that may guide business practice; not infrequently, business may be conducted without paying attention to contract law (Macaulay 1963; Schultz 1952). However, as in the case of law's relevance to democracy, it would be wrong to conclude that law is irrelevant to business planning. A business may prefer to insure rather than to rely on the criminal law to protect from the risk of loss by theft, and businesses may prefer contractual arrangements with customers who have no other source of supply and consequently are forced to accede to reasonable requests to renegotiate contracts already signed, but at least when the risks cannot all be covered in some extra-legal way, law is obviously important to provide basic rules for apportioning loss. By providing a mechanism for enforcing contracts, law reduces to some degree the risks of entering into contracts. To the extent that is so, private planning through consensual agreements is promoted.

But the weak version of the rule seems to provide sufficient guarantees of legality to satisfy those arguments. Do the broad limits on state action provided by the strong version of the rule of law promote the operation of the market? As an empirical matter, it must be conceded that some free market activities have often flourished at various points in history in the absence of the strong version. Individuals may be willing to engage in business, despite the absence of legal controls on state intervention in the market, as long as they believe that they are politically protected, either because they are part of the same elite group that is in control of the state or because the governing group is sufficiently dependent on them for tax revenues or political support. However, levels of political protection sufficient to satisfy entrepreneurs are unlikely to exist if the country is truly democratized because no small elite is then in control. Therefore, as a country begins to institute a meaningful form of democracy, the limitations on the political process provided by the strong version of the rule of law, especially the guarantee of equal treatment, would appear to become increasingly important to promote business confidence in fair treatment by the state.

But beyond guarantees concerning the general political process, the strong version of the rule of law offers little protection against state intervention in the market. Hayek (1960, 220–33) argues that the rule of law should be interpreted to forbid all government regulation of price and quantity of production, but most view the rule of law as neutral on questions of economic intervention. In the early part of this century, the U.S. Supreme Court applied the doctrine of "substantive due process" to limit state intervention in many cases, but the Court has since repudiated the doctrine, so the U.S. Constitution is generally thought to be neutral on the issue of market intervention. A principle requiring just compensation in all cases of public takings of private property, as is found in the U.S. Constitution, might seem to be important to protect the private wealth that is necessary for the free market to operate. But there is controversy over whether the just compensation principle should be regarded as part of the rule of law. (For an argument that it should be, see Sunstein 1993.) There is a broad international consensus that expropriations should be permitted only if in the public interest and done according to law. But there is no international consensus on the requirement to pay full and fair compensation.[19]

To be sure, constitutional rights to equal treatment and to a fair hearing are undoubtedly important procedural guarantees of fairness when the state does decide to intervene in the market. But from the business point of view, the chief contribution the strong version of the rule of law adds to the protections provided by the weak version of the rule of law is to promote trust in the state and the fairness of its regulation of the market by promoting trust in democratic governance.

The Problem of Judicial Review

Any lawsuit can come to have political importance because of the parties or the issues involved, and because of this political salience, the courts' decisions in such cases are particularly likely to be perceived as motivated by partisan politics instead of by law. Lawsuits involving public law issues are especially likely to be politically sensitive because administrative and constitutional law brings the courts into conflict with the other branches of government. Public law litigation (especially that involving judicial review of legislative action) therefore tends to put great pressure on the courts' ability to maintain that their decisions are legal and not political.

The French solved the problem of securing effective review of the legality of executive and administrative action without thrusting the regular courts into such a potentially "political" role by creating special administrative courts for this purpose.[20] Separate administrative courts have been adopted by many—but by no means, all—of the countries of the Civil Law tradition of Western Europe. Countries of the Common Law tradition have preferred to assign review of executive and administrative action to the regular courts despite the potential cost of politicization. The next chapter will demonstrate that both models are found in the post-Communist countries.

Judicial review of legislative action poses a far more sensitive problem for democratic theory. As mentioned previously, the British version of the rule of law with its doctrine of Parliamentary sovereignty is at least superficially the easiest to reconcile with basic principles of democracy. The people's representatives in Parliament decide themselves whether proposed legislation conforms to the constitution, and no other institution infringes on the power of the democratically elected majority in Parliament.

But the British example is also a bit like letting the fox guard the chicken coop. When a Parliamentary majority wants to pass discriminatory legislation or legislation that invades spheres of private action, can one be confident that the members of Parliament will respect constitutional limits? The U.S. system of judicial review, which gives that decision to the courts, may seem a better institutional arrangement for ensuring that legislation conforms to the constitution. The courts are staffed by judges whose training and experience should incline them to take to heart the injunction that law should constrain the exercise of power. At least at the appellate levels, the courts normally justify their legal decisions in a written opinion. The members of Parliament who decide in the English case are not judges—even if they may have legal training, they do not necessarily write opinions on these matters, and the legal argumentation appears as part of the general political debate in Parliament. Most importantly, the U.S. system introduces a neutral third party to decide the issue, while the British MPs are deciding whether their own action is legal.

The American system of judicial review, however, seems to raise a significant conflict with the principles of democracy. Judicial review enables judges to frustrate the will of the democratically elected majority by declaring a duly promulgated statute unconstitutional. This countermajoritarian effect of judicial review is troublesome, and it periodically brings the U.S. Supreme Court into great political controversy. (For example, there were frequent calls for the impeachment of Chief Justice Earl Warren during his tenure on the Court, a time when the Court handed down numerous decisions on civil rights that were not popular with substantial segments of the population.) The countermajoritarian difficulty has deterred some countries from adopting judicial review.

The United States has thought that the benefits of strengthening equality before the law and protection against unwarranted governmental intrusion into private life outweigh the countermajoritarian difficulty and has conferred jurisdiction to conduct constitutional review on all courts, great and small. Many countries, especially those in the Civil Law tradition, have followed the lead of Austria, Germany, and Italy in establishing separate courts—so-called "constitutional courts"—for constitutional litigation. As in the case of administrative review, relegating constitutional litigation to special courts saves the regular courts from the potentially politicizing influence of public law litigation. France—exhibiting strong reservations about judicial review—has provided a particularly limited version of that model by creating a special tribunal for constitutional litigation that can review proposed legislation only before it has been enacted by Parliament. Other countries—like Great Britain, the Netherlands, and New Zealand—have so far rejected the principle of judicial review of legislation though each of those particular countries has begun to develop a form of judicial review to ensure that legislation is consistent with the nation's international commitments. (For Great Britain, see note 6; for Dutch law, see Kortmann and Bovend'Eert 1993, 117–8; for New Zealand, see Palmer 1992,

87–93). Since the end of World War II, there has thus been a clear trend in favor of adoption of some form of judicial review for legislation, though most countries in Europe have insisted on restricting this power to specialized courts.

Consistent with that trend, the post-Communist countries of Eastern Europe and the former Soviet Union have shown considerable enthusiasm for the basic idea of judicial review but also significant caution concerning how to limit its potential for politicizing the regular courts. Not surprisingly, they have tended to adapt forms of judicial review from their Western European continental neighbors, and therefore they have all chosen to create special constitutional courts. Even within that model, however, as the next chapter will demonstrate, they have shown great creativity and willingness to experiment.

TRANSITION TO THE RULE OF LAW

The socialist countries of Eastern Europe and the former Soviet Union had law and legal systems under Communist Party rule, but from the rule of law perspective, they were so seriously deformed that they could not be considered as attempts to institute even the weak version of that ideal. In the pre-Communist period, Russia and some of the other countries in this area had made little progress institutionalizing any form of rule of law. For these countries, the current process of transition entails building a new legal system and a new legal culture with few domestic historical antecedents. Even in countries like Poland and the Czech and Slovak Republics, which shared in the *Rechtsstaat* tradition prior to World War II, the forty-plus years of Communist rule were sufficient to eradicate virtually all but the memory of that tradition. Thus, all of these countries are engaged in trying to build the rule of law culture and its institutions from the ground up.

We have surprisingly little theory to explain how a country without the rule of law can develop it. The definitions set out previously give us an idea of how to define the goal. We can identify the legal institutions and processes a state needs to develop in order to institute the rule of law. At a minimum, a rule of law state requires a constitution that guarantees at least basic civil and political rights (for a country in rapid transition, it seems apparent that the constitution has to be written); court jurisdiction not only over civil and criminal matters, but also over the legality (including the constitutionality) of executive and administrative action; an independent judiciary; an independent bar; and a legal culture, widespread even among the country's politicians, that law, including the constitution, must be obeyed. We know that special court jurisdiction to review the constitutionality of legislation, whether vested in the regular courts or in one special constitutional court, is not a requirement but is a frequent element of the rule of law.

Although the goal may be relatively clear, we have little by way of a roadmap for getting there. Virtually all conscious efforts at transition appear to follow the same general strategy of drafting new laws and constitutions, trying to strengthen the independence of judges and lawyers and educational efforts concerning the rule of law, creating the court jurisdictions necessary for administrative and constitutional law, and hoping that, with time, the requisite legal culture will come into existence. But we can readily see that the trick in the whole process is bringing that legal culture into being. It is easy to write laws and constitutions to guarantee human rights. The Communist era constitutions in Eastern Europe and the former Soviet Union were full of human rights guarantees. It is relatively easy to create new courts or new court jurisdictions. Formal guarantees of independence for judges and the private bar can be adopted. But none of these things are of any avail if the culture does not begin to show, both by words and deeds, that law matters and should matter. In these countries, the problem is, in concrete terms, how to get courts accustomed to "telephone law" to decide cases on their own according to law and how to build the public's confidence that the courts do precisely that.

When one considers the slow, organic development of the rule of law in Great Britain and its former colonies like the United States, Canada, Australia, and New Zealand, it may be tempting to tell the new post-Communist countries that they must similarly "wait a few hundred years" (Elster 1993, 271). But they are understandably in a hurry, and we have no basis to say that the development cannot be at least somewhat compressed though it is reasonable to expect that it may take a "generational effort" (CEELI 1993, 6) to create and stabilize a new legal culture.

The examples of non-Communist countries that have made the transition from authoritarian rule to democracy in this century do not seem very apposite. In some, like Germany and Italy, the period of authoritarian rule was much shorter than Communist rule even in the nations outside of the Soviet Union (twelve and twenty-three years, respectively, in comparison to over forty-five). In Spain and Portugal (Solé Tura 1993), the suppression of democracy and the rule of law may have lasted roughly as long as in Eastern Europe, but nowhere in Europe did it last as long as in the former Soviet Union (almost eighty years). Moreover, in none of the countries of Latin America or the non-Communist countries of Europe did authoritarian rule involve such thorough-going and formal repudiation of the rule of law ideal as it did under Communist rule.

The U.S. government has had considerable experience with problems of transition through its foreign aid efforts to promote the rule of law, but it is not clear what lessons have been learned. In the 1960s and 1970s, U.S. efforts to promote the "development" of Third World countries first began to stress the role of law. "Development" was an amorphous term that included the idea of social and economic modernization but was also linked to growth of democracy and rule of law. Government and private aid agencies recruited lawyers, including academic lawyers, to participate and sponsored numerous studies of law and development. Aid efforts focused especially on the transfer of U.S. methods of legal education and the U.S. culture of socially activist lawyers who try to use law and litigation to achieve social transformation. The aid activities led to the development of a scholarly movement in the United States known as "law and development." But by the mid-1970s leading scholarly members of the movement were increasingly in doubt about whether the aid efforts were in fact contributing to a growth in freedom, equality, democracy, and the other putative benefits of development and increasingly suspicious that the numerous programs to strengthen legal education and legal systems were merely strengthening the hold of anti-democratic elites (Alvarez, 1991; Gardner 1980; Trubek and Galanter 1974). Much of the criticism of law and development had to do with the poor fit between the agents of that movement and the recipient countries. Gardner (1980, 4) characterized the efforts in Latin America as "a rather awkward mixture of goodwill, optimism, self-interest, arrogance, ethnocentricity, and simple lack of understanding." The lawyers and law professors who were sent to provide aid simply did not know the local language, law, culture, economy, or politics. The attempts to transplant the U.S. culture of legally activist judges and lawyers also drew critical fire on the grounds that this particularly American view of law was soon perverted in Third World contexts into a technique for using law to extend the power of the ruling elites. For all of these reasons, law and development projects lost funding and scholarship in this area has not flourished in the United States.

Despite that infelicitous beginning, the United States has persisted in its efforts to promote democracy through assisting the development of legal systems. One program has been designed in conscious reaction to law and development criticism. Since 1985, the U.S. government's Administration of Justice (AOJ) Program has revived a greatly scaled-down version of law and development projects for Latin America, especially Central America. The AOJ Program drew the lesson from the earlier law and development movement that authoritarian regimes block the development of the rule of law, as was previously suggested. Consequently, the AOJ Program has been limited to governments that demonstrate a true commitment to democracy. It has rather clearly rejected the notion that one could encourage the rule of law as a way of preparing the way for a substantially later turn toward democracy (Alvarez 1991, 288). Moreover, the AOJ Program has been limited largely to assistance for the administration of justice, including the training and material needs of the judiciary, such as better libraries and methods of court administration and personnel management. The program has de-emphasized reform of the substantive law or of legal education, and it has tended to use U.S. court administrators and judges in preference to U.S. lawyers or law professors where it has been unable to use Latin Americans (Alvarez 1991, 299). While these limitations may enable the AOJ Program to avoid the kind of critiques of legal imperialism levied at the law and development programs, one may also fear that the limitations will prevent it from accomplishing much to strengthen the rule of law. To date, however, there has been little objective evaluation of the program.

Another program of legal aid, started in 1990 for the post-Communist nations of Eastern Europe and the former Soviet Union, does not appear to be as responsive to the criticisms of the law and development movement. This program, the Central and East European Law Initiative (CEELI), a public service project of the American Bar Association (ABA) funded chiefly by the U.S. government, involves the coordination of massive volunteer efforts by American judges, government lawyers, lawyers in private practice, and law professors to provide assistance to these countries with reform of constitutions and statutes, the judiciary, the legal profession, and law schools. CEELI has also put special emphasis on the development of commercial law. By the end of 1993, CEELI had assisted twenty-one countries in this area through the efforts of over 2,000 U.S. jurists and with the cooperation of 132 U.S. law schools (CEELI 1993, 5). The CEELI programs are also too new to have attracted critical outside evaluation, but the wholesale reliance on U.S. jurists with little or no training in comparative law in general or in the language, history, laws, or culture of the target countries in specific would appear to invite many of the same criticisms made of law and development except for the exceptionally large amount of goodwill that has characterized both the recipients and the providers of this aid, at least so far.

The most important transition issue these legal aid programs raise is whether meaningful legal reform can come substantially before democratization. Critics of law and development claimed that it cannot, and the AOJ Program appears to take that criticism to heart. In the early days of CEELI, it no doubt seemed unnecessary to address that issue because all the post-Communist countries appeared to be committed to moving toward democratic regimes. But the question becomes more pressing as a number of countries in this area of the world appear to be staying in or turning back to an authoritarian form of rule. Thus, together with the critics of law and development, we must ask whether strengthening courts in the absence of democracy will not simply provide authoritarian governments with the means to greater control. Although truly independent courts would seem to minimize this risk, achieving adequate independence for the courts is probably impossible unless the government is committed to democracy.

While conceding discouraging experiences in Latin America that appear to confirm this concern, Schnably (1993, 178–180) argues against assuming that legal reform necessarily must follow political reform. He suggests that restructuring judicial process to conform better to rule of law norms at least affects a group of factors, law and the courts, that are important in the creation of political doctrine and national ideology. Thus, he argues, aid to strengthen the courts' conformity with the rule of law may be worthwhile even in a nondemocratic state. But many of the impediments to democratization frustrate legal reform, as well. For example, as Sajó and Losonci (1993, 333) warn, nationalism and ethnic and religious prejudice are "not particularly tolerant of some of the 'impartial' criteria of law and constitutionalism." It seems reasonable to pursue legal reform in Eastern Europe and the successor states to the Soviet Union as long as there is a reasonable chance that such reform may promote democracy and result in movement toward the rule of law ideal and to discontinue such aid in authoritarian countries if it appears likely to be perverted. But figuring out which prong of that test applies to a given country at a particular time is likely to divide reasonable people for a long time to come in this part of the world.

Beyond that already speculative point, we have only more questions. For example, can the rule of law be expected to develop during times of extreme economic hardship? On the one hand, it is obvious that when everyone has to concentrate on where their next meal is coming from, constitutional litigation—indeed, all litigation—seems like a luxury; thus the attractiveness to some Russians of Pinochet's dictatorship in Chile or authoritarian rule in Singapore as a model for a transition to democracy. On the other hand, the function of law to provide for order seems especially important during times of economic hardship, which tend to be accompanied by political turmoil. Nevertheless, if hard times bring an authoritarian leader to power, as they often do, the foregoing discussion suggests that the strong version of the rule of law will likely be stifled. But as long as economic and political troubles do not lead to suppression of the key public law aspects of the rule of law, it is not clear that economic and political hardships have to prevent the development of the rule of law. Indeed, in view of its importance to democracy, the rule of law is never a luxury. Certainly the Western countries in which the rule of law has been developed all experienced significant economic and political turmoil in the course of the development of the rule of law.

A similar question is raised by the fact that crimes of violence have increased dramatically in post-Communist countries. Can the rule of law develop in the absence of basic law and order? The perpetrators of criminal violence can exploit their protections under the rule of law to frustrate the state's ability to combat violence. While all but perhaps the most repressive societies experience some criminal violence, there may be a point beyond which criminal violence threatens to overwhelm the ability of the government, the police, and the courts to protect society and prosecute suspects in accordance with the rule of law. Such circumstances are particularly likely to lead to pressure to abridge defendants' basic criminal procedure protections, as critics have charged both with respect to the evolution of U.S. criminal procedure since the recent "war on drugs" and with respect to the anti-crime decree Russian President Yeltsin issued during the summer of 1994.[21] Is it ever necessary to abridge fundamental legal protections in order to advance the rule of law? Most defenders of the rule of law would respond that one should bring utmost skepticism to the claim that the point has been reached where society is in danger of being overwhelmed by criminality, but as a theoretical matter, it is not possible to deny that there could be such a point.

Another question is whether the weak version of the rule of law is a necessary stage to prepare the way for the strong version. Most of these countries are attempting to go from the stage of "telephone law" to the strong version without any intermediate step. Thus, even before the regular courts are reliably functioning to decide cases in an impartial manner according to law, these countries are creating constitutional courts. If the regular courts command little respect, it is not apparent that adding courts with the much more problematic public law jurisdictions is necessarily going to improve respect for law. As Sajó and Losonci (1993, 327) have written, "In Poland and Hungary, the spectacular changes in the public law contributed to democracy, but failed to instill respect for constitutionalism or to create the rule of law." The next chapter will explore this issue in light of the experiences in Russia and Poland.

Beyond these issues of timing and sequence, there are particular substantive legal issues that pose minefields for each nation's transition. How a nation's legal system deals with these issues will have a profound effect on the public's trust in the legal system and, hence, on the foundation of a legal culture that supports the rule of law. The most difficult of these issues concern justice for abuses in the communist past, including compensation to former owners for property expropriated by the socialist states, punishment of communist officials who used their power to plunder state property or to harrass or kill others, and the question of "lustration"—purging public offices of individuals guilty of such abuses or guilty simply of providing leadership for the Communist Party at the time abuses were occurring. The most wrenching of these issues is undoubtedly the question of punishment for past abuses. Many would like to simply "draw a veil over the past." Others are burning for retribution. There is pressure to apply new criminal laws retroactively or change the statute of limitations to enable belated prosecutions. "Whichever path is taken, it will be fraught with dangers" (Elster 1993, 273).

CONCLUSION

The task facing legal reformers in this part of the world is thus unprecedented and daunting. They must create not only new courts with new jurisdictions, but a whole new legal culture that differs radically from the culture of legal nihilism fostered by Communist Party rule. Nations with precommunist roots in the *Rechtsstaat* tradition of continental Europe naturally seek to revive those traditions, even in some cases recreating courts or re-enacting laws from the precommunist era. But the precommunist rule of law traditions in most of these countries was weak. The *Rechtsstaat* tradition prior to World War II amounted to no more than the weak form of the rule of law, and that is what the population of these countries tends to understand under the term rule of law even if native legal reformers seem genuinely to be inspired by the strong form of the rule of law. For spreading understanding of the strong form of the rule of law, domestic reformers find international help, both in the form of international standards like the ICJ and CSCE statements on the rule of law and in the form of legal aid from Western countries. But the key problems have to be surmounted by each country on its own because only in that way can each country develop the requisite cultural attitudes and practices.

The next chapter will examine the development of some of the key institutions for implementing the rule of law, especially an independent judiciary, an independent private bar, and the special public law jurisdictions for review of administrative action and the constitutionality of legislation. Such institutional reform is important because the rule of law is not possible without them. But beyond the institutional issues looms the larger question of the development of the necessary legal culture. The progress of efforts to change culture is much harder to measure than the progress at building institutions, but the experience with the functioning of the new institutions will provide important information about the development of legal culture. Whatever the current picture, however, we must keep in mind that, just like the formation of a new democratic political culture, the formation of a new legal culture supportive of the rule of law is a long-term project. Progress will not likely be uniform at all times or for all countries of the area.

Failure to develop a strong version of the rule of law does not mean that law necessarily will become unimportant for society. It is certainly imaginable that authoritarian regimes might develop a weak form of the rule of law in which independent courts adjudicate cases that are not politically sensitive. This is apparently what Gorbachev originally had in mind for the Soviet Union. Moreover, such an outcome may not be so negative for the development of the rule of law. The institutions of the weak form of the rule of law, especially if the courts and the law faculties are given a reasonable degree of independence, may be a good place for nuturing the ideal of the rule of law in its strong form and preparing the appropriate culture. But development of the strong form of the rule of law is not imaginable without democracy. The only certainty therefore seems to be that, just as the strong form of the rule of law has developed in the West in close association with democracy, so too the fates of democracy and the rule of law will be inexorably linked in the post-communist countries of Eastern Europe and the former Soviet Union.

NOTES

1. Acknowledgement: In addition to the Ford Foundation funds that brought the co-authors of this book together for the first time under the Bridging Project in the Summer of 1993, Professor Reitz gratefully acknowledges generous support from the University of Iowa Law Foundation and the University of Iowa Center for Advanced Studies in connection with this chapter. In addition to his co-authors, the author would like to thank the following persons for research help and comments on earlier drafts: Steven Burton, Alexander Domrin, Anselm Erighono, Elena Molodtsova, Mark Osiel, Sir Geoffrey Palmer, Youlian Simidjiyski, and Qiang Zhou.
2. No one disputes that the rule of law includes legal protection against the lawless exercise of private power. Indeed, this is the "primary meaning and purpose of the rule of law" (Walker 1988, 24). The concept thus draws into the definition all of private law—the law that governs relationships among private individuals like contract, tort, and property law. The role of private law is so fundamental that some authors gloss over it in their eagerness to discuss the more difficult questions relating to legal restraints on the exercise of state power. This latter aspect of law is known as public law and includes constitutional and administrative law.
3. In most countries, including Great Britain, administrative agencies generally are subject to the control of the executive. The United States is somewhat unusual in creating a large number of so-called "independent agencies" that have

considerable freedom from direct executive control. However, in all countries, "administrative law" applies generally to the actions of the administrative bureaucracy and judicial review of those actions. In order to cover all countries, this and the next chapter will simply refer to judicial review of "executive and administrative" action, a formulation that recognizes the substantial independence that large and powerful administrative bureaucracies, whether or not formally independent, often have from the head of the executive branch.

4. The "superiority" of constitutional rules is usually expressed in part by the fact that they are more difficult to change than normal legislation. There is, however, great variation in the difficulty of constitutional amendment throughout the world. Many national constitutions, including most of the current ones in Eastern Europe and the successor states to the Soviet Union, are amendable by a special majority in the national parliament (usually two-thirds). The U.S. Constitution is considerably more difficult to amend because it requires ratification by constitutional convention or state legislature in three-fourths of the states. Article 79 of the German Constitution (*Grundgesetz*) permits amendments, as a general rule, by a two-thirds vote of each house of parliament, but parts of the Constitution, including the catalog of human rights and the federal structure of the country, are unamendable.
5. Unlike the Anglo-American Common Law tradition, the Civil Law tradition traces its roots to Roman law, developed as the modern states of continental Europe were formed. Since the nineteenth century, the Civil Law tradition has tended to be characterized by systematic and thorough codification of major areas of law. The process of codification—enactment by the legislature of a statute purporting to state comprehensively the rules for a given area of law—has tended to reinforce for Civil Law countries the strength of legal positivism.
6. One leading German constitutional scholar defines *Rechtsstaatlichkeit* (the "condition of being a *Rechtsstaat*") as one in which there is (1) constitutionalism—that is, the existence of a constitution as the basic and highest legal norm; (2) constitutionally guaranteed principles of liberty and equality; (3) separation of powers; (4) the principle of legality, that is, the principle that all acts on behalf of the state are based on and limited by law; (5) the guarantee of comprehensive and effective protection of legal rights through independent courts and legally prescribed procedures; (6) liability of organs of the state to compensate citizens for injury or violation of their rights in the case of improper action by such a state organ; and (7) the principle of proportionality, i.e., the means of state interventions must be limited to those that are suitable, necessary, and reasonably proportional to their ends (Stern 1988, 26–7). At least points (6) and (7) go beyond limitations that are currently enforceable against organs of government in the United States as a general rule.
7. It is important to note that as a result of Britain's membership in the European Union, British courts have begun to assert the power to review British legislation to ensure its conformity to European Union law, e.g., Regina v. Secretary

of State for Transport, ex parte Factortame Ltd., [1991] 1 All ER 70 (House of Lords, 1990).

8. The great British public law scholar of the Victorian period, A. V. Dicey, for example, insisted on Parliamentary sovereignty in absolute terms and defined rule of law in terms of legal limitations on executive power (Wade 1961, cxvii–cxviii; Wade and Bradley 1993, 100–3). However, he also recognized the force of conventions—that is, rules binding on Parliament that were not enforceable in a court (Dicey 1961, 417–73; see also Wade and Bradley 1993, 26–9).

9. The ICJ (quoted in Marsh 1959, 4) recognized this claim in these words:

> In many societies, particularly those which have not yet fully established traditions of democratic legislative behaviour, it is essential that certain limitations on legislative power . . . should be incorporated in a written constitution, and that the safeguards therein contained should be protected by an independent judicial tribunal; in other societies, established standards of legislative behaviour may serve to ensure that the same limitations are observed, . . .

10. Article 126, guaranteeing the right to unite in public organizations, stated that the Communist Party "is the vanguard of the working people in their struggle to build communist society and is the leading core of all organizations of the working people, both public and state" (Hazard 1992, 6).

11. The party hegemony clause was supplemented by a clause stating that "[a]ll Party organizations operate within the framework of the USSR Constitution" (Sharlet 1978, 78), raising, as Sharlet noted (49), the possibility of "limited government," a promise that was not, however, fulfilled at that time.

12. Poland eliminated its comparable constitutional provision in December 1989 (Brzezinski 1991, 109).

13. The British version of the rule of law shows that the phrase does not mean that a court must have the power to rule on the legality of all exercises of power, including the constitutionality of legislation.

14. Many legal philosophers have maintained that a distinguishing feature of law is that it is comprised solely of rules of general application. Neumann (1986, 212–22) claims that both French and German legal theory embraced this postulate in the eighteenth and nineteenth centuries, but that English law did not. The U.S. Constitution prohibits bills that punish named individuals (bills of attainder), but the U.S. Congress passes many special bills that provide benefits to named individuals and have the force of law. However, even if particularized rules can have the force of law, laws of general application have a much greater claim to justice.

15. Dworkin (1985, 1986) argues that, because of the inherent indeterminism of legal texts, judges cannot and should not avoid deciding cases on grounds of political or moral principle. However, even he would have the judges' reasoning in a case start with the texts (constitutional, statutory, etc.) that are binding and arguably relevant. That is the only point of the formalism upon which I am insisting. The rule of law can accommodate a variety of theories of interpretation.

16. In the United States, if the rule in question is a rule of Common Law, the highest court in the jurisdiction does have the freedom to reconsider the wisdom of the rule in light of its policy bases because the Common Law courts have the power to "find"—or, in effect, make—the law to the extent the legislature has not already specified the rule. The highest court in a jurisdiction that has spoken on a question can even overrule its previous rulings on the issue. However, it should be remembered that these complications of the Common Law do not apply to any of the countries of the Civil Law tradition, including all of the countries of Eastern Europe and the successor states to the former Soviet Union. Widespread codification and legal positivism have produced a style of legal reasoning in the Civil Law that requires one to start with applicable statutory and constitutional texts.

17. Sharlet (1991, 23), for example, illustrates this effect of the rule of law in the following remarks about recent Soviet legal reformers:

> . . . they will have recognized the contractual nature of a democratic constitution as an instrument through which the people convey legitimacy and empowerment to government, which in return performs vital social functions on behalf of the entire society. Implied in such a social contract have been limits and restraints on the powers delegated to government, in order to ensure the freedom and viability of the civil society embodied within the constitutional system.

18. Authoritarian regimes that have come to power in countries already possessing developed forms of judicial review have typically dealt with the courts' challenge to their power by creating new courts they could control and restricting the jurisdiction of the regular courts to the point that they could not decide any politically important cases. Thus, typically all politically sensitive criminal prosecutions are taken out of the hands of the regular courts (for Franco's Spain, see Toharia 1975).

19. The CSCE's Copenhagen Document, for example, affirms only that "everyone has the right peacefully to enjoy his property either on his own or in common with others. No one may be deprived of his property except in the public interest and subject to the conditions provided for by law and consistent with international commitments and obligations" (*International Legal Materials* 29, 1311 (1990)).

20. The French have never even called these review bodies "courts." Officially, they are part of an administrative agency, the Council of State, with oversight authority over all other administrative agencies. However, it is well understood that these bodies are in fact courts, and they operate like courts today. The Germans and Austrians have also created separate administrative courts, but they recognize them as courts and staff them with judges who have the same training as those on the regular courts. All of these countries have been influential models in the Civil Law tradition.

21. The decree was the subject of hefty debate in the Russian media, with many newspaper commentaries criticizing it for violating the Constitution. Sergey Stepashin, the Director of the Russian Federal Counterintelligence Service, defended the decree by stating on Russian television, "I am in favor of the violation of human rights, if the person involved is a bandit and criminal." ("Procuracy Collegium Discusses Anticrime Decree," text of program from "Russia" Television Channel, broadcast at 12:00 GMT, June 23, 1994, translation available in LEXIS, Nexis Library, Txtee File.)

REFERENCES

ALLAN, T. R. S. 1985. "Legislative Supremacy and the Rule of Law: Democracy and Constitutionalism." *Cambridge Law Journal* 44:111–43.

ALTMAN, ANDREW. 1990. *Critical Legal Studies: A Liberal Critique.* Princeton: Princeton University Press.

ALVAREZ, JOSÉ E. 1991. "Promoting the 'Rule of Law' in Latin America: Problems and Prospects." *George Washington Journal of International Law and Economics* 25:281–331.

BERMAN, HAROLD J. 1991. "The Rule of Law and the Law-Based State (*Rechtsstaat*) (with special reference to developments in the Soviet Union)." *Harriman Institute Forum* 4(5, May):1–12, (Slightly revised version in Donald D. Barry, ed. 1992. *Toward the "Rule of Law" in Russia?* Armonk, N.Y.: M.E. Sharpe, 43–60.

BRZEZINSKI, MARK F. 1991. "Constitutional Heritage and Renewal: The Case of Poland." *Virginia Law Review* 77:49–112.

BUERGENTHAL, THOMAS. 1991. "The CSCE Rights System." *George Washington Journal of International Law and Economics* 25:333–86.

BURTON, STEVEN J. 1985. *An Introduction to Law and Legal Reasoning.* Boston: Little, Brown and Co.

———. 1992. *Judging in Good Faith.* New York: Cambridge University Press.

CEELI (Central and East European Law Initiative of the American Bar Association). 1993. *Annual Report*: Author. Washington, D.C.

COLLINS, HUGH. 1982. *Marxism and Law.* Oxford, U.K.: Clarendon Press.

DAHRENDORF, RALF. 1977. "A Confusion of Powers: Politics and the Rule of Law." *Modern Law Review* 40:1–15.

DICEY, A. V. 1961[1959]. *Introduction to the Study of the Law of the Constitution*, Tenth Edition. London: McMillan & Co. Ltd.

DWORKIN, RONALD. 1985. "Political Judges and the Rule of Law." In Ronald Dworkin, *A Matter of Principle*. Cambridge: Harvard University Press, 9–32.

———. 1986. *Law's Empire*. Cambridge: Harvard University Press.

ELSTER, JON. 1993. "The Necessity and Impossibility of Simultaneous Economic and Political Reform." In Douglas Greenberg et al., eds., *Constitutionalism and Democracy*. New York: Oxford University Press, 267–74.

FRANKOWSKI, STANISLAW. 1991. "The Independence of the Judiciary in Poland: Reflections on Andrzej Rzeplinski's *Sadownictwo w Polsce Ludowej* (The Judiciary in Peoples' Poland (1989))." *Arizona Journal of International and Comparative Law* 8:34–50.

FULLER, LON. 1969. *The Morality of Law*, Revised Edition. New Haven: Yale University Press.

GARDNER, JAMES A. 1980. *Legal Imperialism: American Lawyers and Foreign Aid in Latin America*. Madison: University of Wisconsin Press.

HAYEK, FRIEDRICH A. 1960. *The Constitution of Liberty*. Chicago: Henry Regnery Co. (Gateway Edition).

HAZARD, JOHN N. 1992. "Soviet Law Takes a Fresh Breath." *Harriman Institute Forum* 5(6, February):1–13.

HUSKEY, EUGENE. 1991. "A Framework for the Analysis of Soviet Law." *The Russian Review* 50(January):53–70.

———. 1992. "From Legal Nihilism to *Pravovoe Gosudarstvo*." In Donald D. Barry, ed., *Toward the "Rule of Law" in Russia?* Armonk, N.Y.: M.E. Sharpe, 23–42.

HUTCHINSON, ALLAN C. 1989. "Democracy and Determinacy: An Essay on Legal Interpretation." *University of Miami Law Review* 43:541–76.

———, and PATRICK MONAHAN, eds., 1987a. *The Rule of Law: Ideal or Ideology*. Toronto: Carswell.

———, and PATRICK MONAHAN. 1987b. "Democracy and the Rule of Law." In Allan C. Hutchinson and Patrick Monahan, eds. *The Rule of Law: Ideal or Ideology*. Toronto: Carswell, 97–123.

KENNEDY, DUNCAN. 1973. "Legal Formality." *Journal of Legal Studies* 2:351–98.

KORNAI, JÁNOS. 1992. *The Socialist System: The Political Economy of Communism*. Princeton: Princeton University Press.

KORTMANN, CONSTANTIJN A. J. M., and PAUL P. T. BOVEND'EERT. 1993. *The Kingdom of the Netherlands: An Introduction to Dutch Constitutional Law*. Boston: Kluwer Law and Taxation Publishers.

KRYGIER, MARTIN. 1990. "Marxism and the Rule of Law: Reflections After the Collapse of Communism." *Law & Social Inquiry* 15(4, Fall):633–63.

LAPOLOMBARA, JOSEPH. 1974. *Politics within Nations*. Englewood Cliffs, N.J.: Prentice-Hall.

LIEN, MOLLY WARNER. 1994. "Red Star Trek: Seeking a Role for Constitutional Law in Soviet Disunion." *Stanford Journal of International Law* 30:41–114.

MACAULAY, STEWART. 1963. "Non-Contractual Relations in Business: A Preliminary Study." *American Sociological Review* 28:55–67.

MARKOVITS, INGA. 1990. "Socialism and the Rule of Law: Some Speculations and Predictions." In David S. Clark, ed., *Comparative and Private International Law*. Berlin: Duncker Humblot, 205–45. Also published in *Law & Society Review* 23(1989):399–447.

MARSH, NORMAN S. 1959. *The Rule of Law in a Free Society*. Geneva: International Commission of Jurists.

MATHERNOVA, KATARINA. 1992. "Czecho ? Slovakia: Constitutional Disappointments." *American University Journal of International Law and Policy* 7:471–501.

NEUMANN, FRANZ. 1986. *The Rule of Law*. Leamington Spa, U.K.: Berg.

PALMER, GEOFFREY. 1992. *New Zealand's Constitution in Crisis*. Dunedin, New Zealand: McIndoe.

POMORSKI, STANISLAW. 1984. "Controversies over the 'Leading Role' of the Polish United Workers' Party: 1976 Constitutional Amendment." In Kenneth R. Redden and Linda Schlueter, eds., *Modern Legal Systems Cyclopedia* 8 (Eastern Europe). Buffalo, N.Y.: William S. Hein & Co, 8.100.1 to 8.100.14.

QUIGLEY, JOHN. 1990. "The Soviet Union As a State Under the Rule of Law: An Overview." *Cornell International Law Journal* 23:205–25.

SAJÓ, ANDRÁS and VERA LOSONCI. 1993. "Rule by Law in East Central Europe: Is the Emperor's New Suit a Straightjacket?" In Douglas Greenberg et al., eds., *Constitutionalism and Democracy*. New York: Oxford University Press, 321–35.

SCHNABLY, STEPHEN J. 1993. "The Judicial Process in Context." In Irwin P. Stotzky, ed., *Transition to Democracy in Latin America: The Role of the Judiciary*. Boulder, Colo.: Westview Press, 175–83.

SCHULTZ, FRANKLIN M. 1952. "The Firm Offer Puzzle: A Study of Business Practice in the Construction Industry." *University of Chicago Law Review* 19:237–85.

SHARLET, ROBERT. 1978. *The New Soviet Constitution of 1977: Analysis and Text*. Brunwick, Ohio: King's Court Communications, Inc.

———. 1991. "The Path of Constitutional Reform in the USSR." In Robert T. Huber and Donald R. Kelley, eds., *Perestroika-Era Politics*. Armonk, N.Y.: M.E. Sharpe, 17–32.

SHELLEY, LOUISE I. 1992. "Legal Consciousness and the *Pravovoe Gosudarstvo*." In Donald D. Barry, ed., *Toward the "Rule of Law" in Russia?* Armonk, N.Y.: M.E. Sharpe, 63–76.

SOBCHAK, ANATOLY A. 1990. "The New Soviet Union—Challenges in the Development of a Law-Abiding State." *Stetson Law Review* 20:211–16.

SOLÉ TURA, JORDI. 1993. "Iberian Case Study: The Constitutionalism of Democratization." In Douglas Greenberg et al., eds., *Constitutionalism and Democracy.* New York: Oxford University Press, 287–99.

SOLOMON, PETER H., JR. 1990a. "Gorbachev's Legal Revolution." *Canadian Business Law Journal* 17:184–94.

———. 1990b. "The U.S.S.R. Supreme Court: History, Role, and Future Prospects." *American Journal of Comparative Law* 38:127–42.

STERN, KLAUS. 1988. "Staats- und Verfassungsrecht." In *Einführung in das deutsche Recht,* Second Edition. Munich: C.H. Beck (Deutscher Taschenbuch Verlag), 13–39.

SUNSTEIN, CASS R. 1993. "The Negative Constitution: Transition in Latin America." In Irwin P. Stotzky, ed., *Transition to Democracy in Latin America: The Role of the Judiciary.* Boulder, Colo.: Westview Press, 367–82.

TOHARIA, JOSÉ JUAN. 1975. "Judicial Independence in an Authoritarian Regime: The Case of Contemporary Spain." *Law and Society Review* 9:475–95.

TRUBEK, DAVID M., and MARC GALANTER. 1974. "Scholars in Self-Estrangment: Some Reflections on the Crisis in Law and Development Studies in the United States." *Wisconsin Law Review* 1974:1062–102.

URABE, NORIHO. 1990. "Rule of Law and Du Process: A Comparative View of the United States and Japan." *Law and Contemporary Problems* 53:61–72.

WALKER, GEOFFREY DE Q. 1988. *The Rule of Law.* Melbourne, Australia: Melbourne University Press.

WADE, E. C. S. 1961[1959]. "Introduction." In A. V. Dicey, *Introduction to the Study of the Law of the Constitution,* Tenth Edition. London: McMillan & Co. Ltd, XIX–CXCVIII.

———, and A. W. BRADLEY. 1993. *Constitutional and Administrative Law,* Eleventh Edition. Revised by A. W. Bradley and K. D. Ewing, with T. St. J. N. Bates. New York: Longman.

CHAPTER
6

PROGRESS IN BUILDING INSTITUTIONS FOR THE RULE OF LAW IN RUSSIA AND POLAND

JOHN REITZ[1]

This chapter concentrates on the building of legal institutions for the implementation of the rule of law on the theory that without the necessary institutions, there is no chance that the legal system will actually institute the rule of law. By "legal institutions," this chapter means the primary social and legal structures of the legal system, such as courts, the judiciary, and the bar. As the last chapter argued, if law is to set limits to state power, it is necessary that the courts and the lawyers who provide access to them have sufficient independence from the state and that there be court jurisdiction at least to review the legality and constitutionality of executive and administrative action. The post-communist democracies of Eastern Europe and the former Soviet Union have also been eager to adopt a form of court jurisdiction to review the constitutionality of legislation, in part, no doubt, as a concrete symbol of their commitment to democracy and the rule of law. This chapter will describe the ambitious reforms that Poland and the Russian Federation have made in this regard. The description of structural reforms will also give us glimpses of how these key institutions are functioning to institute the rule of law. The final section attempts to summarize what this institution building tells us about the development of the rule of law in these countries.

The reader should not chafe at the level of detail in the ensuing chapter. Specific details, including intermediate steps in the reform, are provided to demonstrate the complexity of this kind of institution building. Indeed, a major part of the trick of getting legal institutions to function in accordance with the ideal of the rule of law lies in such details as how judges and lawyers are chosen for their careers, how and how well they are paid, what limits or exceptions are placed on the jurisdiction of the courts, and who has the right to bring suit. Moreover, while the new post-communist democracies have not been reluctant to experiment with these details, among the nations that have pursued significant legal reform there is beginning to emerge a kind of pattern, born of similarities in history and in current political and economic situations, so that many of the details presently in force may be expected to last for some time or at least to provide the models toward which legal reform will once again tend if it is interrupted and set back by political conflicts that tear down rule of law institutions in these countries.

While there is considerable English-language literature on the building of certain of these institutions crucial to the rule of law in certain post-communist countries—for example, the various new constitutional courts or the development of the bar in specific countries—there is a surprising lack of studies that attempt to assess institution building across the full range of institutions addressed in this chapter. It is therefore not feasible at this stage to provide an overview of legal development generally in the post-communist countries of Eastern Europe and the former Soviet Union. Instead, this chapter will attempt to remedy the lacunae in the literature by providing a comprehensive picture of the development of an independent judiciary and bar and the building of court jurisdictions for administrative and constitutional review in the Russian Federation and Poland through the end of 1994. The chapter focuses on these two countries in part because they have been in many ways among the leaders in legal reform in this part of the world, initiating important reforms with respect to some aspects of the rule of law earlier than most neighboring countries and carrying those reforms further. In part, the focus on Russia and Poland reflects the simple fact that there is much more information about these countries available in Western European languages than for the others of the region. The rather stronger focus on Russian developments within the chapter likewise reflects the greater abundance of English-language literature about Russia and the greater access to Russian legal documents in the United States.

This chapter is also extensive because it is comparative. It seeks to set the Polish and Russian developments in comparative context because, as the previous chapter has already shown in the discussion of judicial review, there is more than one way to set up legal institutions for the rule of law. No sensible assessment of a system's institutions can be made without understanding how they compare, not only to those of the United States, but also to those of other nations thought to institute the rule of law to a meaningful degree, such as the countries of Western Europe. Not surprisingly in view of history and geography, this chapter will show that most of the legal institution building in this part of the world has followed the model of the Civil Law countries of continental Western Europe. The chapter, therefore, also seeks to provide some understanding of the strengths and weaknesses of the Civil Law forms of institutions in comparison with the Common Law counterparts with which we are familiar in the United States.

Finally, this chapter is also comparative in a temporal sense. The sense of the recent evolution—and particularly its limitations—cannot be understood without an appreciation of the history to which it is reacting and on which it is building. This chapter shows that both Russia and Poland have already moved a considerable distance from the systems with which they started prior to the advent of reform communism.

STRENGTHENING THE INDEPENDENCE OF THE LEGAL PROFESSION

Judicial Independence

The previous chapter established that judicial independence is the linchpin of the strong version of the rule of law. But judges under Communist Party rule were not independent. Fundamental aspects of their life and service rendered them particularly susceptible to extrajudicial pressures. These factors facilitated "telephone law" during the period when socialist constitutions recognized the "guiding role" of the Communist Party. Reform communism introduced some important changes designed to strengthen the independence of the judiciary and the private bar, and the new post-communist states continue to make changes. This subsection will discuss (1) methods of judicial selection, (2) material support for the judges and their courts, (3) oversight by the *Prokuratura* and the Ministry of Justice, and (4) the introduction of juries in Russia.

Selection and Supervision of Judges

There are basically two models of judicial selection: (1) selection in a way that uses political as well as professional criteria and therefore makes judges politically accountable (the political model) and (2) selection solely according to politically neutral criteria bearing on professional competence (the professional model). (For a similar typology, see Cappelletti 1989, 104–13). While all selection systems have the tendency to subject the judges somewhat to control by the selectors, the professional model minimizes that infringement on judicial independence, and the political model tends to ensure that judges come to their offices with specific political predispositions or commitments. This is especially the case in a system, like that used for most state judges in the United States, in which the judges have to stand for re-election after fixed terms. In such a system, the judge may at least occasionally think about how his or her decision in a particular case will affect re-election chances. The system used for U.S. federal judges—appointment by the President, subject to approval by the Senate, for lifetime terms—is thought to counteract the effect of political selection by (1) the participation of both other branches of government and (2) the guarantee of freedom that comes with a lifetime term.

In continental Western Europe, judicial selection systems tend to emphasize the professional model and strengthen the political insulation of the judges with lifetime terms. Thus German and French judges are chosen by the Ministry of Justice at the outset of their careers largely according to scores on state examinations and then join a judicial bureaucracy in which they receive tenure (after a short probationary period) and begin serving typically on one of the lower courts (Bell 1988, 1758; Clark 1988, 1816–26). However, even such judges may be subject to a kind of political pressure coming from periodic supervision and reviews for promotion to a higher or more desirably located court. Western European systems try to guard against this source of politicization by emphasizing peer review of the judges by other, and especially more senior, judges, but to the extent the Ministry of Justice remains involved in the process, a degree of political influence cannot be ruled out. It is even thought desirable in selecting the judges for the highest courts (for Germany, see Clark 1988, 1822–6). Thus, we see that some degree of political control over the judges is found in most systems, though the Western European systems emphasizing professional control tend to de-emphasize political control far more than the U.S. systems.

In most communist countries, judicial selection emphasized political control in a manner not too dissimilar from those systems used in the United States. Thus, in the Soviet Union prior to Gorbachev, the judges of the highest court were appointed by the national parliament (the *Supreme Soviet*), and the judges of lower level courts were directly elected by the local population[2] (Garlicki 1991, 8.120.15 and n.49). Socialist Hungary, Czechoslovakia, and Poland preferred systems that ensured complete independence of all judges from local governmental organs. In Poland, the Council of State, the collegial executive power under the 1952 constitution, which was replaced after the 1989 roundtable negotiations with Solidarity by a strong presidential office, appointed all of the judges[3] (Garlicki 1991, 8.120.15 and n.49; Frankowski 1991, 48; Gostynski and Garfield 1993, 274 n.184, 275). The responsiveness of Soviet judges to political control was enhanced by fixed five-year terms, and judicial terms in other socialist countries were similarly short. In socialist Poland, only the judges on the Supreme Court had fixed terms, of five years. All other judges were appointed for life (Garlicki 1991, 8.120.15 and n.49).

While the Soviet Union's system of explicit political control over judges helped enforce "telephone law," the Polish system came closer to the French and German system of professional control by giving the chief executive the power of appointment but requiring of all appointees a full university legal education, postgraduate court training, and the passing of a special state examination for judges and prosecutors (Garlicki 1991, 8.120.15 and n.49). Of course, as long as the Polish Communist Party in effect ruled the country, it was able to control the nomination process to ensure that only reliable communists came to the position of judge. But once Communist Party power waned, Poland had in place a judicial selection system for the lower court judges that did not look too different from those in Western Europe.

Negotiations between the Communists and Solidarity resulted in changes to the Polish judiciary that further made it look more like its Western European counterparts. In 1989, justices of the Supreme Court were also given lifetime tenure (up to age 65) by constitutional amendment[4] (Frankowski 1991, 48–50). In the same year, the process of executive appointment for all judges was amended by legislation providing that the President can appoint only candidates recommended by the National Council of the Judicature, a body consisting of representatives from the judicial, legislative, and executive branches (Gostynski and Garfield 1993, 275). Thus, judicial independence in most Polish courts is now protected by the requirement for passing a professional examination, lifetime tenure, and the checks-and-balances device of the National Council, which ensures that the office of the President does not entirely control the appointment process.[5] The resulting system is similar to that used in continental Western Europe.

In the Soviet Union, the system of judicial elections for short terms of office, combined with the power of the electing bodies to recall judges, subjected the judges even more effectively to Communist Party control than in Poland. Reforms begun during the Gorbachev era and continued in the post-communist Russian state have strengthened the judges' independence but also increased executive branch control of the selection process.

The Gorbachev reforms concentrated on breaking the power that local party bosses could exercise over judges as a result of the system of local elections for the lower level judges. A 1989 all-Union Statute on the Status of Judges changed the system of direct elections so that judges were elected by the parliamentary assembly (*soviet*), not at their level (district, city, area, region, or territory), but by the next highest level (their "superior *soviet*"). (Justices of the Supreme Court continued to be elected by the Supreme Soviet.) At the same time, professionalization of the judiciary was encouraged by requiring, for the first time in the history of the Soviet Union, that judges have completed "higher legal education," at least two years of work in a legal specialty, and a qualifying examination.[6] Nominations were in the hands of the Ministry of Justice and the courts' own "judicial qualifying boards," which were intended to professionalize and depoliticize the selection process by certifying that candidates have the required qualifications and by making recommendations to the electing *soviets* for the recalling of judges who do not follow the rule of law. The Gorbachev reforms also sought to strengthen the judges' independence from their selectors by increasing the term of office from five to ten years. Finally, to combat "telephone law," a new law was also passed to criminalize official interference with the resolution of a specific case (Barry 1992, 260–3; Huskey 1992, 224; Solomon 1990, 186–7).

These changes substantially reduced the ability of local Party leaders to subvert judicial independence, but left the courts exposed to influence from their "superior" *soviets*. Despite the new criminal law, some of these bodies attempted in blatant ways to use their power to influence individual court decisions (Lawyers Committee 1993, 72; Huskey 1992, 225). One Russian judge complained to the Lawyers Committee that "the tyranny of the Communist Party has been replaced by the tyranny of the legislators" (Lawyers Committee 1993, 71).

The 1989 statute on judges seemed to give control over the selection process to the (next-superior) *soviet*, but observation of the cursory way that the Congress of People's Deputies debated and elected candidates for the new Constitutional Court (Lawyers Committee 1993, 46–7), suggests that the Russian legislature was not taking judicial elections very seriously. The nomination power, which under the 1989 statute was given to the Ministry of Justice, was apparently a more significant control. However, the involvement of judicial qualifying boards provided a mechanism for placing a premium on professional, as opposed to political, qualifications, thus somewhat insulating the judges from political control by the executive. In fact, the process of judicial selection under the 1989 statute was apparently controlled by the nomination of the chief judge of each respective court (Savitsky 1993, 648). However, this procedure also contributed to judicial independence from the state because it constituted a form of professional control over the process.

Despite these changes, the position of the Russian judge remained precarious. The judges on the Russian Constitutional Court created in 1991 had lifetime tenure (up to a mandatory retirement age), but the other judges were still exposed to political control both because they had no assurance of re-election after a ten-year term if they offended either the electing or nominating bodies and because they could even be recalled during their terms by the body that elected them (Savitsky 1993, 643). Accordingly, Russian reformers pushed for lifetime terms for all judges, as in Western Europe and the U.S. federal courts, and on June 26, 1992, the Russian Federation adopted a new Statute on the Status of Judges, which promised them an "unlimited" term, explicitly stated that they are responsible to no political body but only to the law, and abrogated the threat of recall[7] (Lawyers Committee 1993, 69; Savitsky 1993, 643–5). Life terms could not initially be given effect because the ten-year term had been written into Article 164 of the Russian Constitution. However, the new Constitution adopted for the Russian Federation by referendum in December, 1993, contains no mention of term limits for judges. It therefore clears the way for the 1992 statute on lifetime terms to take effect though it does not anchor that reform in the constitution.[8]

At the same time, the new Constitution also greatly enhances executive power in judicial selection by giving the President of the Russian Federation the power to appoint all of the lower federal judges. Only with respect to the three highest courts of the country, the special Constitutional Court, the Supreme Court (the highest court for the regular court system), and the Superior Court of *Arbitrazh* or Arbitration (the highest court for disputes on contracts with state companies and between commercial entities), does the President have a mere power of nomination. The judges of those courts are elected by the Federation Council, the new Federal Assembly's upper house, which corresponds to the U.S. Senate. Valery Savitsky (1993, 649), of the Institute of State and Law in Moscow, has argued that the enhancement of executive power in judicial selection raises the danger of executive control over the judges. Nevertheless, that control is significantly counteracted by lifetime terms. Moreover, the 1992 legislation strengthened the role of the judicial qualifying boards. As long as either these boards or the chief judges of the respective courts continue to play a significant role in presidential appointments and nominations of judges, the Russian judicial selection system will look very much like the Polish system and not so different from the selection process for German and French judges. In each country, what is probably crucial for the public's perception that the selection system does not undermine the judges' independence is, first, that they have lifetime tenure and are not subject to recall, except for grave crimes,[9] and, second, that because of professional input no obviously unqualified persons are appointed.

An important issue related to judicial selection is the question of purging or lustration. The general issue was raised at the end of the previous chapter. The problem is especially delicate for judges because under the old regime judges in these countries had to have been regarded as loyal Communist Party members in order to have obtained their jobs. Moreover, at least in the Soviet Union, many of the judges had come to the bench when there were scarcely any professional education requirements. Their ability and willingness to give allegiance to the rule of law are therefore both suspect. But it is not possible, consistent with the rule of law, to purge the judiciary of unregenerate communists except for extraordinary breach of office, such as taking bribes. In view of the indeterminate nature of much of legal argument, impeaching sitting judges merely for reaching what appears to some—or even to most—knowledgeable observers to be the wrong decision entails the risk of fatally damaging judicial independence.

Moreover, the newly democraticizing countries need people to serve as judges, and at least at the beginning of the transition, except in Poland, people who had the necessary legal training but who were not implicated in the previous regime were scarce. Thus, in Hungary, Sajo (1993, 294–5 n.1) reports that only a minor portion of the sitting judges changed with the regime change.[10] In Russia, the problem has been exacerbated by the lengthening of judicial terms. Perhaps the use of judicial qualification boards will prevent reappointment of incompetent judges, but no system appears to have been devised to avoid conferring lifetime appointments on judges who under Communist Party rule convicted people pursuant to "telephone law" in clear violation of statutory law (Lawyers Committee 1993, 77; Savitsky 1993, 650–1). In Poland, Sajo (1993, 294–5 n.1) reports, there have been larger changes in the judiciary because during its ten or so years of opposition, Solidarity was able to train a class of young lawyers who were ready and able to replace the politically compromised judiciary when they came to power. Still, the judges' lifetime tenure was a barrier to an outright purge, so finding a way to "cleanse" the judiciary without undermining their dignity and independence has been a subject of considerable discussion (Sabbat-Swidlicka 1992, 27).

Lack of Material Support

The material conditions for both the judges and their courts in most of the communist countries were appalling. Perhaps the situation is not so dire in Poland. At least accounts of recent reforms with respect to the judiciary there have not focused on this aspect (Frankowski 1991; Gostynski and Garfield 1993; Sabbat-Swidlicka 1992). But the conditions in Russia may be taken as representative of the problems in most of the other countries.

The average judicial pay in the Soviet Union in 1989, for example, was said to be below the national average (Henderson 1990, 312–4). For that reason, the Gorbachev reforms of that year provided for a doubling of judges' salaries. Nevertheless, Thorson (1992, 45) reports that even in 1991, "an estimated 4,000 judges were unable to survive at all on their state salaries and another 7,000 judges had a very low standard of living." Thus, it appears that most of the judges were very poorly paid.[11] This situation obviously failed to attract the best legal talent to the bench.

Low pay also put the judges at the mercy of local officials, even after the local officials' power over judicial selection was eliminated, because local officials continue to dispose over such vital matters as housing and heat. RSFSR Deputy Minister of Justice Cheremnykh wrote in *Izvestia* in 1989 that "more than 3,000 judges either do not have a residence of their own or lead an existence on the brink of homelessness" (quoted in Henderson 1990, 312). For this reason the 1989 law "impose[d] on local *soviets* the duty to secure 'amenable living premises in the form of a separate apartment or house' for any judge within six months of their election" (quoted in Henderson 1990, 325). But this provision was not backed up by an allocation of money to pay for these facilities, so it appears likely that many financially strapped local *soviets* were unable to fulfill this duty.

The 1992 legislation on judges addressed these material concerns by providing that judicial salaries may not be decreased and by pegging judges' salaries (exclusive of supplements for qualifications and years of service) to those of the chief judges of their respective courts and to those of the Chief Justices of the Supreme Court of the Russian Federation and of the Supreme *Arbitrazh* Court (Article 19). Apparently, as a result of that legislation, judicial salaries have risen to more satisfactory levels.[12] Articles 19 and 20 of that statute also continue the tack of the earlier legislation in promising judges substantial fringe benefits, including the house or apartment promised by the 1989 legislation or, as an alternative, a no-interest loan for housing. But the 1992 statute expands the fringe benefits in almost incredible fashion to cover liberal vacation leave including reimbursement for travel costs, medical care, use of public transportation, service uniforms, insurance, and even assistance in obtaining telephones and places for children in preschools. Under present financial conditions in Russia, these provisions obviously make judgeships quite attractive, but judicial applicants must wonder to what extent the already overstrained local units of government, who are to pay for most of the benefits, can do so, especially in view of the difficulties already evident under the 1989 legislation.

Much less progress appears to have been made with respect to the material conditions for the courts themselves. Even during reform communism, court buildings were "in a state of dilapidation and ill equipped with such basic essentials as conference rooms where defense lawyers can meet clients" (Henderson 1990, 312). On September 3, 1991, President Yeltsin signed a decree on emergency measures for the Russian courts. At that time, it was estimated that some 39 percent of the People's Courts were housed in "unsatisfactory" conditions (Thorson 1992, 45). The general lack of financial support for the courts even led to a judges' strike in Chelyabinsk, Russia, in 1992 (Thorson 1992, 45). Lawyers Committee (1993, 76) investigators "learned first-hand of judges' poor working conditions" in 1991 and 1992. It is to be feared that even in 1994 the courts remain dilapidated and without such basic equipment as microphones and file cabinets, not to mention computers. The lack of sufficient budgets for the courts gives local officials a continuing opportunity for leverage over judges. The poor working conditions may also be a significant barrier to attracting the best candidates to serve on the bench.

Supervision by *Prokuratura* and Ministry of Justice

All socialist countries used two executive agencies to exert control over the courts: the *prokuratura* or procuracy and the Ministry of Justice. Reformers have recognized that a truly independent judiciary must be shielded from both.

Of the two institutions, the Ministry of Justice represents the lesser threat. The USSR Ministry of Justice was a fairly weak institution. Khrushchev had abolished the central offices of the Ministry, and it was only reconstituted in 1970 (Huskey 1992, 223). Under 1980 legislation the Ministry of Justice exercised "organizational guidance" over the courts (Quigley 1990a, 66). This power did not apparently present as serious a threat to the independence of the judiciary as did the procuracy because the "Ministry of Justice remained one of the smallest and least influential ministries at the end of the Soviet era" (Huskey 1992, 235). Nevertheless, according to Huskey (1992, 226), there were complaints that the Ministry of Justice set guidelines for the percentage of persons convicted of crimes who should be imprisoned and that those guidelines were used as performance standards for the judges. In 1989 Soviet legislation eliminated the Ministry's power of guidance (Quigley 1990a, 68). Poland passed similar legislation in the same year giving the judges a considerable measure of self-governance (Frankowski 1991, 48–50). The elimination of the Ministry's supervisory control undoubtedly strengthened judicial independence, but it must be remembered that the executive branch continues to exercise some control through the appointment process.

The greater threat to judicial independence came from the procuracy. This institution was an important legal office in all socialist legal systems. The procuracy included the state's prosecutors but under traditional socialist law its authority ran far beyond the bounds of criminal law matters to include general supervision over the execution of the laws by all parts of the administrative bureaucracy, including the courts. It was actually modeled on an office established by Peter the Great and known as the "eye of the tsar" (Butler 1988, 107). Under Communist Party rule, the procuracy came to be a powerful and elite group of lawyers with general investigative powers to ensure that citizens and the lower bureaucracy adhered to the law (Butler 1988, 111). The members of that office have traditionally had better legal qualifications, higher pay, and brighter prospects for advancement than the judges (Huskey 1992, 222–3, 228). The office of the procuracy has also apparently outnumbered the judiciary by a substantial margin in recent years.[13] Most importantly, the procuracy has had a type of supervisory power over the courts through its power to monitor them, to participate in any case where necessary to protect "state interests," and to appeal from "incorrect" decisions, whether or not the procuracy had participated in the case previously (Cappelletti 1975, 819–21; Huskey 1992, 223). The procuracy could not change the decision—it could only appeal to the next highest court to do so—but in an era of an all-powerful Communist Party, the office of the procuracy could very effectively extend the reach of Party supervision. It thus acted as a formal supplement to "telephone law" and as an institutional rival to the courts. As such, the procuracy has been an institution fundamentally at odds with the rule of law.

The procuracy apparently did not pose as much of a threat to judicial independence in Poland as in the Soviet Union. At least by the 1980s Garlicki reported that the Polish procuracy's power to supervise the courts consisted solely of broad rights to appeal from decisions they believed to be wrong. According to him, a procurator "has no power to give binding instructions to the courts, nor has he any influence on the personal status of the judges. His position toward the courts, then, is apparently weaker than that of the Minister of Justice" (Garlicki 1991, 8.120.18). In March 1990, Poland abolished the Soviet-style office of procurator and incorporated within the Ministry of Justice a much more modest office with its role limited chiefly to prosecuting criminal cases (Frankowski 1991, 50; Gostynski and Garfield 1993, 274).

But in Russia, the procuracy has retained its autonomy and many of its former powers, even those concerning court proceedings. Although 1989 legislation was apparently intended to eliminate any basis for the procuracy to exercise supervisory functions over the courts, Quigley (1990a, 70), and Huskey (1992, 226–7) reported that the procuracy closed its departments for supervising the courts, the Russian Federation Procurator's Office Act, passed on January 17, 1992, maintained broad language about the procurator's supervisory powers in general. As the Lawyers Committee (1993, 94) notes, Articles 2 and 9 of the new law eliminate the procuracy's power to take up cases pending in court. It is therefore restricted to participating in pending cases as a party in court, but Article 31(3) still grants the procurator the right to intervene in any case at any time to protect "the rights and legitimate interests of citizens, the society and the state," and a procurator can still apparently try to resolve citizen complaints as long as they are not pending in court. If Article 32 limits the procuracy's power to appeal from court decisions to those cases in which it participated in court,[14] then its current powers in civil cases do not appear too dissimilar to those of the office of the *ministère public* in France, upon which Peter the Great modelled the Russian office. The French office similarly represents the public interest in matters not limited to criminal ones. However, in civil cases, the *ministère public*'s appeal can never change the outcome for the private parties unless one of them also appeals (Cappelletti 1975, 804, 820–1), while the Russian procurator's appeal can apparently change the outcome for all parties in the case. In France the office has come to play a very restricted role outside of the criminal prosecutor's usual role, but the Russian procuracy remains a powerful office with wide-ranging authority. Most importantly, with respect to criminal matters, the procuracy "retains primary authority over all pre-trial decisions, including arrests, searches, seizures, and detention" (Lawyers Committee 1993, 94). Thus there is no judicial control over some of the most important aspects of the pretrial criminal process.

The Lawyers Committee (1993, 93) concluded that "[t]he clear focus of the [1992] law is to protect the procuracy's prerogatives and power. While this law does decrease procuracy control over the work of the courts and the preliminary investigation [in criminal cases], it does not sharply reduce its role to that of state accuser only," as Russian reformers had sought to do and as was done in Poland. That the procuracy was able to resist the reform efforts is some measure of its continuing power in Russia.

One might expect the procuracy to develop considerable independence from either the executive or the legislative branch. Under Article 129 of the 1993 Constitution, the Procurator General is elected (and recalled) by the Federation Council upon nomination by the President. (The 1992 law provided a selection method that was similarly split between legislature and executive.) The Procurator General appoints all other procurators, although each component (republic or autonomous region) of the Russian Federation must agree to the appointment of the procurator for that component. However, in the long-drawn-out struggle between Parliament and the President over control of the newpaper *Izvestia*, Foster (1993, 730) reports that the procuracy became the "de facto investigatory arm of the Russian legislature." After the assault on Parliament, Yeltsin was able to secure the appointment of a longtime ally as Procurator General. Thus, the procuracy apparently remains highly politicized, and a strong body under current Russian law—possibly even a rival to the courts. It constitutes an elite body of lawyers that could bring considerable pressure to bear on the courts, though their ability to do so in a manner that subverts judicial independence has been considerably reduced. Moreover, as a repository of some of the best legal talent in the country that is expressly charged with the duty to represent the public interest, the procuracy has the potential to contribute greatly to the development of the rule of law, especially in connection with the development of administrative law (see the section on the development of forms of judicial review, executive and administrative acts).

The Jury System

One additional institution in which the Russians have shown great interest as a way of enhancing the independence—and hence, the legitimacy—of court decisions is the jury system of Anglo-American law. The lay jury, which decides questions of fact—including the ultimate question of guilt or innocence—out of the hearing of the judge, is a signal feature of the Common Law tradition. Following the French Revolution, a number of Civil Law countries, including Russia, tried various forms of the jury system but most quickly abandoned it. Instead, the Civil Law countries tend to involve lay persons only in the decisions of certain specialized courts, and then through the device of "lay judges" who sit with the professional judges and decide all aspects of the case together with the professionals. The jury system actually took root fairly well in Tsarist Russia, which introduced it in 1864 and kept it until the 1917 Revolution, but communist leaders distrusted the jury system. Socialist law therefore adopted an expanded version of the Western European system, so that the panel hearing a case the first time in socialist countries generally consisted, and still is supposed to consist after the fall of communism, of one professional judge and two "lay assessors."[15] As in the case of the jury system, there is no lay participation at any appellate level.

Russian judicial reformers have shown great interest in bringing back the jury system, in part because it is thought to assure greater independence of court decision than the lay assessors, who, because of their lesser numbers and greater contact with the professional judge, are thought to be too easily influenced by the professional judge (they are known colloquially as "nodders.") (Huskey 1992, 230; Quigley 1990a, 72–4). Russian interest was also stimulated by U.S. lawyers teaching about the subject in Russia (CEELI 1993, 21; Stead 1993). In November 1989, the Supreme Soviet of the USSR authorized the republics to adopt a jury system the parties could choose for the most serious criminal charges but left the details to each federal republic to establish by legislation (Quigley 1990a, 73–4). The 1993 Constitution does not guarantee the right of jury trial, but Article 123(4) does authorize jury trials "in circumstances stipulated in federal law." Finally, at the end of 1993 and the beginning of 1994, jury trials for criminal matters were reinstituted in a limited number of Russian regions on an experimental basis at the option of the accused.[16]

Development of Independent Legal Profession

In socialist countries, what corresponded to the private bar in Western countries was divided into the *advocatura* or advocates, those who represented private parties in court, and the jurisconsults, those who gave legal counsel to state-run businesses. The latter were salaried employees of state-owned institutions who did not have the right to represent private individuals in the regular courts, though they did have the right to represent state businesses, which primarily litigated in the special *arbitrazh* courts established to resolve disputes among the state and the state-owned enterprises. But the advocates had a monopoly over the right to represent individuals in the regular courts, and especially in criminal matters (Garlicki 1991, 8.120.18 to .19; Gostynski and Garfield 1993, 272–3). Together advocates and jurisconsults served as gatekeepers and professional guides to the courthouse door. Their independence from the state was therefore crucial to the rule of law.

As employees of their state-owned clients, the jurisconsults had virtually no independence. The advocates by contrast were corporately organized in local monopolistic "colleges," nominally self-governing, that maintained their own offices, charged fees to private individuals for their services, and drew no salary from the state. They thus were one of the few groups in socialist society with the potential to operate as a real exemplar of "civil society" (see Chapter 3). It has been claimed that the Polish advocates substantially realized this potential. "Despite constant political pressure, the Polish bar maintained a lack of subservience unique in the Soviet bloc," (Kondracki, Dawson, and Davies 1988, 918), unlike the Polish judges who were subject to the political domination of the Party (Frankowski 1991). In Poland, the advocates' independence was apparently protected somewhat by national bodies of self-government. Advocate's colleges were organized into regional advocates' chambers, which participated every three years in a National Congress of the Advocatura, which in turn elected central bodies for self-government, such as the Chief Council of the Advocatura, the Higher Disciplinary Court, and the Higher Revisory Commission. Through these bodies, the Polish advocates self-regulated and continue now to self-regulate questions of professional responsibility, finances of the profession, and provision of legal aid. They also decide which graduates to admit into the profession, a power they have used sparingly to enhance their monopoly and to favor families with long traditions of serving as advocates (Gostynski and Garfield 1993, 271–3). The Polish Ministry of Justice has only limited powers of administration over the bar, including the right to veto admission of an individual, but subject to court review (Gajewska-Kraczkowska 1992, 1126). The loss of Communist Party control has certainly strengthened the autonomy of the Polish *advocatura* by eliminating Party attempts to keep control over the advocates by political means, but building an independent bar has not required significant structural changes in post-communist Poland.

The situation was quite different in Russia where a number of structural features undermined the advocates' independence. They were heavily regulated by the Ministry of Justice, which set low limits for overall incomes and fees as well as numbers of lawyers admitted to practice as advocates (Burrage 1990, 444; Huskey 1992, 234). Most important issues, instead of being left to self-governance, were thus determined by the state in ways calculated to keep the advocates from constituting a significant political force. Although on paper local advocates' colleges were each to be run by an assembly of all of the collegiate members, in reality the Communist Party and the Ministry of Justice so thoroughly controlled the colleges—in contrast to Poland—that self-governance was a fiction. The one significant power of self-government the Russian advocates exercised was to examine applicants for entry into their profession and select individuals (Burrage 1990, 454–5; Huskey 1990, 105).

Reforms in the twilight of communism changed these features. In February 1989, a national bar association was created for the first time for the Soviet Union, against the wishes of the Ministry of Justice.[17] In an unprecedented example of public participation in the legislative process, the national bar association prepared its own draft in opposition to the government's draft of a new law on the legal profession (Huskey 1990, 115–6). At the end of 1989, the Ministry of Justice lifted its income ceilings and fee schedules, freeing the advocates to negotiate with clients over fees. This reform made the Russian advocates even less regulated than their Polish counterparts, who as of 1993 were still bound by a statutory fee schedule (Gostynski and Garfield 1993, 273). In 1991, the Soviet Ministry of Justice lifted membership ceilings imposed on local colleges of advocates (Huskey 1992, 234). Thus executive branch control of the Russian advocates' colleges was substantially curtailed by 1991.

Debate since then has centered around whether the Ministry of Justice should play any role in admission to the bar. In 1992, Yeltsin's Ministry of Justice proposed to do away with the colleges' complete control over admission to the profession of the advocates. Instead, the Ministry advocated that it take charge of the admission process, which would include examination of candidates by qualifications committees consisting of advocates, judges, and professors, in a manner similar to bar examination committees in Germany (Burrage 1993, 583–5). But that proposal was never adopted, and in 1994 a new draft on the advocates was published that would leave admission entirely to the individual colleges.[18] It therefore seems unlikely that the Ministry of Justice will soon be given enhanced powers over the advocates' colleges. They thus have become truly self-regulating since the disintegration of the Communist Party.

In addition, as part of the overall decentralization of post-communist life, the advocates' colleges are losing their courtroom monopoly. First, advocates have been free to practice outside of the old system of colleges, in Poland since 1982 (Gajewska-Kraczkowska 1992, 1126),[19] and in Russia since the late 1980s (Huskey 1992, 234). This liberalization allows advocates to practice without regulation by the colleges, though it has not resulted in the exodus from the colleges that might be expected for a number of reasons: Advocates practicing on their own are personally liable for malpractice and there is no well-developed malpractice insurance market; lawyers used to practicing in the shabby but insulated environment of a college have no experience in renting office space and attracting clients; legal regulation of the profession has not kept up with the change to a free market system, so that, at least in Poland, advocates find that they lose the right to represent individuals in court if they form group practices with other advocates outside of a college (Gajewska-Kraczkowska 1992, 1126–7).

More importantly, the scope of cases subject to the advocates' monopoly has been contested. In Poland, the *arbitrazh* courts have been abolished and disputes between businesses are heard by the regular courts, but the jurisconsults have been given the right to represent private and state-owned businesses in the regular courts. Polish advocates have therefore been able to maintain their monopoly over the representation of private individuals in civil matters and over the representation of defendents in criminal matters, but they have not been able to extend their monopoly to the more lucrative business litigation (Gostynski and Garfield 1993, 273). In Russia, the *arbitrazh* courts have not been abolished, but transformed into general commercial courts, and the jurisconsults continue to have the right to practice in those courts. In both countries, seasoned jurisconsults probably have advantages over the advocates in securing business clients because of their long-standing contacts among business managers and their greater familiarity with the relevant legal issues. But in Russia, the advocates' monopoly in the regular courts is also crumbling. About the only advantage advocates currently have is that only advocates who are members of a registered college can take part in the preliminary investigation in criminal cases. In civil cases and in all other phases of criminal cases, jurisconsults and even non-legally trained individuals can participate as long as the parties and the judge agree.[20]

Thus, in both countries, the unregulated jurisconsults compete with the advocates for much, if not most, of the legal business. The Russian legal profession is so unregulated that law students have formed law firms while still in school to pursue lucrative commercial law practices (Granik 1993, 972). The total lack of regulation of the profession cries out for some regulation in the name of consumer protection and the maintenance of professional standards, but the wide open competition is good news from the standpoint of professional independence from the state. A healthy market for advocates' services provides an important guarantee of independence from state control.

One crude measure of the importance a society attaches to law is whether the legal profession provides a good way to earn a living. In this respect the news from Russia and Poland is also encouraging. While the Polish *advokatura* generally retained a positive reputation and has long been the top choice for young law graduates (Gostynski and Garfield 1993, 271–3), the Russian advocates under socialism did not enjoy that position, but the recent healthy market for their legal services has apparently improved their prestige. Burrage (1993, 581) tells us that, "[i]n sharp contrast to 1963, the 1989 law graduates of Moscow University considered the *advokatura* to be by far the most attractive legal career." Granik (1993, 974 n.28) questions whether the prestige of the Russian *advokatura* has improved. She believes that the sense widespread among the advocates themselves that their professional image has improved is simply a "false equation of increased demand for services with increased prestige" (Granik 1993, 974n.28). But the introduction of criminal jury trials in Russia may enhance the *advokatura*'s role by giving the lawyers the chance to address panels of their fellow citizens on fundamental issues of justice.

The disappearance of the Russian advocates' monopoly raises a serious issue concerning fair access to justice. The advocates can be expected to compete vigorously with the jurisconsults for lucrative commercial business, leaving individuals of modest means and the destitute to seek civil and criminal counsel from among the least capable of the unregulated providers of legal representation. Unlike the situation in Poland, in Russia there is no longer a system of advocates' colleges to assure representation at fixed prices. As in the West, unless the state intervenes in the market with state-funded legal aid, the legal profession itself will eventually feel pressure to shoulder the burden of ensuring a reasonable level of representation by well-trained professionals as a public service. At present, however, there appear to be neither state nor private structures for the provision of legal aid.

The surge in demand for legal services suggests that more legally trained personnel are required to build the rule of law in these post-communist countries. Burrage (1993, 585) writes, "it is difficult to imagine Russia continuing as a growing market economy with the existing minuscule legal profession." In fact, there were thought to be fewer advocates per capita in 1988 than in prerevolutionary Russia (Huskey 1990, 106). But we actually have surprisingly little factual basis to support the claim that more lawyers are needed for the rule of law.[21] Nevertheless, it seems likely that the creation of broad-based societal support for the rule of law is enhanced by an increase in the number of citizens with substantial exposure to legal education. Moreover, in view of the traditional communist disparagement of the rule of law and all of its institutions, it seems obvious that the transition to the rule of law requires an upgrading of the support for and the quality of legal education, especially in Russia.

Already under reform communism, the Soviet Union had taken steps to upgrade the quality of legal education and reduce the number of evening and correspondence students (Markovits 1990, 242). With the turn toward the free market, an increased demand for legal education is reported for both Russia and Poland (Gostynski and Garfield 1993, 285; Granik 1993, 964), and the Russians, at least, have responded to market pressures by permitting the opening of new private law schools to supplement the traditional, state-run schools and by opening a special evening program at Moscow State University for students pursuing law as a second career (Huskey 1992, 227–8; Granik 1993, 964–5). Moreover, hundreds of young Russian judges have been sent abroad for education (Huskey 1992, 227–8), and both the ABA's CEELI and U.S. AID, among others, have begun bringing legal academics from Eastern Europe and the former Soviet Union to the United States for retraining and exposure to U.S. methods of teaching and law school administration.

Despite these efforts, conditions for Russian legal education are reported to remain daunting. Academic salaries are so low that law professors have to hold other jobs to make ends meet. Libraries lack resources and new legislation is not available. Paper is in such short supply that there is a shortage of teaching materials, library materials are stolen, and there are inadequate facilities to permit faculty to compile and copy new legal materials to distribute to students[22] (Granik 1993, 968–70). The Russian Federation's lack of a system to disseminate authoritative texts of new legislation quickly and widely is the most serious of these problems, for it affects not just legal education, but the whole legal system.[23] But the free press has at least partially filled the void by publishing new and proposed laws, and, as Granik (1993, 968) points out, the low academic salaries have had the positive effect of insuring that many professors, through the law practices they pursue on the side, are intimately involved with and knowledgeable about the latest changes in Russia's legal system. But their involvement in practice also means that they lack the time to write and publish the kind of scholarship that could fulfill the "Greek chorus" function described in the preceding chapter as a crucial support for the rule of law. There are thus significant resource problems that currently limit the ability of especially the Russian legal profession to play the roles an independent legal profession should play in a state subject to the rule of law.

DEVELOPMENT OF FORMS OF JUDICIAL REVIEW

This section will describe the considerable progress in creating and expanding court jurisdiction for the exercise of judicial review over executive, administrative, and even legislative acts. The section will treat the development of judicial review of administrative action first because significant expansion of judicial review first occurred in this area. Indeed, the long historical roots of the drive to develop administrative law jurisdiction in socialist courts deserve emphasis. Moreover, as the previous chapter discussed, judicial review of administrative and executive action is a less controversial element of the rule of law than review of legislation.

Review of Executive and Administrative Acts

Under early Soviet law, the principal means of testing the legality of executive action was the *prokuratura* or procuracy, discussed previously. In the Soviet state—and, indeed, in all socialist states—that office could and did provide some measure of relief for citizen complaints about unlawful bureaucratic action. However, as one would expect, given the origins of this office under an absolute monarch and its adoption by modern authoritarian regimes, it was concerned chiefly to ensure that the lower bureaucracy and citizens adhered to the law, not to enforce legal limitations on the highest agencies of state power (Butler 1988, 111). Solomon (1990, 191) says that the procuracy rarely acted against the powerful central ministries.

Starting as early as the 1950s, however, there was a modest movement within socialist legal circles to introduce some limited forms of judicial review over administration.[24] In the Soviet Union, "[t]he role of the courts in controlling administrative activity [had] traditionally been a minor one" (Barry 1989, 69), but there had been considerable academic debate within socialist legal circles about the desirability of judicial review of administrative action. The Brezhnev Constitution of 1977 contained an article promising judicial review of all unlawful administrative action (Barry 1989, 66, 68–76), but it took ten years before the Gorbachev reforms resulted in the legislation necessary under that constitution to implement the promise. In the meantime Soviet legislation had come to provide for regular court review of the lawfulness of bureaucratic decisions in specific instances. For example, even before the Gorbachev reforms, the regular courts had been empowered to countermand the order of a state factory manager dismissing a worker if the dismissal was not based on one of the grounds set forth in the relevant statute (Quigley 1990b, 216).

As in so many other legal matters, Poland was the leader in the turn toward judicial review of executive and administrative action. In January of 1980, just before Solidarity forced the Polish communists to share power, Poland re-established a court structure it had had before World War II, a special administrative court, now called the Highest or Supreme Administrative Court.[25] In fact, the legislative initiative that led to establishment of the court started in 1977, and the creation of the administrative court was the last important legislative measure of the Gierek government (Kuss 1989, 477). The court has jurisdiction to determine the legality of an enumerated list of administrative actions, but the list is quite broad. The judges of the Supreme Administrative Court are chosen in the same way as the regular Polish judges (discussed in more depth later in the chapter), have lifetime tenure (until age 65), and are paid the same salaries as Supreme Court judges (Wiersbowski and McCaffrey 1991, 8.110.10).

The Polish concept of an administrative court was originally influenced by the Austrian model, which like the French one, uses a specialized court to insulate the regular courts from potential politicization due to this kind of judicial review (see Chapter 5), though the perception that a special body of judges could better develop expertise in administrative matters was undoubtedly also influential. No other communist or post-communist state has followed suit to date. There is indication, however, that the Polish experiment with an administrative court has been successful. One of the court's early decisions (in 1981) established the principle that "administrative measures imposing any kind of obligation on the citizen must be based on statutes or implementing provisions explicitly mentioned in the statutes" (Kuss 1986, 361), a principle confirmed in Articles 45 and 54 of the current Polish Constitution. Relying largely on Polish scholars' studies of Supreme Administrative Court decisions, Markovits (1990, 227) has expressed the opinion that the special Polish administrative court under reform communism had become an advocate and protector of citizens' rights against the bureaucracy, even indirectly reviewing the fairness of the administration's exercise of discretion by examining the factual basis for administrative decisions, the bureaucracy's interpretation of law, its observance of procedural rules, and sometimes even its motives.

Poland continued its path-breaking reform of administrative law by creating the Constitutional Tribunal in 1982. This Polish version of a constitutional court, like the other constitutional courts subsequently adopted in Eastern Europe and Russia, has the power of judicial review not only of the constitutionality of legislation, but also of regulations issued by the highest levels of administrative and executive power (described in Article 33a of the Polish Constitution as "normative acts enacted by main and central State organs"). Because the Polish administrative structure is highly unified, with local authorities operating as branches of the central government (Reid 1987, 818–9), the Tribunal's jurisdiction would appear to cover all important administrative regulations within the fields subject to its jurisdiction. It is thus a very important part of judicial review of the executive branch even though the Tribunal's power is sharply curtailed by provisions limiting who can bring suit in this court (see the subsection on review of constitutionality of legislation and constitutional courts). In fact, this function has been the most important aspect of its operation (Brunner 1992, 539; Kuss 1986, 366), and Schwartz (1992, 779–80) indicates a large percentage of cases resolved in favor of the individuals whose complaints were brought to the Tribunal by the Ombudsman (described below).

No doubt, an important reason for splitting the administrative review jurisdiction in this manner was the fact that issues of administrative law often involve issues of constitutional law. For example, the Polish Constitution, like the Russian Constitution and most other modern European constitutions, provides that executive and administrative actions are limited by the statutory law (law passed by the legislature). Thus, questions of the limitation of executive and administrative power, especially at the highest levels, are questions of both statutory interpretation and constitutional law, and the idea was to bring all constitutional questions under one roof. It may also have been thought that a court with the stature of the Constitutional Tribunal was needed to annul regulations issued by the top administrative bodies or the Council of Ministers.[26]

The Soviet Union began the significant expansion of judicial review of administrative action in 1987 with the adoption of a "Law on Appeals" that created general jurisdiction in the regular courts to review the legality of administrative action. This first statute was, however, too limited. For example, the statute did not apply to decisions made by a collegial body, apparently a rough attempt to exempt the politically most sensitive cases from judicial review on the premise that most politically sensitive actions, including the issuing of norms of general applicability, would be by collegial bodies (Oda 1989; Quigley 1988).

A second statute was enacted at the Union level in 1989 to eliminate that feature and expand judicial review to all action by any "state administrative agency or official" (Article 1 of 1989 Act on the Procedure for Judicial Review of Illegal Administrative Actions). However, it also proved unsatisfactory for several reasons: (1) The term "state administrative agency" was understood to exclude many state organs that were not deemed to be part of state administration (Savitsky 1993, 657–8) indicates that state schools, hospitals, and enterprises, for example, were not included); (2) the statute exempted "normative acts" (Article 3(2)); and (3) it carried forward the 1987 statute's exception for cases for which the law provided for review by superior administrative officers instead of court review (Article 3(1)). In addition, Savitsky (1993, 659) indicates that the 1989 statute's requirement that individuals first seek relief from superior officials within the agency before suing under the statute was felt, especially by the judges, to be a burdensome impediment to court review. In view of these limitations, it is not surprising that relatively little litigation resulted from these statutes.[27]

In 1993 the newly independent Russian Federation passed its own administrative review statute seeking to address each of the above-listed limitations of the 1989 Union act. The 1993 Russian Act creates court jurisdiction to hear appeals from "all state organs [not just state administrative organs], local governmental organs, institutions and enterprises and their associations, social associations, and officials" (Savitsky 1993, 658). It eliminates the exemption for normative acts, and it exempts cases governed by other statutes only if the other statute provides for a form of judicial review. Finally, it makes the prior appeal to a superior official optional; the plaintiff can choose to go directly to court (Savitsky 1993, 659). The chief exception to the administrative law jurisdiction created by this statute is similar to the one in Poland to accommodate the constitutional court. As described in the next section, Russia has also created a constitutional court, and under the 1993 Constitution, that court has jurisdiction to review "normative enactments (regulations) of the president of the Russian Federation . . . or the government of the Russian Federation," as well as regulations issued by the governments of the republics and other components of the Russian Federation (Article 125 (2) (a) and (b)). The 1993 administrative review statute respects this Constitutional Court jurisdiction, which was similar under legislation in force prior to the 1993 Constitution, by exempting cases that come within the jurisdiction of the Constitutional Court.[28]

Thus, by stages, Russia has developed an all-embracing jurisdiction in the regular courts to review executive and administrative action, except for the issuance of normative rules (decrees) by the two highest bodies of the executive branch, the President and the Government, but these actions are reviewable by the Constitutional Court. But how the regular court administrative jurisdiction is functioning in practice is not clear.[29] Two different Russian scholars reported that during 1988 the courts decided about half of the cases filed under the 1987 statute against the government (cited in Barry 1992, 266; Lesage 1990, 207), and Barry (1992, 267) reports a Russian Supreme Court case from 1990 in which the court protected a cooperative from illegal acts of the executive committee of the local *soviet* (city government council). But Quigley (1990a, 62–3) reports an incident that signals the magnitude of the problem Russia has faced. In a case under the 1987 statute in which lower court judges ruled against the executive committee of a local *soviet*, the representatives of the committee who visited the judges after the ruling were able to traumatize them to such an extent that one of them burst into tears and the bench of that particular court was thereafter disinclined to rule against the city officials. However, the subsequent upgrading of the judges' positions—especially lifetime tenure—may have given them the institutional strength to withstand this kind of political pressure.

A bigger obstacle to the implementation of the rule of law is undoubtedly the attitude of the citizenry toward the judicial system. Under socialism, the preferred method of seeking redress of grievances against the state was to make an official complaint in the hope that the officials, especially the procuracy, would provide redress (Markovits 1990, 232–4). In 1990, it is estimated that millions of citizens sent letters to the press, Communist Party, and government officials complaining that executive agencies had violated their rights, but fewer than 4,000 brought cases in court (Huskey 1992, 228). At least as of the end of 1991, "the [Russian] population did not yet view the court as a reliable source of justice" (Huskey 1992, 228). Even in Poland, with its special administrative law court, there is a similar, albeit smaller, disparity (reported by Markovits (1990, 232) at about one million complaints to officials to less than 10,000 administrative law suits in 1983). Socialist citizens did not expect to have to litigate against the state; they expected state officials to take care of them, and it is not clear that such an attitude can be changed quickly.

The Poles have intelligently accommodated that attitude by borrowing the Western European idea of the ombudsman. This office, established in Poland in 1987, does not have the authority to nullify administrative action but can try to mediate disputes between citizens and the state and call attention to administrative illegality in order to create pressure for its correction, thus providing the kind of state-sponsored alternative to litigation that the formerly socialist populations seem to want (Markovits 1990, 232, 237). The Polish Ombudsman also has standing to bring suit before the Constitutional Tribunal, and in fact, most of the cases decided by that court from 1986 through 1991 were brought by Poland's capable and popular first Ombudsman, Professor Ewa Letowska (Schwartz 1992, 779).

Unlike the Poles, the Russians have not eliminated the broad powers of the socialist procuracy, and its traditional functions outside of criminal law have included trying to resolve citizen complaints outside of court, somewhat like an ombudsman. However, the procuracy also has the right to intervene in all manner of lawsuits, and that power could be used to help private citizens vindicate their rights in court against the state. As the best funded "public interest" law office in the country, the Russian procuracy thus has even greater potential than the Polish Ombudsman to promote the rule of law. One indication that they may be starting to play such a role is that in the small group of published Supreme Court decisions under the 1989 administrative review statute, the procuracy generally appears to have been the moving party.[30] While the Western European version of this type of office has not proven a very effective "watchdog" of the public interest in noncriminal law matters (Cappelletti 1975), the Russian procuracy may well represent the best hope for developing administrative review in Russia until private interests learn to use it and develop ways of funding such litigation. Much depends, however, on how independent that office proves to be from other state powers.

Review of Constitutionality of Legislation and Constitutional Courts

As mentioned in the previous chapter, the post-communist countries of Eastern Europe and the former Soviet Union have demonstrated great enthusiasm for constitutional review, including judicial review of legislation, but also considerable creativity in the development of Western models. By mid-1994, at least Poland, the Czech and Slovak Republics (and Czechoslovakia before its demise), Hungary, Romania, Bulgaria, Russia, the Ukraine, and Kazakhstan had each adopted its own form of constitutional court.

Poland

As we saw in the last section, the current development of constitutional courts in Eastern Europe and the former Soviet Union begins with Poland.[31] The Poles amended their constitution in 1982 to provide for a Constitutional Tribunal, and the Tribunal went into operation at the end of 1985. The Tribunal is staffed by eight judges, who each serve an eight-year, nonrenewable term. Like the French model, which is limited to pre-enactment review (described in Chapter 5), the Polish one maintains the supremacy of parliament, at least in a formal sense, through the provision that the Tribunal's finding that a statute violates the Constitution must be referred to the *Sejm* (the lower house) where a two-thirds vote can override the Tribunal's decision (Brunner 1992, 538–9; Schwartz 1992, 760). However, in a functional sense, the Polish Constitutional Tribunal is more like the typical Western European constitutional courts, because its review also operates after enactment of the law in question, and the two-thirds majority necessary to override the Tribunal's decision is the same requirement for amending the constitution, a response that can be made to a constitutional court ruling in any system.[32] Moreover, it is not easy to marshall that kind of majority, especially in a parliament as fractious as the Polish one. In the first ten years of its operation, only one minor decision was overridden by the *Sejm* (Schwartz 1992, 760). Thus, the Polish Tribunal's decision against a statute has more or less the same practical effect of nullifying that statute as the decision of any other constitutional court. Decisions invalidating high executive and administrative regulations do not have to be referred to the *Sejm* to take effect (Brunner 1992, 538–9; Kuss 1986, 361–3).

The Polish Constitutional Tribunal's powers to set limits to legislation, or even to high-level executive and administrative regulations, are sharply restricted by rules having to do with (1) who can bring suits before the court and (2) whether the legal challenge may only be brought in the context of challenging the application of the rule to an individual case. These rules in Poland are strikingly different from those in the United States but are similar to those found elsewhere in both Western and Eastern Europe. The first of these types of rules addresses what is called the issue of "standing" (i.e., who has the right to sue with respect to a specific action), and the second addresses the difference between "abstract" and "concrete" review. Abstract review refers to a system in which court review can be had merely because a party with standing wishes to secure the court's view on the constitutionality of the statute, whether or not it has been applied to anyone. In concrete review, the court has jurisdiction over a question of a statute's constitutionality, for example, because the statute in question has been applied against a party who then has raised the claim of unconstitutionality as a defense to the application of the statute. In the latter situation, there is a concrete case pending in court involving a specific party and specific facts. It is obvious that at least the affected party should have standing to sue. In the former situation, the only issue before the courts is the constitutionality of a statute or regulation in the abstract. If, as is the case in most countries, it is thought undesirable to let everyone have standing to seek abstract review, then it is not so obvious how that right should be restricted.[33]

Constitutional review in the United States is in principle chiefly by way of concrete review. U.S. courts use a variety of so-called "justiciability" doctrines, including standing rules that generally require an individual and concrete interest on the part of the plaintiff, "to avoid deciding many questions of major constitutional significance" (Schwartz 1992, 752). While U.S. courts do in limited circumstances stretch these rules to allow parties to assert the rights of those not before the court (especially in freedom of speech cases) or otherwise to challenge a statute "on its face" instead of "as applied," the strong tendency in the U.S. is to avoid abstract review[34] (Nowak, Rotunda, and Young 1986, § 2.12; Schwartz 1992, 752–9). This limitation on the court's power of constitutional review is thought wise because that power might otherwise be used as a kind of general warrant to disrupt the other two branches of government. It is also a feature of U.S. law that helps maintain a separation between law and partisan politics because political factions who lose in Congress are not so easily able to pursue their battle against the statute in the courts. They can do so only if they find an individual with a concrete legal dispute, generally someone against whom the statute in question is being applied. Finding such a plaintiff takes time, slows down the rush to the courthouse, and permits the government the opportunity to try to cure or minimize constitutional defects in the way the statute is applied.

Poland, like most Western European countries, permits abstract review and gives standing to certain public officials to invoke the court power to review legislation and executive action without regard to whether it has been applied yet to individuals. In Poland, the list of authorized plaintiffs for constitutional litigation includes parliamentary committees, the chief executive (formerly the Council of

State, now the President), the Council of Ministers, all higher-level courts,[35] the Presidium of the *Sejm*, the Ombudsman, and groups of fifty or more legislators (Brunner 1992, 546; Kuss 1986, 364). Like French and Italian law, Polish law makes no general provision for private parties to sue directly in the constitutional court, but Poland has gone a step farther than those Western European countries by allowing certain private organizations like trade unions and trade associations to bring suits for abstract review before the Constitutional Tribunal concerning matters affecting them (Kuss 1986, 364; Schwartz 1992, 755).

Given the long-standing European skepticism toward judicial review, it is perhaps ironic that modern European systems of constitutional review tend to permit public-official standing and abstract review, devices that are calculated to plunge the constitutional courts more directly into political controversy than the U.S. version. In particular, provision for suit by fifty or more deputies invites legislative blocs who lose in parliament or who object to executive policy to pursue their political fight through suits before the Tribunal, though the requirement for at least fifty deputies somewhat dampens that effect. But abstract review is useful, and every system allows it to some extent, even arguably the United States, because there are some cases in which it is simply unfair or unwise to force parties to wait until a statute or regulation is applied against individuals before the legality of the statute or regulation can be tested. However, every system also limits the use of abstract review because of its potential to overwhelm the courts' dockets and its tendency to blur the line between political and legal disputes. Because of their long history of distrust in government, Americans may look askance at a system of abstract review that limits standing to specific public officials, but—as discussed in the previous section—the general population in Eastern Europe and the former Soviet Union is accustomed to looking to state actors to solve important problems. The European practice of public official standing and abstract review may therefore be especially suitable for these post-communist democracies.

The only mechanism for concrete review of individuals' claims in Poland is the standing given to the other courts to refer abstract legal issues that are relevant to resolving concrete cases before them. As Brunner (1992, 546) notes, this procedure "blurs the procedural line dividing concrete from abstract review." It provides a way for claims that a statute has been unconstitutionally applied to an individual to get to the constitutional court, but it makes the other courts a kind of filter. Polish legislation tries to prevent the filter from being a complete block for all but the most obviously warranted claims by providing that the courts are to refer all "serious" constitutional questions even if they are not sure the constitutional claims are valid (Schwartz 1992, 759). In fact, so far few judges have been willing to refer constitutional questions to the Constitutional Tribunal because they do not come out of a culture comfortable with judicial review (Brunner 1992, 547; Schwartz 1992, 779–80). A system like the German one that provides individuals with a right to sue directly in the constitutional court if none of the regular courts are willing to refer the constitutional claim would obviously give the Constitutional Tribunal the opportunity to recognize constitutional claims the regular judiciary is not willing to recognize, but the Polish system is like the Italian system in that it gives individuals no right of direct suit (Merryman, Clark, and Haley 1994, 801).

The standing rules also affect the operation of the Tribunal's currently more important function to review high executive and administrative action. Because of the limitations on direct access to the Tribunal, individuals cannot directly contest, for example, a central administrative regulation that arguably violates a parliamentary statute. However, even if none of the designated official parties bring an action for abstract review, the concrete review system offers an opportunity for the individual to raise his or her legal and constitutional claims before the Supreme Administrative Court when the regulation is applied against that person. The Constitutional Tribunal will decide this claim under two conditions: (1) The action complained of is within the enumerated list of actions subject to administrative court review, and (2) the Supreme Administrative Court is willing to recognize the constitutional issue as serious enough to refer the question. Since the jurisdiction of the Supreme Administrative Court is actually quite broad, the limitations inherent in a system of concrete review by reference from the other courts are likely to be the most important barrier.

The standing restrictions do not necessarily prevent the judicial review of executive and administrative action that is required by the strong version of the rule of law. Every individual claim of illegality, including every claim of nonconstitutionality, can be presented at least to the Supreme Administrative Court (unless the official action falls outside the administrative court's enumerated jurisdictional bases). It is hard to argue that the rule of law requires more unless, as a practical matter, the administrative courts consistently fail to fulfill their obligation to refer serious constitutional questions. Of course, if the standing restrictions are unobjectionable with respect to administrative review, then it should be clear that they are even less objectionable with respect to review of legislation, which is not a necessary part of the strong version of the rule of law. Moreover, as discussed above, public official standing to seek abstract review beneficially complements the private standing rules.

In sum, the Polish Constitutional Tribunal has been established in the mold of the typical European constitutional court. The main litigants who can invoke the court's power are public officials with standing to bring cases seeking abstract review. A system of reference from the other courts gives private litigants a limited opportunity to secure concrete review. Despite the limitations on its powers and on the rules of access to it and despite criticism that the judges of the Tribunal are too sympathetic to the *Sejm*, the Tribunal has issued some controversial rulings. Since the end of Communist Party control in early 1989, the Tribunal has been free to take a more critical look at parliamentary statutes, and in that year, out of eight cases challenging statutes, it invalidated six (Brzezinski 1993, 195). In its most important case through the end of 1992, it struck down two key statutes that comprised part of the "shock therapy" of 1991 to reduce pensions and freeze salaries of state employees. The *Sejm* did not overturn the decision even though it threatened to inflate the state deficit unacceptably, with the result that the Finance Minister resigned and the decision jeopardized an International Monetary Fund loan (Brzezinski 1993, 196–8; Schwartz 1992, 780). Based on this rather limited information, it appears that constitutional review has begun to function in a meaningful way in Poland, though unfortunately Western scholars have not commented on the legal reasoning employed by the court.

Russia

Developments on Russian soil started later and have been much more fast-paced, radical, and dismaying, though not without some rays of hope. The story starts in late 1989 with the creation of the Committee of Constitutional Supervision of the USSR, a body that bore some resemblance to the Polish Constitutional Tribunal in that it had both pre- and post-enactment power to review legislation and regulations issued by high executive and administrative bodies and its decisions were subject to override by a two-thirds majority of the Congress of People's Deputies. Like the French but unlike the Polish model, this Soviet experiment was limited to abstract review; it could not decide concrete cases (Hausmaninger 1990, 302–3, 306; Barry 1993, 25–6). Like both the French and Polish examples, the Soviet creation was not denominated a "court" and the Soviet model was, perhaps more clearly than in the French or Polish cases, nothing more than a special committee of the parliament, much like the current Finnish parliamentary Committee for Constitutional Law (Scheinin 1993, 40–2). Even at its birth, it was viewed as temporary, and many expected the Committee to evolve into a constitutional court[36] (Hausmaninger 1990, 322). Instead, it was disbanded at the end of 1991 together with the Union itself in the wake of the August 1991 coup attempt. In spite of its weaknesses, the Committee demonstrated the utility of this intermediate model of judicial review for initiating legal debate over constitutional issues and received generally "high marks for its decisions on individual and political rights" (Barry 1993, 27). Members of the Committee, however, especially Chairman Alekseev, developed the habit of speaking out publicly on important political issues not before the Committee, and this practice damaged its image of neutrality (Barry 1993, 27).

Even before the August coup attempt, the first Russian Constitutional Court was created by constitutional amendments in December 1990, and passage of a Law on the Constitutional Court in mid-1991 (Barry 1993, 28–9). The first thirteen judges were confirmed by the Congress of People's Deputies in October 1991. The remaining two positions for the Court's full complement of fifteen judges were never filled, but the Court commenced working without them. The Court was in the mold of the more typical Western European constitutional court with full power to annul legislation enacted in violation of the constitution. It also had the power to review decrees by the President or the Council of Ministers. The 1991 Law on the Constitutional Court established a long list of high public officials and bodies with standing to bring cases for abstract review, including the President, the Procurator General, and individual parliamentary deputies. It also gave individuals the right to sue directly in the Court under certain conditions to obtain review in concrete cases (Schwartz 1992, 755).

In addition, the Court had a variety of other powers that seemed to broaden its powers in a dangerously unlimited way. For example, it was charged to review the constitutionality of federal treaties and to issue a report on concrete breaches of the constitution, thus in some cases in effect initiating actions on its own, without a complaining party (Schwartz 1992, 756). Moreover, the Russian Constitutional Court was given the power to initiate legislation, a provision Schwartz (1992, 756) criticized as a "serious encroachment on separation of powers principles." Thus, despite an express limitation against deciding "political questions," a puzzling and probably unimportant limitation,[37] the Russian Constitutional Court was armed with sufficient powers to intrude very forcefully on the actions of the other two branches of government.

Sharlet (1993b, 331) has trenchantly summarized the history of this first Russian Constitutional Court: "Following the Court's meteoric rise in public esteem during its first year of operation, 1992, its star began to fall in the spring of 1993, with the institution plummeting to its nadir by the end of the First Republic [which ended with the adoption of the new Constitution in December 1993]." In the wake of his fateful military attack on the Russian Parliament, Yeltsin suspended the operation of the Court and the 1993 Constitution has significantly reshaped it, so that we might speak now of a second Russian Constitutional Court. By the end of 1994, however, this new Constitutional Court has not yet started to operate. A review of the first Court's brief career provides some signs of hope for the rule of law in Russia and much that is cautionary. Indeed, the experience with the first Constitutional Court reveals just how risky the whole project of judicial review is.

One of the most dramatic cases came first. In that case, the Court struck down a decree by the then popular President Yeltsin merging the Ministries of Security and Internal Affairs. The Court ruled that the Constitution vested the power to create ministries solely in the legislature and that the Supreme Soviet had not delegated that power to the President. Yeltsin was reportedly surprised by the decision and only acquiesced in it after Chief Justice Valery Zorkin held an hour-long personal conference with him and called publicly through the press and a televised session of the Supreme Soviet for compliance (Barry 1993, 31; Sharlet 1993a, 6; Schwartz 1992, 763–8).

Other important early cases saw the Court tangling with the federal legislature and autonomous republics of the Russian Federation, respectively. Thus, the Court ruled unconstitutional an attempt by Khasbulatov, the Chair of the Supreme Soviet of Russia, to revive in Russia the infamous USSR Copyright Agency. The Court also invalidated a proposed referendum on autonomy by the autonomous Republic of Tatarstan. The latter case proved to be the most bruising for the Court because Tatarstan held its referendum in open defiance of the Court's order. Moreover, at least one Western scholar has strongly criticized the legal basis for the decision (Lien 1994, 95–6).

The Russian Constitutional Court's most celebrated case was the "CPSU" case (Sharlet 1993a, 16–31). A group of communist deputies of the Russian Federation sued in the Russian Constitutional Court in late 1991 for a declaration that

President Yeltsin's edicts banning the Communist Parties of the Soviet Union and the Russian Federation and seizing their assets following the August 1991 coup attempt were unconstitutional. The Russian Constitution does not give the President the power to ban political parties, but in addition to rather technical arguments,[38] Yeltsin's legal defense team argued that the bans were in accordance with law on the grounds that the Communist Parties had illegally arrogated to themselves the power of the state and therefore were not true political parties, but illegal state structures. In April, 1992--four months after the suit was filed—constitutional amendments were adopted giving the Constitutional Court the power to rule on the constitutionality of political parties and public associations.[39] Shortly thereafter, a group of deputies led by respected constitutional specialist Oleg Rumyantsev filed a countersuit asking the Court to exercise its power to ban the Parties.

As if each suit alone did not already contain too much political dynamite, the Court combined the two suits into a single "case of the century." A little over a year after suit was first filed, after fifty-two sessions, during which the Court heard forty-six witnesses and received in evidence a mountain of documentary evidence—some of it obtained from secret Communist Party archives—and after a drawn-out and infelicitous skirmish with Gorbachev over whether he would testify—he successfully defied the Court's orders to do so—the Court issued its ruling in late 1992. The Court held that Yeltsin could constitutionally ban all activities by the Soviet Union and Russian Communist Parties insofar as the ban applied to the leadership structures of the Parties. But, while adopting the chief idea advanced by the President's side, the Court held that the Constitution did not permit him to ban the local or primary party organizations, which did not operate as state structures. The Court similarly gave each side a partial victory with regard to the property issue. The Court upheld the decision with regard to property that belonged to the state but which the Parties had held and used as their own, but the Court invalidated Yeltsin's decrees to the extent that they seized property that actually belonged to the Communist Party or as to which ownership was unclear. Finally, the Court refused to decide the countersuit on the grounds of mootness, finding that the Communist Parties had collapsed in the wake of the August 1991 putsch attempt. Moreover, the Court ruled that outstanding property matters, including the question of return of the confiscated Party property, would have to be dealt with by the regular courts, a ruling that left for other courts the issue of who among the various new groupings claiming to represent the old Communist Party interests could claim the Party property.

Thus, the most important part of Yeltsin's decrees—the ban on the leadership structures of the USSR and Russian Communist Parties—was upheld, and the Communist Parties had to give up state property and faced the prospect that they might not even be able to recover their own property. But Yeltsin did not emerge unscathed. The Court invalidated parts of each of his decrees and conceded him no power to ban any true political party, including the Communist Parties, or confiscate its property.

The Court's decision in the CPSU case was widely seen, both inside Russia and outside, as an adroit compromise, but one driven by political, rather than legal, considerations (Barry 1993, 35–6; Sharlet 1993a, 30; Wishnevsky 1993, 6). In essence, the criticism is that political considerations led to a decision contrary to law. One of the two judges of the Court who wrote dissenting opinions explicitly raised that charge, calling the CPSU ruling a "flawed, reprehensible decision" decided by judges acting "not as legal experts but as politicians" (Barry 1993, 35). But it is not clear that this is a fair criticism. The central idea behind the Court's decision—the idea that the Communist Parties had taken over state functions and therefore were not operating simply as political parties—is an idea that was apparently well supported by evidence adduced at the trial and is, indeed, generally accepted as accurate among foreign and domestic observers alike. Moreover, it seems arguable that their subversion of state power and property should change the Parties' legal status on these issues.[40] The disturbing aspect of the CPSU decision is not that the Court accepted this argument, but that it failed to develop the argument in its opinion at all, merely implying the argument in a phrase and not otherwise justifying its decision (Barry 1993, 35). The Court's argument was a controversial one, and in order to persuade some part of the legal community that it should be accepted, it would have been desirable for the Court to have argued the legal and moral justice of the position in some detail (See Chapter 5).

After the decision in the CPSU case, the Court continued until September 1993, deciding a series of cases in which it limited now Yeltsin's power as President, now the parliamentary power, though apparently demonstrating much greater caution with respect to the ethnic regions after its experience with the Tatarstan case. Western commentators have not suggested that any of these decisions were demonstrably unreasonable applications of law (Foster 1993, 734–5; Lien 1994, 99–102; Sharlet 1993b, 324–5). But the result was that the Court, in the phrase quoted by Sharlet (1993b, 323), was "asked to do 'too much heavy [political] lifting.'" Its cases brought it constantly into confrontation with the other two branches of government in a way it did not have sufficient institutional strength or "legitimacy" to sustain.[41]

There were other problems as well. The Court began to be overwhelmed by the flood of petitions and delays were aggravated by the Court's cumbersome procedures (Sharlet 1993b, 323). But those problems are normal ones for all courts and might have been susceptible to cure through procedural tinkering or the creation of inferior courts. They suggest the success of the rule of law rather than a problem. More worrisome was the problem of the Court's off-the-bench activism, particularly on the part of Chief Justice Zorkin, who gave numerous press interviews and public speeches. In some of his extra-judicial comments, Zorkin exhorted other state officials to comply with Court rulings, in some he even addressed pending cases, something that was clearly prohibited by Article 20 of the 1991 Law on the Constitutional Court (Barry 1993, 36–8; Schwartz 1992, 777–8; Slater 1993).

He also had begun playing the role of broker in the ever-worsening disputes between President Yeltsin and Chairman Khasbulatov of the Supreme Soviet. At first, this role as mediator appeared to garner considerable support for the Court both inside and outside Russia (Wishnevsky 1993, 8). The Court's great "hour of triumph" came in December 1992 when Zorkin achieved momentary success in mediating the dispute between Yeltsin and Khasbulatov over a referendum Yeltsin proposed to see whether the Russian people sided with him or with the Parliament concerning the pace and direction of economic reform (Wishnevsky 1993, 7–8). However, by mid-1993, Zorkin had come increasingly to side with Khasbulatov against Yeltsin (Slater 1993) and therefore appeared less and less like an unbiased mediator.

A low point in this development came in March 1993, when Yeltsin suggested in a televised speech that he would issue a decree to increase his powers and the Court, working all night at Zorkin's insistence, ruled that this putative decree was unconstitutional. Before the Court had decided the case, Zorkin said in a speech to the Russian Parliament that Yeltsin's speech had been "an attempt at a coup" (quoted in Slater 1993, 2). When Yeltsin finally did issue the decree, it avoided many of the constitutional problems the Court had identified.[42] Sharlet (1993a, 32) suggests that Zorkin's efforts should be credited with having forced Yeltsin to moderate his position, but for many observers, the incident sharply undercut any claim the Court could make to be engaged in something different from partisan politics.

In the end, the Court was so deeply involved in the epic struggle between the executive and legislative branches in Russia that it inevitably became a casualty of that battle. When in September 1993 Yeltsin issued a decree suspending Parliament, the Court went into emergency session to hold it unconstitutional. Shortly after that came the assault on the parliament building, Zorkin's resignation as Chief Justice, and Yeltsin's suspension of the Court (Lien 1994, 102–3; Sharlet 1993b, 325–6, 332).

Thus, the first Russian experiment with a constitutional court seemed to end in disaster. The immediate result, knocking the Court out of action and severely tarnishing its image, was certainly not a good result for the rule of law. However, there is one bright ray of hope. Despite strong criticism of the Court and of Zorkin in particular and despite earlier drafts that Yeltsin had sponsored for the new Constitution (Lien 1994, 104–8), the actual draft adopted in December, 1993, preserves an important and reasonably independent role for the Constitutional Court. Journalists who had been among the sharpest critics of Zorkin and the Court, as well as the principal dissenting justices who had publicly criticized the Court's decisions, lobbied strongly and successfully to save the institution (Sharlet 1993b, 332).

The idea of a constitutional court is thus apparently to get a second chance in Russia, but the 1993 Constitution introduces some important changes in this second Constitutional Court, most of which seem reasonably calculated to make it a more successful body. The number of justices has been increased from fifteen to nineteen. Because the thirteen justices from the first Constitutional Court, including Zorkin, who resigned only as Chief Justice but remains on the Court, are grandfathered in by the transitional provisions of the new Constitution (Section 2, Article 5)—apparently with the lifetime tenure for which they were elected—Yeltsin has the opportunity to "pack" the Court with up to six new sympathizers, but the additional judges should also better enable the Court to divide into panels in order to process more cases. As mentioned in the previous section, the method of selecting new judges for the Court involves the executive and legislative branches in a manner very similar to the method for appointing federal judges in the United States. The new Constitution is silent on the term of office for the new justices, but Article 12 of the Russian Federal Law on the Constitutional Court, adopted in July 1994, fixes the term at twelve years or until age 70 and forbids reappointment. Thus, Russia has adopted term limitations for the Constitutional Court similar to those that apply to Polish and Western European constitutional courts.

Most importantly, the new Constitution restricts public official access to the Court in at least two important ways. First, Article 125(2) narrows public official standing by eliminating the provision for a single deputy to bring suit for abstract review. It requires a full one-fifth of the members of either house of the legislature, or ninety deputies from the Duma (Sharlet 1993b, 333). While this provision still permits a legislative minority to seek review of bills that it does not have the votes to stop, the new requirement reduces the ease (and speed) with which legislative fights can be carried to the Court. Such a provision will not, however, shield the Court from having to decide cases in which a majority of the legislature is at odds with the President, as was often the case during Russia's first republic, but perhaps that kind of epic conflict will be reduced by the dominant position the new Constitution gives the president over the legislature.

Second, the new Constitution does not give the Procurator General standing to sue for abstract review. This omission takes away from the procuracy the opportunity to play an overtly political role by invoking abstract review—probably a good thing—but does not eliminate its opportunity to play a significant role in developing the rule of law. Through its broad powers to participate in cases in the regular courts, the procuracy will have the chance to urge the courts to refer important questions of constitutional law to the Constitutional Court. These changes may well reduce somewhat the dimensions of the political role the new Court can play, but they also reduce the risk of another political failure.

Finally, the opportunity for the new Court to repeat the disastrous tendency the first Court had toward overt political activism is narrowed by the omission of power to ban political parties or to consider cases on its own initiative. But the Court can still interfere in external affairs by reviewing—in a case brought by one or more of the public officials given automatic standing—the constitutionality of international treaties of the Russian Federation that have not yet entered into force (Article 125(2)(d)). The Court has been given a role to play in any impeachment of the President of the Federation, a proceeding that would inevitably carry a high political charge,[43] and the Court still has the dubious power of legislative initiative.[44] Thus, the Court still has substantial power to play a significant political role, perhaps even too much power.

One of the most significant of all of the features of the new Court is the retention of the jurisdictional feature of direct access by individual litigants. Article 125(4) of the new Constitution might be construed to eliminate the right of individuals to sue directly in the Court, in which case the only means for concrete review would be by reference from other courts.[45] However, Article 96 of the 1994 Law on the Constitutional Court maintains the right of direct suit by individuals whose rights or freedoms are violated by a law in a specific case. This feature is important because the individual right of direct access provides an important guarantee of judicial review in concrete cases affecting individuals. If individuals had to rely on the regular courts to refer constitutional questions, experience from other countries teaches that there would be fewer decisions on constitutional claims. Like any other feature that brings cases to the Court, it may involve the Court in political controversy. But, in fact, review of concrete cases, to which judicial review in the United States is restricted, seems to carry less danger of politicizing the Court's work than public official standing to bring cases of abstract review.

The new Court is thus not stripped of powers, but the Court's powers and access to the Court appear to have been restricted in ways that may make it somewhat less likely that the second Court will become involved in a replay of the first Court's disaster. However, by the end of 1994, the new Court had not yet started functioning, though apparently only for want of agreement on a candidate for the last position to be filled on the Court. When that problem, which has already lasted roughly half a year, is overcome, the Russian experiment with a constitutional court apparently will begin again.

CONCLUSION

This chapter has shown that both Poland and the Russian Federation have made substantial progress in building key legal institutions for the rule of law. In view of the precommunist history of these countries, it is not surprising that their new institutions tend to look like Western European ones, not like U.S. legal institutions (with the exception of Russia's current experiment with the jury system). This chapter has argued that when one compares bench, bar, and public law jurisdictions in Russia and Poland with comparable institutions in Western Europe, one has to conclude that the Eastern European legal institutions are, at least in design, reasonable variants of Western European models. Polish and Russian judges now have roughly the same structural guarantees of independence as Western European judges: lifetime tenure (except for the judges on constitutional courts), professional input into the judicial appointment process to ensure professional standards, and maybe even adequate levels of pay. Neither Russian nor Polish advocates are controlled by the state. Increasing demand for their services and self-governing professional organizations give advocates and jurisconsults in both countries their most important guarantees of independence from the state. With respect to judicial review of executive and administrative action, Poland has reestablished the special administrative court it had before World War II and Russia has established general jurisdiction in the regular courts. Both countries have adopted constitutional courts for the review of legislation and high executive branch regulations. In the manner of Western European constitutional courts, the Polish and Russian courts provide opportunities for both abstract review (through suits brought by designated public officials) and concrete review (at least through references from other courts).

There are some aspects of these new Polish and Russian structures that cause concern. The limitations on the jurisdiction of the Polish High Administrative Court prevent it from exercising judicial review over all administrative and executive acts, but the omitted cases do not appear to be too significant, and every legal system commits some action to the unreviewable discretion of administrative or executive officials. There are more serious problems in Russia. The new Russian Constitutional Court has not yet started to function, though it seems likely that it soon will. Working conditions for the regular courts still appear bleak, dissemination of new legislation and other legal texts is chaotic, and law schools appear to be badly in need of more resources. The Russian procuracy is still powerful and therefore has the potential to reassume its socialist role as a dangerous rival to and supervisor of the courts though recent changes have considerably tamed its power. However, as a result of these changes, the procuracy also has the potential to be a powerful agent to promote the rule of law. The most glaring rule of law defect concerning the Russian procuracy is the lack of judicial oversight over its powers to arrest and search in criminal cases.

Nevertheless, from the anecdotal evidence presented in this chapter, one must also conclude that these new legal institutions are functioning reasonably well, at least insofar as the legal community is concerned. For example, for all their controversy, the opinions of the first Russian Constitutional Court seem to have been on the whole quite defensible, maybe at times even brilliant, though perhaps not always argued in a sufficiently explicit way to persuade the public. With the exception of Zorkin's out-of-court activism, discussed above, fault for the ultimate demise of the Court does not appear to have lain with the legal culture of the Russian legal community; the chief problems were caused by politicians, who have refused to obey law and court decisions or threatened to do so. Yeltsin's military attack on the parliament in October 1993 was only the most extreme example. Foster's (1993, 729) detailed study of the dispute between the president and parliament over control of the newspaper *Izvestia* concludes that both sides consistently bypassed the courts. Hoffmann (1994, 54) writes recently that "[o]ne still has the queasy feeling that Russia's executive branch leaders are talking about 'rule *by* law,' not 'rule *of* law'."

It is thus the more general legal culture, and especially the legal culture of political elites in Russia, that appears problematic. This is hardly surprising in view of the short time that has elapsed since reform communism began the turn toward the rule of law. Nor is the picture uniformly bleak. The fact that both countries have succeeded in accomplishing the impressive institution building described in this chapter suggests that there is considerable support for the rule of law among at least some political elites, probably even among those who have at times resisted court decisions, like Yeltsin.

It is also clear, however, that there is quite a contrast between Russia and Poland in this regard. The previous chapter showed that Poland had much more of a rule of law culture before World War II; one has to go all the way back before 1917 to find such a culture in Russia. Even then it was a culture shared by only a very small circle of people with scarcely any tangible effects on the Tsarist government. The recent institution building reflects that history. Poland has been well ahead of both the Soviet Union and Russia in fostering an independent and vigorous judiciary and legal profession. Similarly, Poland has been the leader in creating both types of public law jurisdiction. Most importantly, Poland has always had proportionately far more legally trained individuals than Russia. It seems likely that the development of the rule of law will continue to proceed in a much smoother manner in Poland than in Russia.

The contrast between Poland and Russia also raises an important question. The Polish versions of judicial review (High Administrative Court and Constitutional Tribunal) have both been designed in a more "cautious" manner than the corresponding jurisdictions in Russia. Polish administrative review is limited to a defined list of official actions; access to the Polish Constitutional Tribunal is much more limited than was access to the first Russian Constitutional Court and still does not include direct suit by individuals. Moreover, the Poles started with judicial review of the more mundane issues of the legality of administrative action. Constitutional litigation came later. In Russia, the sequence has been reversed. Whether the Polish "caution" resulted from its jurists' prudential concerns to conserve fledgling judicial power from overextension or from political realities governing the compromises that could be negotiated, one wonders whether the Polish path has not been a better choice, if only because it has not so far led to the kind of disaster suffered by the first Russian Constitutional Court. Such an argument, however, is speculative at best in view of the many differences between Poland and Russia, including the much better preservation of a legal culture supportive of the rule of law in Poland.

If the Russian Constitutional Court has emerged from its first political disaster with its wings somewhat clipped and the Polish Constitutional Court has yet to be given the power to spread its wings as broadly, neither case demonstrates fundamental flaws in the attempts to institute the rule of law in these countries. The "high-wire act" of constitutional adjudication seems to require courts with strong public support, at least among political elites, and as already discussed, courts in this part of the world, especially in Russia, are not yet supported by a strong legal culture. But, strong constitutional courts should not be regarded as the touchstone for the strong version of the rule of law. It is significant that the predominantly English language literature surveyed in this chapter provides considerable information about the constitutional court cases, especially in Russia, but hardly any information about decisions of other courts. Western scholars seeking to assess progress toward the rule of law need to pay at least as much attention to the workings of the regular courts and especially of the courts charged with administrative review. For it is as much here in the review of mundane administrative action or criminal procedure, for example, as in the review of constitutional issues that the pledge against arbitrary government has to be redeemed. While such cases are part of the weak form of the rule of law, they are also included in the strong form, and they are functions that socialist courts scarcely performed. If we could confirm that these jurisdictions are working well, that would be good news indeed for the rule of law.

There is one important lesson for legal development strategy that the history recounted here teaches unambiguously. The negative examples of Alekseev and Zorkin show quite dramatically that in order to preserve the appearance of neutrality so vital to the courts' legitimacy, judges—especially justices of the constitutional court—must avoid public involvement in political disputes in any capacity other than that of a judge resolving a specific dispute. No doubt, the power to give abstract review, as well as the plethora of special powers conferred on the first Russian Constitutional Court, obscured the importance of this point, but the justices in the new democracies have to see that they must limit their involvement to cases properly before them, whether for abstract or concrete review, and limit their pronouncements chiefly to the issuance in court of well reasoned judicial opinions. Courts can become a "third power" alongside the executive and legislative powers only if they do not forsake their judicial role.

In attempting to draw up a balance sheet for the progress toward the rule of law, it is important to realize what an interim balance sheet it is. Not only are there gaps in our information in the West about how these legal systems are functioning, but the changes are so new, especially in Russia, that the current legal institutions have scarcely had a chance to begin functioning. It was only in 1988 that Gorbachev first publicly endorsed the turn toward the rule of law. We will not know for some time whether the new institutions that have been built since then are going to function well, but their chances of doing so would be enhanced by a period of stability so that lawyers and judges can master the basic rules now in force. I do not mean to disparage the kind of tinkering that constantly goes on in most modern legal systems to try to improve the quality of legal institutions, but fundamental restructuring of legal institutions, however necessary it may sometimes be, is very disruptive and slow evolution is usually to be preferred. Whether the pace of legal change will slow down depends on the stability of the political system. Another constitutional upheaval in Russia would likely cause major changes in the design of the Constitutional Court or prevent it from commencing to function, and such changes would surely have a negative effect on the other courts as well. Finally, even if the legal systems of Poland and Russia do get a period of relative quiet in which to develop their powers, it is also important to remember that in all countries, progress toward the rule of law ideal is never finished. It is something which must be produced every day in the interaction of the legal and political systems.

NOTES

1. Acknowledgement: In addition to the Ford Foundation funds that brought the co-authors of this book together for the first time under the Bridging Project in the Summer of 1993, Professor Reitz gratefully acknowledges generous support from the University of Iowa Law Foundation and the University of Iowa

Center for Advanced Studies in connection with this chapter. In addition to his co-authors, the author would like to thank the following persons for research help and comments on earlier drafts: Alexander Domrin, Jason Kilborn, Elena Molodtsova, Mark Osiel, Youlian Simidjiyski, and Qiang Zhou.

2. Bulgaria followed the same system. In Romania, East Germany, and Yugoslavia, the judges were appointed to lower level courts by local *soviets*.

3. In Hungary and Czechoslovakia, the appointment power for all judges was shared by the national parliament and the national executive.

4. Only the eight judges of the new Constitutional Tribunal, discussed in the next section, still serve fixed terms of eight years. In the case of the judges wielding the special power of judicial review of legislative and high executive and administrative power, it was thought desirable to limit the power individuals could exercise by limiting their terms. The tendency of short terms to undermine a judge's independence is counteracted by the rule that the judges cannot be reappointed (Kuss 1986, 359; Schwartz 1992, 759).

5. Judges of the Constitutional Tribunal are elected by the *Sejm* (Brzezinski 1993, 177).

6. Commenting on the low status of the Soviet judiciary prior to these reforms, Professor Ginsburgs (1985, 308) wrote that "the cultural level of the average local judge remains low and, better training notwithstanding, the stereotypical judge does not cut a 'patrician' figure on the social scene or command popular respect by virtue of intellectual prowess." Even in 1993, Savitsky claims that many of the judges have received their legal education through correspondence or evening schools (Savitsky 1993, 644).

7. In September 1992, the Russian Parliament amended this provision of the statute to provide that a judge must first serve a five-year probationary period in order to qualify for a lifetime term (Savitsky 1993, 644).

   The 1992 Law on the Status of Judges also strengthened the courts' power and independence in both symbolic and actual ways by requiring judges to wear robes while presiding, by providing that their salaries may not be diminished while in office, and by giving the courts some power to punish those who act in contempt of court. The 1992 legislation also prohibits judges, as in Poland, from being members of any political party (Lawyers Committee 1993, 70; Savitsky 1993, 645). The similar Polish measure has been criticized as unfairly depriving judges of their rights to participate in political life, but Savitsky (1993, 646) argues strongly in favor of such restrictions, which also used to apply in West Germany.

8. Nor does the 1993 Constitution fully guarantee the independence of the judges. Article 121 provides that a judge's powers may be terminated "in accordance with the procedure and on the grounds laid down by federal law." The 1992 Statute on the Status of Judges provides greater protection, as discussed above, but one can, of course, worry that statutes may more easily be amended than constitutions.

9. In the United States, federal judges can be impeached by Congress but the power is thought to be reserved generally for serious crimes and is sparingly used. In promising that the judges may not be removed from office, the 1992 law on judges may seem to go too far because it does not make any provision for impeachment of judges for such grave offenses, although in view of the abuse of the power of recall under the Soviet system it is understandable why the Russian legislators chose an absolute prohibition on recall. Article 121 of the 1993 Constitution provides that a judge's powers may be terminated or suspended "in accordance with the procedure and on the grounds laid down by federal law." For justices of the second Constitutional Court, Article 18 of the 1994 Law on the Constitutional Court sets out specific grounds for impeachment under a complex procedure that involves, depending on the specific grounds invoked, (a) a simple ruling of the Constitutional Court itself, (b) a decision of the Federation Council (the upper house of the new legislature) upon charges brought by the Constitutional Court, or (c) a decision by the Court upon charges brought by the Federation Council.
10. The experience of West Germany in re-establishing its judicial system after World War II suggests that wholesale purging of the judiciary may not be necessary. Despite the broad support the German judiciary gave the Nazi regime and despite the large number of judges appointed by the Nazis, there was no wholesale purging of German judges after World War II (Müller 1991). But there are many differences between Naziism in Germany and state socialism in Eastern Europe and the Soviet Union, not the least of which is the considerably shorter duration of Naziism.
11. There were only about 11,000 to 12,000 judges in all of the Soviet Union in 1985 (Ginsburgs 1985, 307).
12. Neither the Lawyers Committee (1993) nor Savitsky (1993) mentions judicial salaries as an important problem for judicial independence.
13. Huskey (1992, 232) reports that the number of procuracy personnel was planned to rise to 39,500 in 1992 for the Russian Federation alone. Compare the number of judges (15,781) reported for the entire Soviet Union in 1988 (Huskey 1992, 227).
14. The language of Article 32 (1) applies that limitation literally only to a "procurator's assistant, the procurator of a directorate, and the procurator of a department."
15. It has apparently become increasingly difficult to get people to serve as lay assessors because of the economic dislocation (Lawyers Committee 1993, 71).
16. "Russia: Further Nine 'Regions' to Introduce Trial by Jury," ITAR-TASS News Agency (World Service), Moscow, December 10, 1993, translation available in LEXIS, Nexis Library, File Txtee.
17. A rival association was created for lawyers working in state agencies (Jones 1992, 90–1).

18. "Draft Statute on the Advocatura of the Russian Federation," *Rosiiskaia Gazeta,* October 22, 1994, page 4.

19. Approval by the Minister of Justice is required to open a private law office, but Gajewska-Kraczkowska (1992, 1127) says that it is always given.

20. Based on communications to me by Dan McGrory, serving with the ABA's CEELI office in Moscow during spring 1995, with special responsibility for the development of the Russian bar.

21. Statistics on lawyers are notoriously difficult to obtain and, because of differences in the way the term "lawyer" is defined in different countries, to compare (Galanter 1993, 78–9). Such comparative studies as we have tend to show enormous variation in the proportion of population acting as lawyers. One of the more careful students of the subject gives the following as estimates of the number of lawyers per million population for western countries for the years noted: Belgium (1972), 389.7; Canada (1972), 890.1; England-Wales (1973), 606.4; France (1973), 206.4; Italy (1973) 792.6; Netherlands (1972), 170.8; United States (1980), 2348.7; West Germany (1973) 417.2 (Galanter 1986, 166). However, some of these figures include judges and some do not. Nevertheless, even taking account of the considerable increase in number of lawyers that the United States and other countries experienced in the 1970s and 1980s, the United States stands out as a country with an unusually high ratio of lawyers to total population.

Japan is often put forward as the example of a country that employs a very small proportion of its population as lawyers, but that is only true if one limits the definition of lawyer to the narrow class of persons the Japanese call lawyers (the *bengoshi*), who are entitled to represent parties in court. Galanter (1986, 166) gives the figure of 91.2 lawyers registered with the bar association for 1975, but he also reports the figure of 807.1 for 1982 as an estimate of the total number of persons engaged in providing the full range of legal services—consultation and advice as well as representation—a number that boosts Japan above many Western countries though not the United States. It should also be borne in mind, however, that there are reasons to doubt whether Japan is a country that adequately institutes the rule of law (Urabe 1990).

Russia, a land of roughly 150 million people, was estimated to have approximately 16,000 advocates in 1992 (Lawyers Committee 1993, 104), or about 106.7 advocates per one million population, on a par with the figure for Japanese *bengoshi.* Poland, a land of about 40 million, was estimated to have 7,000 advocates in 1992 (Gajewska-Kraczkowska 1992, 1126), or about 175 advocates per one million population, more than the figure for the Netherlands for 1972. And if one adds in the figures for jurisconsults, who typically accounted for the bulk of the legal profession in socialist countries, the totals for Russia and Poland approach or exceed those for much of the rest of Western Europe. For example, there were estimated to be 60,000 jurisconsults, or approximately three times as many jurisconsults as advocates in the Soviet Union in 1981 (Feldbrugge and Collignon 1985, 445–7). If the same proportions hold for Russia today, the figure for 1992 for the ratio of people engaged as advocates or jurisconsults per one million population would be 426.8. Thus it is not apparent on the basis of statistical comparison that Russia and Poland need more lawyers.

22. Recent accounts of legal education in Poland do not remark on these same problems, so the situation is apparently better there. Moreover, it is claimed that even under socialism Polish legal education, like the Polish bar, retained considerable independence from state or Communist Party control (Gostynski and Garfield 1993, 256–7, 271).

23. Granik (1993, 969) writes,

> It might be more charitable to describe legal research as a variant of investigative reporting . . . For law students, as well as lawyers, legal research involves perusing the newpapers to which one subscribes; running from kiosk to kiosk to stand in lines to purchase additional newpapers and Western journals if available; telephoning one's contacts in the private sector and every area of the municipal and national governments to determine what new legislation has been passed, how it is interpreted and implemented, and what new legislation might be contemplated.

24. In 1952, Yugoslavia adopted fairly broad judicial review of administrative action, largely through a separate judiciary specialized in administrative matters (Kuss 1989, 487–8). Yugoslavia may have been driven to this bold experiment with judicial review by the necessity of using law to mediate severe ethnic conflict within the Yugoslav state (Markovits 1990, 207). A number of other countries in Eastern Europe (Hungary in 1957, Romania in 1967, and Bulgaria in 1970) began to give the regular courts jurisdiction to review the legality of executive and administrative action. Hungary did so through a clause listing a limited number of types of decisions that could be appealed to the courts. Romania and Bulgaria made administrative decisions generally appealable, subject to some exceptions, though at least in the case of Romania the result was that only politically unimportant matters were subject to court review (Wiersbowski and McCaffrey 1991, 8.110.7; Kuss 1989, 482–4, 490–6).

25. Despite the name, there is only one administrative court and there is also provision for appeals to the Supreme Court of Poland in certain extraordinary circumstances (Wiersbowski and McCaffrey 1991, 8.110.10).

26. Because the Constitutional Tribunal does not have jurisdiction over nonnormative action (that is, decisions taken with respect to specific individuals) at the highest levels of administrative and executive power, this action would escape judicial review in Poland if it were not included within the enumerated actions subject to the High Administrative Court. It is not clear whether this gap creates a significant hole in the rule of law fabric.

27. Lesage (1990, 197), relying on Russian scholars, reports for 1988, 4,789 cases filed for review under the 1987 statute; of which 1,920 were dismissed as improperly filed, leaving a balance of 2,869. Savitsky (1993, 657) claims that in 1992, under the 1989 statute, only 9,965 complaints were filed.

28. Unlike the situation in Poland, however, because of the comprehensive nature of the 1993 administrative review statute, there do not appear to be any types of high executive action that would completely escape judicial review.

29. Study is hampered by the fact that, as in most Civil Law countries, most court decisions are not published. Only the Supreme Court of the Russian Federation publishes its decisions, and then only a selection and generally in edited form that omits much of the factual detail.

30. The decisions are reported in the Russian Supreme Court's official journal, *Biulleten' Verkhovnogo Suda Rossiiskoi Federatsii.* The comment in the text reflects my attempt, with translation and analytical assistance by Youlian Simidjiyski, to find cases under the 1989 statute reported at the end of 1992 and most of 1993. Of course, it is possible that the Supreme Court chiefly selects for publication cases in which the procuracy participated.

31. Leaving aside the short-lived period in the 1920s when the Supreme Court of the Soviet Union developed modest powers of judicial review (see Chapter 5), Yugovslavia was the first socialist country to develop a constitutional court. The various Yugoslav constitutional courts (a federal one and one for each republic) were created in 1963. But they seem to have played a minor role in the political life of the country under communism and have been casualties of the vicious war that has engulfed that country since the fall of communism though there are efforts to renew constitutional courts in some of the successor countries (Brunner 1992, 537–8).

32. There is a procedural difference. The reference to the *Sejm* can change the outcome in the specific case, whereas constitutional amendment after a court decision cannot affect the specific case. However, this difference is only important in the case of concrete review, and as explained below, that type of review is not currently an important part of the Polish Tribunal's jurisdiction.

33. The one country that so far has chosen to grant everyone standing is Hungary. Largely for this reason, Brunner (1992, 539) calls the Hungarian Constitutional Court "the most powerful and perhaps even most active specimen of its kind in the world."

34. The United States Constitution limits the federal courts to "cases and controversies," a phrase which has been taken generally to prohibit abstract review as involving "advisory opinions."

35. Standing was originally confined to the Presidents of the Supreme Court and the Supreme Administrative Court, but since 1990 it has been extended to "all judicial bodies of these two courts as well as to all higher-level courts" (Brunner 1992, 546).

36. Russian attitudes were undoubtedly influenced by the rapid evolution in Hungary, which already in 1984 had established a special committee to advise parliament on the constitutionality of proposed and enacted legislation. At the end of 1989, amendments to the Hungarian Constitution converted that body into a true constitutional court with powers of both abstract and concrete review (Brunner 1992, 539–40).

37. Schwartz (1992, 757) notes that the Russian Court was the only one of the new post-communist constitutional courts under such a ban, but he says it is unclear what the nature of this limitation was meant to be. The U.S. Supreme Court has developed a rule of withholding judgment in "political questions" without an express clause in the Constitution restricting its authority in that manner. The basis for the United States doctrine is that the Constitution treats certain questions as questions that for purposes of federal law are left for resolution not by the courts but by one of the other two branches. An obvious example is the determination to remove from office in the impeachment of a federal officer, a determination the Constitution leaves to the Senate. The U.S. form of the doctrine thus does *not* mean that certain legal issues are so politically sensitive that the Court should not decide them, although some scholars have charged that the doctrine amounts to that position (see generally Nowak, Rotunda, and Young 1986, 102–10; but see Sharlet 1993a, 17, 23 [arguing that Russian Court should not have taken the CPSU case because it involved political questions]). Nevertheless, experience both with the U.S. Supreme Court (Schwartz 1992, 757 n.77) and the Russian Constitutional Court suggests that this limitation will not prevent courts wielding the power of judicial review from deciding questions of great political moment. The new 1994 Law on the Constitutional Court omits any mention of a "political question" exception to the Court's jurisdiction.

38. The technical defense had to do with (1) gaps in the way USSR law had been adopted in Russia after its 1990 declaration of sovereignty, (2) technical flaws in the Parties' compliance with the USSR law on public associations, and (3) a 1932 Stalinist decree that purported to give the executive authority to ban political parties and that had not yet been revoked at the time of Yeltsin's bans though it subsequently was (Sharlet 1993a, 26).

39. This amendment was modelled on similar rules in Germany, Romania, Bulgaria, and the former Czechoslovakia (Schwartz 1992, 751).

40. But it should be conceded that the distinction between leadership structures and the local party organizations may be more difficult to justify.

41. Sharlet (1993b, 323) notes that the Russian Constitutional Court declared executive and legislative acts unconstitutional in seven of its first nine cases. By contrast, during its first seventy-five years, the U.S. Supreme Court invalidated only two federal statutes; its chief role was one of defining the balance between federal and state power (Baum 1992, 185–90; Wilson 1986, 83). Since its establishment in 1947 under a constitution expressly granting the right of judicial review, the Japanese Supreme Court has used its power very cautiously, invalidating statutes only five times up to 1980 (Bolz 1980, 88–90).

42. The decree did, however, reserve to the President the right to ban parties and media that "inflame social discord," a provision Lien (1994, 100) sensibly criticizes.
43. Article 125 (7) limits the Court's role to "ruling on whether the presentation of a charge against the president of the Russian Federation of treason or the commission of some other grave crime complies with established procedure."
44. Article 3 (6) of the 1994 Law on the Constitutional Court suggests a limitation on this power but in words so vague as to constitute no real limitation: The Court "takes legislative initiatives on questions within its own purview."
45. As is often the case in questions of legal interpretation, the nub of the problem is the slippery word *and.* Article 125 (4) gives the Court the power to review the constitutionality of a law as applied to an individual "on the basis of complaints regarding the violation of citizens' constitutional rights and freedoms *and* at the request of judges." If both are required in a single case, then the new Constitution permits only a system of judicial reference. If *and* means *or* in this context, as it often can, then the Constitution preserves a system of direct suit as well.

REFERENCES

CONSTITUTIONS AND STATUTES

Poland

Polish Constitution: for bilingual edition of "Constitutional Act of 17th October, 1992," see Gisbert H. Flanz. 1993. "Poland Supplement." In Albert P. Blaustein and Gisbert H. Flanz, eds., *Constitutions of the Countries of the World.* 15. Dobbs Ferry, N.Y.: Oceana Publications, Inc., 1–76.

Soviet Union

Law on the Procedure for Appealing to the Court Unlawful Actions by Officials That Infringe the Rights of Citizens. 1987. In George Ginsburgs et al., eds. 1989. *Soviet Adminstrative Law: Theory and Policy.* Boston: Martinus Nijhoff Publishers, 80–3.

Law on the Procedure for Judicial Review of Illegal Administrative Actions, November 2, 1989. In Zigurds L. Zile, ed. 1992. *Ideas and Forces in Soviet Legal History*, No. 392. New York: Oxford University Press, 526–7.

Russian Federation

Constitution of the Russian Federation, adopted in December, 12, 1993 referendum: For English translation, see "Draft Constitution Approved by Constitutional Conference," November 11, 1993, LEXIS, Nexis Library, Txtee File.

Zakon o Konstitutsionnom Sude RSFSR, 12 iyulya 1991 goda [Law on the RSFSR Constitutional Court, July 12, 1991]. *Vedemosti RFSFR*, No. 30, Item 1017 (1991). For English translation, see "RSFSR Constitutional Court Act," July 12, 1991, LEXIS, Nexis Library, Sovleg File.

Zakon o Prokurature Rossiiskoi Federatsii, 17 yanvarya 1992 goda [Law on the Procuracy of the Russian Federation, January 17, 1992]. *Vedemosti RFSFR*, No. 8, Item 366 (1992). For English translation, see "RF Procurator's Office Act," January 17, 1992. LEXIS, Nexis Library, Sovleg File.

Zakon o Statuse Sudei v Rossiiskoi Federatsii, 26 iyunya 1992 goda [Law on the Status of Judges in the Russian Federation, June 26, 1992]. *Vedemosti RFSFR* No. 30, Item 1792 (1992).

Zakon ob Obzhalovanii v Sud Deistvii i Reshenii, Narushayushchikh Prava i Sbobody Grazhdan, 27 aprelya 1993 goda [Law on Complaints to the Court about Actions and Decisions That Violate the Rights and Freedoms of Citizens, April 27, 1993]. *Vedemosti RFSFR*, No. 19, Item 685 (1993). [This is referred to in the text as the 1993 statute on administrative review.]

Federal Law on the Constitutional Court, signed by President Yeltsin and dated July 21, 1994. *FBIS Daily Report* (Supplement): Central Eurasia. Washington, D.C.: U.S. Government Foreign Broadcast Information Service, July 28, 1994 (FBIS-SOV-94-145-S).

Projekt Federal'nogo Zakona "Ob Advokature Rossiiskoi Federatsii" [Draft Federal Law "On the Advocates of the Russian Federation"]. *Rossiiskaia Gazeta*, October 22, 1994, pages 4–5.

SECONDARY LITERATURE

BARRY, DONALD D. 1989. "Administrative Justice: The Role of Soviet courts in Controlling Administrative Acts." In George Ginsburgs, ed., *Soviet Administrative Law: Theory and Policy.* Dordrecht: Martinus Nijhoff Publishers, 63–83.

———. 1992. "The Quest for Judicial Independence: Soviet Courts in a *Pravovoe Gosudarstvo*." In Donald D. Barry, ed., *Toward the 'Rule of Law' in Russia?* Armonk, N.Y.: M.E. Sharpe, 257–75.

———. 1993. "Constitutional Politics: The Russian Constitutional Court as a New Kind of Institution." In George Ginsburgs et al., eds., *Russia and America: From Rivalry to Reconciliation.* Armonk, N.Y.: M.E. Sharpe, 21–42.

BAUM, LAWRENCE. 1992. *The Supreme Court*, Fourth Edition. Washington, D.C.: CQ Press.

BELL, JOHN. 1988. "Principles and Methods of Judicial Selection in France." *Southern California Law Review* 61:1757–94.

BOLZ, HERBERT F. 1980. "Judicial Review in Japan: The Strategy of Restraint." *Hastings International and Comparative Law Review* 4:87–142.

BRUNNER, GEORG. 1992. "Development of a Constitutional Judiciary in Eastern Europe." *Review of Central and East European Law* 18:535–53.

BRZEZINSKI, MARK F. 1993. "The Emergence of Judicial Review in Eastern Europe: The Case of Poland." *American Journal of Comparative Law* 41:153–200.

BURRAGE, MICHAEL. 1990. "Advokatura: In Search of Professionalism and Pluralism in Moscow and Leningrad." *Law & Social Inquiry* 15:433–78.

———. 1993. "Russian Advocates: Before, during and after Perestroika." *Law and Social Inquiry* 18:573–92.

BUTLER, W. E. 1988. *Soviet Law*, Second Edition. Stoneham, Mass.: Butterworths Legal Publishers.

CAPPELLETTI, MAURO. 1975. "Governmental and Private Advocates for the Public Interest in Civil Litigation: A Comparative Study." *Michigan Law Review* 73:793–884.

———. 1989. *The Judicial Process in Comparative Perspective*. Oxford, U.K.: Clarendon Press.

CEELI (Central and East European Law Initiative of the American Bar Association). 1993. *Annual Report*: Washington, D.C.

CLARK, DAVID S. 1988. "The Selection and Accountability of Judges in West Germany: Implementation of a *Rechtsstaat*." *Southern California Law Review* 61:1795–847.

FELDBRUGGE, F. J. M. and JEAN-GUY COLLIGNON. 1985. "Lawyers." In F. J. M. Feldbrugge, G. P. van den Berg, and William B. Simons, eds., *Encyclopedia of Soviet Law*, Second Edition. Boston: Martinus Nijhoff Publishers, 444–7.

FOSTER, FRANCES H. 1993. "*Izvestiia* as a Mirror of Russian Legal Reform: Press, Law, and Crisis in the Post-Soviet Era." *Vanderbilt Journal of Transnational Law* 26:675–748.

FRANKOWSKI, STANISLAW. 1991. "The Independence of the Judiciary in Poland: Reflections on Andrzej Rzeplinski's *Sadownictwo w Polsce Ludowej* (The Judiciary in Peoples' Poland [1989])." *Arizona Journal of International and Comparative Law* 8:33–52.

GAJEWSKA-KRACZKOWSKA, HANNA. 1992. "The Bar in Poland: Professional Ethics and the Legal Position of the Defense Counsel in Criminal Cases." *Capital University Law Review* 21:1125–44.

GALANTER, MARC. 1986. "Adjudication, Litigation, and Related Phenomena." In Leon Lipson and Stanton Wheeler, eds., *Law and the Social Sciences*. New York: Russell Sage Foundation, 151–257.

———. 1993. "News from Nowhere: The Debased Debate on Civil Justice." *Denver University Law Review* 71:77–113.

GARLICKI, LESZEK. 1991. "The Legal Profession in Poland." In Kenneth R. Redden, ed., *Modern Legal Systems Cyclopedia* 8. Buffalo, N.Y.: William S. Hein & Co, 8.120.1 to .25.

GINSBURGS, GEORGE. 1985. "The Soviet Judicial Elite: Is It?" *Review of Socialist Law* 11:293–311.

GOSTYNKSI, ZBIGNIEW, and ALAN GARFIELD. 1993. "Taking the Other Road: Polish Legal Education during the Past Thirty Years." *Temple International & Comparative Law Journal* 7:243–86.

GRANIK, LISA A. 1993. "Legal Education in Post-Soviet Russia and Ukraine." *Oregon Law Review* 72:963–75.

HAUSMANINGER, HERBERT. 1990. "The Committee of Constitutional Supervision of the USSR." *Cornell International Law Journal* 23:287–322.

HENDERSON, JANE. 1990. "Law of the USSR: On the Status of Judges in the USSR." *Review of Socialist Law* 16(3):305–38.

HOFFMANN, ERIK P. 1994. "Challenges to Viable Constitutionalism in Post-Soviet Russia." *The Harriman Review* 7(10–12, November): 19–56.

HUSKEY, EUGENE. 1990. "Between Citizen and State: The Soviet Bar (Advokatura) Under Gorbachev." *Columbia Journal of Transnational Law* 28:95–116.

———. 1992. "The Administration of Justice: Courts, Procuracy, and Ministry of Justice." In Eugene Huskey, ed., *Executive Power and Soviet Politics.* Armonk, N.Y.: M.E. Sharpe, 221–46.

JONES, ANTHONY. 1992. "Professionalization." In David Lane, ed., *Russia in Flux: The Political and Social Consequences of Reform.* Brookfield, Vt.: Edward Elgar, 85–100.

KONDRACKI, JERZY A., ANDREW HUTCHINSON DAWSON, and NORMAN DAVIES. 1988. "Poland." In *Encyclopedia Britannica*, 25, Fifteenth Edition. Chicago: Encyclopedia Britannica, 911–37.

KUSS, KLAUS-JÜRGEN. 1986. "New Institutions in Socialist Constitutional Law: The Polish Constitutional Tribunal and the Hungarian Constitutional Council." *Review of Socialist Law* 12:343–66.

———. 1989. "Judicial Review of Administrative Acts in East European Countries." In George Ginsburgs, ed., *Soviet Administrative Law: Theory and Policy.* Dordrecht, Netherlands: Martinus Nijhoff Publishers, 467–98.

Lawyers Committee for Human Rights. 1993. *Human Rights and Legal Reform in the Russian Federation.* New York and Washington, D.C.: Lawyers Committee for Human Rights.

LESAGE, MICHEL. 1990. "Le contrôle de la légalité des actes administratifs en URSS." *Etudes et Documents du Conseil d'Etat* 42:189–210.

LIEN, MOLLY WARNER. 1994. "Red Star Trek: Seeking a Role for Constitutional Law in Soviet Disunion." *Stanford Journal of International Law* 30:41–114.

MARKOVITS, INGA. 1990[1989]. "Socialism and the Rule of Law: Some Speculations and Predictions." In David S. Clark, ed. *Comparative and Private International Law.* Berlin: Duncker Humblot, 205–45. Also published in *Law & Society Review* 23, 1989, 399–447.

MERRYMAN, JOHN HENRY, DAVID S. CLARK, and JOHN O. HALEY. 1994. *The Civil Law Tradition: Europe, Latin America, and East Asia.* Charlottesville, Va.: Michie Co.

MÜLLER, INGO. 1991. *Hitler's Justice* (Schneider, Deborah L., translator). Cambridge: Harvard University Press.

NOWAK, JOHN E., RONALD D. ROTUNDA, and J. NELSON YOUNG. 1986. *Constitutional Law*, Third Edition. St. Paul, Minn.: West Publishing Co.

ODA, HIROSHI. 1989. "Judicial Review of Administration in the U.S.S.R." *Public Law,* 111–30.

QUIGLEY, JOHN. 1988. "The New Soviet Law on Appeals: *'Glasnost'* in the Soviet Courts." *International & Comparative Law Quarterly* 37:172–77.

———. 1990a. "Law Reform and the Soviet Courts." *Columbia Journal of Transnational Law*, 28:59–75.

———. 1990b. "The Soviet Union As a State Under the Rule of Law: An Overview." *Cornell International Law Journal* 23:205–25.

REID, COLIN T. 1987. "The Approach to Administrative Law in Poland and the United Kingdom." *International & Comparative Law Quarterly* 36:817–37.

SABBAT-SWIDLICKA, ANNA. 1992. "Toward the Rule of Law: Poland." *RFE/RL Research Report* 1(27, July 3):25–33.

SAJO, ANDRAS. 1993. "The Judiciary in Contemporary Society: Hungary." *Case Western Reserve Journal of International Law* 25:293–301.

SAVITSKY, VALERY. 1993. "Will There Be a New Judicial Power in the New Russia?" *Review of Central and East European Law* 19:639–60.

SCHEININ, MARTIN. 1993. "Constitutional Law and Human Rights." In Juha Pöyhönen, ed. *An Introduction to Finnish Law.* Helsinki: Finnish Lawyers' Publishing, 27–58.

SCHWARTZ, HERMAN. 1992. "The New East European Constitutional Courts." *Michigan Journal of International Law* 13:741–85.

SHARLET, ROBERT. 1993a. "The Russian Constitutional Court: The First Term." *Post-Soviet Affairs* 9:1–39.

———. 1993b. "Russian Constitutional Crisis: Law and Politics under Yeltsin." *Post-Soviet Affairs* 9:314–36.

SLATER, WENDY. 1993. "Head of Russian Constitutional Court under Fire." *RFE/RL Research Report*, 2(26, June 25):1–5.

SOLOMON, PETER H., JR. 1990. "Gorbachev's Legal Revolution." *Canadian Business Law Journal* 17:184–94.

STEAD, DEBORAH. 1993. "Russia Trying to Revive a Tradition So Old It's Revolutionary: Trial by Jury." *New York Times*, Friday, July 2, B9, col. 1.

THORSON, CARLA. 1992. "Toward the Rule of Law: Russia." *RFE/RL Research Report* 1(27, July 3):41–9.

URABE, NORIHO. 1990. "Rule of Law and Due Process: A Comparative View of the United States and Japan." *Law and Contemporary Problems* 53:61–72.

WIERSBOWSKI, MAREK, and STEPHEN C. MCCAFFREY. 1991. "The Supreme Administrative Court—Judicial Control of Administrative Authorities: A New Development in Eastern Europe." In Kenneth R. Redden, ed., *Modern Legal Systems Cyclopedia* 8 (Eastern Europe). Buffalo, N.Y.: William S. Hein & Co, 8.110.1 to 8110.17.

WILSON, JAMES Q. 1986. *American Government: Institutions and Policies*, Third Edition. Lexington, Mass.: D.C. Heath.

WISHNEVSKY, JULIA. 1993. "Russian Constitutional Court: A Third Branch of Government?" *RFE/RL Research Report* 2(7, February 12):1–8.

CHAPTER
7

Political Institutions and Democratic Governance in Divided Societies

VICKI L. HESLI [1]

Although the concept of democracy is difficult to define, very few would argue against the assertion that the major principle on which democracy is based is that of popular sovereignty. In other words, government can be legitimated only by the will of those whom it governs. Democracy therefore implies the right of self-determination. Nationalism also rests on the principle of self-determination and, thus, the two concepts of nationalism and democracy are theoretically and practically linked together in a complementary and yet uneasy union.[2] According to Fukuyama (1992, 23), the ideology of nationalism embodies the "belief that homogeneous cultural linguistic groups should be organized into sovereign states." Sovereignty by definition is supreme power—or for a "national" group, full autonomy.

The importance of building a democracy on a culturally homogeneous foundation is an idea advanced by many philosophers. John Stuart Mill, for example, asserted that it "is in general a necessary condition for free institutions that the boundaries of governments should coincide in the main with those of nationalities" (1958, 232–3). In contrast, the presence of diversity has been considered by other philosophers as a favorable factor in the preservation of democracy. Lord Acton, in *Essays on Freedom and Power*, maintained that "the combination of different nations in one state is as necessary a condition of civilized life as the combination of men and women in society" (1948, 186).[3] The overriding tendency among liberal theorists, however, is to assume that cooperation and accommodation across groups is more difficult to achieve when the basis of group identity is ethnicity rather than some other characteristic that is considered less immutable and less all-encompassing. The prospects for democracy are seen as best when individuals have a multiplicity of identities that criss-cross rather than reinforce each other (Bentley 1967). The generally accepted assumption is that the intensity and disruptive consequences of political disagreements will be reduced and cohesion enhanced when citizens identify with a broader, all-encompassing state, as well as or rather than with ethnic subgroups within a state. The likelihood of such multiple or universal identities, however, declines when different cultural groups are isolated in separate territories or regions of the state.

Indeed, when the sense of identity of individuals is based primarily upon their membership in an ethnic group, then associations built for the purpose of advancing the interests of citizens (such as political parties and interest groups) tend also to be based upon an allegiance to specific ethnic groups. If a territorially based ethnic group comes to perceive that its interests are being systematically ignored or undermined by the prevalent state structures, then the group may adopt an ideology of national separatism. Smith (1976, 3) defines the fundamental goals of a separatist movement as the realization of citizen self-government, the establishment of a territorial home, and the maintenance of a distinctive ethnic history. In addition to the fundamental goals, we would expect that the motivations behind support for separatism would include a range of political, economic, and cultural grievances against the central state.[4]

Nationalist leaders from the independence-minded republics of the Soviet Union were acting in the name of self-determination. Thus, in the decline of communism, "movements for democracy and movements for independence" often became one and the same (Nodia 1992, 9). Nationalism as an ideology, however, has shown itself to have two faces. One face is a positive historical force that has provided the political basis for democratic government (Nodia 1992, 7). The second face of nationalism is negative and brings forward images of genocide, ethnic cleansing, forced assimilation, and many other potentially aggressive and hostile components of group assertiveness. Nationalism as an ideology, therefore, has many variants depending upon the place and the time.

Given the intensity of the nationalist orientations characteristic of the emergence of democracy in Eastern and Central Europe and the former Soviet Union, we can expect that the stabilization and preservation of these new democracies will depend critically on their ability to manage existing ethnic tensions within their borders. Ethnic conflicts persist throughout the region, varying in level of violence from parliamentary confrontation in the former Czechoslovakia, to full scale war in Chechnya, Abkhazia (Georgia), and Nagorno-Karabakh (Armenia and Azerbaidzhan). The newly established independent states may disintegrate further, as the minorities living within these states come to see the majority as oppressors. Would-be nations will continue to demand their collective right to national self-determination. New states may be replaced by ever more new states based upon finer divisions of national identity—unless democracy itself, and the democratic procedures that are adopted, can provide a way to resolve ethnic conflict within the existing states.

The purpose of this chapter is to evaluate the prospects for the successful resolution of ethnic conflict through democratic procedures. To this end, the first part of the chapter will be devoted to a discussion of the nature of ethnicity. We are interested here in reviewing those theories that attempt to explain the existence and the strength of ethnic identities in modern society. In the second section we move from the theoretical to the empirical. We overview the relationship between nationalism and the demise of the Soviet empire. The same nationalist forces that led to the emergence of democracy in the former republics of the USSR, however, now pose critical challenges for the consolidation of democracy. Nationalism and its potential to severely constrain the assemblage of democratic principles is the focus for the third section. In the final section we ask whether there are ways to arrange a state, such as federalism or the adoption of constitutionally mandated group rights, that will reduce ethnic conflict and its propensity to turn into violence.

THEORIES OF ETHNIC CONFLICT

We begin with a review of five theoretical frameworks that have previously been employed for analyzing and evaluating the emergence of ethnic identities and the development of nationalist movements. The theories differ not only in their assumptions but also in their goals. Some approaches attempt merely to explain identity, while others seek to go beyond identity to describe the origins of ethnic mobilization and nationalism. Certain approaches, such as the cultural pluralist, expect that hostilities will occur whenever ethnic groups with unequal power come together in the same political system. Other perspectives are more optimistic about the prospects for ethnic harmony. Thus, for instance, Marxists believe that nationalist identities are characteristic of the capitalist stage of a society's historical development, and that, with further progress toward socialism, nationalism would become obsolete. Clearly, the theories about the foundations of ethnic identity are diverse, as are theories about the transformation of identity into mobilized nationalism.

To begin our overview of the theoretical approaches to the study of ethnicity and nationalism we present the following definition: ethnicity or ethnic identity refers to the self-definition of a group of people as distinct from others according to some common traits or culture within the group. People may use language, religion, race, or some other characteristic to define themselves as a group. Each of the five approaches discussed below—Marxism, modernization, cultural pluralism, relative group worth, and rational choice perspectives—would accept this basic definition of ethnicity. Each of the approaches, however, attempts to explain a different aspect of how and why ethnicity becomes politicized.

Marxism

The Marxist-based theories that have addressed the "national question" were incorporated into the ideological foundation of the Soviet state. Marxism, however, tends to treat ethnic conflict as a diversion from the real problem of class struggle between the bourgeoisie and the proletariat (Tucker 1972). National identities are understood as masks imposed by the bourgeoisie on the working class to provide them either with a patriotic identity that attaches them to a bourgeoisie that exploits them, or, where the proletariat is ethnically split, gives them divisive identities to prevent them from uniting against the ills of capitalism. Thus, Marxism views the cultural and religious symbolism of identity merely as a tool of the ruling class that can be used to perpetuate the submissiveness of the workers.

There is a Leninist variant of this viewpoint that focuses on the imperialist expansion of capitalism into Africa, Asia, Latin America, and, for that matter, the expansion of the Russian Empire of the nineteenth century. The colonial and imperialist policies of capitalist states often involved the recruitment of particular ethnic groups in these areas for the purpose of performing certain tasks. These policies created economic disparities among the affected groups. In addition, migrants into colonial territories often took jobs that others would not, leading to a further concentration of certain ethnic groups into specific areas of labor. As a result, competition over scarce resources—and ultimately over control of the means of production, both in the colonies of imperialist states and in the new, post-colonial states established by "national bourgeoisies"—is likely to mirror ethnic differences. Because in many societies ethnic differences are thus reflected in the division of labor, what are really class antagonisms tend to look like ethnic antagonisms.

The most extensive treatment of the "national question" was provided by an Austrian Marxist, Otto Bauer. According to Bauer, a nation could be distinguished by its national character, which includes shared historical experiences, habitation in a common territory, and a common language (Bauer 1907). The development of capitalism led to increased competition between nations. Advanced education, industrialization, and migration to cities all contributed to an "awakening" of historical nations and to increased rivalry among newly mobile populations. Bauer's solution to the problems of nations in the capitalist stage was to grant limited autonomy to national communities.

More contemporary Marxist theories include a body of literature called dependency theory. This body of work has its origins in Lenin's own writings about the "carving up of colonies" by the international capitalist class (Lenin 1964, 186–8), while Johan Galtung (1971) was instrumental in pointing out the conflicting interests of the metropolitan center and the periphery nation. The work of Michael Hechter (1975) is the most useful for clarifying the coincidence between both a cultural gap and economic inequality between the center (the core) and the periphery.

The Marxist perspective is important for highlighting the relevance of economic competition for understanding ethnicity and nationalism, but economic deterministic arguments alone cannot account for the willingness of large groups of people to sacrifice economic well-being for the sake of values such as religious and linguistic autonomy. Nationalist movements do not emerge solely as the result of perceived economic injustice. The Marxist perspective, which sees class conflict as the major force in history, has also been criticized by those who observe that nationalist movements often unite people across class lines.

Modernization

According to the modernization perspective, the process of modernization alters society in ways that lead to changes in the nature of ethnic identities. In the immediate post–World War II period, the prevalent assumption among scholars was that ethnic conflict was a relic of traditionalism doomed to be overtaken by modernity. Nonetheless, ethnic identities, as a stubborn remnant of the past, were impeding the process of modernization in many of the post-colonial societies of Africa and Asia. By the mid-1960s, this view had fallen out of favor, as scholars began to recognize the persistence of ethnic identities in even the more "modern" European societies, such as France and the United Kingdom.

The idea of the link between modernization and the abatement of ethnicity, however, was later revived with a new directional emphasis. Intensely felt ethnic identities, mobilized into nationalist movements, came to be seen as an integral part and even a product of the modernization process. The link between modernization and the resurgence of nationalism is based upon defining modernization as expanding industrial and service sectors, widening markets, increasing secularism and literacy among the people, and rapid urbanization. Each of these processes brings about increased interaction among diverse peoples. Modernization also tends to have an unequal impact, with some groups and regions benefiting more than others. Modernization generally involves more competitive access to the market and employment opportunities and unequal economic development across groups, which tend to breed ethnic-based and regional hostilities. The dual processes of urbanization and education simultaneously serve to equip national elites and ordinary people with the resources that they need to challenge a central state (Gould 1966; Weiner 1978; Pye 1979; Katzenstein 1979; and Gellner 1983).

This revised modernization thesis would account well for the emergence of the Popular Front movements in the Baltic states in 1988 and 1989. Estonia, Latvia, and Lithuania were among the most urbanized, well-educated, and materially well-off of the republics of the former Soviet Union. Because of their more modern character, Baltic nationalists were the first to establish independence movements, doing so just as soon as Moscow showed signs of weakness and vacillation in response to sporadic protests.

The problem, of course, is that the revised modernization thesis cannot account for the many historical manifestations of nationalism and for the pervasiveness of ethnic conflict in some of the less-modern regions of Europe and Asia. Predictions about the rise of nationalism cannot be found in a straightforward correlation between modernization and the intensity or salience of ethnic identities; yet processes such as urbanization and education are surely relevant to the politicization of ethnicity.

Cultural Pluralism

The cultural pluralist perspective is important because it recognizes that ethnic conflict arises when groups with mutually incompatible traits (including, for example, distinct value structures and contrasting social structures) attempt to coexist in a single society (Furnival 1948; Smith 1965). Groups form closed sociocultural units. Yet because they share a single territory, they must interact intermittently in shared markets and in a shared central political system. Within the shared political and economic spheres, one group may come to dominate all others. When distinct institutional systems come together—when values and modes of behavior appear to be incompatible—the tendency is for the dominant group to force the assimilation of the subordinate groups into the dominant culture. Because groups tend to come together with unequal resources, there is little incentive for the more powerful group to accommodate the subordinate groups. Power inequality, accompanied by forced assimilation, may ultimately lead to resistance on the part of the subordinate groups. The cultural pluralist approach highlights a number of dimensions that play a role in the development of ethnic-based politics, including the amount of differentiation between groups, the distance between their beliefs and day-to-day rituals, and the historical legacy associated with the manner in which two cultures first come into contact.

An application of this argument would be the attempted Russification of the non-Russian peoples of the USSR. The USSR was constitutionally a multinational, federal political system, in which each constituent subunit (for our purposes, the fifteen republics) was ethnically based. Although each of the titular nationalities had its own union structures of administration and varying degrees of cultural and linguistic autonomy, the long-term Soviet goal was the assimilation of all Soviet citizens into a more unified culture that was clearly dominated by the Russians. The non-Russians were threatened by Russian language requirements and religious repression, and, although under severe constraints, resisted to try to save their separate cultures and ethnic identities.

The problem with this perspective is that it does not explain why groups that are quite similar on a variety of historical, linguistic, and religious dimensions are no more successful in finding peaceful solutions to their differences than are groups that are wholly differentiated. Nationalism can arise where differentiation between groups is small as easily as it can rise when groups differ more visibly in terms of language, religion, or other important characteristics.

An example of the impact of rising nationalism upon historically and culturally similar nations is the declaration of independence by Ukraine at the end of 1991. In the aftermath of the failed August 1991 coup against Mikhail Gorbachev, Moscow was clearly amenable to renegotiating the character of Ukraine's participation in a restructured Soviet state. However, Ukrainian leaders were unwilling to discuss a new power-sharing arrangement with the Russian Federation. Rather, Ukrainians used the opportunity of a weakened Soviet state to distance themselves from their Russian "brothers."

Ukraine has a history of struggle with Russian forces. It tried to escape Russian control during the Civil War following the 1917 revolution and was reattached to Russia in 1920 only after two years of bitter fighting. Armed nationalist resistance continued during the inter-war years when Western Ukraine became a part of Poland, as well as during the war when a Ukrainian division joined the Germany army's thrust deep into the Russian heartland. All this happened despite the facts that, in many ways the Ukrainians are similar to Russians and the Ukrainians had closer ties with the Russians than did most other minority nationalities within the

USSR. Large portions of the Ukrainian population have historically been characterized as "well Russified"—at least those living in major cities—and have been adequately represented in the upper ranks of the CPSU and the government. In addition, a sizable Russian population resides within the republic. Nonetheless, in December of 1991, when Ukraine held a vote on the independence question, 90.3 percent of those voting voted yes.

Relative Group Worth

The relative group worth perspective attempts to address the question of why national identities are, at times, held so intensely and why group differences appear to be so immutable. According to this perspective, ethnic groups are to be understood as extended kinship clusters, and thus, the ethnic group fulfills functions similar to those filled by family ties and obligations (Horowitz 1985). When the "worth" of a group is low as a result of unflattering comparisons, or when group status is threatened through government policies (such as the policy of Russification) or societal change, ethnic ties become a natural base for political organization. Assertions of group separateness facilitate group solidarity and the preservation of group worth. Thus, movements of national separatism tend to emphasize those characteristics—such as language—that make the group distinctive.

The approach makes an important contribution to existing theory because it allows for group status to be evaluated in both symbolic and material terms. A subordinate group may achieve economic success, but may still feel deprived because of a lack of adequate political power. The approach recognizes that control of state structures conveys the ultimate in group power and prestige. By focusing on the psychological aspects associated with the preservation of group status, and the human needs fulfilled through the security of brotherhood, the emotive power of ethnic affiliations can be better appreciated. The most important aspect of ethnicity is that it provides a sense of familiarity, community, and emotional support for the members of a group. Such identities are likely to play an especially powerful psychological role during periods of cognitive uncertainty, such as is the case when a society undergoes a major transformation. The ethnic tie provides a sense of security during the transition period.

The problem with the perspective is that it predicts the greatest levels of hostility on the part of those whose group bears the greatest burden of negative or invidious comparisons. The lower the position of the group, the stronger the desire to break the shackles of oppression. In fact, however, the most oppressed groups may have few of the human and material resources necessary to challenge the state. In addition, relative group status as a motivation behind political mobilization must be evaluated in the context of the policies and strategies undertaken by the central state apparatus and by the groups operating within the territory of state authority—such strategies will serve to define the alternatives and options available to all competing parties.

The relative group worth and cultural pluralist perspectives are a part of a broader category of explanations for the salience of ethnicity that has been labeled primordialist. For the primordialists, ethnic identity fulfills the basic human need to feel worthy. By identifying with a group that is deemed worthy, an individual can gratify his or her own need for esteem. However, while primordialist explanations seem useful in explaining the existence and/or strength of ethnic identity, they offer less assistance in understanding the mobilization of some ethnic identifiers into nationalist movements. Scholars studying ethnic-based political action now often grant that the observed behavior reflects a combination of primordialist orientations and what has been termed instrumentalist motivations (Brass 1991). According to instrumentalists, the flames of ethnic passion are fanned by political leaders who employ ethnic-based symbols in pursuit of their own power or materially oriented goals. Ethnic identities are no more intractable than any other social identity, but ethnicity, because of its symbolic aspects, is readily available for manipulation by elites.

Rational Choice

The rational choice approach provides a mechanism for merging theoretically the primordialist and the instrumentalist perspectives. According to the rational choice approach, individuals make choices on the basis of calculations about the costs and the benefits of their behavior. Individuals will take part in collective actions, such as joining a political movement, only when the benefits to the individual derived from such activity outweigh the costs. As an example of the application of the rational choice perspective, the nationalist mobilization that took place in the Soviet Union in the period from 1988 to 1991 can be explained by reference to a set of incentives that were provided to citizens as a by-product (Hardin 1982) of their participation in the movements for republican independence. Among these by-products were a sense of solidarity, a chance to address perceived social injustices, and the opportunity to participate in a great historical event. Most outside observers were rather skeptical about the probability of success for the popular front movements when they first took up the demand for fully independent states, but the people were "rationally" motivated to participate in these collective action endeavors. Their commitment grew in strength with mounting evidence that the popular movements did indeed have a very high probability of victory.

The achievement of independence by the Baltic states represents the successful provision of a public good for those citizens who supported national separatism in those republics (Motyl 1990). Independence, once provided, is analogous to a collective good because it is characterized by jointness of supply and the impossibility of exclusion. That is, once the goal of independence was achieved, the benefits entailed (as well as the costs associated with independent statehood) came to be shared by all citizens in the republic. The goal of independence, therefore, could only become a movement for independence when a core of participants decided that the benefits of actively supporting the call for independence exceeded the costs.

Thus, the rational choice perspective is useful for understanding political behavior in divided societies not because it posits that political actors are rational beings, but because it brings attention to the fact that in order for an ethnic-based political organization to be successful, it must develop an incentive program and must build a perception of viability for the nationalist party or association (Meadwell 1989). Once the organization begins to coalesce, it must offer rewards for participation that override the negative consequences (such as sanctions imposed by central authorities) associated with support (Motyl 1990). The rational choice perspective, however, does not explain why ethnic identities and nationalist aspirations first arise; rather the approach focuses on clarifying the dynamics of collective action among populations that are already conscious of their national identities.

NATIONAL SEPARATISM AND THE DEMISE OF THE SOVIET STATE

The above theoretical overview highlights the importance of ethnicity in politics. It leads into the question of minority empowerment—an issue that provided the justification for demands for independence that emanated from several republics of the USSR in the late 1980s, in 1990, and in 1991. These movements for independence provide examples of a category of nationalism called national separatism—defined as ideas or actions that promote the establishment of a new, territorially based state structure. The new state is expected to promote the interests of an ethnic community that perceives that its needs have not been adequately addressed through existing state structures.

National separatist movements are widespread throughout the world. With diverse locations and historical contexts come diverse characteristics, which make analyzing these movements quite difficult. Yet, an understanding of ethnically based political participation and political organization must be incorporated into a general study of regime transformation and/or democratization. The demise of the Soviet Union can be attributed in large part to mobilized anti-state collective action on the part of national groups, and yet the focus of many scholars has not been on citizen action, but rather on the weakness of the internal core of the Union. These analysts marvel at the rottenness of the central core, exposed by the cracking of the external shell. The concentration has been on the center's inability to control the periphery with methods that had previously been proven effective. In their focus on the decay of the center, activities in the periphery have received short shrift. And yet it was a tug of war between the center and the periphery, culminating in the victory of republican-based nationalisms, that accounts for the emergence of new states from the remnants of the Soviet empire.

In this section, therefore, we will concentrate on studying the role that nationalism played in the rise of democratic movements in the Soviet Union and the resulting demise of the USSR. The framework to be employed is the rational choice perspective. This perspective highlights the fact that a variety of incentives were operating in the late Gorbachev era that led many individuals in the Baltic republics,

Georgia, Byelorussia, Azerbaidzhan, and parts of Ukraine to make the choice to support national separatism in their republics. By interpreting the concept of incentives rather broadly, and also by making reference to the development of conventions (new routines for behavior), we can provide explanations for why anti-state collective action was successful in the Soviet context.

In 1987 and 1988, citizens of the Baltic Republics held several mass rallies and demonstrations that openly questioned the legitimacy of Soviet rule, and these were not suppressed by the Soviet police. The successes of these early demonstrations contributed to a perception that Moscow would not proceed with the use of force, and would not employ its formidable coercive tools to smash the rising challenges to Soviet authority. Since there was no punitive response from the Kremlin, nationalist leaders found it relatively easy to convince others that the open expression of grievances was physically safe. Among those who took part, a convention of participation in anti-state demonstrations began to develop.

The role of open and relatively uncensored electronic and printed media became a critical second factor in mobilizing support for the independence movements. Through the open media, individual citizens were given access to images of nationalist success. Success compounded itself as it was communicated to the people. Pictures of hundreds of thousands of nationalists filling the streets, together with a lack of a violent response from the authorities, provided an incentive to participate—a desire to be a part of a great historical transformation. Public opinion polls, regularly published in the press, provided evidence that alienation from the regime was widespread.

These behavioral changes and emotive forces, however, could not have coalesced into a successful movement without the emergence of a national leadership and the development of organizational structures. Ironically, the organizational framework of the Communist party provided structural support for the nationalist movements as many Communists either gave up their party membership or became simultaneously members of both the Communist party and the nationalistic Popular Fronts that had begun to develop in the Baltics. In some cases, the former party members became leaders of the Popular Front movements. Nationalist movements in the Baltic republics were able to absorb elites from the state and party structures, as well as recruit members of the national intelligentsia who had been discriminated against as a result of policies of Russification. (The 1992 presidential contest in Lithuania represented competition between these two leadership strands—Landsbergis as a nationalist who arose from within the Lithuanian intelligentsia, and Brazauskas as a nationalist who had served as the Communist Party leader in Lithuania.) Thanks to a few early successes, such as the proliferation of republic-level laws privileging local languages in 1989, these new national leaders began to acquire legitimacy. By providing positive examples that could be followed, and by making personal sacrifices in support of the cause, the leaders themselves contributed to the strength of the movement.

The church as well had historically provided a base for resistance to Soviet domination, and church buildings became a convenient meeting place and site for political discussions. In Lithuania, for example, the Catholic religion provided a common thread of group identity and solidarity, together with an institutional focus. It had played the same role earlier in Poland. In Ukraine, the legalization of the Ukrainian Catholic Church provided a powerful symbol of freedom for the Ukrainian people. Western Ukrainians have made the charge that easterners are less nationalistic, in part because of their adherence to a Russian-style Orthodox Church, rather than Catholicism. Thus, cooperation with regime sponsored institutions, including adherence to the Russian Orthodox faith, came to be interpreted as anti-Ukrainian. Negative social pressures added costs to any lingering orientations toward support of Soviet institutions.

The language issue also became a powerful symbol underlying the cause of national separatism. The Lithuanian language, for example, although not recognized as an official state language until 1989, could be heard throughout the republic even during the height of the Stalinist era (Venclova 1991). With the decline of Soviet repression in the late 1980s, national flags came to be displayed prominently, songs representing cultural continuity with pre-Soviet culture were broadcast regularly, and holidays and public ceremonies were used to commemorate events important to each nation's history.

The Baltic peoples have been especially apprehensive about the effects of Russian domination on their national cultures. In Estonia and Latvia, fears about national survival stemmed from the massive in-migration of Russians. In the last Soviet census (1989), 52 percent of the population of Latvia were ethnic Latvian, while 34 percent were Russians. The comparable figures for Estonia were 61.5 percent Estonian and 30 percent Russian.

Language, religion, culture, and even concerns over environmental degradation became unifying forces and provided symbols for the mobilization of the people. In many republics there was widespread concern about ecological damage, and the nationalist leaderships were readily inclined to tie the environmental destruction of their homelands to Russian hegemony.

As the national front movements gained strength, they could offer more specific incentives for support. They could offer the possibility of land grants and voting rights to future citizens in exchange for an oath of support. The nationalists of Estonia provided a potent example: anti-draft laws were adopted giving young men a legal foundation for refusing service in the Soviet Army, other laws were passed requiring public sector employees to speak the Estonian tongue, payments were offered to non-Estonians who would vacate their homes and relocate to elsewhere within the USSR, and suffrage was limited to those who met language or strict residency requirements. Such laws discouraged the continued presence of non-natives who were perceived as a bloc of potential opposition to the Estonian national cause.

Nonetheless, it was not until the nationalists could demonstrate relative self-sufficiency by promising a viable state upon the achievement of independence that the movements came to be taken seriously by the more risk-adverse residents of the republics and by the members of the international community. The problem with developing self-sufficiency rested with overcoming the hegemony of the overarching Soviet state, and promoting the full diversification of the republican economy, either by internal differentiation or by trading internationally (Meadwell 1989). Economic specialization, such as the near-full reliance of the Uzbek economy on capital from the cotton-growing industry, can serve as a constraint on the development of self-sufficiency. In Central Asia, income and wealth levels were low. People living on the margin of subsistence tend to be risk averse and desire stability and security. Such orientations may operate as obstacles to the promotion of group mobilization.

The Baltic states, in contrast, could point to their recent, inter-war period of independence and argue that this period demonstrated their potential for self-sufficiency. Their more immediate experience with independent status made the idea of independence less inconceivable than it was for the Central Asians. In addition, the proximity of the Baltic states to the West contributed to the belief that Estonia, Latvia, and Lithuania would be able to enter the world trading system. Indeed, there was a widespread belief among the Baltic peoples that their underdevelopment in comparison to the West was directly attributable to their involvement in the Soviet system. They believed that a break with the Union would bring an improved standard of living.

A reference to state viability and the use of selective incentives also provides an explanation of why economic stagnation had such a devastating impact on the power of the Kremlin. The center lost resources that it had used to "buy" the support of the *apparatchiki* (the communist party and state bureaucrats), the military, and the internal security administration (Motyl 1990). The government was perceived to have lost the capacity to force compliance, either through monetary rewards or through the threat of punishment. The state's power decreased with prolonged economic decline, rapid social change, failed policies, corruption, and incompetence on the part of the leaders. In contrast, the republics increased their resources and their relative power through social development, economic growth, and organized political activity. With decentralization, republics were forced to become more self-sufficient and were encouraged to advance the interests of their region.

THE ETHNIC FACTOR IN POLITICAL DEVELOPMENT

National separatism contributed directly to the breakup of the Soviet Union, Yugoslavia, and Czechoslovakia. The question that remains is whether these same nationalist orientations will eventually lead to the destruction of the fragile democracies that exist in the new states that rose from the rubble of the Soviet empire. The study of ethnic identities needs to be included in an evaluation of the possibilities and pitfalls associated with the consolidation of democracy. To achieve a stable, democratic regime, the state must develop strategies for conflict management, or more idealistically, conflict resolution. How can ethnic competition best be managed (resolved) within the structures of a democratic state? What decision rules and institutions should a society adopt in the hope of reducing rather than enhancing ethnic conflict? If democracy is the end goal of the transitional regimes of Eastern and Central Europe and Eurasia, how can democracy be structured so that it has the best possible chance for survival in these multi-ethnic and often deeply divided societies?

Despite the fact that the achievement of political stability is to a large degree dependent upon the nature of the divisions within a society, many scholars have neglected to incorporate ethnicity systematically into the study of political change. Several reasons have been put forward for the omission of the ethnic factor.[5] One such reason is the unwarranted exaggeration by western scholars of the influence of materialism in human affairs. The assumption has often been that the wellsprings of ethnic discord are in fact economic, and that an ethnic minority can be placated if its standard of living is improved. Another reason has been the unquestioned assumption that greater contacts among ethnic groups will lead to a greater awareness of what groups have in common, rather than what makes them different. Related to this is the optimistic belief that increased ties between groups lead to more harmonious relations and eventually to assimilation. A third reason for the neglect of ethnicity is that political scientists tend to study states rather than regions within states. The focus has been primarily on identifying statewide political cultures, with little recognition of separate political cultures for ethnic minorities.

Most observers now agree that ethnonationalism and national separatism are serious threats to stability in those Eastern and Central European and Eurasian states attempting a transition to democracy. The psychological and emotional hold of ethnicity can no longer be ignored. If we accept the premise that ethnic identity is a natural basis for political organization and that nationalism as an ideology has proved its functional power through history, then any theory of democracy must incorporate contingencies for the resolution of ethnic conflict. Most states in the international system are composed of more than one major ethnic group, and within these states, each ethnicity may well demand the right of self-government. Unfortunately, however, the difference between the promotion of one group's rights and the violation of the rights of another group tend to be slim. Consider the resolution adopted by the Latvian parliament (October 1991) that outlined principles for a future law on citizenship. The criteria for naturalization included knowledge of Latvian and residence of at least sixteen years in Latvia. Thus, anyone who did not speak Latvian and who had not lived in Latvia for sixteen years would not be able to become a citizen. In practice, this meant that close to half of all the residents in the country would be denied citizenship. Under such conditions of competition for the constitutional protection and enhancement of group rights, the consequences of each policy and legal-normative choice must be carefully considered.

This example of Latvian citizenship restrictions demonstrates that the positions adopted by political leaders are just as often divisive as they are conciliatory. Political leaders in their efforts to mobilize people for mass action can be quite adept at making blatant appeals to a group's belief in its common heritage and descent. Democracy implies competitive elections and ethnicity provides a convenient core of symbols upon which to mobilize supporters for the competition. Only if such proclivities are limited will the prospects for accommodation and compromise among competing ethnic groups be enhanced. Politicians can either contribute to or work against the rise of ethnic conflict. If candidates for public office draw upon the cultural forms, values, and practices of an ethnic group in their competition for political power and economic advantage, they contribute to the development of ethnic consciousness (Brass 1991). If, however, political leaders seek to promote cooperation and collaboration with state authorities and with the leaders of other ethnic categories, then differences across groups can be minimized.

Our evaluation of the rise of national separatism in the Soviet Union, however, has already revealed that ethnic-based political participation is more than just manipulation of the masses by their leaders. The beliefs held by the people do place constraints on the activities of elites. Leaders cannot move too far afield from the mood of the people or the people will quickly find new leaders more to their liking. Leaders are compelled to respond to the demands of their constituency. Leaders ride the waves of mass opinion.

Ample evidence is now available showing that loyalty to an ethnic group does not disappear even if an individual is also loyal to a multi-ethnic state. In the Soviet context, research has confirmed that national groups living within their own homeland are particularly hostile to non-natives who have migrated into native territory. Hostilities often arise when one group perceives that the sanctity of its own homeland is being infringed upon by ethnic strangers (Horowitz 1985). The notion of a homeland is intimately associated with the myth of an ancestrally related people. Indigenous people living in their own homelands manifest greater resistance to accultural assimilation than do those who have left their homelands to become immigrants in a new territory (Connor 1987, 209).

The newly established Russian Federation is an example of a highly heterogeneous state, with a multitude of ethnic groups living in traditional homelands. These ethnically based political units had a degree of formal autonomy under the Soviet government. Thus, recognition by the new Russian state of the rights of minorities to self-determination (i.e., home rule) has become a strategic necessity in Moscow's effort to hold the new Russian Federation together. With the demise of the Soviet Union, several national republics located within Russia declared their intention to govern themselves. On August 30, 1990, a year before Gorbachev resigned as General Secretary of the Communist Party, the Supreme Soviet of the Tatar autonomous republic (located within the territory of Russia) passed a declaration of sovereignty and on March 21, 1992 the residents of Tatarstan participated in a referendum and voted in favor of establishing Tatarstan as a sovereign state, by a margin of 61 to 37 percent.[6] With the resource of popular support in hand, the leadership of Tatarstan successfully sidestepped the signing of the Russian Federation treaty (March 29, 1992) and chose rather to negotiate bilaterally with Moscow regarding such issues as autonomy, control over natural resources, and economic arrangements.

Regional autonomy may take some pressure off the center, but will not necessarily reduce ethnic tensions in the local areas. The referendum of sovereignty for

Tatarstan passed by large margins in ethnic Tatar areas, but passed by much smaller margins in the cities where most Russians live. In the five districts where Russians form a majority, and in the capital, Kazan, the referendum was defeated. Tatars account for just 49 percent of the peoples living within Tatarstan; 43 percent are Russian, with the remainder coming from other regional populations. Although a significant number of Russians voted in favor of sovereignty for Tatarstan, the upsurge of Tatar nationalism has been resisted by *Soglasie*, a multi-ethnic but mostly Russian group, and by the Democratic Party of Russia, both of which campaigned for a "no" vote in the March referendum. Those opposing the referendum claimed that visions of future wealth for Tatarstan are unrealistic and that the region has received more from Russia than it has given.

As has previously been the case in other declarations of sovereignty or independence, the Tatar leadership asserted that the region had been exploited by Moscow, and that greater local autonomy and control over resources would serve to check these "colonialist" tendencies. Although the Russian Federation constitution was not approved in December of 1993 in Tatarstan, on 3 February, 1994 a bilateral power-sharing agreement with Moscow was signed that committed Tatarstan to participation in the Federation in exchange for a high degree of economic autonomy.

Chechnya, in contrast, has not yet been able to resolve its differences with Moscow. The Chechens have not signed the Federal Treaty and have not participated in recent Russian Federation elections. Fighting in the region has been endemic since late 1991 when President Dudaev declared his region fully independent from Moscow. During 1994 opposition forces within Chechnya, backed by Russian forces, were engaged in a civil war against forces loyal to Dudaev. Beginning in December 1994, the Russian army became more directly involved with an assault on the Chechen capital city of Grozny. The situation in the region is complicated by unsettled border issues and by refugees and armed mercenaries from contiguous conflicts—most notably Abkhazian and Ingush refugees and infiltrators. The Chechen Republic is more ethnically homogenous than is Tatarstan, and it could more practically achieve separate statehood as it shares an external border with Georgia.

A variety of roads can be followed in rearranging the political, economic, and social relations between the Russian center and these national regions, but in all cases the driving principle from the perspective of the regional players will be self-determination and the protection of minority rights. If violence is to be avoided in the future, minority populations must have guarantees that their interests will be protected in areas such as language and school curriculum, the distribution of resources, and the opening of employment opportunities in the private and public sectors. They should have a secure expectation of fair treatment under the law. Repression, restricting the activities of minorities, and forced integration ultimately have only negative consequences.

Russia is but one of the new countries emerging from the breakup of the USSR. Each of the fourteen other new non-Russian independent states must also make decisions on the basic treatment it will give to the Russians and other minorities who reside within its territory. The fate of the Russians is crucial, given the widespread dispersion of Russians throughout the former USSR, and the possibility that mistreatment of these people could invoke political, military, or economic retaliation from Russia (see Chapter 9). The most explosive example of the predicaments faced by Russians living in what has suddenly become non-Russian territory is the bloody conflict in the trans-Dniester region. Here Russians are fighting to maintain their preeminence within a military-industrial enclave located within Moldova. Other examples of potentially explosive situations abound, including the Russians living in both the Crimea, part of the Ukraine only since 1954, and in Central Asian republics where anti-Russian sentiment, although not overtly violent, remains strong. Nonetheless, a December 1994 public opinion poll conducted in Kazakhstan and Estonia indicated that Russians living in the "near abroad" consider changing economic circumstances (i.e., low living standards) to be a much worse problem than ethnic discrimination. Many Russian respondents reported that they had never had any problems with the local populations (Mihalka 1995).

Indeed, ethnic tensions do not necessarily lead to violence. Groups are not inevitably separated by permanent cultural boundaries. Ethnicity, although prevalent and powerful, is by no means invariant. For different groups in different situational contexts, national identities can be more or less salient in comparison to other forms of group identity. And even within any ethnic category at one specific time, great variation exists among individuals in their levels of nationalist passion. In Eastern Europe and Eurasia generational differences are currently apparent, with the younger people being more eager to assert their national identity and the older people displaying more "internationalist sentiments."

In some cases, nationalist fervor can be found to be lacking in exactly those areas where it is most expected. The fact that Ukrainian nationalists had a more difficult time mobilizing mass support for independence than did the Baltic independence leaders can be accounted for by a variety of factors, including Stalin's assertions of Ukrainian collaboration with the Germans, which provided a rationale for the ruthless elimination of Ukrainian nationalists during the 1940s and 1950s, the persecution of Ukrainian nationalists in the late 1960s and early 1970s (Beissinger 1988, 74) and the conservatism of Volodymyr Shcherbitsky, Communist Party leader of the Ukraine during the 1970s and 1980s (Nahaylo 1991, 110–1). Another contributing factor is the assimilation of many Ukrainians to Russian language, religion, and identity. In addition, Sysyn argues that the Ukrainian nation was incompletely formed prior to its incorporation into the USSR: "Ukraine at the turn of the century was merely a geographical notion, amorphous in its limits and not widely acknowledged by those who did not adhere to the Ukrainian national movement" (1991, 853). Consequently, the level of Ukrainian national consciousness has been uneven.

The relatively recent revival of interest in Cossack history has provided a focus for Ukrainian national self-identification. The attention to the Cossack *Sich* has emphasized the Cossacks' role as representatives of Ukrainian statehood. The Ukrainian Popular Front (*Rukh*) drew on this symbolism by embracing a proposal to celebrate the 500th anniversary of the Zaporozhian Cossacks. Once local elections brought Ukrainian nationalists to power, the rediscovery of Ukrainian history proceeded at full speed. Thus we see a stalled, but revived, development of Ukrainian national consciousness.

Similarly, when the Uzbek SSR was created in 1925, the process of national consolidation had hardly begun. When nepotism and corruption in Central Asia became the target of Moscow's wrath, the Uzbeks' resentment of Russian encroachment produced strong nationalist reactions. Uzbek nationalism, relatively latent after the brutal repression of armed rebellions against Soviet rule, suddenly awakened with the arrest of Uzbek officials accused of corruption in the cotton industry (Carlisle 1991, 34–5).

STRATEGIES FOR ACCOMMODATING ETHNICITY THROUGH DEMOCRATIC STRUCTURES AND PROCEDURES

Unfortunately for the stability of the states of the former Soviet Union and Eastern and Central Europe, ethnic mobilization is now a given. This heightened consciousness of ethnic affiliations is unlikely to fade away for some time. Thus, we return to the question of how to accommodate the demands of politically mobilized ethnic constituencies through democratic processes. Governments must adopt policies and institutional mechanisms to deal with ethnic-based demands.

Arent Lijphart (1977) has described certain institutions that together may make stable democracy possible within a multi-ethnic state: a multi-party system, a multi-party cabinet, proportional representation, political decentralization, and official rights for minority groups. To make these institutions effective, the ruling coalition and the government administration must include representatives from all significant communities, all communities must have the right to veto decisions affecting their interests, and each ethnicity must have the freedom to run its own affairs. These structural and institutional features will only work if supported by certain conditions within the broader society: a balance of power among groups, small size of the polity, patriotic feelings or a common religion, and a "tradition of cooperation."[7] He labels a polity that meets these conditions a "consociational democracy." This is a stringent list of conditions, and one that seems to exclude Russia and most other post-communist states.

The idea of consociational democracy was put forward by Lijphart as a means for accommodating the interests of the segmented cultures within a divided society. But the idea was developed to analyze the politics of established Western European systems, most notably the Netherlands, whose divisions fell along religious and to some extent linguistic lines. The Netherlands has never been characterized by the profound cleavages that separate the peoples of the former Soviet Union. Even though most of the multi-ethnic states of Eastern and Central Europe and Eurasia share the goal of a stable democracy, many of these states also share a near vacuum of the basic conditions necessary for success—most notably they lack a tradition of cooperation. Beissinger (1991) argues that a consociational approach is unlikely to work in the USSR because of the numerical imbalance of ethnic groups, the huge size of the territory, the lack of political parties representing the major segments of society, and the relative intermixing of the various groups. In addition, the consociational solution, focusing upon elite negotiation, tends to ignore the role of the ordinary citizen, and does not address the possibility that one or another cultural group may lack elite representation at the center.

Given these reservations about the applicability of the full consociational solution, the most basic structural technique available for providing a degree of self-determination to regionally based ethnic groups appears to be the building of a federal system that involves the devolution of real decision-making authority to ethno-regional territories.[8] The decentralization of political power may allow for the satisfaction of ethnic demands within the existing framework of the political system. If the people find that their needs are being met at the subnational level they control, they may have no rationale and motivation for national separatism. Although a substantial devolution of authority to ethnoterritorial administrative units is characterized by a certain amount of risk from the perspective of the center, it remains a powerful tool for the accommodation of ethnic interests emanating from a regionally based minority.

The Polish minority living within Lithuania provides an example of where violent conflict has been avoided through the creation of an autonomous national-territorial region. The Poles and the Lithuanians have a long history of interaction, and during the nineteenth century the Poles operated as an urbanized elite in a largely agrarian Lithuanian society.[9] Poles tended to see themselves as representing a more advanced culture, and after World War I the capital city of Vilnius (and surrounding regions) was incorporated into Poland. After World War II, Vilnius came under Soviet rule as a part of the republic of Lithuania. Poles now constitute approximately 8 percent of the population of Lithuania and are concentrated in Vilnius and three other regions.

The passage of the January 1989 language law—which mandated the use within two years of the Lithuanian language in official, business, educational, and social spheres of life—provided a catalyst for the organization of Poles in what they saw as self-defense against overbearing Lithuanian nationalism. Spokespersons associated with the Lithuanian Popular Front responded by saying that they would guarantee Polish national rights, but that they rejected ideas of regional autonomy. In September 1989, the soviets (local councils) of the Vilnius and Salcininkai regions declared their domains to be Polish national-territorial regions. Two weeks later, the Lithuanian Supreme Soviet declared the decision unconstitutional and invalid. In October of 1990, after Lithuania's March 1990 declaration of independence, Polish leaders proclaimed the formation of a Polish National Territorial District within Lithuania, encompassing five southeastern regions.

In early 1991, the Lithuanian nationalists took a number of steps to accommodate the interests of the Polish minority. The 1989 language law was amended to allow for the equal use of minority languages in areas where non-Lithuanian speakers comprised a majority. The state obligated itself to aid cultural organizations of ethnic minorities, it guaranteed the right to education in native languages, and work was begun on drafting plans in which the Salcininkai and Vilnius regions would have some degree of autonomous administration.

Concessions to local demands for political influence may be a necessary condition, but not the only adaptation required for the consolidation of democratic institutions. Thus, in addition to building federal structures, each new regime must formulate a program for managing and resolving ethnic conflict. Part of this program will include policies to be implemented or legislation to be passed that involves the sharing of power and resources within the system. Ways must be found to guarantee minorities access to political influence. For example, each ethnicity must have the chance to build its own associations and these organizations must have an opportunity for influence in the system. Unfettered participation in organizations—pluralism—is one of the precepts of democracy. Especially at the regional level, all major groups should have some associational representation and government leaders must be accountable to local organizations.

This analysis suggests that a substantial dispersion of political power is a necessary, but not sufficient, measure to reassure frightened ethnic minorities. Such dispersion can take many forms: from national to regional governments, from executives to legislatures, and from governments to ethnic associations. In the former communist states, however, power had only reluctantly and, in most cases, haphazardly, been devolved to regional and/or representative institutions. For now, the executive branch in Russia, although weak by international standards, is much more powerful than the legislative branch. In addition, with the adoption of the new Russian Federation constitution in December of 1993, the chaotic drift of authority from Moscow to the regions has been halted. Until a party system develops, together with multiple associations for representing social, economic, ethnic and regional interests, the executive is likely to retain a monopoly of power.

Elected representatives within legislative bodies, as well as elected executives, have a tendency to enact laws that guard their own power. We know from experience that social welfare programs for the underprivileged and other altruistic pieces of legislation that promote the interests of minorities are also passed by legislators. But tendencies toward the promulgation of discriminatory legislation and tendencies toward the neglect of minority interests are better held in check when the legislative and executive branches contain representatives with real political power from each ethnicity within a society. How can such representatives be brought into the decision-making arena?

The structure of the electoral system is critical for the fair representation of ethnic-based interests. Elections provide an important forum within which groups organize. They provide the prizes for the most effective political associations and leaders. The critical challenge becomes how to structure the multiple aspects of the electoral process so that the multiple interests of the society will be adequately represented.

Rational choice has not only tackled the problem of collective action in the form of nationalist movements (Meadwell 1989; Motyl 1990), but has also addressed the challenge of determining a fair decision-rule for society (Mueller 1979). Arguments have been made that group preferences cannot be aggregated, without the possibility of incongruence between group and societal preferences, unless the groups have some overlapping interests. With wholly separated ethnic communities, however, the areas in which interests overlap may be dangerously limited. The rule of law and the protection of minority interests becomes especially critical when majority rule is accepted as the unquestioned principle at the base of democracy. Ethnic tensions may be reduced if minorities perceive that a credible court system exists to enforce equal treatment rules (nondiscrimination) or affirmative action programs (attempts to address the inequalities already inherent in the system).

According to an argument offered by Linz and Stepan (1992), elections can heighten or reduce the political relevance of ethnicity. These authors claim that founding elections (the first elections held within a new state) are particularly crucial, and to reduce the salience of ethnicity, statewide elections should be held prior to local or regional elections. Of course, the relationship between elections and the salience of ethnic identity is more multifaceted than this analysis suggests. Nationalists often organize and press their demands on the state outside of the framework of any electoral contest. In the case of the Baltic states, the Popular Fronts had held their founding congresses prior to the passage of the new electoral laws that opened up competition for delegates to the USSR Congress of Peoples Deputies and later to the republic-level Supreme Soviets. Given the openness of glasnost and the alleged weakness of Moscow, the platforms of the Popular Fronts would have evolved and their movements would have grown in strength even without the prospect of elections on the horizon.

Donald Horowitz provides other suggestions on ways that electoral systems can be structured to reduce ethnic conflict. Unfortunately, the task is not an easy one. "Societies that are deeply riven along a preponderant ethnic cleavage . . . tend to throw up party systems that exacerbate ethnic conflict" (Horowitz 1985, 291). Where ethnic loyalties are strong, parties tend to organize along ethnic lines. It is a proclivity that is cumulative: Once one party organizes along ethnic lines, others are inclined to follow suit (Horowitz 1985, 293–306). The problem is that once this occurs, the results of elections, in terms of each party's share of the vote, correspond very closely to the ethnic demography of the population.

Under such circumstances, the choice between some variant of majoritarian versus proportional voting systems becomes critical. Overall, as has been demonstrated by Rae (1971), proportional representation voting systems tend to inflate less the strongest party's share of the seats in a legislature than do first-past-the-post electoral rules. Proportional systems can be designed with large, multi-member constituencies and no minimum percentage cutoff, so as to reduce disparity between votes and seats (Rae 1971, 151–70). The drawback of strict proportionality is that it may contribute to fragmentation of the party system—with each party drawing support from one ethnicity. Voters tend to cast their ballot for the party identified with their own ethnic group, no matter who the individual candidates happen to be (Horowitz 1985, 319–20). A majoritarian electoral system may contribute to the ideal of having a few large, broad-based, multi-ethnic parties in the sense that coalitions form at the grassroots level prior to elections.

The danger of minorities being completely left out of decision making occurs when a mere plurality of the votes for one party leads to solid majority control by that party of the legislature, plus control of all major executive and administrative offices.[10] To avoid this possibility, the ethnic composition of the legislature may be prescribed by law and certain offices within the executive branch may be reserved for named ethnic groups. For reserved seats, there is still competition, but the competition is restricted to members of the same group (Horowitz 1985, 633–4). An option that requires cooperation across ethnic groups is to institute a presidential election formula where, to be elected president, the candidate must win a plurality of the vote unionwide, plus at least 25 percent of the vote in no fewer than two-thirds of the autonomous regions.[11] The expectation is that such a formula would produce candidates, and hopefully political parties, with multi-ethnic support; otherwise it would be impossible for a presidential candidate to be elected (Horowitz 1985, 636). Another electoral tool that has been used to secure inter-ethnic cooperation and communication is the requirement that voters list second and third preferences for each office. Whenever there are three candidates, voters must indicate their second choice; and when there are more than three candidates, second and third choices must be stated. Thus bargains can be struck across ethnic parties and negotiation over second- and third-preference votes will occur (Horowitz 1985, 639–40). James Coleman (1992) suggests that voting rules should incorporate a compensation principle, that is, compensation is made to the minority group members whenever policies are adopted that would make those who oppose the policy worse off.

The above list only touches the surface of the many possible ways in which electoral rules can be adjusted in an effort to reduce conflict and enhance cooperation in divided societies. Decisions made about voting rules must be considered just as carefully as decisions made about federal structures and the devolution of authority to autonomous regions. Elections must certainly be held regularly, and thus the referenda held in 1995 that extended the presidential terms of Central Asian leaders, including the presidents of Turkmenistan and Kazakhstan, may not be conducive to the representation of diverse or regionally based interests.

A case can also be made for going beyond structural solutions and moving into the realm of investment policies and affirmative action programs in an effort to meet the concerns of ethnic minorities. In those cases where an ethnicity is not only numerically and politically weak but also underprivileged in the economic and social spheres, preferential treatment policies may be necessary to raise the economic status and well-being of a group so that they are better equipped with the resources needed to compete with the dominant group (Horowitz 1985). The Abkhazian minority living within Georgia provides a case in point. This group, comprising only 1.8 percent of the population of Georgia, claims that it has been discriminated against both economically and culturally. The Abkhaz believe that their rights have not been respected within the Georgian state (and previously as part of the Georgian SSR). By 1989 the Abkhazians were a minority even within their designated autonomous region, and the Georgians, who accounted for 46 percent of the population in the Abkhaz ASSR (Abkhazians accounted for only 18 percent), did not support more autonomy for an Abkhaz government, and they certainly did not support a secessionist movement.

The Transcaucasian region—including Georgia, Abkhazia, Armenia, and other small nations—was incorporated into the Russian Empire when the resistance of the indigenous people was finally put down in 1864. The Russian conquest led to an influx of Russians and Ukrainians to the area, and by the end of the nineteenth century, Abkhazians made up only slightly more than 53 percent of the population of Abkhazia (Otyrba 1994, 283). In 1917, as a result of the breakdown of centralized control associated with the Bolshevik seizure of power, Abkhazia, as part of a North Caucasus Federation, became temporarily independent. Eventually, in 1921, the Bolsheviks reestablished Russian control over the region, and for ten years, between 1921 and 1931, Abkhazia had the status of a soviet socialist republic within the USSR. In February of 1931, however, the status of the region was downgraded to that of autonomous republic within Georgia. Significant migrations of Georgians into the region followed, especially as a result of the deportations of the 1930s and 1940s. This resulted in the reduction of the Abkhazian portion of the population to only 18 percent. The Abkhazians tried to upgrade the status of their region during the negotiations over a new 1978 Soviet constitution, and, although this effort was unsuccessful, the Brezhnev government did make some concessions to the region in terms of affirmative action programs.

With the onset of perestroika, several prominent Abkhazians revived the effort to gain true self-governing powers for the region. In 1989, a petition was signed by thirty thousand people demanding the restoration of Abkhazia's pre-1931 sovereign status (Otyrba 1994, 286). The reaction from Georgia was very negative and ethnic clashes occurred in July 1989. During the same period, Georgian language laws were passed that further threatened the maintenance of Abkhazian culture. Negotiations, however, did result in a new formula that was used when elections were held to the Abkhazian Supreme Soviet (parliament) in 1991. The ethnic mix of the parliament was predetermined: Of 65 seats, 28 were reserved for the Abkhaz, 26 for Georgians, and 11 for other nationalities.[12] In fact, Abkhazians were overrepresented in administrative structures in their autonomous regions—to the detriment of proportional representation for Georgians, Russians, and Armenians living in the region (Slider 1991, 75). These rules, however, did not prevent the growth of national separatism, once Georgian politicians began to promote a more exclusive concept of a new Georgian state.

With the passing of laws on privatization, and given the ultranationalism displayed by Georgian leaders such as ousted President Gamsakhurdia, Abkhazians perceived that their economic security was threatened. They believed that they would have difficulty in maintaining their status and well-being. To allay these fears, they might have been provided, in addition to quotas in the political sphere, with preferential economic programs. To avoid separatism, affirmative action programs that guaranteed employment and educational opportunities to Abkhazians may have been necessary. In addition, the forced use of the Georgian language in the Abkhaz autonomous region would have to be ended in order to allay fears of cultural extinction.

But instead of making concessions in the cultural and economic spheres, as well as in the political realm, the Georgian state remained firm. With the Abkhazian majority in the Abkhaz Supreme Soviet, the Georgian minority eventually walked out. During this same period, a violent overthrow of the elected Georgian president occurred and the country moved toward civil war. When the Georgian government made its decision to reinstate the old Georgian Constitution of 1921, which did not provide for a federated structure, what was left of the Abkhazian parliament voted to reinstate the old Abkhazian constitution of 1925. This constitution provided for the secession of Abkhazia from both the USSR and the Transcaucasian Federation. This constitutional confrontation deteriorated into military confrontation in August 1992. Units of the Georgian National Guard were sent to take control of Sukhumi, the capital of Abkhazia. After months of heavy fighting, a cease-fire agreement was partially implemented, but the differences that separate the two nations remain unresolved. Indeed, by the end of 1993, Georgia had lost control of the breakaway region.

The acknowledged goal of preferential treatment programs is to help disadvantaged groups catch up or maintain themselves. Although such programs often generate resentment on the part of the better-positioned groups, social justice within a society is unlikely to be achieved without some degree of economic parity between groups. When substantial economic and social differences are superimposed upon communal differences, an argument can be made that equality of political influence cannot be achieved without adopting measures to achieve greater economic equality. Investments, subsidies, and various other developmental programs can be channeled toward the region.

The Russian Federation has come to be marked by ever-increasing regionally based disparities in economic well-being and the Yeltsin administration appears to be considering a more aggressive targeted investment strategy. The Russian Federation's most depressed areas include four ethnoterritorial republics: Adygeya, Dagestan, Mordovia, and Chuvashia. Special assistance to these areas is expected to be included in the 1996 budget of the Russian Federation Individual members of disadvantaged groups could also be given favored access to education and employment. Of course, all such preferential programs will be considered as temporary, with the ultimate aim being equal opportunity and treatment for all members of the society.

In general, economic prosperity enhances inter-ethnic cooperation. With economic scarcity, ethnic affiliations become stronger, operating as a kinship social welfare network. The tendency is to turn inward in times of trouble. Regional protectionism and discriminatory practices become especially prevalent when resources are sparse. Thus, policies that not only provide opportunities for the underprivileged, but that also promote economic growth more generally, yield an atmosphere most supportive for the development of ethnic harmony.

CONCLUSION

In conclusion, ethnic conflict may destroy post-communist states, as it has the USSR, Czechoslovakia, and Yugoslavia, and threatens to do in Russia. Failing that, it can reduce the likelihood of successful democratization. Thus, scholars and politicians must find ways to accommodate ethnic interests so that democracy can proceed. A few of the possible strategies for the reduction of ethnic-based political conflict include the generous devolution of power to ethnoregional territories, the adoption of electoral rules that encourage inter-ethnic bargaining, and the promotion of opportunities for increased prosperity among economically disadvantaged minorities. If such strategies are not adopted, then we must predict that, in ethnically divided states, the prospects for a successful consolidation of democratic rule are bleak.

Election rules and governmental programs do not create ethnic divisions and cannot make these divisions vanish once they have appeared, but political decisions do have consequences for ethnic rivalry and competition. The institutional arrangements adopted by Eastern and Central European and former Soviet countries will affect the prospects for a democratic transition. Ethnic rivalry and conflict place constraints on the development of democratic institutions, but these challenges can be reduced with the introduction of policies and procedures that are deemed to be acceptable from the standpoint of the majority while simultaneously protecting the status of minorities. Without the introduction of such procedures, these countries may disintegrate into subregions of rival ethnic camps, rather than move toward the institutionalization of democratic practices within a multi-ethnic state.

NOTES

1. Acknowledgment: The author would like to thank Robert Grey for his creative and careful suggestions on improvements for this paper. The author also gratefully acknowledges Patrick Fisher's assistance in compiling references. She is also indebted to William Reisinger, John Reitz, Donald Smith, and John Mutti for comments they offered on earlier versions of this manuscript.
2. This description of the relationship between nationalism and democracy comes from Ghia Nodia (1992).
3. Both the Mill and Acton quotations are drawn from Nodia (1992, 13).
4. For more on the definitional and structural components of secession, see Premdas (1990).
5. The reasons why ethnonationalism has previously failed to receive adequate treatment are taken directly from a discussion by Walker Connor (1987).
6. See *Report on the Tatarstan Referendum on Sovereignty,* prepared by the staff of the U.S. Commission on Security and Cooperation in Europe, April 14, 1992.

7. Nordlinger (1972) identifies additional conditions that may motivate the elite representatives of the various groups to cooperate: the united desire to fend off an external threat, a cross-cutting commercial class, an inability of one group to control political office without support from another, and the threat of serious civil strife.
8. Federal solutions do not work for addressing the needs of diaspora nationalities, such as the Jews of the former Soviet Union. The Russians and the Ukrainians in particular have had to deal simultaneously with the revival of their own culture while attempting to hold in check latent features of anti-Semitism. In part to overcome a reputation tainted by historical anti-Jewish acts, the leadership of Ukraine was the first among former republics to give diplomatic recognition to the state of Israel.
9. The primary source for the information on Lithuania Poles is *Minority Rights: Problems, Parameters and Patterns in the CSCE Context,* Commission on Security and Cooperation in Europe, Washington, D.C.
10. In creating governing coalitions minorities may, under certain conditions, not only acquire power, but disproportionate power.
11. This is the basic formula put forward by the framers of the Nigerian constitution. For a discussion of additional formulas to be used in the case of a deadlock, see Horowitz (1985), 197–201.
12. *Svobodnaya Gruziya,* August 21, 1991, cited by Slider (1991, 76).

REFERENCES

ACTON, LORD. 1948. *Essays on Freedom and Power.* Boston: Beacon Press.

BAUER, O. 1907. *Die Nationalitatenfrage und die Sozialdemokratie*. Vienna: Verlag der Wiener Volksbuchhandlung Ignaz Brand.

BEISSINGER, MARK R. 1988. "Ethnicity, the Personnel Weapon, and Neo-Imperial Integration: Ukrainian and RSFSR Provincial Party Officials Compared." *Studies in Comparative Communism* 26(1): 71–85.

_____. 1991. "The Deconstruction of the USSR and the Search for a Post-Soviet Society." *Problems of Communism* 40 (November/December): 27–35.

BENTLEY, ARTHUR F. 1967. *The Process of Government.* Cambridge: Harvard University Press.

BRASS, PAUL R. 1991. *Ethnicity and Nationalism: Theory and Comparison.* Newbury Park, Calif.: Sage.

CARLISLE, DONALD S. 1991. "Uzbekistan and the Uzbeks." *Problems of Communism* 40 (September/October): 23–44.

COLEMAN, JAMES S. 1992. "Democracy in Permanently Divided Systems." *American Behavioral Scientist* 35(4/5, March–June): 363–74.

CONNOR, WALKER. 1987. "Ethnonationalism." In Myron Weiner and Samuel Huntington, eds., *Understanding Political Development.* Boston: Little, Brown, 196–220.

FUKUYAMA, FRANCIS. 1992. "Comments on 'Nationalism and Democracy.'" *Journal of Democracy* 3(4): 3–28.

FURNIVAL, J. S. 1948. *Colonial Policy and Practice.* London: Cambridge University Press.

GALTUNG, JOHAN. 1971. "A Structural Theory of Imperialism." *Journal of Peace Research* 8(2): 81–117.

GELLNER, ERNEST. 1983. *Nations and Nationalism.* Ithaca: Cornell University Press.

GOULD, HAROLD A. 1966. "Religion and Politics in a U. P. Constituency." In Donald Eugene Smith, ed., *South Asian Politics and Religion.* Princeton: Princeton University Press, 51–73.

HARDIN, RUSSELL. 1982. *Collective Action.* Baltimore: Johns Hopkins University Press, Chs. 2 and 7.

HECHTER, MICHAEL. 1975. *Internal Colonialism: The Celtic Fringe in British National Development, 1536–1966.* London: Routledge & Kegan Paul.

HOROWITZ, DONALD L. 1985. *Ethnic Groups in Conflict.* Berkeley: University of California Press.

KATZENSTEIN, MARY FAINSOD. 1979. *Ethnicity and Equality: The Shiv Sena Party and Preferential Policies in Bombay.* Ithaca: Cornell University Press.

LENIN, V. I. 1964. *Collected Works, Volume 24, April–June 1917.* Moscow: Progress Publishers.

LIJPHART, ARENT. 1977. *Democracy in Plural Societies.* New Haven: Yale University Press.

LINZ, JUAN J., and ALFRED STEPAN. 1992. "Political Identities and Electoral Sequences: Spain, the Soviet Union and Yugoslavia." *Daedalus* 121(2): 123–39.

MEADWELL, HUDSON. 1989. "Ethnic Nationalism and Collective Choice Theory." *Comparative Political Studies* 22(2): 139–54.

MIHALKA, MICHAEL. 1995. "As many as three million Russians may migrate to homeland." *OMRI Daily Digest*, No. 75, Part 1, 14 April, 1995. <omripub @omri.cz>

MILL, JOHN STUART. 1958 [1861]. *Considerations on Representative Government.* New York: Liberal Arts Press.

MOTYL, ALEXANDER. 1990. *Sovietology, Rationality and Nationality*, New York: Columbia University Press.

MUELLER, DENNIS C. 1979. *Public Choice.* Cambridge: Cambridge University Press, Ch. 12.

NAHAYLO, BOHDAN. 1991. "Baltic Echoes in Ukraine." In Jan Arveds Trapans, ed.,

Toward Independence: The Popular Front Movements. Boulder, Colo.: Westview Press, 109–22.

NODIA, GHIA. 1992. "Nationalism and Democracy." *Journal of Democracy* 3(4): 3–22.

NORDLINGER, ERIC A. 1972. *Conflict Regulation in Divided Societies.* Cambridge: Harvard Center for International Affairs.

OTYRBA, GUEORGUI. 1994. "War in Abkhazia: The Regional Significance of the Georgian-Abkhazian Conflict." In Roman Szporluk, ed., *National Identity and Ethnicity in Russia and the New States of Eurasia.* Armonk, N.Y.: M.E. Sharpe, 281–309.

PREMDAS, RALPH R. 1990. "Secessionist Movements in Comparative Perspective." In Ralph R. Premdas, S. W. R. de A. Samarasinghe, and Alan B. Anderson, eds., *Secessionist Movements in Comparative Perspective.* New York: St. Martin's, 12–29.

PYE, LUCIAN W. 1979. "Political Modernization: Gaps Between Theory and Reality." *The Annals of the American Academy of Political and Social Science* 442: 28–39.

RAE, DOUGLAS W. 1971. *The Political Consequences of Electoral Laws.* New Haven: Yale University Press.

SLIDER, DARRELL. 1991. "The Politics of Georgia's Independence." *Problems of Communism* 40 (November/December): 63–79.

SMITH, ANTHONY D. 1976. "Introduction." In Anthony D. Smith, ed., *Nationalist Movements.* New York: St. Martin's, 1–30.

SMITH, M. G. 1965. *The Plural Society in the British West Indies.* Berkeley: University of California Press.

SYSYN, FRANK. 1991. "The Reemergence of the Ukrainian Nation and Cossack Mythology." *Social Research* 58 (Winter): 845–64.

TUCKER, ROBERT C., ed. 1972. *The Marx-Engels Reader.* New York: W.W. Norton.

VENCLOVA, TOMAS. 1991. "Lithuania: The Opening and the Hand of the Past." *Salmagundi* 90/91 (Spring/Summer): 1–11.

WEINER, MYRON. 1978. *Sons of the Soil: Migration and Ethnic Conflict in India.* Princeton: Princeton University Press.

CHAPTER
8

Economic Policy and Democratization in the Former Communist States

JOHN H. MUTTI

THE AMBIGUITIES OF ECONOMIC AND POLITICAL TRANSITIONS

Many scholars link the fate of democracy, a political phenomenon, to various economic phenomena. The modernization school (see Chapter 3) argues that a higher level of economic development is a prerequisite to the achievement of democracy (Lipset 1959; Dahl 1989; Vanhanen 1990). These observers note the relatively high level of economic development, industrialization, urbanization, and education found among the long standing democracies. They view such conditions as especially conducive to mobilization of the public and the creation of countervailing powers within the society to limit authoritarian rule and to promote democracy (Vanhanen 1990). They further note the relatively high rankings of the former communist states on world indices of economic development, industrialization, urbanization, and education. In consequence, they make the optimistic prediction that a successful transition to democracy can be expected to occur in these former communist states.

There is indeed strong empirical evidence linking economic development and democracy. While correlations are strong, such correlations provide neither a prediction of how long it will take to achieve democracy once a given level of development is attained nor an explanation of the process by which democracy will be established. Some critics of modernization theory note that the type of development that occurred in the former communist states was not based on private property and a diffusion of economic power, and that, therefore, the hypothesized linkage between economic development and a transition to democracy may prove in this case to be false. These scholars argue that a Soviet-style command economy is incompatible with political democracy. Only a market economy, they say, will sustain democracy. Most leaders of the former communist states, accepting this proposition, have declared their commitment to achieve simultaneously both a democratic form of government and a market-oriented economy.[1]

There are several problems with such an analysis. The first is that the modernization model assumes that economic development precedes a move to political democracy, and both makes possible and motivates such a move. Such diverse scholars as Marx and Barrington Moore (1966) argued that democratization is an inevitable (Marx) or one possible (Moore) outcome of capitalist industrialization. Both scholars assume a long period of industrialization, with democracy emerging sometime at the end of this process.

Historically, however, the attempt to simultaneously move from a command economy to a market one, and from a dictatorial political system to a democratic one, is unprecedented. This dual transition (Pei 1994) involves special problems unknown in earlier democratic transitions. The move to a market economy will, at least in the short run, distribute its rewards and costs relatively unequally. Some small number of people, because they occupied strategic positions or developed extremely useful contacts under the command economy, will be able to use these valuable resources effectively in the new system, and will become the privileged of that new system. Others—the young, the educated, and the adventurous—will successfully master the requirements of the new system and also do very well. A new criminal class may join these two groups.

However, the great mass of the people have suffered a severe decline in their standard of living. In nearly all of the countries in transition, production dropped sharply and inflation raged, hitting those on fixed incomes especially hard. Unemployment will likely grow further from its 1995 levels. There are substantial impediments to government action to alleviate such suffering. While most Western economists perceive such phenomena as the (short-term) costs of the transition to a market economy, the greater the duration of hardships, the less convincing such arguments will seem to the mass publics of the former communist states.

The simultaneous introduction of political democracy distributes its rewards and costs much more equally. Ordinary citizens may lack the privileged access to the political elites that the wealthy are likely to possess. But the vote is not a totally irrelevant political resource, and large numbers of economically deprived citizens are likely to manifest their dissatisfaction at the polling booth.

The resulting clash between a new economic elite committed to the full (and rapid) flowering of the market economy and an enfranchised mass population determined at the very least to moderate the harshness of the transition can have several possible outcomes. The economic elite, frustrated by politically imposed delays and/or limits on the transition to the market may lead or join efforts to repudiate democracy in the name of economic reform. There are Russians who look with admiration on the economic achievements of the military regime of Pinochet in Chile, and on the growth rates of the relatively authoritarian East Asian countries: Taiwan and South Korea.

Hough (1994) reminds us that in the magnitude of the changes in the socioeconomic system the former communist countries have experienced—if not in the way these changes occurred—there has been a revolution, not reform. Revolutionaries tend neither to tolerate opposition nor to support democracy. A return to authoritarianism to promote the transition to the market would demonstrate that, at least in the special circumstances of the dual transition, relative economic prosperity and a market economy need not lead to democracy.

A less dramatic, and thus more probable, outcome, is that the citizens of these countries will elect politicians who will moderate the magnitude, and certainly the pace, of the economic reforms. By early 1995, the most fervent supporters of the market had been electorally repudiated in Poland, Hungary, and Lithuania, and market reform had been stalled in much of the former communist world. As I shall show below, many economists would argue that a gradual transition to the market may have substantial economic costs, but this outcome would preserve at least some market reforms and some degree of political democracy.

There is a second, very different, problem with the purported linkage between economic phenomena (a high level of development and a market economy) and democracy. While the development of capitalism in the West may have, over the centuries, produced societies in which income and wealth are more equally distributed than was true of the precapitalist societies—this remains a contested scholarly proposition—communist societies have tended to value, and communist political economies to produce, a greater degree of economic equality than is found in capitalist societies (Lane 1992, 168–72). The move to the market from communism presupposes increased inequality. While such increased inequality may be consistent with definitions of political democracy that emphasize such formal institutions and procedures of democracy as competitive elections and multiple political parties, many would raise questions as to how truly democratic a political system can be when a resource as politically potent as wealth is horribly unequally distributed (Sakwa 1995).

These are major problems in the linking of economic phenomena to political phenomena. They are discussed in some length in other chapters of the book (2 and 9, among others). Nevertheless, both politicians in the former communist states and western politicians and academic analysts assume that, for these new democracies to endure, there must be a simultaneous and successful transition to a free market economy. In this chapter, therefore, I shall take as a given, not as an issue still to be debated, the desirability of creating a market economy. If that starting point is accepted, though, there is considerable controversy among economists over the best way to achieve a market economy, particularly the pace at which to proceed. Just as there is no generally applicable theory of political transitions to use in predicting how democratization will be achieved in the former communist states, there is no generally applicable theory of transitions in the economic literature to use in predicting how market-oriented economies will emerge in these states. This chapter will consider the primary obstacles to establishing a market economy and will assess how the economic policies chosen to deal with these obstacles in turn are likely to influence the process of democratization.

The economic policy choices that confront the former communist states cover a bewildering array of issues. A distinction between two different types of economic policy choices is useful, because the two major international lending agencies, the International Monetary Fund (IMF) and the World Bank, generally divide their responsibilities in this way. The first set of policies deals with the overall stability of the economy in the short run and they are commonly labeled macroeconomic stabilization measures. They are directed at the following sorts of potentially conflicting goals: preventing high inflation, avoiding a flight of capital out of the country when there is no confidence in its currency, restoring the ability of the country to borrow in international markets, generating full employment, and ensuring that all citizens can achieve some basic standard of living. Policy choices that face the government include the size of the budget deficit, the rate of growth of the money supply and the availability of credit, and the value of the currency internationally.

The second set of policies is no less urgent but the goals can only be achieved sometime in the future, since they require major adjustments in the structure of the economy and not just stabilization based on the current structure. Common goals are to use workers and resources more efficiently in order to increase economic output and to make investments in people and productive capacity in a way that will promote economic growth that can be sustained in the future. In the case of the former communist states, that transformation means shifting workers and equipment away from uses that were high priorities to the state in a centrally controlled command economy toward the production of goods and services demanded by individual consumers and enterprises or by foreign markets. The objective is not simply to correct past imbalances in the allocation of resources, but to adopt a system that encourages innovation and can accommodate future changes. The policy measures often include deregulation of prices, elimination of subsidies, the removal of barriers to international trade and investment, and privatization of state enterprises.

Issues of Timing—Shock Therapy versus Gradualism

No matter which of these specific policies happens to be under consideration, a basic conflict is likely to arise between advocates of an immediate change, or "shock therapists," and those who favor a more phased implementation, or "gradualists."

At one level, shock therapists have offered suggestive analogies to support their position: if an owner is to cut a dog's tail off, do it all at once rather than an inch at a time; or, if a country is to shift from driving on the left-hand side of the road to the right-hand side, do not start with only trucks making the change. These quips do not suggest that pain and suffering can be avoided in an immediate transition, but they suggest that more pain and suffering will occur in a gradualist scenario and that many changes must be made simultaneously rather than sequentially. This judgment is based on the belief that a gradualist approach pushes the benefits from a reformed economy far into the future or perhaps denies them entirely, especially if attempting only modest reforms initially allows the currently centralized system to perpetuate itself. Thus, a key motivation for shock therapy is political, based on the observation from Latin America and elsewhere that a new regime will accomplish little against the opposition of entrenched interests if it gives its opponents time to organize against it.

In the gradualist context, proponents of shock therapy argue, lobbies have an incentive to spend money to influence the political decision-making process rather than to transform the economy. The possibility of frequent changes in laws governing the character of the economy reduces the credibility of any plan for gradual change. Unless there is some way for the government to bind itself to a permanent change, it will be difficult to produce the economic certainties crucial to promoting economic investment. Confidence in government policy and the rules of the game is necessary to convince individuals to keep their money at home to invest rather than send their funds elsewhere. Sometimes treaties and agreements with other countries or multilateral institutions increase government credibility and thereby promote investment, but those alternatives often are not under the control of the newly emerging democracies. Therefore, shock therapists particularly stress the advantage of making a once-and-for-all change in the economic structure.

With respect to the scope of reforms to attempt, if only one policy is changed while many other distortions remain, the economy may become worse off. For example, removing price controls when only one domestic producer exists may result in a monopoly outcome of lower output and higher prices, if competition from imports still is prohibited and state banks lend only to existing state enterprises. Shock therapists view simultaneous reform on several fronts as necessary, in contrast to a sequential plan that attempts to resolve one problem before moving on to address another.

Gradualists reject the premise that the initial costs of both a complete change and a partial change are the same, as implied in the analogy of the dog's tail. In terms of competing analogies, gradualists note that if an owner wants to teach a dog to jump, he progressively increases the height the dog must clear, rather than starting at the final objective. Gradualists also argue that even if a radical change can be accomplished all at once, it is likely to be extremely wasteful.

Apply this reasoning to the U.S. military buildup in the 1980s. Suppose a country seeks to enhance its defense capability by acquiring 1,000 new tanks, but it insists on attaining this goal in one year rather than two. The cost will be much higher in terms of the production of other goods that must be given up, since the resources required for tank production must be drawn from other uses that are progressively less similar to this new use. Furthermore, the benefits from having the first 500 tanks likely are greater than those provided by the second 500 tanks. If the country delays acquiring the second 500 tanks, its benefits are reduced by less than half. Further, the country may gain from lower costs of tank production that are possible in the future given the opportunity to retrain workers and invest in new facilities—strategies that additional time allows. The fact that slower adjustment allows for a bigger reduction of costs than benefits argues for the gradualist position.

In the former communist states a more relevant perspective is the appropriate rate of decline in industrial production. In the long run a decline in industrial production may be desirable, because the Stalinist emphasis on heavy industry means that other sectors of the economy, such as services, are much smaller than in the West. Very rapid reductions, however, simply result in many workers being laid off, and the availability of those resources to produce elsewhere in the economy provides little benefit if there is no way to ensure their transfer to areas where demand exists or may develop in the future. Sometimes this failure may be attributable to the difficulty of forming new ventures (when company law is uncertain), receiving credit (when banks favor existing state enterprises), acquiring necessary inputs (when imports are limited and domestic production is inadequate), or marketing the output (in a country where middlemen and distributors previously were viewed as nonproductive parasites on the society). Unemployment may be a long-term problem, moreover, because workers who are laid off may not have the right skills and/or may not be located in the right geographic areas to take advantage of eventual increases in demand. Workers will have particular difficulty finding new jobs when a single enterprise is the major employer in the community. This feature of the USSR economy is a source of inflexibility that is compounded by severe limitations on the opportunity to find housing elsewhere.

If transferring resources to alternative uses proves difficult, but the government still must provide workers some basic standard of living to avoid social unrest and a loss of political power, then the government must somehow raise the revenue to make those expenditures. That step will likely introduce other distortions into the economy. Therefore, slowing down the rate of economic change and the resultant congestion in labor markets may result in less economic distortion than an immediate break with the past. A similar logic lies behind the western practice of phasing in multilateral tariff reductions over ten-year periods or longer.

When a government continues to subsidize a failing enterprise simply to maintain current employment, concurrent reforms that call for decentralization and privatization may leave it with little control over the way the subsidy is spent, a further reason for gradualism. From either perspective, however, the government must assess whether a policy that seems attractive in the short run is reasonable in the long run. For example, would expenditures on worker retraining or new capital equipment be preferable to subsidized missile production, because once a worker has shifted from producing missiles to producing household appliances there is no continuing budget commitment? Or, will Russia emerge as a dominant market force in the international satellite launching business, so that subsidies to maintain current missile capacity are a preferable way of investing in the future? While governments cannot know these probabilities very precisely, they must think in these terms to use their limited funds most effectively.

That the optimal pace of adjustment may depend upon both the initial condition of the economy and public preferences of the society should not be surprising. In an analogous context, countries must determine how much to save in order to promote investment and faster growth. Saving more now means less consumption and a lower standard of living, which may be politically unacceptable in spite of its long-run promise. Making a more rapid transition and accepting more unemployment or lower wages for more than a year or two may be politically unacceptable in spite of the long-run gain from shifting workers and equipment to new uses. Westerners often point to the very high rate of forced saving and rapid industrialization of Stalinist Russia as an example of a large initial sacrifice to achieve a long-run goal. Perhaps Russia will not choose to make such an extreme choice again.

A further gradualist concern is that changing all policies at once simply creates chaos that does not reinforce progress in economic or political reform. Few legal and social institutions exist to support the functioning of a market, and past experience in these states demonstrates little tolerance for a system of clear rules but unforeseen outcomes. As discussed in Chapter 5, important institutions that evolved only gradually in the West are the establishment of a system of commercial law to enforce contracts and a regulatory framework to give buyers adequate information about the value of goods or assets that they purchase. In the absence of these conditions, an immediate shift in policy on all fronts may be counterproductive. Dismantling the old centralized system too rapidly may create a political and economic vacuum that is filled by the few groups, such as the *nomenklatura* and the mafia, that are immediately ready to take advantage of new opportunities; these groups in turn may dominate decision making for decades to come.

These conflicting claims and insights demonstrate why the debate between the two approaches continues. In the discussion below these ideas are elaborated further but no agenda universally applicable to all of the economies in transition is suggested. Rather, the economic situation in the former communist states is assessed, the transition policies they have pursued are explained, and the effects on different groups within their societies are identified. This information provides an important part of the background necessary to predict the course of democratization in these countries.

STABILIZATION POLICY

Nearly all of the former communist states have experienced explosive inflation (greater than any U.S. rate of price increase in the past 100 years), decreases in industrial production (as large as those of the United States during the great depression of the 1930s), and a drastic drop in their standard of living. Central European countries such as Poland, Hungary, and the Czech Republic have overcome these initial setbacks, controlling inflation and generating positive growth again. Their success, however, has not come from trying to turn the clock back to the pre-1989 era. Rather, they have been able to stabilize their economies and to restructure them. Consider some of the key stabilization issues to address.

Inflation

A critical sign of instability is inflation, which exceeded 25 percent a month in Russia during 1992–1993 and reached much higher rates in countries such as Ukraine and Belarus that attempted even fewer economic reforms. Due to rapid increases in the money supply and declines in real industrial output, prices continued to rise as more currency chased fewer goods.

What dangers does inflation pose for an economy and for political stability? As stated by J. M. Keynes (1920, 220):

> There is no subtler, no surer means of overturning the existing basis of society than to debauch the currency. The process engages all the hidden forces of economic law on the side of destruction and does it in a manner which not one man in a million can diagnose.

When the inflation rate reaches 50 percent a month, which economists label hyperinflation, a ruble owned at the start of a year becomes completely worthless by the end of the year. Unexpected inflation serves as a tax on those who hold rubles and causes drastic redistributions of wealth and income.

Citizens of the former Soviet Union (FSU) accumulated large ruble balances because few consumer goods were available to purchase. In Russia this large number of rubles in potential circulation was a potential source of instability, because as Russians became convinced that the ruble would lose its future purchasing power as a result of inflation, they converted their rubles into foreign exchange or hoarded nonperishable goods. The first response caused the ruble's international purchasing power to fall, while the second response contributed to more demand, higher prices, and lower purchasing power of the ruble domestically. That process will continue until speculators are convinced that prices will not continue to rise in the future. In the meantime, though, rubles change hands quickly and rapid price increases shake confidence in the economic strategy of the government. These effects are not confined to some small group, either. Those who saved and those who received fixed incomes denominated in rubles have clearly suffered great losses. To some extent, however, they have convinced the government to compensate for their losses or to raise pensions and salaries.

Because few domestic assets could be expected to retain their value, the threat of inflation gave those who held rubles a strong incentive to convert their savings into foreign currencies such as dollars or marks. For example, in 1991 when the inflation rate in Russia was 50 percent but the interest rate was only 4 percent, savers had little incentive to hold rubles. In 1994 Russia had some of the highest real interest rates in the world, or a nominal interest rate 10 percentage points greater than the monthly inflation rate (*The Economist* 7/9/94, 11). Such a high rate was necessary to offset the risk that the government might abandon its commitment to reduce inflation. Capital flight still was estimated to have reached $25 billion per year (Maital and Milner 1993). As Russia is discovering, it is difficult to create the expectation of constant or lower future inflation if past policy has demonstrated little commitment to this goal.

Unpredictable inflation also makes it difficult to know how future revenues and costs will change. When future profits cannot be predicted, investors will risk little in long-run commitments. This confusion over future prices and costs results in a pattern of investment that only by luck will be consistent with the world market conditions to be faced by an outward-oriented economy.

A Declining Standard of Living and a Short-Run Solution: Imports

Another challenge that has faced economies in transition has been a large drop in domestic production and the standard of living. Even countries that have been timid reformers have not avoided this fate. A decline in output is difficult to avoid because most prior production relationships no longer exist. The pattern of specialization in production within the eastern bloc, the implicit subsidies from one republic to another, and the trading relationships within the Council for Mutual Economic Assistance (CMEA), no longer can be relied upon.

In Central European countries that began the transformation process earlier, industrial production is rising again, but increasing domestic output should not be seen as an easy short-run solution. The Russian situation is typical of what faces many former republics. Industrial output fell by over 25 percent in both 1992 and 1993, and leaders hope that the contraction in 1994 was limited to this amount. If an economy produces much less, individuals must consume and invest much less, unless the government gives up its claims on current production or additional goods can be obtained from abroad. Given the difficulties of reducing government spending in any economy, the basic question considered here is how the FSU might pay for more imports.

Exports

One method of financing more imports is to export more goods and services. Retooling production to meet foreign tastes and standards is a long-run process, however, and in the short run exports are constrained by the limited attractiveness on the international market of goods the FSU currently produces. Aside from natural resources such as oil and gas, there is one obvious exception: armaments. Given the decline in military expenditures within Russia and the large existing capacity to produce sophisticated weaponry, Russia hopes to sharply increase its exports of military goods to developing countries, particularly China and India (RFE 1/18/93). Russia's share of the world arms market declined to 5 percent in 1994 (RFE 7/9/94), which indicates that many traditional customers cannot afford to buy from it if concessionary terms are not available and new customers have not yet been found. The Russians also hope to exploit their existing expertise in nuclear power to sell plants to China, Iran, and Pakistan (RFE 12/9/92).

With respect to natural resource sales, if Russia cuts deliveries to former allies at subsidized prices, its total earnings may rise in spite of declining domestic production. The sale of these products in world markets, however, does not guarantee that the foreign exchange earned will become available to the government to finance needed imports. Exporters instead have tended to keep these earnings for themselves in foreign bank accounts. Moreover, expansion of these exports is limited by quotas, imposed by the Russian government to restrict sales abroad in order to maintain a sufficient supply of inputs for domestic industries (RFE 10/7/92). Continuing to make such energy available at subsidized rates is one way of postponing the immediate pressure to adjust in industries that use much more energy than their international competitors, but it imposes different costs on the economy. To achieve greater export earnings will require instead that prices of other goods drop enough to make them competitive internationally and thereby promote nonenergy exports.

Other problematic aspects of the trade situation of these transition economies arise from external restrictions. For example, Russia has an excess of installed capacity and the ability to divert sales to foreign customers in sectors such as steel, aluminum, uranium, and textiles. Western countries, however, have their own excess capacity and noncompetitive producers in these same sectors, and their long-run adjustment problems are compounded by an economic recession just when Easterners seek to enter world markets. As a result, Westerners have sought to limit sales from the former communist states. The European Union's agricultural policy also poses a major barrier to neighboring countries that in an unrestricted market would have a competitive advantage in producing many agricultural commodities.

Foreign Investment

An alternative way to finance more imports is by attracting foreign investment. One category is foreign direct investment, which implies foreign control of an enterprise and often involves the transfer of technology. This possibility will be most significant in host countries that define property rights clearly and demonstrate consistency in applying commercial legal procedures. Geographic proximity also plays a role in the ability of former communist states to attract investment, as countries that border on Western Europe are more likely to play a role in the plans of multinational corporations to serve an integrated European market. Yet, ambitious foreign firms that took over some of the most successful Eastern European firms—such as General Electric, which invested in Tungsram of Hungary (light bulbs), or Volkswagen, which invested in Skoda of Czechoslovakia (automobiles)—have retreated from early expansion plans (RFE 9/17/93).

With respect to the actual scope of such investment, the figures are ambiguous. As reported in the United Nation's *World Investment Report 1992*, accumulated foreign equity exceeded $1 billion only in Hungary ($2.1 billion) and the FSU ($5.7 billion). World Bank figures suggest that the Czech Republic exceeded this threshold in 1992. Russian officials, however, noted that in 1994 foreign investment in Russia was less than in Estonia.

Most investments have been made by European firms. Within Russia, foreign interest has been greatest in natural resource development and in high-technology military goods, but Russian leaders have been anxious to keep domestic control of these operations. A joint venture announced between Pratt Whitney and Energomash on rocket engine technology is an example of a potentially successful match of Russian capabilities and foreign interests (RFE 10/27/92), but few such arrangements have been concluded.

Aside from legal prohibitions and ownership uncertainties, another deterrent to foreign investment is the outstanding debt of many former communist states. A country with a large debt will have to devote most of its earnings of foreign exchange to paying interest on the existing debt. As a result, companies that consider new investments in the former communist states often are concerned that they will not be able to convert future profits into foreign currency. A large debt also may raise the prospect that the government will increase its taxation of capital income. While the 1980s were a period when the Latin American debt crisis meant those countries had little access to international credit markets, Eastern European countries were judged to be creditworthy and they were able to increase their borrowing. Many of these funds, however, were used to maintain high consumption. Because they were not invested, they did not result in greater productive capacity that would allow the loans to be repaid without cutting future consumption.

Total external debt in 1989 for several states on the eve of reform in 1989 is reported by the World Bank as follows: Bulgaria $10 billion (7.6%), Czechoslovakia $8 billion (3.0%), Hungary $21 billion (12.5%), Poland $43 billion (5.9%), Romania $1 billion (0.8%), and Russia $54 billion[2] (World Bank 1994). The figures in parentheses indicate the interest due on this debt as a share of export earnings, a proxy for the country's ability to service its debt without first making major changes in its economic structure. The low figure for Romania reflects its negative reaction to a debt crisis in 1981 and its decision to pay off its foreign debt. Thus, it entered the reform period without a large burden created by past obligations. The high figure for Hungary may represent an initial vote of confidence by the international banking community in Hungarian economic prospects, but it also suggests that Hungary is unlikely to be able to rely on a rapid expansion of debt to finance greater imports that might ease its adjustment process.

Foreign Aid

Foreign aid also can be used to pay for imports, and advocates of proposals for Western countries to provide foreign aid often compare its role to that of the Marshall Plan in the reconstruction of Western Europe after World War II. The actual scope of the Marshall Plan should be noted: Its transfer of $12 billion over four years represented 2 percent of GDP in the recipient countries (Summers 1992, 31). Although measurement of GDP in the recipient countries in dollar terms is problematic, Summers calculates that a comparable transfer to Eastern Europe today would require about $5 billion a year, a figure high enough to be an unlikely contribution by the United States, Europe, and Japan.

Moreover, if Russia is included in the discussion, the figures become much larger. One estimate (Bhagwati, 1994) uses the Harvard Plan's call for $30 billion per year over five years, an important part of which was intended to allow more imports and to limit the decline in the standard of living. Western nations pledged $24 billion in 1992 and $28 billion in 1993 but did not deliver on these promises, an outcome Bhagwati cites in rejecting shock therapy and supporting a gradualist policy.

Recent experience with aid programs demonstrates that they often carry the disadvantage that the recipient is given little choice from whom to buy or at what price. Such aid is conditional on political factors as well, as demonstrated by the cool western reception to Russian requests in 1991 and 1994 when Russia's treatment of the Baltic Republics seemed aggressive.

Even if these drawbacks are overcome, obtaining aid will be difficult when major western economies are mired in economic recessions. Also, far poorer countries feel their claims for development assistance should rank above those of the former communist states in Europe. Nevertheless, the concessionary terms under which half of Polish debt to Western governments was forgiven in 1991, while African countries were unable to reach a comparable agreement, does suggest that strategic political interests may favor the former communist states. These states are especially likely to receive aid in the form of goods sold at highly subsidized prices when the sales satisfy politically important groups in the European Union or the United States, such as farmers.

The International Monetary Fund and Conditionality

Possible financing through the IMF has received much publicity, in part due to the reluctance of individual countries to face more directly the budgetary consequences of providing assistance. IMF loans traditionally have been short term, to offset a balance of payments deficit that may have arisen from temporary conditions such as a poor harvest, a drop in export prices, or an increase in import prices. The borrowers, though, may prefer to receive resources for a longer period of time to invest in long-run economic development. These divergent interests may be partially reconciled if the IMF's focus on short-run macroeconomic stabilization improves the likelihood that the borrower can repay its loan and again become creditworthy in international capital markets.

The IMF has come to play a key role as an international financial policeman, certifying the appropriateness of economic policy pursued by sovereign borrowers who supply no collateral to foreign lenders. An IMF stamp of approval can make the borrower's change in economic policy appear more credible to private financial institutions, who otherwise would be unwilling to lend where little recourse is available in case the country does not repay the loan. Nevertheless, if private lenders are not convinced by the IMF involvement, then IMF financing may simply replace outstanding private loans, bailing out banks without increasing the funds available to the borrowing country.

The IMF diagnoses most loan applications as resulting from the country living beyond its means. The remedy seen as appropriate is for the country to reduce its spending relative to its production. Critics often complain that the IMF emphasizes cutting spending rather than increasing production. For instance, if a country suffers a severe recession so that residents have less income to spend on imported goods, that solution will prove quite costly for a large country such as Russia, because it devotes a small share of income to imports. As a result, a large reduction in income and in increase in unemployment would be necessary to generate much improvement in the balance of trade.

For a comparably large economy such as the United States, a preferable means of reducing a trade deficit has been through a fall in the value of the dollar internationally, which makes U.S. goods more attractive to foreigners and foreign goods more expensive to U.S. buyers. If there is adequate capacity in the economy, output can rise to improve the trade balance and the government need not rely on a cut in spending to reduce import demand and increase export supply. In Russia this approach has not been as successful, because a weaker ruble has little impact on Russian exports and primarily means Russians can no longer afford to buy as many imports. Thus, adjustments that might occur on the supply side are limited. With no immediate replacement for the centralized planning system, it is not clear how more inputs can be bought, workers with the appropriate skills hired, new machinery installed, or new factories built. One of the goals of the longer-run transition is to achieve an economy where production can expand more easily in response to price incentives. The sooner this type of restructuring occurs, the smaller the decline in income or the value of the ruble that will be necessary to improve Russia's trade balance.

Why do countries accept conditions imposed by the IMF? Borrowers typically have exhausted all other sources of credit and are seeking some way to reduce the cutback in expenditure that otherwise must occur if they are to balance export receipts with import spending. This situation is even more severe if citizens are taking funds out of the country or converting their savings into foreign currency, since those actions create another claim on available foreign exchange. Some critics regard the conditions the IMF imposes before granting a loan to be too harsh and to demand too rapid an adjustment. In the absence of such a loan, however, the potential borrower would have to reduce its demand for foreign exchange even more. That alternative is likely to be even less attractive since it typically will require a further depreciation of the currency or a greater reduction in national income.

In order to receive a loan, the borrowing country must prepare a letter of intent that indicates various economic performance targets it intends to meet if the IMF grants it a loan. If the targets are not met, then further loan disbursements are in jeopardy. These targets constitute the major elements to be negotiated by the borrowing country and the IMF.

One central target is the government budget deficit as a share of gross domestic product (GDP). For example, Poland converted a budget deficit of 7.4 percent of GDP to a surplus of 3.8 percent in 1990 (Sachs 1992). While Poland did not maintain this surplus in subsequent years, based on continued satisfactory policy performance the IMF signed its fourth agreement with Poland in 1994. In contrast, the Russian budget deficit was 20 percent of GDP in 1991 and it has only gradually declined since then. To receive IMF support in 1994 the government proposed policies that would result in a deficit of 9.6 percent of GDP. While that figure exceeds typical IMF targets, such as the 5 percent figure that served as the basis for negotiations in 1992, the United States and the European Union pressured the IMF to reconsider the application of its traditional standards in 1994.

Large budget deficits have resulted from an inability to collect taxes to pay for government expenditures (Fischer 1992; McKinnon 1992). Part of this shortfall is due to the collapse of the command system in which the government automatically received the difference between a firm's receipts and expenditures. While taxation represents another way of capturing this surplus, it requires a new administrative capability that does not yet exist. Lagging revenue collections have been a particular problem for the central government, as opposed to lower levels of government that now make more direct claims on the natural resources extracted in their jurisdictions (Wallich and Nayyar 1993). Proposals to re-establish the state liquor monopoly represent a gradualist approach to rely upon more familiar administrative mechanisms to close this budgetary gap.

Another source of the budget deficit is spending to cover the losses of state enterprises. A bankruptcy law was passed by parliament in the summer of 1993, and a Federal Bankruptcy Agency was established in September 1993. In mid-1994 the head of the agency estimated that half of all enterprises could not meet their financial obligations, but only sixty firms appeared on a list of insolvents and proceedings had been initiated against only three (*Economist* 3/19/94, 79). As a sign of the political dangers of stringent action, in 1994 President Yeltsin requested a bailout plan for the giant auto maker ZIL and promised never to let it go bankrupt.

Aside from the prestige attached to certain enterprises, the state is under pressure to keep failing enterprises operating because they provide many of the social services workers expect and would find difficult to obtain if unemployed. In other words, there is not an independent social safety net that is adequate to deal with the unemployed. Yet, covering the losses of these failing firms accounted for 12.5 percent of GDP in 1992 and 7.4 percent in the first quarter of 1994 (*Economist* 7/16/94, 46). The IMF particularly monitors the budget deficit because a government that spends far more than the revenue it collects often is under pressure to finance its spending by printing more money, a second target the IMF watches. A rapid increase in the money supply creates additional macroeconomic imbalances. In a command system with controlled prices, individuals end up holding additional currency, because the quantity of goods available to consumers already has been determined and will be rationed at the regulated price. The consequence of greater government demand for goods is longer lines of consumers trying to buy the smaller quantity of goods available to them, while they accumulate rubles that have little value in official markets. In a market system a large increase in the money supply tends to cause inflation, particularly when the growth in the money supply far outpaces the growth in the production of goods. The consequence of greater government demand for goods is higher prices of the goods available to consumers.

A third target of the IMF, that a country maintain a realistic foreign exchange rate, is more difficult to achieve in highly inflationary economies. Instead, the international exchange rate can easily become overvalued. That label applies when the value of the ruble (measured as dollars per ruble) is not allowed to fall enough to offset the ruble's decline in its domestic purchasing power under highly inflationary conditions. A frequent problem in many developing countries has been that an overvalued currency causes imports to appear cheaper than domestically produced goods, while exports priced on the basis of rising domestic costs of production become less attractive to foreign buyers. Thus, the country's price competitiveness erodes and its balance of trade is likely to deteriorate.

In the first half of 1992 overvaluation was not a problem, because the ruble fell far faster in exchange auctions than Russian prices rose. That result probably reflected the action of many who had ruble savings and converted them into foreign currency. As the dollar price of the ruble stabilized in late 1993 and 1994, however, and Russian domestic prices continued to rise more than 10 percent a month, the prospect of overvaluation became a relevant concern.

Treatment of the exchange rate was a striking aspect of Poland's shock therapy program, given the decision in 1991 to depreciate the zloty sharply and then to make it convertible into hard currency. By way of contrast, western European countries after World War II allowed their currencies to be freely exchanged for foreign currency only after a ten-year adjustment period. In the Polish case convertibility was intended to demonstrate a commitment to a less pervasive role for the government in rationing foreign exchange to favored buyers at some overvalued official rate.

Estonia also adopted a bold adjustment strategy. Not only did the government make its new currency, the kroon, convertible into foreign currency, but it also pegged the value of the kroon to the German mark. To maintain such a position means that the central bank gives up its ability to independently control the money supply; otherwise a rapid increase in the supply of kroons that individuals are not willing to hold may exhaust the Central Bank's holdings of marks. A small country is particularly likely to consider such a strategy as a way to build confidence in its conduct of a stable economic policy. Most of the former communist states, however, have been less willing to forego the opportunity of printing money to finance government budget deficits, and therefore they have let their currencies fall in value relative to Western currencies in order to avoid their goods becoming noncompetitive internationally.

A fourth target the IMF monitors is a country's real interest rate (the interest rate minus the expected rate of inflation). In communist states the interest rate historically played no role in the allocation of capital or in determining which sectors of the economy expanded or contracted; it was not higher interest rates, but rather the government production quotas, that limited new car sales or the number of new houses built. If the interest rate is to ration scarce capital among potential borrowers, however, negative real interest rates where the inflation rate exceeds the borrowing rate will not serve that function. Positive real interest rates also are necessary to stem capital flight, which occurs when Russians deposit funds in Swiss bank accounts or when they hold their savings at home in dollars or marks rather than rubles.

A fifth element of most letters of intent to the IMF is some target regarding wage increases. If a depreciation of the exchange rate makes imports relatively more expensive, an attempt to raise wages to offset this rise in the cost of living will increase domestic costs and counteract the initial incentive to purchase fewer foreign goods. Unless productivity rises, there is limited scope to offer higher wages; the IMF sees little prospect of being repaid if loans are simply used to maintain the current standard of living. When the state directly controls wages that are paid, the administrative steps to fulfill this condition can be taken directly. Once enterprises are no longer bound by central directives, then less direct measures must be relied upon. For example, Poland imposes a tax on wage increases that exceed a given norm. When this authority lapsed in 1994, growth in wages was four percentage points higher than the rate of inflation in spite of rising unemployment.

These five aspects of IMF stabilization plans emphasize factors that increase a country's ability to repay whatever funds are borrowed from the IMF. As government spending is cut, however, the reduction in demand may not automatically be replaced by greater private investment or foreign demand, and unemployment may result. The expectation of IMF advisers is that this unemployment will be temporary, due to a temporary drop in demand (Kahn 1990). A portion of the IMF loan may be used to provide a safety net that limits the drop in the standard of living, but the IMF generally does not monitor whether these funds benefit those most hurt by the government's policies.

To what extent has economic stabilization been an elusive goal for the former communist states? Difficulties in stabilization often are due to the initial disequilibrium positions of these economies when reforms were initiated. Countries with large foreign debts and large currency overhangs are less likely to demonstrate stable performance. Although most economic statistics in the former communist states are imprecise indicators of performance, one suggestive item that poses fewer problems of measurement is the value of the exchange rate before liberalization occurred and afterward. Table 8–1 shows the average exchange rate reported by the IMF for 1988–1994.

A country that has been able to avoid a drastic decline in the value of its currency has likely pursued macroeconomic policies that are more consistent with the standards suggested by the IMF. Smaller budget deficits, slower monetary growth, and lower inflation rates create less pressure for currency depreciation, as well as positive real interest rates that discourage capital outflows. By this indirect standard, the Czech republic appears to have created the most stable macroeconomic conditions. In Russia the general exchange rate for tourists moved from 5.5 rubles per dollar at the outset of 1991 to 400 rubles per dollar at the end of 1992 and to 2,000 rubles per dollar in early 1994. Countries such as Belarus and the Ukraine

TABLE 8–1. National Exchange Rates

	Units of domestic currency/US$ (end of year, except 1994 = June)*						
Country	**1988**	**1989**	**1990**	**1991**	**1992**	**1993**	**1994**
Bulgaria	.82	.89	.84	2.19	17.18	25.46	49.1
Czechoslovakia	14.31	14.29	28.00	27.84	28.90	29.96	28.27
Hungary	52.54	62.54	61.45	75.62	83.97	100.70	—
Poland	503	6,500	9,500	10,957	15,767	21,344	22,450
Romania	14.37	14.44	34.71	189.00	460.00	1,276	1,677

*Domestic currency: Bulgaria, lev; Czechoslovakia, koruny; Hungary, forint; Poland, zloty; Romania, lei.
Source: International Monetary Fund (1994), Central Intelligence Agency (1993).

have seen their currencies fall markedly relative to the ruble, and thus even more relative to hard currencies. Continuing rapid depreciation of the currency typically is a sign that consensus has not been reached within the government to control the budget deficit and to limit the expansion of credit. By default government expenditures are financed by an inflation tax on those who hold the domestic currency, and the goal of economic stabilization remains unfulfilled.

STRUCTURAL ADJUSTMENT AND ECONOMIC POLICY IN THE LONGER RUN

While greater macroeconomic stability is necessary in moving toward a market economy, it certainly is not sufficient. A second set of policies involves changing the basic structure of how goods are produced and sold in the economy. Such changes are likely to take much longer to implement than a macro stabilization plan, although most countries have taken initial steps in both areas. Some of these changes are complementary with a stabilization plan and some conflict. For example, greater reliance on market prices and less state subsidization will reduce the budget deficit (a macro goal addressed above) as well as give some producers an incentive to expand production and others an incentive to contract (a longer-run restructuring of the productive capacity of the economy). On the other hand, austerity plans to reduce a trade deficit (a macro goal) may dry up the funds that new enterprises need to meet new market demands (a restructuring goal).

Simply maintaining the status quo of five years ago is not a viable option for the former communist states. Their command economies were already in serious decline despite large borrowing from Western lenders. Production had become progressively divorced from any market test of efficiency. The gradual decentralization of power away from a Stalinist form of control resulted in less accurate information being reported to the center while competing interests shifted attention away from the goal of expanding national output (Olson 1992). More recently, the expectations raised by glasnost meant that consumers would not accept a permanent commitment to high defense production and limited availability of consumer goods. Additionally, the inefficiencies of the old regime no longer could be offset by the 1970s windfall from high energy prices.

The situation of the states of the FSU is particularly severe because the pattern of specialization within the Soviet Union was so extreme. Some former republics are entirely dependent upon the production of a single commodity—such as cotton in Uzbekistan—or the output of a single large factory intended to serve the entire USSR market—such as the giant Kamaz truck factory in Tatarstan. The breakdown of trading relationships within the FSU has made firms vulnerable to supply interruptions. Cigarette production in Russia, for example, came to a halt, not because of a tobacco shortage or the unavailability of paper, but because the glue used in making cigarettes came from a single plant in Armenia that was shut down as the result of rising ethnic tensions (Maital and Milner 1993).

One problem is that too many workers and too much equipment are concentrated in sectors where costs of production exceed world market prices. These economies are unbalanced in other respects, too, given the general Stalinist emphasis on the development of raw materials and heavy industry (steel and machinery) and the large role played by military production. Conversely, production of consumer goods and the service sector are both generally underdeveloped. Large changes in economic structure are necessary.

Decontrolling Prices and Production

A first step in moving toward a market economy is shifting away from a central plan that determines how much of a good is produced, where it will be sold, and at what price. Giving enterprises the freedom to choose what inputs to use and what goods to produce is one initial reform. Another is to free prices from the controlled levels that prevailed earlier, when goods were allocated by a "first come, first served" system, with long lines and political influence rather than price. Price liberalization gives an incentive for some industries to expand output and others to contract output, and for buyers to shift away from goods whose relative prices rise.

Gradualists advocate a phased removal of price controls, because allowing prices of subsidized necessities to rise immediately to world market levels will reduce the value of savings and current incomes and create tremendous pressures to raise wages. In some sectors the cost of inputs valued at world prices will exceed the value of output at world prices, and those enterprises will be forced out of business. In some sectors there will be only a single monopoly producer who can take advantage of the collapse of planning to restrict output and raise prices. If other policies are not introduced at the same time to deal with these consequences, even the first steps toward establishing market relationships will be contentious.

The impetus for action is clear, however, when the enormous budgetary impact of state subsidies is recognized. In Poland subsidies represented 5 percent of GDP before reforms were initiated (Sachs 1992). In Russia import subsidies for basic commodities equaled roughly 12 percent of GDP in 1991 (*Economist* 7/16/94,

45). Bread subsidies in 1993 were budgeted for over $2 billion (RFE 1/7/93), yet such low prices created an incentive to feed it to livestock. From the standpoint of income distribution, providing subsidies to all buyers of a product means that no effort is wasted in determining who should be eligible for this benefit, though total expenditures will be larger and fewer funds will be available to support those most in need. As commodity subsidies are eliminated, purchases of the subsidized goods can be expected to decline.

A comparable price distortion that does not show up as a subsidy in the Russian budget is the practice of keeping export products at home and selling them at domestic prices far below world prices (an effect equivalent to a subsidy), as in the case of oil. Only in 1994 were such controls relaxed. Another input rationed at nonmarket rates within the Russian economy was capital. Because there was no market test to consider the cost of working capital in an industry, Russian enterprises tended to carry very large inventories and maintain works in progress for much longer times than in the West. Immense investments in capital equipment have been made, although the low productivity of the new capacity argues against its efficiency. In addition to the inefficiency caused by mispricing energy and capital, Russian firms had no incentive to take environmental costs into account, so pollution-intensive industries overexpanded. Price liberalization and an effort to consider true costs of production in the former communist states will result in a reduction in output of industries that are energy intensive, capital intensive and pollution intensive.

The high degree of concentration in the Russian economy means that price liberalization often allows the sole producer of a good to increase the price charged to a level far above cost. For 600 key goods there is only one producer within the Russian economy, a situation said to represent 30 to 40 percent of industrial output (Kahn and Peck 1991, 65). Less extreme cases are even more common, as suggested by the market share of the largest plant for the following products: sewing machines 100 percent; washing machines 90 percent; diesel locomotives 95 percent; polypropylene 73 percent and reinforced steel 55 percent (*Economist*, 8/11/90, 67). In those circumstances firms have considerable power to set prices. If there are no barriers to entry, the firm's high profits will soon attract competitors. But potential competitors may not be able to raise the necessary funds, acquire the technology, or arrange a distribution network necessary to enter this business. Gradualists have argued that the de facto limitations on new entrants argues against an immediate liberalization of prices. Shock therapists favor prompt liberalization, even if monopoly prices result, because producers now must consider whether output should be expanded or contracted on the basis of market conditions.

Removing Controls on International Trade

Another potential source of competition is from imported goods. Even though a firm may be the sole producer in the home market, it will not be able to set monopoly prices if it faces competition from producers in other countries. Imports from abroad limit the prices that domestic producers of competing goods can charge in taking advantage of a captive domestic market. Firms that sell in export markets face this discipline even more directly, because they gain little by appealing to their own government to limit sales by foreigners in the home market. For nontraded goods where a single producer serves the market, market economies often regulate the prices charged to limit monopoly power, as in the case of electric and telephone utilities. The fewer the restrictions on trade, the smaller the nontraded sector will be and the less the government will have to establish elaborate regulatory mechanisms.

Shock therapists favor a rapid dismantling of current trade barriers to provide a benchmark by which enterprises in the former communist states can judge whether more investment in a sector is warranted. Gradualists advocate a slower opening to foreign competitors, because so much installed capacity is not efficient at world prices. Some competition may be necessary to limit monopoly power, but immediate adjustment to world prices would drive too many firms out of business. Furthermore, they note that in economies long characterized by excess demand at controlled prices there is likely to be a surge of imports and a large balance of trade deficit if all controls are dismantled.

The breakdown of trade within the Eastern bloc (CMEA) in March 1991 and the shift toward using hard currencies for payment have made the possibility of foreign competition more difficult, especially for goods where transportation costs are important. As trade among neighboring countries recovers, the monopoly power of isolated domestic producers will decline. A contrary trend is illustrated, however, by Russia's increase in import barriers in 1994 to protect its ailing domestic producers whose costs have risen faster than prices. An ominous lesson from the West is that once protection is offered it is difficult to remove, and in the meantime investment in noncompetitive sectors of the economy rises.

Which economies face the largest adjustments in reallocating resources in response to market forces? No single measure provides an unambiguous ranking among the former communist states, but some suggestive indicators are shown in Table 8–2.

Columns 1 and 2 reflect one important aspect of the country's economic structure, particularly its dependence on trade with other former communist states. The smaller a country's share of total exports sold to CMEA partners, presumably the more it already has been subject to market discipline in maintaining the quality of its production, catering to the demands of customers, and becoming familiar with Western business practices. If trade with Western economies already is a significant share of GDP, then market influences are more pervasive at the outset of reform. The figures reported are quite sensitive to the exchange rate chosen to convert CMEA trade or GDP into dollar amounts, but despite the different procedures applied in columns 1 and 2, similar interpretations emerge: Hungary and Poland appear to have least dependence on nonmarket oriented transactions within CMEA and the greatest exposure to western markets. The USSR's trade with Western Europe represents less than 2 percent of its GDP, a sign that market influences have been particularly small.

TABLE 8–2. Indicators of the Prospects for Economic Adjustment prior to Reform

Country	Exports to CMEA/Total Exports	Exports to EC & EMTA/ GDP	Prices Administered (%)	State Ownership (%)	GDP/Capita	
					ICP**	Current
Bulgaria	69	—	100	Economy wide except ag	7,900	2,250
Czechoslovakia	60	4	100	Economy wide	—	3,140
Hungary	43	11	15	90	6,190	2,780
Poland	41	10	100 excluding food	70	4,530	1,690
Romania	39*	—	80	Economy wide	6,780	1,640

*_Source:_ Columns 1, 3, and 4 from Bruno (1992). Column 2 calculated from the United Nations (1991). Columns 5 and 6 from the World Bank (1992, Tables 1 and 30).
**United Nations International Comparison Project, an effort to measure GDP in terms of the purchasing power of the domestic currency.

Columns 3 and 4 crudely measure the state role in determining production patterns. The more prices it controls and the more productive capacity it controls, the larger the scope for government intervention and nonmarket forces to determine the allocation of resources. Earlier steps toward reform that liberalized prices and allowed for private enterprise in Hungary and Poland again suggest they will face less traumatic adjustment to market conditions.

The final column of the table, GDP/capita, tempers these suggestions, however. GDP/capita is an indication of the productivity of the economy, which is related to the education and skill level of the work force. If higher worker productivity also is a sign of greater flexibility and adaptability, then the larger the GDP/capita, the easier time an economy will have in transforming itself into a market economy. High GDP/capita also may indicate a country's good fortune in having important natural resources or an advantageous geographic location. Based on GDP/capita, Czechoslovakia (one of the ten wealthiest countries in the world in the 1930s) appears in a promising position in spite of its initially large dependence on CMEA trade and the high degree of governmental control exercised. That optimistic conjecture is reinforced by Czechoslovakia's low foreign borrowing and macroeconomic stability cited earlier.

External economic factors will play a role in the transformation of the former communist states. Possible membership in the European Union is a particularly important issue. Under an optimistic scenario, Hungary, Poland, and the Czech republic may join the European Union early in the twenty-first century. While political factors will be important determinants of the timing of such an expansion, underlying economic factors merit attention, too, because the European Union already is aware of the strains of accepting members with very divergent levels of economic development.

Consider the United Nations' human development index (a composite measure of education, health, and economic development) for a relevant set of comparison countries (Table 8–3).

There has been vigorous debate within the European Union over the proper scale of transfers from richer to poorer countries within the union. Poorer Southern-tier members—such as Portugal, Spain, and Greece—have argued for much larger transfers from the North than were included in the 1993 budget. Such demands would likely be even greater if the Eastern European nations were to join, since their HDI measures are all lower than those reported for Spain and Greece. The Eastern bloc countries are more reliant upon agricultural production as well, and that is a highly subsidized sector within the union. Therefore, the wealthier EU members may be reluctant to extend full membership to former communist states very rapidly.

Aside from any social transfers received or markets that open to them, the former communist states place great importance on joining the European Union because it offers them a way to establish greater credibility for the policy choices they make. When a government issues a decree or a parliament passes a law that changes economic policy, there still remains the possibility that the next government or par-

TABLE 8-3. Human Development in Selected Countries

Eastern Bloc Countries	HDI Value	Other Countries	HDI Value
Romania	0.733	Turkey	0.671
Albania	0.791	Mexico	0.804
Bulgaria	0.865	Portugal	0.850
USSR	0.873	Greece	0.901
Poland	0.874	Spain	0.916
Hungary	0.893	Ireland	0.921
Czechoslovakia	0.897	Italy	0.922

Source: United Nations Development Programme (1992)

liament may reverse this change. Treaty commitments are a way of binding the hands of future governments, making it more difficult for policy reversals to occur and thereby creating more certainty for those deciding where to invest or build houses or obtain training. Therefore, countries that already seem to have the best prospects for reforming successfully and becoming members of the European Union are likely to widen the gap that currently exists between them and those states that have barely begun the reform process.

Privatizing State Assets

Liberalizing prices, abandoning central planning, and opening the economy to international trade are all steps that will allow markets to play a more important role in allocating resources, but those reforms can be carried out within an economy that continues to be based on market socialism: Firms that produce the new bundle of goods are still owned by the state. A further reform is to privatize state-owned enterprises (SOEs). A first step is to recognize the legal right to hold private property and to grant it the same protection as state property.

The actual process of privatization has differed across countries and the type of assets to be sold. One of the least controversial steps in Russia has been to privatize housing, where long-time residents have the opportunity to buy the apartments they inhabit. These are not open market transactions, though, and conditions often are imposed on the length of time land must be held before it can be sold (or perhaps it can only be passed on to heirs) and the way in which the property can be used (restricted to residential housing or private gardens).

There was never significant agricultural collectivization in Poland. In countries where there was, there often has not been pressure for immediate privatization. In Russia few steps to break up collectives were taken through 1993, although a land decree issued in April 1994 calls for the national application of a successful privatization experiment in Nizhny Novgorod. Under that approach laborers and pensioners were given vouchers that represent claims on land and equipment, but they were encouraged to form and bid as viable groups rather than to operate individual farms. Uzbekistan's initial program privatized 700 unprofitable state farms by allowing the new owners to assume the outstanding debt to the government, but the new owners had to sell 80 percent of their cotton production to the state. Less than 5 percent of arable land was to be allocated to small farms (RFE 1/11/93). Thus, private ownership does not mean total freedom from government intervention. Even when no formal change in ownership occurs, however, major restructuring of the agriculture sector may be possible, as demonstrated in China under a system of long-term leases to individuals.

Small-scale private enterprises have sprung up in the distribution and service sector. Many opportunities exist for expansion given the low priority this area received previously. Low initial capital requirements in this sector may explain its rapid growth, too, since state banks have tended to fund state enterprises and forced most new entrepreneurs to rely on unofficial finance.

The most complicated issues of privatization arise in the case of large-scale enterprises. An initial step is to convert large SOEs into joint stock corporations that operate independently from government ministries. The government then must decide how to allocate shares of stock in these enterprises and how the board of directors is to be appointed. Each alternative strategy has its own drawbacks. Simply transferring control to current workers and managers can be accomplished quickly, but it provides no revenue to the state. It also raises a serious question of equity, since workers in sectors that happen to face strong demand for their output in the newly restructured economy will receive a claim on a much more profitable future than workers in sectors where facilities are outdated and demand for production has declined.

If enterprises are auctioned off to the highest bidder, who will be able to bid? Politically, it may be unacceptable for foreign bidders to buy assets at what local residents feel are unfairly low prices; similar sentiments were expressed in the United States when Japanese investors made major purchases in the United States as the value of the dollar fell sharply in 1986–1987. Domestic buyers may be regarded with suspicion as well, if their ability to bid is due to a favored position in the state hierarchy or to gains from illegal activity and extortion in mafia-like operations. If property instead is to be leased, so that state assets do not pass simply to those who already have the most capital, what process will determine which people are eligible? Or, is a bidding process possible to establish the appropriate rent to charge?

Bidders will find it difficult to determine a fair price for state property. In a capitalist system, the price of a factory would reflect the anticipated value of profits earned from operating it. In most former communist states there is little basis to predict what price will be received for production, what input costs will be, which taxes will be imposed, and whether there will be restrictions on selling the asset in the future. Therefore, bidders may place a low value on assets in these countries undergoing major transitions.

For foreign buyers there is even greater uncertainty, since they cannot be sure of their ability to send profits out of the country, the rate of exchange that will be applicable, or the likelihood that they will be subject to discriminatory taxes and regulations. When Russia imposed a $5 per barrel export tax on oil, the initial euphoria over a potential Western role in reversing the decline in Russian production quickly evaporated. Nationalistic feelings have restricted most foreign participation to joint ventures, thereby limiting the types of firms that might consider entering the market and transferring technology or hard currency to it.

With the exception of Hungary, the goal of most privatization plans to date has not been to attract an inflow of hard currency or to raise revenue for the government. Rather, a primary goal appears to be achieving broad ownership of shares across the population, a possible reflection of socialist concerns over income distribution, equity, and the prospective ability of all to participate in a market economy and democratic society. Czechoslovakia was the first country to establish a program under which citizens could buy vouchers that would subsequently be used to bid for shares of stock in a variety of state enterprises. The program did not result in universal ownership, because to participate individuals had to buy a voucher book for $35. Yet, the initial offering in 1992 resulted in 8.5 million participants. Several investment groups emerged to operate as mutual funds, receiving vouchers from individuals to invest among 1,400 companies as they saw most appropriate. The division of the country into the Czech and Slovak Republics interrupted this process, but a second wave of privatization occurred in the spring of 1994 in each country (RFE 4/11/94).

In late 1992 Russia began a program to distribute privatization vouchers to all citizens. The first reported auction in Moscow where these vouchers were used, for a single confectionery factory, occurred in December 1992, but the subsequent pace of privatization was very rapid. By June 1994 80 percent of enterprises with employment under 200 workers had been privatized and 70 percent of larger enterprises. Nearly all the vouchers had been used by the time the program expired. One of the great successes of the program was that 45 million new stockholders were created by it.

Voucher sales, however, accounted for a minority share of most privatizations, and therefore they should not be regarded as the key characteristic of the Russian transition to private ownership. Rather, when most state enterprises were converted into corporations, two options could be followed. One called for 25 percent of the shares to be nonvoting and to be awarded to workers and managers, while the other 75 percent would be sold to outsiders for vouchers. The second option allowed 51 percent of the shares to be sold to workers and managers, in exchange for vouchers or cash, 10 percent were given to local governments, and 30 percent were auctioned to outsiders for privatization vouchers.

The first option represented an outcome similar to a western-style enterprise, and it was adopted in 20 percent of privatizations, primarily in situations where managers were unsure that workers would continue to support them. Because each firm generally designed its own privatization plan rather than have it imposed from above, it is not surprising that the second option, which gave control to insiders, was adopted in 80 percent of the cases. Furthermore, workers and managers could buy their shares at a price equal to 1.7 times the firm's book value in 1991. By 1993 the price level was fourteen times higher than in 1991, and therefore this clause represents a great advantage for insiders (Boycko, Shleifer, and Vishny 1993).

In comparison with other former communist states, privatization was accomplished quickly in 1993–94. The sense of urgency that drove this strategy is not surprising given the see-saw battle for control of the government in 1993 between the President and the parliament. In April President Yeltsin appeared victorious in a referendum that supported economic reform, but his subsequent actions to dissolve parliament did not generate much certainty regarding political or economic reform. A World Bank loan to support privatization and to create a social safety net was not approved by parliament, which instead preferred to subsidize troubled state enterprises. In the elections for the new state Duma in December 1993, the reform parties did not gain operating control and the President retained even fewer of his advisers that favored shock therapy. Rapid action, therefore, may have seemed appropriate for political reasons, but a closer examination of what was accomplished through privatization is warranted.

Given the de facto control of newly privatized enterprises by management, what checks exist to control inefficient managers? In the U.S. economy where the stock market plays an important role for firms seeking to raise new capital, inefficient management must contend with hostile takeover bids to buy a controlling interest in the firm, name a new board of directors, and replace existing managers. Or, a firm that keeps the same inefficient management team can expect to see its price fall in the marketplace, which makes it more costly for the firm to try to raise new capital. Nevertheless, these checks do not operate too stringently in the United States, where management compensation is only weakly related to the performance of the firm. A more activist role by U.S. pension funds in challenging current managers may make the system more responsive to shareholder interests.

In Russia these possible external checks are even less likely to be effective. The rights of minority shareholders are not well defined, and few enterprises have paid dividends. Although investment companies may develop a stronger voice than an individual shareholder, such companies are limited to holding 15 percent of the shares in an enterprise in Russia. The failure of the Russian investment company (and pyramid scheme) MMM in 1994 raises further questions about the viability of this outside influence, if such companies focus most of their attention on acquiring firms with assets that can be readily sold and on attracting new customers to meet withdrawals from old ones. A more effective system of external control seems to be emerging in Czechoslovakia, where 40 percent of the vouchers came to be held by five funds (Rutland 1994).

If minority owners are unlikely to have success in replacing inefficient managers, another possible model of outside control is the one utilized in Germany where banks play a more active oversight role. While existing Russian banks are state enterprises, too, they are not monolithic and some appear to be developing expertise in allocating credit on the basis of market criteria (Sachs 1993).

Although workers hold a majority of the shares in most privatized firms in Russia, worker control has not often emerged as a separate issue. A temptation in worker-owned enterprises is to raise wages rather than declare profits or retain earnings for further investment. Minority shareholders have little way of defending their interests in such a situation. Boycko, Shleifer, and Vishny (1993) attribute the extremely low values at which shares of Russian firms trade to the claims of managers and workers on potential profits. Capital flight out of Russia demonstrates that savers are much more certain of the return from foreign assets.

One expectation of privatization is that it will result in less need to subsidize inefficient state enterprises, which should face hard budget constraints. That outcome did not occur in Russia in 1993, when state subsidies to firms continued to be 15 percent of GDP. In 1994 the government was able to reduce this expenditure. Nevertheless, under the previous system managers ensured the success of their enterprises by convincing the government to provide more credit or cash, and the same managers still look to the government to provide the same solution.

Attempts to save failing companies are observed in the United States under the "too big to fail" doctrine. Government bail out plans for Lockheed, Chrysler, and Continental Illinois Bank demonstrate the fact that even in a capitalist system the discipline of the market is not always accepted politically. That pressure will be much greater in Russia. Yet, dealing effectively with large enterprises must depend on other factors as well. Pinto, Belka, and Krajewski (1993) report that Poland has been successful in imposing hard budget constraints and forcing restructuring even without privatization, especially where firms face foreign competition.

The complexities of privatization have caused some observers to conclude that too many scarce entrepreneurial resources are being used here, when in reality a more effective way to build a market economy would be to promote the creation of new enterprises (Murrell 1992). This view is consistent with the Hungarian economist Kornai's assessment: "We will have to reckon for the next two decades with the dual economy that emerged in Hungary over the past ten to twenty years, and with its two constituent parts, the state and private sectors" (1990, 101). Kornai suggests that dismantling a large state sector immediately is unlikely to be successful. The government's goal should be to "prevent the state sector from siphoning off excessive resources to the detriment of the private sector" and to adopt policies that "promote the private sector's fast and energetic development." While the rationale for this strategy is clear, achieving it may be difficult. Limiting the availability of funds to large SOEs will prove difficult if they continue to account for the majority of GDP and employment and thus political power.

CONCLUSION

The former communist states are making progress in converting their economies into market-oriented ones, but the process is far from smooth, even in the most promising countries. Poland and Hungary have had IMF loans frozen when they deviated substantially from their stabilization goals. The problems are reflected in the judgment of Standard and Poor's, a private company that evaluates the riskiness of borrowers. In 1994 it considered only debt from the Czech Republic to be investment grade and rated Hungarian and Polish debt as speculative. The course of future policy in the former communist states remains uncertain to many observers.

Political difficulties exacerbate economic problems. The cry for political independence and sovereignty within both the Eastern bloc and the USSR resulted in a breakdown of the somewhat tightly integrated economic institutions of the CMEA and the far more tightly integrated Soviet economy. The collapse of these relationships would have forced major changes even if all of the new governments had ignored calls for economic reform. The breakdown of trade with neighboring countries imposed a high cost on the former communist states; the smaller the country and the greater its reliance on the non-market system, the larger and more immediate the adjustments it had to make. There simply are not markets for many of the goods produced in abundance during the communist era, and for many others world market prices are far less than the cost of production when inputs must be bought competitively.

As resources are reallocated within the economy, not all sectors suffer proportionally. The wealthy and the powerful push for government expenditures that promote their interests, while the poor use their limited political power to push for government welfare programs. Under these circumstances government budget deficits are financed by printing more money, and the result is a less visible inflation "tax" on those who hold the national currency. Groups that bear high costs can be expected to seek political solutions. When just a few people are affected because the scope of change is small, a political strategy to ignore them may be successful because those displaced can more likely find satisfactory economic alternatives. When large numbers are forced to change, and they are represented by those with political power, then a democratic government will find it difficult to proceed on the article of faith that any losses will be small and temporary and adjustments to new alternatives will be straightforward. These concerns help explain why Polish reformers lost a vote of confidence in the *Sejm* in May 1993 and Russian reform parties were rebuffed by voters in elections for the new state Duma in December 1993.

The changes in government personnel that followed these electoral losses did not result in a wholesale rejection of stabilization and adjustment programs. The new leaders also recognized the inevitable need for some changes to occur. Some commentators have argued that authoritarian regimes are better suited than democratic ones to enforcing the rigors of stabilization and adjustment programs, although others note that changes hammered out in a democratic setting are more likely to be permanent. Within the fledgling democracies of Eastern Europe some agreement on the need for economic reform appears to be emerging. However, the compromises necessary to achieve such agreement limit the rate and magnitude of economic change.

For those states that do not benefit from an external pull into the European Union, the question is particularly pointed: Will the attempt to buy the assent of managers and party members from the communist era lock into power a group that will take advantage of the current chaos to ensure its own monopoly position? In particular, will this group arrest the reform process in midcourse and leave the Eastern states with the poor capitalism and unstable democracy of the South rather than the rich capitalism and participatory government of the North (Przeworski 1991)?

This chapter has focused on the processes of, and obstacles to, a successful transition to a prosperous market economy. It is obvious that the obstacles are great, and that, therefore, achievement is problematical. While it is not clear whether such a success is a prerequisite to successful democratization, failure would impose severe strains on the new democratic institutions and practices of the former communist world.

NOTES

1. Commitment by political leaders in the former communist countries to the creation of a market economy is, of course, largely motivated by the perceived economic benefits of such a conversion. The hypothesized political benefits are presumably an important, but secondary, motivation.
2. The World Bank reports no figure for Russia, as Russia has no series for exports or national income.

REFERENCES

BHAGWATI, JAGDISH. 1994. "Shock Treatments." *The New Republic*, March 28: 39–43.

BOYCKO, MAXIM, ANDREI SHLEIFER, and ROBERT VISHNY. 1993. "Privatizing Russia." *Brookings Papers on Economic Activity* 2:139–81.

BRUNO, MICHAEL. 1992. "Stabilization Plans in Eastern Europe." *International Monetary Fund Staff Papers* 39(4, December): 801–24.

CENTRAL INTELLIGENCE AGENCY. 1993. *CIA World Factbook.* Washington, D.C.: Central Intelligence Agency.

DAHL, ROBERT A. 1989. *Democracy and Its Critics.* New Haven: Yale University Press.

Economist, various issues.

FISCHER, STANLEY. 1992. "Privatization in East European Transformation." In Christopher Clague, and Gordon Rausser, eds., 1992, *The Emergence of Market Economies in Eastern Europe*. Cambridge, Mass.: Blackwell Publishers, 227–44.

HOUGH, JERRY F. 1994. "The Russian Election of 1993: Public Attitudes Toward Economic Reform and Democratization." *Post-Soviet Affairs* 10(1): 1–37.

INTERNATIONAL MONETARY FUND, BUREAU OF STATISTICS. 1994. *International Financial Statistics.* Washington, D.C.: International Monetary Fund.

KAHN, ALFRED E. and MERTON J. PECK. 1991. "Stabilizing the Soviet Economy." In Merton J. Peck and Thomas J. Richarson, eds., *What Is To Be Done? Proposals for the Soviet Transition to the Market Economy.* New Haven: Yale University Press, 38–82.

KAHN, MOHSIN. 1990. "The Macroeconomic Effects of Fund-Supported Adjustment Programs." *International Monetary Fund Staff Papers* 37(2, June): 195–231.

KEYNES, J. M. 1920. *The Economic Consequences of the Peace.* London: Macmillan and Company Limited.

KORNAI, JANOS. 1990. *The Road to a Free Economy Shifting from a Socialist System: The Example of Hungary.* New York: Norton.

LANE, DAVID. 1992. *Soviet Society under Perestroika.* New York: Routledge.

LIPSET, SEYMOUR M. 1959. "Some Social Requisites of Democracy: Economic Development and Political Legitimacy." *American Political Science Review* 53(1, March): 69–105.

MAITAL, SHLOMO, and BEN-ZION MILNER. 1993. "Russia and Poland: The Anatomy of Transition." *Challenge* 36(5, September/October): 40–7.

MCKINNON, RONALD. 1992. "Taxation, Money, and Credit in a Liberalizing Socialist Economy." In Christopher Clague and Gordon Rausser, eds., *The Emergence of Market Economies in Eastern Europe.* Cambridge, Mass.: Blackwell Publishers, 109–28.

MOORE, BARRINGTON. 1966. *Social Origins of Dictatorship and Democracy: Lord and Peasant in the Making of the Modern World.* Boston: Beacon Press.

MURRELL, PETER. 1992. "Evolution in Economics and in the Economic Reform of the Centrally Planned Economies." In Christopher Clague and Gordon Rausser, eds., *The Emergence of Market Economies in Eastern Europe.* Cambridge, Mass.: Blackwell Publishers, 35–54.

OLSON, MANCUR. 1992. "The Hidden Path to a Successful Economy." In Christopher Clague and Gordon Rausser, eds., *The Emergence of Market Economies in Eastern Europe.* Cambridge, Mass.: Blackwell Publishers, 55–76.

PEI, MINXIN. 1994. *From Reform to Revolution: the Demise of Communism in China and the Soviet Union.* Cambridge: Harvard University Press.

PINTO, BRIAN, MAREK BELKA, and STEFAN KRAJEWSKI. 1993. "Transforming State Enterprises in Poland: Evidence on Adjustment by Manufacturing Firms." *Brookings Papers on Economic Activity* 1:213–70.

PRZEWORSKI, ADAM. 1991. *Democracy and the Market.* New York: Cambridge University Press.

Radio Free Europe/Radio Liberty Daily Report (RFE), various issues.

RUTLAND, PETER. 1994. "Privatization in Russia: One Step Forward, Two Steps Back?" *Europe-Asia Studies* 46(7): 1109–31.

SACHS, JEFFREY. 1992. "Building a Market Economy in Poland." *Scientific American* (March): 34–40.

———. 1993. "Comments on Maxim Boycko, Andrei Shleifer, and Robert Vishny, 1993, Privatizing Russia." *Brookings Papers on Economic Activity* 2:184–8.

SAKWA, RICHARD. 1995. "Problems of Democracy and Democratisation Theory: The Case of Russia." In Joni Lovenduski and Jeffrey Stanyer, *Contemporary Political Studies 1995*, Volume I. Belfast: The Political Studies Association of the United Kingdom, 100–10.

SUMMERS, LAWRENCE. 1992. "The Next Decade in Central and Eastern Europe." In Christopher Clague and Gordon Rausser, eds., *The Emergence of Market Economies in Eastern Europe.* Cambridge, Mass.: Blackwell Publishers, 25–34.

United Nations Development Programme. 1992. *Human Development Report 1992.* New York: Oxford University Press.

United Nations. 1992. *World Investment Report 1992, Transnational Corporations as Engines of Growth.* New York: United Nations.

United Nations, Department of International Economic and Social Affairs, Statistical Office. 1991. *International Trade Statistics Yearbook.* New York: United Nations.

VANHANEN, TATU. 1990. *The Process of Democratization: A Comparative Study of 147 States, 1980–88.* New York: Crane Russak.

WALLICH, CHRISTINE, and RITU NAYYAR. 1993. "Russia's Intergovernmental Fiscal Relations: A Key to National Cohesion." *Challenge.* 36(6, November/December): 46–52.

WORLD BANK. 1992. *World Development Report.* New York: Oxford University Press.

WORLD BANK. 1994. *World Debt Tables 1994–95.* Washington, D.C.: The World Bank.

CHAPTER 9

The Impact of External Factors on the Future of Democracy in the FSU and Eastern Europe

ROBERT D. GREY[1]

Many analysts of democratization have focused heavily on identifying economic and social determinants or prerequisites for the process.[2] Challenging these deterministic arguments are scholars who argue that, although such conditions do limit and constrain the options available to political leaders, these leaders do have substantial room for maneuver (DiPalma 1990; Huntington 1991: Przeworski 1991; Kitschelt 1992).

Significant as are the disagreements between these competing schools, they nevertheless share one important feature. For both approaches, domestic phenomena are the sole or primary determinants of whether democracy emerges and/or persists. In this chapter, I will argue that international forces also shape the processes of the emergence and/or the consolidation of democracy.

In some cases, external forces have been indisputably decisive. For example, the United States imposed democracy upon Germany and Japan at the end of World War II; the USSR brought down a fledgling democracy in Czechoslovakia in the late 1940s and suppressed the possible emergence of democracy in Hungary in 1956 and its reemergence in Czechoslovakia in 1968. However, such situations, in which invasions, accompanied by subsequent occupations, permit an outside power to essentially overwhelm all domestic forces, are unusual. More typically, external and internal forces interact. It is likely that, in this interaction, international factors play a very important role (Huntington 1991, 85–99; Whitehead, 1986).

Some scholars, in attempting to assess the nature and magnitude of outside influences on democratization, focus on deliberate efforts by outside actors to encourage or support democracy. There are analysts of American foreign policy, for instance, who believe it is both possible and desirable for America to deliberately export, or, at least, promote, democracy (Muravchik 1991; Diamond 1992; Allison and Beschel 1992; Mroz 1992/93; Lowenthal 1991). Analysts of Soviet-East European relations during the cold war period emphasized the inhibiting effects of Soviet policies on whatever internal dynamics promoted democratization in the area. In the late 1980s, it could be argued, the USSR "removed the veto" (DiPalma 1990, 184).

Other analysts, however, emphasize the indirect influence of the international context, rather than specific policy measures by supportive or repressive states. Thus DiPalma (1990, 184), although he contends that democracy emerges essentially as a compromise among competing domestic forces, does devote the last chapter of his recent book to "democracy by diffusion, democracy by trespassing." Similarly, Starr (1991) analyzes "diffusion approaches to the spread of democracy in the international system." I will examine such concepts in greater detail below.

INTERNATIONAL POWERS AND THE PROMOTION OF DEMOCRACY DURING THE COLD WAR

In the pages below, I will distinguish between these two distinctly different strands of analysis, the one emphasizing intentional action by outside actors to affect the emergence or consolidation of democracy, the other highlighting more indirect, diffuse impacts of the international setting. I will first examine arguments that powerful international actors may be able to influence the likelihood that democracy will emerge in nondemocratic countries or last in countries that have achieved democracy. International influences on democratization need not, of course, be positive. Powerful states may attempt to promote democracy or to prevent its emergence.

It must first be acknowledged that all states pursue multiple goals in the international arena, and that the promotion of democracy has seldom been a high priority goal for major international actors, despite some idealistic rhetoric to the contrary. Distinctions must be made among the different powers. Whitehead (1986), for instance, distinguishes between the foreign policies of Western Europe and those of the United States. He argues that the foreign policies of such European states as France and Germany, as well as those of lesser powers like Belgium, Holland, and the Scandinavian states, have been quite supportive of the democratization of authoritarian states. In part, he suggests, such policies reflect the strength of socialist parties in these countries, and their abhorrence of right-wing authoritarianism. In part, the policies emerge out of the historical conflicts of these states with Naziism and Fascism. However, the assigning of a high priority to promoting democracy also reflects the lesser role, compared to America, that these states have assigned during the cold war period to a worldwide conflict with communism. Unlike the United States, they have not tended to tolerate right-wing authoritarian regimes because such regimes have been strongly anti-communist.

Thus, France and Germany are credited by scholars with contributing in the 1970s to the successful efforts of Spain and Portugal to democratize. Furthermore, by imposing the requirement that only democratic nations could join the European Economic Community, the EEC offered support to the forces supporting democracy in Greece. As the former communist states have moved toward democracy, Western European states, with Germany in the lead, have offered financial assistance, technical advice, and constitutional guidance (Höhmann, Meier, and Timmerman, 1993; Koch, 1993; Oldenburg, 1993; Pridham and Vanhanen 1994; Pridham, Herring, and Sanford 1994).

Within America, however, thinking about international politics has largely been dominated by what is called the "realist" school of international politics. Members of this school emphasize that states both do, and should, pursue a foreign policy based primarily on their most pressing national interests. These interests are usually interpreted as, first, military security, and second, economic prosperity. It seems to the realists that the promotion of democracy has little to do with the achievement of these goals. Those who advocate the promotion of democracy have usually been seen by members of this school as naive moralists, whose insensitivity to national interests is "fortunately" offset by their political impotence.

Challengers to this "realistic" viewpoint have emphasized that America has more than two foreign policy goals and they have pushed the desirability of foreign policies based, at least in part, on the promotion of such "moral" goals as democracy and human rights. A more subtle version of the argument posits that the promotion of democracy (particularly if it is accompanied by a move from a command economy to a market economy) is likely to be not only desirable in and of itself but also to be an effective means to enhance both American national security and economic prosperity. Proponents of the view that "democracies do not go to war with each other" certainly see democratization of the former Soviet Union as enhancing American national security. For many analysts, the conversion of communist economies to market ones is seen as promoting not only the prosperity of the converted economies, but also the prosperity of the international (capitalist) economy. Thus, for these critics of realism, there is no inherent conflict between promoting national security and economic prosperity while simultaneously working to spread democracy and human rights.

Has America included support for democracy as one of its foreign policy goals? American rhetoric in support of democracy has certainly been strong (Whitehead 1986; Huntington 1991, 91–8). The stated goals of the Kennedy administration's Alliance for Progress as well as the promotion of human rights during the Carter administration certainly suggested such a desire. So, too, did some of the justifications offered by the Johnson administration for its intervention in the Dominican Republic; the Reagan administration for its invasion of Grenada; and, finally, the Bush administration for its invasion of Panama. However, it is difficult to determine either the mix of goals that lay behind these actions or the priority assigned to promoting democracy in that mix. Other possibly relevant goals have included the promotion of perceived national security, in the form of anti-communism (central to the Grenadan case), as well as regional political stability (the Dominican Republic), the protection of Americans abroad (Grenada, again), and a purported attack on the international drug trade (Panama).

Creation by the Reagan administration of a National Endowment for Democracy (NED) added rhetorical flourish to what seemed to have been a low-priority American goal. However, the NED has never received the kind of funding that would suggest that promoting democracy had climbed substantially higher in the hierarchy of American foreign policy goals.

With the collapse of communism in East Central Europe in 1989 and the subsequent disappearance both of the Soviet Union and of communism as a powerful force within Russia, the primary successor state, there was a substantial growth in American verbal commitment to playing a significant role in promoting democracy in that part of the world. In 1992, the Bush administration promoted legislation to demonstrate its support for democratization in former communist countries. However, passage of the "Freedom for Russia and Emerging Eurasian Democracies and Open Markets Support Act of 1992" was no guarantee of a substantial, well-financed effort to, in fact, provide such support. The Clinton campaign of 1992, while de-emphasizing foreign policy, nevertheless argued that more had to be done to ensure democracy's emergence and survival in the former communist countries. The new Clinton administration brought to the Russian administration of Boris Yeltsin promises of assistance and came to Congress with requests for such assistance.

Yet the historical record suggests that the narrower perspective of the realists has tended to predominate in American foreign policy and does so still. Whitehead (1986), for example, treats American rhetorical commitment to the promotion of democracy as a thin veneer for a foreign policy dominated for decades by cold war conflict with the Soviet Union, a conflict in which strong support of anti-communist authoritarian regimes was one American strategy. Both Diamond and Huntington, however, argue that, starting with the Carter administration and continuing with the Reagan administration, commitment to the promotion of democracy became a real, if not central, goal for the United States (Diamond 1990; Huntington 1991).

Western European states and the United States have not been the only international actors whose actions have affected the spread of democracy. Contrary to conventional wisdom, the Soviet contribution to the spread of world democracy, while unintentional, nevertheless has been substantial. In the 1950s, 1960s, and 1980s the Soviet Union had acted decisively to squash tiny shoots of political liberalization in Poland, Hungary, Czechoslovakia, and Poland again. In the late 1980s, however, the USSR itself embarked upon a substantial liberalization and both permitted and encouraged parallel liberalization in Eastern Europe, China, and Cuba. Gorbachev's goal was to reform communism to save communism. Nevertheless, when developments[3] carried East Germany, Czechoslovakia, Hungary, and Poland past liberalization to democratization, and when, if communism of any variant were to be saved, it could only have been saved by the military intervention of the Soviet army, the Soviets stood aside and permitted the democratization of these countries. Gorbachevian support for reform and passivity in the face of its escalation contributed far more to the emergence of democracy in the communist world than did American "activism."

While one tends to think of international influences as state-to-state, intergovernmental organizations (IGOs) such as the United Nations, the Council of Europe, the European Economic Community (EEC), and the Conference on Security and Cooperation in Europe have also been active. Moreover, a number of nongovernmental organizations (NGOs) such as the Catholic Church[4] and the Socialist International (Whitehead 1986) have worked to promote democratization. In the democratization of Spain, European political parties worked closely with their Spanish counterparts. The fall of communism found Western European corporations, political parties, and trade unions moving into Eastern Europe as well.

INTERNATIONAL POWERS AND THE PROMOTION OF DEMOCRACY AFTER THE COLD WAR

With the demise of the Soviet Union and the collapse of communism on its territory and in eastern and central Europe, however, the context of international politics changed dramatically. The twenty-two formerly communist states of central and eastern Europe and central Asia initially all claimed to be developing democratic political systems, and outside support was seen as crucial for the success of this transition. Thus, Russian Foreign Minister Kozyrev stated in 1992: "The main evolutionary trends in Russia and the political maturity of its citizens enables us to expect that the country will not lapse into absolutism. The course of our internal processes, *in conjunction with the favorable 'external background'* (emphasis mine), give hope that we shall continue to seek answers to questions about the fate of Russia not by looking for a new 'strong arm' but through the elimination of the inadequacy of our own lives as compared with normal countries" (Kozyrev 1992, 7–8). Similarly, then Russian Ambassador to the United States Vladimir Lukin stressed:

> . . . the obvious U.S. interest in successful Russian democratic reforms. Russia needs American understanding and support in its complex geopolitical situation; it needs the United States as a source of economic and technical assistance, as a market for some of its products, as a partner in mutually beneficial cooperation to strengthen both countries' position in global technology competition, and, finally, as a leading Western country that will largely determine whether Russia is fully integrated into the community of developed countries (Lukin 1992, 73).

Russian leaders and their counterparts from the fourteen other states of the former Soviet Union and the states of eastern and central Europe sought external assistance to ease the transition from communism. As political leaders, forced by their jobs to be realistic, they argued that other states should help them, not out of idealism, but from the realization that it was in the interests of potential donor states that these countries become politically democratic and, in the economic sphere, join the international capitalist economy.

It is now but a short time since the emergence of some democratic states in East Central Europe and what are at least nominally democratic states there and in the former Soviet Union. Yet even in that brief time, concrete western commitment to support of democracy has proved to be quite limited, and the leaders of the former communist world have become very disillusioned.

The historical record suggested that European states, for both practical reasons and idealistic ones, were most likely to respond positively to this appeal (Inotai 1992; Dabrowa 1992; and Karaganov 1992). During the cold war, the military might of the Soviet Union threatened Europe more seriously than it did the United States. The military might of Russia has not disappeared, and that might, in the service of a Russia returned to authoritarianism and possible expansionism, would pose a comparable threat to Europe. To the extent that a democratic Russia is perceived in Europe as less likely to be an aggressive Russia, the European states have incentives to promote democratization. Since the other smaller, weaker former communist states do not directly threaten Western Europe, European states will lack this particular incentive to aid them. However, creation of a possible buffer zone between a powerful Russia and Western Europe might provide the incentives to promote friendly states, if not democratic ones, in eastern and central Europe.

Similarly, a successful transition to a prosperous market economy, while it would undoubtedly benefit the world economy in general, would have special relevance for Europe. The proximity of potentially massive markets for European goods, the availability of attractive investment opportunities for European capital, and the existence of relatively cheap labor for new Western European businesses in the East, all make a successful conversion to a market economy attractive to Europe.

A third incentive exists. Failure either in the political transformation or the economic one could well lead citizens of the former communist countries to flee their homelands. Western Europe has already been traumatized by relatively small numbers of immigrants from Africa, the Middle East, and southern Europe. In a number of countries, including most recently Germany, immigration laws have been made much more restrictive than they used to be. To these countries, the image of large numbers of Eastern or Central Europeans crossing their borders, seeking political asylum or economic opportunities, is quite frightening.

However, these practical incentives are not the only factors operating. Strong currents of opinion in Western Europe favor the promotion of democracy as a morally appropriate policy for their governments to follow. This is especially true on the left, among socialists and social democrats.

Thus, while there exist strong incentives for Western Europe to actively promote democracy, there exist, as well, powerful constraints. Much of the thinking about the most effective ways to help the transition has focused on the need of the former communist states for substantial capital during the early and difficult days of the transition to a market economy. European ability and willingness to provide massive amounts of capital is limited.[5] For Germany, the richest of the West European states, the effort to revitalize the economy of its newly added Eastern Lander (states) has absorbed most of its available resources. The continuing world recession has remained an obstacle, as has the recognition that there are many other claimants, particularly poorer third world states, on the limited funds available for this purpose. Nevertheless, Western Europe has continued to be the major source of financial assistance to its eastern neighbors. Thus, Germany contributed *annually* (emphasis mine) to Russia, from 1990 through 1993, a sum equal to total Marshall Plan aid (Oldenburg, 1993, 21).

While much of the help that Western Europe has provided and will provide is bilateral, state-to-state aid, assistance has taken many other forms. The overwhelming majority of foreign private capital investment in the east has come from European sources. European political parties have rushed to provide technical assistance to their counterparts in the east. The European Economic Community, now European Union, has been negotiating with Eastern European states about assistance in the short run and membership in the long run. In 1992, Poland, Hungary, and the Czech Republic signed association agreements with the EEC and can reasonably anticipate membership in the future. For Western Europe, it is important that eastern states become truly members of a common (democratic and capitalist) European home.

For America, the incentives have been both less clear and less powerful (Saunders 1993; Bodie 1993; Breslauer 1993; Porter and Saivetz 1994; Zelikov 1994; Brzezinski 1994). For realists, it is no longer clear that the former communist countries pose a threat to America security. Yet for some analysts, such as Hopf (1992), the possible failure of Russian democratization—with its threat of a restoration of a militarily strong, expansionist, and dictatorial Russia—makes support for Russian democracy an American national security issue of the highest priority. Others, however, in thinking about a "new world order," assign less importance to developments in Russia and emphasize greater American interests in, for instance, the Middle East. Concern about a possibly revived Russian dictatorship and its propensity to aggression does not, of course, imply great concern about whether other former communist states revert to dictatorship. However, there are analysts committed to the position that America has a moral obligation to, as well as an interest in, promoting democracy everywhere, who urge assistance to all of the former communist states in their effort to achieve stable democracy.

While Western European states and private investors see attractive economic opportunities opening up, from the other side of the Atlantic, Americans are less likely to see substantial economic stakes, at least in the short run. Similarly, the United States, given its distance from the countries of the east and the protection an ocean provides—if not from ICBMs, at least from large numbers of refugees—lacks the intense fear of immigrants from the East that, in Europe, promotes greater assistance to the former communist states.

It is not only the apparent lack of major incentives that has limited and will limit U.S. efforts to assist democratization and the move to a market economy. Like Europe, the United States has endured, at the end of the 1980s and the beginning of the 1990s, a major recession. The election campaign of 1992 was almost wholly fought on domestic issues, and the repudiation of President Bush can be seen, at least in part, to be a result of his "overemphasis" on foreign affairs. With a very large government deficit, a political commitment to reduce it, a substantial domestic agenda, and a reluctance to raise taxes to fund that agenda (and reduce the deficit), the Clinton administration has found it difficult to justify major expenditures to assist the transition from communism. Mroz (1992/93) saw the Bush administration as having failed both to recognize the need for and to take advantage of the opportunity to aid the east. He argues that the time for successful intervention may be rapidly disappearing. The first three years of the Clinton administration provide support for that argument.

An additional factor has been operating. As the Yeltsin administration in Russia has been settling in, it has added to its agenda not only (and, perhaps, not primarily) achievement of democracy and of a market economy. It has begun to define its foreign policy and to identify Russian national interests (Sestanovich 1994). The invasion of Chechnya in 1994, seen by Russian leaders as a domestic issue, raises the possibility of comparably aggressive policies toward the "near abroad" (the other new countries, formerly Soviet Republics, emerging from the collapse of the USSR). Russia identifies this as the primary area of its concern and promotion of Russian political and economic interests as the primary goal (Goble 1993). Russian leaders have also argued that it is up to Russia to protect the interests of the 25 million ethnic Russians who now find themselves subjects of the governments of these other new countries.

To many leaders of the new countries and to many American foreign policy decision makers, these rhetorical concerns and policies seen to emerge from them suggest a Russian interest in recreating the Soviet Union/Russian Empire. The American response to this perceived Russian neo-imperialism has been a cooling of the enthusiasm to "help Russia" (Brzezinski 1994; Arbatov 1994; Kozyrev 1994). William Bodie (1993) nicely summarizes the resulting U.S. ambivalence:

> Today, the United States clearly seeks to cultivate democratic institutions on the territory of the former Soviet empire. But American policy also seeks objectives in post–cold war Europe—arms reductions and non-proliferation, Russian economic stabilization, amelioration of ethnic conflict—which, though favorable to U.S. interests, may actually hinder the rapid adoption of democracy in the region. *To date, it is not clear whether the United States is more interested in the internal pluralism of the Soviet successor regimes or their external behavior.* (Bodie 1993, 509. Emphasis mine.)

Government assistance is not the only source of American support. American NGOs—such as corporate associations, labor unions, or political parties—while sympathetic to the transition, lack the incentives, the priorities, or the means to do much. The primary channel for American support has been through U.S. influence in such intergovernmental agencies as the IMF or the World Bank.

There are numerous economic components to a multilateral strategy of external assistance. Membership in the IMF and World Bank, a stabilization fund to support the convertibility of the ruble and the other currencies of the area, most favored nation status, debt relief, emergency food relief, and other measures are important parts of the strategy and are discussed more fully in Chapter 8.

MODES OF ASSISTANCE: SUPPORT FOR A MARKET ECONOMY

Thought on how best to promote democracy is complicated by the complexity of perceived interconnections between the fate of political democracy and economic concerns. There seem to be three basic ways of conceptualizing that relationship. First, some analysts seem to regard the existence of a market economy as equivalent to political democracy. The two are seen as one, and to promote the former is to promote the latter. British parliamentarians who, in February 1992, gave Russian President Boris Yeltsin a standing ovation when he said he would promote market reform even if he had to dissolve parliament to do so, were clearly espousing this position. A somewhat different but complementary position is that, in the long run, democracy and a market economy go together, that the dispersion of economic power, attendant upon a market economy, would prevent dictatorial concentration of political power (see Chapter 3).

I would however, offer, a sharply divergent view. At least in the short run, the simultaneous movement to political democracy and to a market economy seem to pull the political economy in opposing directions (Pei 1992, 1994). Movement toward a market economy necessitates higher unemployment and, at the same time, vastly increased inflation. Movement toward democracy provides to the population real political power. A population that is both economically battered and has the political clout to resist this buffeting is likely to do so. One result of this situation is a possible retreat from economic reform.

During 1992, the elected Russian parliament resisted greatly the push by Yeltsin and his then Prime Minister, Gaidar, for a more aggressive economic transition. Commentary in the West explained this parliamentary opposition as due to the undemocratic character of the parliament. Elections had occurred prior to the collapse of communism and a large number of seats had been reserved for communists. Moreover, additional seats were held by industrial managers who had both an economic and political interest in preserving as much as possible of the old system. While both of these factors were at work and may, in fact, adequately explain parliamentary opposition, it is also probable that such opposition paralleled, if it did not reflect, popular opposition to the consequences of, if not the goal of, market reform. In polls taken in 1992, two-thirds of Russian respondents went so far as to reject continuing Western humanitarian aid if it were tied to the continuation of the Yeltsin administration's economic policies (Mroz 1992/93, 47). In the new, more democratic elections of December 1993, parliamentarians equally hostile to rapid and drastic economic reform were returned to office. Although movement toward a market economy continues, democracy has been solidified at the expense of rapid movement toward the market.

It is possible that those most committed to market reforms may decide that it is impossible, in the context of a democratic competition for popular support, to effectively promote such reforms. Hostile to these recent developments, they may reassert dictatorial control in order to better manage the transition to capitalism. There are those in Russia and elsewhere in the former communist world who find attractive the perceived economic successes of authoritarian rule in Chile under Pinochet, in Taiwan or South Korea before they democratized, or even in the People's Republic of China under continuing rule by the communist party. While not hostile to democracy, they argue that it must follow successful conversion of the economy and achievement of a reasonable level of prosperity. Yeltsin's dissolution of parliament in the fall of 1993 suggests such a prioritizing of economic reform.

If this analysis is correct, exclusive or overemphasis by the various sources of external support on pushing market reforms, and particularly pressure by such sources for rapid conversion, may undermine rather than support democracy. Instead of insisting on linking economic assistance to a rigorous and rapid transition to a market economy, the emphasis of Western economic assistance should, therefore, be on reducing the suffering of the peoples of these countries as they undergo the economic transition, reducing the likelihood of a popular repudiation either of democracy or of economic reform. However, few scholarly analysts and almost no government decision makers outside of Russia itself seem greatly concerned about this danger.

Given the tendency to see such tight linkages between economic phenomena and successful democratization, much of the thinking as to how most effectively to support the transition to democracy has focused on providing support for a shift from the command economy to a market economy, rather than focusing on somehow promoting democracy per se. Proponents of this shift assume that successful democratization depends upon and will automatically follow from the success of such a transition and the prosperity it is assumed it will bring. My analysis suggests the superficiality of such a view.

NONECONOMIC MODES OF EXTERNAL ASSISTANCE

Much of the literature on consolidation of democracy emphasizes the crucial role of political elites in so fully accepting democracy that they never seriously consider attacking the basic democratic institutions and practices (DiPalma 1990). While the various incentives for elites to buy into democracy will, for the most part, be domestic ones, it may be possible to structure some additional international incentives (Allison and Beschel 1992, 90–7). Thus, for instance, the leaders of present democratic states should make it clear that membership in elite international institutions such as the IMF and the World Bank, attendance at elite gatherings such as the meeting of the G-7, or even less elite ones such as environmental summits, may depend on continued adherence to democracy. "Only democrats need apply." Adherence to democracy must be made to seem the only political option that is internationally respectable or acceptable.

In addition to providing the highest political elites with incentives to preserve democracy, outsiders might provide assistance in such tasks as constitution writing and revamping of law codes (see Chapters 3 and 5). To those who stress the role not of the highest political elites but of leaders of "civil society," for example, trade union leaders, party officials, and chairs of various business associations, another strategy suggests itself (see Chapters 3 and 4). Assistance in institution building may contribute to democratic stability. Delegations to the former communist states to assist these leaders of intermediary organizations in figuring out how to organize and operate their institutions effectively might be of great help. Similarly, inviting these leaders to visit democratic states (and paying for their visits) to watch democracy in action might both help them to build their institutions and remind them that such perks are unlikely to accrue to anti-democrats. A particularly vital group might be personnel from the media. To those who think of the media as the fourth branch of democratic governance, working with such personnel would seem to be a highly positive and inexpensive means of strengthening democracy.

All of these strategies are desirable means for the international community to promote the consolidation of democracy but they are likely to play a minimal role in the long term fate of democratic institutions and practices. The general international, economic, political, and military context may have more impact on the fate of democracy than these explicit, deliberate efforts to promote it.

THE INTERNATIONAL CONTEXT AND DEMOCRATIZATION

While the probability of successful democratization may be affected by explicit attempts by foreign actors to promote or constrain it, it will also be affected by general characteristics of the international context. Conditions in the political, economic, and security spheres will have an impact. Concepts such as international diffusion (DiPalma 1990, 183–99), imitation (Huntington 1991, 31–108), and demonstration effect capture some of the subtle ways that the international political environment and the domestic one interact.

Diffusion involves, in part, what DiPalma calls the "demonstration effect." Dictatorial leaders see their peers in other countries fall and understand, as a result, that they, too, may be vulnerable. Their increased sense of vulnerability may lead them to negotiate their way out of dictatorship, as a way of preserving more than they might if their regimes were overthrown: their lives, their freedom from prison, or perhaps even continuing, if lessened, political power. Conversely, democratizers are encouraged by the success of democratization efforts elsewhere. They develop not only an increased appreciation of the likelihood of success, but some sense of potentially effective strategies.

In addition to demonstration effects, diffusion may work by narrowing the apparently available alternatives for political change. For example, the transition away from communism in Eastern and Central Europe conceivably could have taken the form of coups by Eastern European militaries and the imposition of military regimes. This, after all, has been the world's most common regime change in the post-war era. However, as a result of the wave of world democratization occurring since 1974, democracy undoubtedly seemed, even to the military in these countries, the only plausible arrival point for the departure from communism. Of course, this effect, while promoting the emergence of democracy in the area, could be followed by a later wave of dictatorial/military takeovers, should there be a failure of democratic consolidation.

A strong case can be made, I would argue, that such effects were at work in a very powerful way in the emergence of democracy in Eastern Europe in 1989–90. However, it is not nearly as clear that such effects will play much of a role in the consolidation of democracy, and might, in fact, play a significant role (as they almost certainly did in the same part of the world during the interwar period) in a possible "ebbing of the wave."

While the international political context may have an impact on democratization efforts, so too will the international economic context. For instance, the world recession of the late 1980s and early 1990s made much less likely substantial external assistance for the former communist countries. It also made less likely strong export markets for the products of these countries. To the extent that the international community seems to be turning away from free trade and toward heightened protectionism, this will also adversely affect the economic health of the former communist countries. Most analysts feel that the greater the economic difficulties, the less likely the chances for successful consolidation of democracy.

It is the security sphere, however, that has the greatest likelihood of seriously affecting the prospects for democratic consolidation. I would argue that the greater the security threat a state confronts, or thinks it confronts, the higher the concentration of political power it is likely to be willing to accept. The higher the concentration of political power, the less likely its politics will be democratic.

While I know of no definitive proof for these propositions, there does exist some supportive evidence. Even in the consolidated democracies of the West, wars have been times of reduced democracy, and even cold wars have tended to erode their democratic character. For example, during WW II the "constitutional rule" that British parliamentary elections must take place at least every five years was put on hold for the duration of the war. Many students of American politics saw the period of the cold war as a time of heightened executive influence over the legislature and as a time of enhanced political influence for a "military-industrial complex."

Conversely, security assurances may reduce the sense that consolidated power is necessary in the face of danger. Measures that heighten the sense of security of the elites of the area would be useful. A number of such measures have been pursued recently. For instance, Russian troop reductions and withdrawals have promoted greater international confidence, not only among their former enemies, but also among their former allies of the Warsaw pact, as well as among the other states of the former Soviet Union. Troop withdrawals from these countries have now taken place.

To the extent that anyone in the former Soviet bloc saw NATO's military strength as threatening, western troop reductions may also be seen as reassuring. However, to the extent that the states of central and eastern Europe, as well as the fourteen other states created out of the old USSR, see threats to their security as asymmetrically coming from Russia, they might be more reassured by continued NATO strength, accompanied by some sort of security guarantees. The recent debate on possibly extending NATO membership to former Warsaw Pact members reflects a Western sense of the desirability of heightening the sense of security of these countries. Unfortunately, such a move is clearly seen as threatening by Russia. The perception that Europe will be aggressive in punishing aggression might also be reassuring, although the recent passive response of Europe to Serbian aggression is likely to suggest to the former communist states that they had best depend on their own military capabilities to defend their interests.

There is another component to the relationship between a severe external environment and low probability of democratic consolidation. One strategy for coping with a hostile world is concentration of power. A second strategy is the building up of a powerful military to cope with that hostile world. Powerful militaries, however, are likely to constrain democratic consolidation in several ways. First, powerful militaries are themselves likely to become important actors in domestic politics. While the Soviet Union and the communist states of Eastern Europe achieved a level of civilian control of the military comparable to that of the industrialized democracies of the West, with the possible exception of the Jaruzelski takeover in Poland in the early 1980s, there is no guarantee that the successor states will be equally successful. Certainly one of the main mechanisms of civilian control—party infiltration of every level of the military—has been destroyed everywhere in the area. Since military takeover of the political system is by far the most typical path by which democratic consolidation in the world is thwarted, the strengthening of militaries that will follow heightened perceptions of external threat will increase the fragility of domestic democratic institutions and practices.

There is a second important way in which a military buildup might constrain democracy. Such a buildup would be very expensive. At a time of severely limited state economic resources, and in a situation in which state resources have a crucial role to play in "buying time" for democratic consolidation, the "diversion" of resources into the military might well so limit the money available for social safety nets as to make much more likely popular support for a return to dictatorship. In much of the third world, military coups are greeted with enthusiasm or at least relief.

The initial naive view of analysts was that the end of the cold war and the collapse of the Soviet Union created a net gain in security for everyone. With the disappearance of what was considered Soviet expansionism in the third world, and Soviet willingness to forgo its "obligations" under the Brezhnev doctrine to intervene in Eastern Europe, it was felt that there were no significant international aggressors left.

Contributing to this view is a body of literature that holds that democratic states don't fight each other. Whatever the validity of that view, it is not to argue either that democratic states don't fight, or that they are incapable of being aggressors. Their democratic character hardly prevented the French and British from creating their vast world empires nor has it prevented the sending of American troops off to fight in numerous places over the last century and a half.

At the time of its accession to independence, Russian foreign policy, like that of the USSR under Gorbachev, seemed to abjure the use of force in international politics, and even to deny the existence of Russian national interests, equivalent to those of other states. Such an idealistic viewpoint could hardly have been expected to last long. Though the primary spokespeople for such views, President Yeltsin and Foreign Minister Kozyrev, continued in office until 1996, Russian foreign policy has changed dramatically.

Yeltsin, Kozyrev, and other Russian centrists now advocate an "assertive" and "aggressive" foreign policy, and appeal for western understanding of the "natural" character of such a foreign policy for a major power (Sestanovich 1994; A. Arbatov 1993; G. Arbatov 1994; Bodie 1993; Zelikov 1994). Although initially only extreme nationalists espoused Russian use of force, Russian troops were, by early in 1995, fighting not only in Chechnya but in Tajikistan. The Russian army has been active in Moldova, with the 14th Army occupying the Transdniester region and in Georgia.

It is true that the dramatic decline of Soviet/Russian strength vastly reduced Russian influence in Eastern Europe and freed fourteen former republics from actual control by Moscow. However the weakness of these states both makes them vulnerable to continuing Russian influence and makes them more accessible to influences emanating from other states.

The successor states of the old communist bloc face substantial security threats. In part this is a function of their weakness. They are small and their economies are in shambles. Their armies are small and poorly trained. Their military equipment is second-rate and deteriorating. Almost no one will be significantly deterred by their military strength, nor will that strength enable them to use military force to promote their international interests. Of course the present possession of nuclear weapons by the Ukraine, Kazakhstan, and Belarus at least makes them less plausible as targets of aggression.

In greater part, however, security is threatened because of the crazy-quilt distribution of ethnic groups in the area (For a more extended discussion of this topic, see Chapter 7). Some states are ethnically homogeneous—that is, almost all of their inhabitants share the same ethnicity. Poland and some of the central Asian states fall into this category. In addition, these states are fortunate in having most members of their "national group" resident in their own country. Such states are unlikely either to be a target for other's irredentism, or to fall victim to the temptation to themselves expand outside their borders.

While Hungary is internally homogeneous, there are large numbers of Hungarians in Romania, Slovakia, and Serbia. Thus Hungary, while safe from other's covetous eyes, may either contemplate the creation of a greater Hungary, at the expense of its neighbors, or wish to protect Hungarians who are victims of discrimination elsewhere. However, its small size and military weakness make aggression on its part implausible.

Unfortunately, most of the former communist states are both more ethnically heterogeneous than these states, and have more members of their group outside of the national territory. Both of these situations may well create a heightened security problem. For the ethnically heterogeneous states, ethnic divisions are likely to form the structuring cleavage of their politics. If politically subordinate or demographically less numerous groups feel themselves victimized, and are geographically concentrated, they may well develop secessionist movements. So far, such situations have led to the collapse of the USSR, Yugoslavia, and Czechoslovakia, and violent conflict in Georgia between the Georgian majority and the Abkhazian and Ossetian minorities, but there are numerous other countries where the potential for such a conflict is high. Even if no outside involvement occurs, civil war conditions are not conducive to democratic politics.

If to secessionist politics is added outside support for secession, an international war is likely to ensue. The victimized minority of one state is frequently the aggravated majority of another state. The conflict between Armenia and Azerbaijan over Nagorno-Karabakh demonstrates the potential for international conflict in such situations, but tensions between Russian and the Ukraine over the Crimea and between Russia and Moldova over the Transdniester area threaten to turn into major conflicts, affecting domestic politics.

There do exist causes of invasion other than ethnic irredentism, and other sources of civil war than ethnic heterogeneity and conflict. Thus, although the analysis so far has treated Russia as a probable source of danger to the other states of the area, it is not itself totally free from danger. Several of its neighbors, including the Ukraine, possess nuclear weapons, and thus are not totally helpless in the face of possible Russian threats. Nevertheless, the former states of the Soviet Union seem unlikely to threaten Russia. However, it must be remembered that along much of Russia's southern border lies China. If China, with its massive population, large army, nuclear weapons, and claims on Soviet (now Russian) territory has at times in the past seemed a major security threat to a large and powerful Soviet Union, how much greater a potential security threat must it seem to a smaller and weaker Russia? While those in the West treat as axiomatic pacific American, European, and Japanese stances toward all the former communist states, their statesmen would be remiss in their duties if they did not consider the possibility that traditional enemies, now putative friends, might not someday again become enemies. The world is a dangerous place, and the more dangerous it seems, the more domestic politics must be arranged to deal with whatever perils seem on the horizon. Democracy will suffer as a result of the necessary concentration of power in the face of dangers.

CONCLUSION

The international environment is a source both of possible support for movement toward and consolidation of democracy and of threats to those goals. The rhetoric of international politics in the early 1990s suggests that the rich democracies of the world were committed to helping the former communist countries make a transition to democracy. Their efforts to do so, however, have been constrained by their limited resources, competing priorities, and the wrong-headed assumption that the promotion of moves toward a market economy is equivalent to providing support for a movement toward democracy. Negative reactions toward an increasingly assertive Russian foreign policy have further weakened Western commitment to help Russia.

Despite these obstacles, some state-to-state support, financial and otherwise, has been provided and limited increases in such support will occur. Intergovernmental and nongovernmental organizations will add these efforts. In addition, international political "currents" are supporting democracy. In Africa and Asia, as well as Eastern and Central Europe, more and more states are moving toward democracy. Democracy is on the agenda.

However, the international arena is a source of threats, as well as support. The worldwide recession of the past few years raises obstacles to economic growth and presumably democratic consolidation. The vulnerable security situation of many of the new political systems is likely to encourage dictatorial concentrations of power. The analysis so far has suggested that the security problems will be highest for states that are weak, ethnically heterogeneous, and whose minority population(s) shares ethnicity with another state. From this perspective, Russia, given its strength and the fact that no other nearby state "wants" either its territory or its population, has the least to worry about. On the other hand, there are substantial numbers of Russians outside Russia, Russia is significantly stronger than its neighbors, and there is a growing nationalist movement within Russia. In late February 1992, Boris Yeltsin, President of Russia, declared that Russia should have "special status on the territory of the former Soviet Union to monitor conflicts and prevent ethnic clashes." Russia, the heart of the former hegemon, is therefore likely to be, and to seem to be, a great threat to its neighbors, and thus to limit their potential to achieve lasting democratic rule.

In this chapter, I have focused on external factors that might affect the successful consolidation of democracy in the former communist states. However, I tend to assume, with most scholars, that internal political and economic developments are likely to have a far more potent effect on the future political direction of these states than any external factors, and that the latter factors will have at most a marginal effect. The exception I would make to this general rule is that severe security threats rise instantly to the top of any state's agenda, and, in doing so, have a very great impact on their politics and economics. Thus, unfortunately, to the extent that outside forces are likely to impact substantially on the possibility of consolidation of democracy, it is most likely to be in a negative direction.

NOTES

1. The author would like to express his gratitude to Stephen White, his students, Jill Cetina and Scott Wittstruck, and his colleague, Eliza Willis, for their useful comments on earlier drafts of this chapter.

2. See Chapters 3 and 4.
3. The emergence of democracy in these countries was, I think, largely a consequence of internal dynamics. According to then Deputy Soviet Foreign Minister Aleksandr Aleksandrovich Bessmertnykh, however, the USSR leadership aggressively pushed East European communist leaderships to "reform communism." (Bessmertnykh, personal interview, Oct. 18, 1992). However, I shall argue below that there were also more subtle international influences at work, dovetailing with and strengthening both the internal factors and Soviet pressures.
4. Huntington (1991) particularly emphasizes the contribution of a liberalized Catholic church to the democratization of Latin America. While, given the repression of religion throughout the communist sphere, religious forces were seldom strong enough to have a significant impact on the fall of communism or its replacement by democratizing regimes, the Catholic Church in Poland played a role similar in character to that of the Latin American churches and perhaps one even greater in magnitude.
5. It should be noted, however, that the agreement of the G7 (the world's major industrial powers), announced on April 1, 1992, to provide $24 billion for the transition involved only some $4.35 billion (Treasury Department estimate) to $6.6 billion (State Department estimate) from the United States. Thus, the vast majority of the funding was to come from the IMF, World Bank, and European and Japanese sources.

REFERENCES

ALLISON, GRAHAM T., JR. and ROBERT P. BESCHEL, JR. 1992. "Can the United States Promote Democracy?" *Political Science Quarterly* 107(1, Spring):81–98.

ARBATOV, ALEXEI. 1993. "Russia's Foreign Policy Alternatives." *International Security* 18(2, Fall):5–43.

ARBATOV, GEORGI. 1994. "Eurasia Letter: A New Cold War?" *Foreign Policy* 95(Summer):90–104.

BODIE, WILLIAM C. 1993. "The Threat to America from the Former USSR." *Orbis* 37(4, Fall):509–25.

BRESLAUER, GEORGE. 1993. "Two Years After the Collapse of the USSR: Aid to the Soviet Union: What Difference Can US Policy Make." *Post Soviet Affairs* 9(4):308–11.

BRZEZINSKI, ZBIGNIEW. 1994. "The Premature Partnership." *Foreign Affairs*, 73(2, March-April):67–82.

DABROWA, SLAWOMIR A. 1992. "Security Problems Facing Central and Eastern Europe After German Reunification." In Paul B. Stares, ed. *The New Germany and the New Europe*. Washington, D.C.: The Brookings Institution, 305–30.

DIAMOND, LARRY. 1990. "Beyond Authoritarianism and Totalitarianism: Strategies for Democratization." In Brad Roberts, ed. *The New Democracies: Global Change and U.S. Policy*. Cambridge, Mass.: MIT Press, 227–49.

———. 1992. "Promoting Democracy." *Foreign Policy* 87(Summer):25–46.

DIPALMA, GUISEPPE. 1990. *To Craft Democracies: An Essay on Democratic Transitions*. Berkeley: University of California Press.

GOBLE, PAUL. 1993. "Russia and its Neighbors." *Foreign Policy* 90(Spring):79–88.

HÖHMANN, H.-H. C. MEIER, and H. TIMMERMANN. 1993. "The European Community and the Countries of the CIS: Political and Economic Relations." *The Journal of Communist Studies* 9(3, September):151–76.

HOPF, TED. 1992. "Managing Soviet Disintegration: A Demand for Behavioral Regimes." *International Security* 17(1, Summer):44–75.

HUNTINGTON, SAMUEL P. 1991. *The Third Wave: Democratization in the Late Twentieth Century*. Norman: Oklahoma University Press.

INOTAI, ANDRAS. 1992. "Economic Implications of German Unification for Central and Eastern Europe." In Paul B. Stares, ed. *The New Germany and the New Europe*. Washington, D.C.: The Brookings Institution, 279–304.

KARAGANOV, SERGEI A. 1992. "Implications of German Unification for the Former Soviet Union." In Paul B. Stares, ed. *The New Germany and the New Europe*. Washington, D.C.: The Brookings Institution, 331–64.

KITSCHELT, HERBERT. 1992. "Review Essay: Structure and Process Driven Explanations of Political Regime Change." *American Political Science Review* 86(4, December):1028–34.

KOCH, BURKHARD. 1993. "American and German Approaches to East Central Europe: A Comparison." *World Affairs* 156(2): 86–96.

KOZYREV, ANDREI. 1992. "Russia: A Chance for Survival." *Foreign Affairs* 71(2, Spring):1–16.

———. 1994. "The Lagging Partnership." *Foreign Affairs* 73(3, May/June):59–71.

LOWENTHAL, ABRAHAM F. 1991. *Exporting Democracy: The United States and Latin America*. Baltimore: The Johns Hopkins University Press.

LUKIN, VLADIMIR P. 1992. "Our Security Predicament." *Foreign Policy* 88(Fall):57–75.

MROZ, JOHN EDWIN, 1992/93, "Russia and Eastern Europe: Will the West Let Them Fail?" *Foreign Affairs* 72(1):44–57.

MURAVCHIK, JOSHUA. 1991. *Exporting Democracy: Fulfilling America's Destiny*. Washington, D.C.: The American Enterprise Press.

OLDENBURG, FRED. 1993. *Germany's Interest in Russian Stability*. Köln: Berichte des Bundesinstituts fur Ostwissenschaftliche und Internationale Studien.

PEI, MINXIN. 1992. "The Dual Transition: Analyzing Regime Transition from Communist Rule." Paper presented at the 1992 Annual Meeting of the American Political Science Association, Chicago, September 3–6.

———. 1994. *From Reform to Revolution: The Demise of Communism in China and the Soviet Union.* Cambridge: Mass.: Harvard University Press.

PORTER, BRUCE D., and CAROL SAIVETZ. 1994. "The Once and Future Empire: Russia and the Near Abroad." *The Washington Quarterly* 17(3, Summer):75–90.

PRIDHAM, GEOFFREY, and TATU VANHANEN. 1994. *Democratization in Eastern Europe: Domestic and International Perspectives.* New York: Routledge.

———, ERIC HERRING, and GEORGE SANFORD. 1994. *Building Democracy: The International Dimension of Democratisation in Eastern Europe.* London: Leicester University Press.

PRZEWORSKI, ADAM. 1991. *Democracy and the Market: Political and Economic Reforms in Eastern Europe and Latin America.* New York: Cambridge University Press.

SAUNDERS, HAROLD H. 1993. *The Concept of Relationship: A Perspective on the Future Between the United States and the Successor States to the Soviet Union.* Columbus, Ohio: The Mershon Center, Ohio State University, January.

SESTANOVICH, STEPHEN. 1994. *Rethinking Russia's National Interests.* Washington, D.C.: Center for Strategic and International Studies.

STARR, HARVEY. 1991. "Democratic Dominoes: Diffusion Approaches to the Spread of Democracy in the International System." *Journal of Conflict Resolution* 35(2, June):356–81.

WHITEHEAD, LAURENCE. 1986. "International Aspects of Democratization." In Guillermo O'Donnell, Philippe C. Schmitter, and Laurence Whitehead, eds., *Transitions from Authoritarian Rule: Comparative Perspectives.* Baltimore: The Johns Hopkins University Press, 3–46.

ZELIKOV, PHILIP. 1994. "Beyond Boris Yeltsin." *Foreign Affairs* 73(1, January–February):44–55.

INDEX

A

Accommodating ethnicity through democratic structures and procedures, strategies for, 206–212
Ackerman, B., 28, 29, 38
Acton, Lord, 190
Adams, J. S., 5
Advocatura, 155–156
Allan, T. R. S., 116
Allison, J. T. Jr., 248, 257
Allman, J., 47
Almond, G. A., 56, 81, 92, 105
Altman, A., 112
Alvarez, J. E., 132
Anderson, W., 47
AOJ program, 132
Arbatov, A., 261
Arbatov, G., 255, 261
Arbitrazh courts, 155, 157
Arendt, H., 65, 90, 103
Aristotle, 15
Aron, R., 45
Avis, G., 7

B

Balzer, H. D., 9
Barber, B., 31, 84
Barnum, D. G., 103
Barry, D. D., 148, 160, 163, 168, 169, 171
Barry, M., 81
Bauer, O., 193
Bauer, R., 94, 104
Baum, L., 183
Bawn, K., 70
Beissinger. M. R., 205, 207
Belka, M., 243
Bell, J., 146
Bentley, A. F., 190
Berglund, S., 14
Berman, H. J., 113, 114, 115
Beschel, R. P. Jr., 248, 257
Bhagwati, J., 228
Bobbio, N., 32, 45
Bodie, W. C., 254, 255, 261
Bollen, K. A., 55
Bolz, H. F., 183
Bova, R., 69
Bovend'Eert, P. P. T., 129
Boycko, M., 242, 243
Boyle, H., 84
Bradley, A. W., 113, 143
Brass, P. R., 197, 203
Breslauer, G., 254
Brezhnev doctrine, 11
Brody, R. A., 103
Brown, A., 7
Brunner, G., 161, 164, 166, 182, 183
Brzezinski, Z., 94, 104, 119, 138, 167, 168, 178, 254, 255
Buergenthal, T., 113
Burbulis, G., 43
Burrage, M., 156, 158
Burton, M., 32, 67

Burton, S. J., 123
Butler, W. E., 152, 160
Butterfield, J., 9

C

Campbell, A. et al., 84
Cappelletti, M., 146, 152, 153, 164
Carey, J. M., 72
Carlisle, D. S., 206
Caspar, G., 68
Ceaser, J. W., 27, 28
CEELI, 131, 155
Censorship, 13
Central Intelligence Agency, 233
Chase, W. J., 3
Chechan Autonomous Republic, 13
Choices facing builders of liberal democracy, 24–51
  conditions within a democracy, 38–43
  democracy and the post-communist countries, 43–44
  democratic processes, 29–38
  path to modern democratic ideals, 25–29
Civil society, 59–60
Clark, D. S., 146, 147, 167
Clinton, W., 92
Coleman, J. S., 33, 210
Collignon, J. -G., 181
Collins, H., 117
Communism, decline and fall of, 9–11
Communist rule, strengths and weaknesses, 6–8
  political socialization, 7
  social contract, 8
Comparative historical approaches to democratization,
  theoretical cluster 2, 58–66
  concepts, 59–62
  employing the concepts, 62–64
  evaluation, 64–66
Connor, W., 203, 213
Conquest, R., 19
Constitutional design and the stability of democracy,
  theoretical cluster 4, 70–72
Constitutionalism, 37–38
Constitutionalism and the rule of law, 111–143
  meanings of and communist attitudes toward, 112–121
  relationship to democracy and free markets, 121–130
  transition to, 130–135
Constitutionality of legislation and constitutional courts,
  review of, 164–174
  Poland, 164–168
  Russia, 168–174
Constitutions and statutes, 184–185
  Poland, 184
  Russian Federation, 184–185
  Soviet Union, 184
Converse, P. E., 30
Cook, L. J., 8
Coser, L. A., 90
Cultural pluralism, 194–196

D

Dabrowa, S. A., 253
Dahl, R. A., 15, 29, 30, 32, 33, 39, 40, 55, 56, 57, 84, 86, 90, 217
Dahrendorf, R., 112
Dallin, A., 9
Dalton, R. J., 30, 87, 102
Davies, N., 155
Dawson, A. H., 155
Decalo, S., 17
Decontrolling prices and production, 234–235
de Lauretis, T., 103
Dellenbrant, J. A., 14
Democracy, conditions within, 38–43
  liberty, equality, and the tension between them, 40–41
  peaceful conflict resolution, 42–43
  popular empowerment, 38–40
  protection of rights of individuals, 41–42
Democracy, establishing and strengthening, 52–78
  democratization, 53–54
  theoretical clusters, 54–72
Democracy in the post-communist world, 11–15
  Central Europe, Eastern Europe, and the FSU, 14–15
  Russia, 11–14
Democratic ideals, modern, history of, 25–29
Democratic processes, 29–38
  constitutional constraints on policy, 37–38
  importance of competition, 31–33
  institutional variants, 35–37

methods of representation, 34–35
popular participation, 30–31
voting and rule by majority, 33–34
Democratic theory and post-communist change, 15–18
Democratization, 53–54
Diamond, L., 55, 72, 248, 251
Di Palma, G., 15, 16, 87, 102, 248, 249, 257, 258
Downing, B. M., 28
Downs, A., 35
Duch, R., 89, 95, 96, 98, 101, 103, 104
Dunn, J., 27
Duverger's law, 34
Dworkin, R. M., 42, 112, 138

E

Eckstein, H., 43, 81, 92, 101
Economic policy and democratization in former communist states, 217–247
ambiguities of transitions, 217–223
stabilization policy, 223–233
structural adjustment and economic policy in the longer run, 233–243
Economic and political transitions, ambiguities of, 217–223
timing issues, 220–223
Ekiert, G., 14, 65
Elkins, D. J., 103
Elster, J., 38, 131, 135
Entman, R. M., 102
Epstein, D. A., 42
Ethnic conflict, theories of, 192–198
cultural pluralism, 194–196
Marxism, 192–193
modernization, 193–194
rational choice, 197–198
relative group worth, 196–197
Ethnic factor in political development, 201–206
Etzioni, A., 47, 92
Evans, P. B., 46
Exports, 225–226
External assistance, noneconomic modes of, 257–258
External efficacy, 87

F

Farber, S., 3
Feldbrugge, F. J. M., 181
First, R., 17
Fischer, S., 230
Fitzpatrick, S., 4
Former communist states, how to understand probable future, 1–23
communist rule: its strengths and weaknesses, 6–8
decline and fall of communism, 9–11
democracy in post-communist world, 11–15
democratic theory and post-communist change, 15–18
rise of communism and its transformation to Stalinism, 2–6
Foster, F. H., 154, 171, 175
Frankowski, S., 119, 147, 150, 152, 153, 155
Frentzel-Zagorska, J., 64
Friedgut, T. H., 5
Fukuyama, F., 25, 73, 190
Fuller, L., 142
Furnival, J. S., 194

G

Gajewska-Kraczkowska, H., 156, 157, 180
Galanter, M., 180
Galtung, J., 193
Garfield, A., 147, 150, 153, 155, 156, 157, 158, 159, 181
Garlicki, L., 147, 153, 155
Gelener, E., 194
Getty, J. A., 19
Gibson, J., 89, 95, 96, 98, 103, 104
Giddens, A., 90
Gill, G., 4
Ginsburgs, G., 178, 179
Gladdish, K., 72, 74
Glasnost, 10
Goble, P., 255
Goldfarb, J., 66
Gorbachev, Mikhail, 9–11
Gostynski, Z., 147, 150, 153, 155, 156, 157, 158, 159, 181
Gould, H. A., 194
Gradualism, 220–223
Gramsci, A., 46, 60
Granik, L. A., 157, 158, 159, 181
Grey, R. D., 1–23, 94, 104, 248–266
Grofman, B., 47
Gunther, R., 32, 67

H

Hahn, J. W., 5, 7, 95, 97, 102, 104
Haley, J. O., 167
Hardin, R., 197
Hatch, J. B., 3
Hausmaninger, H., 168
Hayek, F. A., 128
Hazard, J. N., 118, 121, 138
Hechter, M., 193
Held, D., 39, 84, 85
Henderson, J., 150, 151
Herring, E., 250
Hesli, V. L., 95, 96, 97, 102, 190–216
Heywood, A., 46
Heywood, P., 14
Higley, J., 32, 67
Hoffman, E. P., 175
Höhmann, H. -H. C. M., 250
Hopf, T., 254
Hornblower, S., 28
Horowitz, D. L., 74, 196, 203, 209, 210, 214
Hough, J. F., 57, 105, 218
Huber, J. D., 72
Huntington, S. P., 14, 17, 29, 55, 68, 102, 248, 250, 251, 258, 264
Huskey, E., 118, 119, 120, 148, 152, 153, 155, 156, 158, 159, 163, 179
Hutchinson, A. C., 112, 121, 122, 125, 126

I

Impact of external factors of future of democracy in FSU and Eastern Europe, 248–266
  international context and democratization, 258–262
  international powers and promotion of democracy during the Cold War, 249–252
  noneconomic modes of external assistance, 257–258
  support for a market economy, 256–257
Imports, 225
Individual rights, protection of, 41–42
Inflation, 224–225
Influence of ordinary people in democratic societies, 83–86
Inglehart, R., 57, 90, 102, 105
Inkeles, A., 94, 104
Inotai, A., 253
International context and democratization, 258–262
International economic developments, 62
International Monetary Fund and conditionality, 228–233
International powers and the promotion of democracy
  after the Cold War, 252–256
  during the Cold War, 249–252
International trade, removing controls on, 235–239
Interpersonal trust and cooperative social relations, 90–91
Intra-elite bargaining and transitions to democracy,
  theoretical cluster 3, 67–70
Isaac, J. C., 84, 85, 102

J

Jennisch, L., 94, 104
Jones, A., 179
Jowitt, K., 57–58
Joyce, W., 9
Judicial independence, 146–155
  jury system, 154–155
  lack of material support, 150–151
  selection and supervision of judges, 146–150
  supervision by prokuratura and Ministry of Justice, 152–154
Judicial review, forms of, development, 159–174
  review of executive and administrative acts, 160–164
  review of constitutionality and constitutional courts, 164–174
Judicial review, problem of, 128–130
Jury system, 154, 155

K

Kahn, A. E., 235
Kahn, M., 232
Kaplan, C., 97, 104
Karaganov, S. A., 253
Karatnycky, A., 52
Karl, T. L., 24, 46, 68, 82
Katzenstein, M. F., 194
Keane, J., 46, 59
Kennedy, D., 122
Keynes, J. M., 224
Khrushchev, 8

Kim, J. -O., 41, 47, 92
Kiss, E., 95, 96
Kitschelt, H., 74, 248
Knight, A., 6
Koch, B., 250
Komsomol, 7
Kondracki, J. A., 155
Kornai, J., 127, 243
Kornhauser, W., 84
Kortmann, C. A. J. M., 129
Kozyrev, A., 252, 255
Krajewski, S., 243
Krygier, M., 112, 116, 125
Kuss, K. -J., 160, 161, 164, 165, 178, 181

L

Lane, D., 9, 219
La Palombara, J., 114
Lapidus, G. W., 9
Lardeyret, G., 74
Lawyers Committee for Human Rights, 148, 149, 151, 153, 178, 179, 180
Legal profession, strengthening independence of, 146–159
  development of independent legal profession, 155–159
  judicial independence, 146–155
Lempert, D., 97
Lenin, V. I., 62, 193
Lesage, M., 163, 181
Levine, D. H., 74
Lewin, M., 9, 57, 105
Liberty, equality, and the tension between them, 40–41
Lien, M. W., 118, 169, 171, 172, 184
Lijphart, A., 29, 36, 47, 70, 71, 72, 206
Lindblom, C. E., 32
Linz, J. L., 53, 72, 74, 209
Lipset, S. M., 15, 55, 74, 101, 217
Losonci, V., 115, 133, 134
Lowenthal, A. F., 17, 248
Luhmann, N., 90
Lukin, V. P., 252

M

Macaulay, S., 127
MacIntyre, A., 92
MacPherson, C. B., 84, 85
Maher, K. H., 79–110, 95, 102
Mainwaring, S., 52
Maital, S., 224, 234
Majoritarian or plurality voting, 34
Malenkov, 8
Manning, R., 19
Marcus, G. M., 103
Markov, S., 20
Markovits, I., 119, 159, 161, 163, 181
Marsh, N. S., 113, 138
Marx, Karl, 2–3
Marxism, 192–193
Mass values and democratic institutions, relationship between, 80–82
Mass values, role of, 79–110
  do "the people" matter to democracy? 80–86
  orientations supportive of democracy, 86–93
  political ortientations in post-communist countries, 93–99
  what can we expect? 99–101
Mathernova, K., 119
McAuley, M., 105
McCaffrey, S. C., 160, 181
McCauley, M., 9
McFaul, M., 20
McKinnon, R., 230
Meadwell, H., 198, 201, 209
Merryman, J. H., 167
Mestrovic, S., 14
Meyer, A. G., 44, 47
Michels, R., 103
Migranyan, A., 65
Mihalka, M., 205
Mill, J. S., 190
Millar, J. R., 104
Miller, A. H., 95, 96, 97, 102
Miller, B., 14
Miller, R. F., 39
Milner, B. -Z., 224, 234
Mishler, W. T. E., 95, 104
Modernization, 193–194
Monahan, P., 112, 121, 125
Moore, B. Jr., 28, 63, 74, 218
Motyl, A., 197, 198, 201, 209
Mroz, J. E., 248, 255, 256
Mueller, D. C., 209
Muller, E. N.,
Müller, I., 179
Multiparty competition and nonviolent conflict resolution, 86–87
Murachik, J., 248
Murrell, P., 243

Murukami, Y., 45
Mutti, J. H., 217–247

N

Nahaylo, B., 205
National separation and the demise of the Soviet state, 198–201
Nayyar, R., 230
New Economic Policy (NEP), 118
Neumann, F., 138
Nie, N. H., 41, 92
Nodia, G., 191, 213
Nordlinger, E. A., 214
Nowak, J. E., 165, 183

O

Octobrists, 7
Oda, H., 162
O'Donnell, G., 32, 55, 69, 74
Ohn, M. -G., 47
Oldenburg, F., 250, 254
Oliver, J., 5
Olson, M., 233
Ombudsman, 161, 163–164
Ordeshook, P. C., 72
Orientations supportive of democracy, 86–93
 external efficacy, 87
 interpersonal trust and cooperative social relations, 90–91
 multiparty competition and nonviolent conflict resolution, 86–87
 participatory orientation and efficacy, 91–92
 political tolerance, 88–89
 rule of law and democratic constitution, 87–88
 value of individual liberty/rights, 89–90
Otyrba, G., 211

P

Pactadura, 67–68
Page, B. I., 103
Palmer, G., 129
Participatory orientation and efficacy, 91–92
Pateman, C., 31, 84, 85, 91, 92
Peaceful conflict resolution, 42–43
Peck, M. J., 235
Pei, M., 218, 256
Pennock, J. R., 29, 45
Perestroika, 10
Phillips, D. L., 47
Piereson, J. E., 103
Pinto, B., 243
Pipes, R., 94, 104
Poland, 164–168
Political institutions and democratic governance in divided societies, 190–216
 ethnic factor in political development, 201–206
 national separatism and demise of Soviet state, 198–201
 strategies for accommodating ethnicity, 206–212
 theories of ethnic conflict, 192–198
Political orientations in post-communist societies, 93–99
 post-glasnost studies, 94–99
 pre-glasnost studies, 94
Political tolerance, 88–89
Pomorski, S., 119
Popkin, S., 103
Popular empowerment, 38–40
Porter, B. D., 254
Powell, G. B., 36, 43, 45, 47, 71, 72, 105
Premdas, R. R., 213
Pridham, G., 14, 250
Privatizing state assets, 239–243
Prokuratura, 146, 152–154, 160
Proportional representation (PR), 34
Przeworski, A., 15, 32, 38, 45, 46, 67, 102, 103, 245, 248
Putnam, R., 82, 91, 92
Pye, L. W., 101, 102, 194

Q

Quade, Q., 74
Quigley, J., 120, 152, 153, 155, 160, 162, 165

R

Rae, D. W., 47, 209
Rational choice, 197–198
Rechtsstaat, 114–115
Reform commission, 120–121
Reid, C. T., 161
Reiman, M., 4
Reisinger, W. R., 24–51, 51–78, 95, 96, 97, 98, 102, 104, 105
Reitz, J., 111–143, 144–189
Relative group worth, 196–197

Remington, T., 7
Roberts, N. S., 89
Rockman, B. A., 47
Roeder, P., 14
Roper, J., 33, 44
Rose, R., 95, 104
Rothberg, A., 9
Rotunda, R. D., 165, 183
Rueschemeyer, D., 46, 61, 63, 64
Rule of law, definition of and communist attitudes toward, 112–121
Rule of law and democratic constitution, 87–88
Rule of law and its relationship to democracy and free markets, 121–130
- law and politics, 122–126
- problem of judicial review, 128–130
- rule of law and democratic order, 121
- rule of law and free markets, 127–128

Rule of law, progress in building institutions in Russia and Poland, 144–189
- development of forms of judicial review, 159–174
- strengthening independence of legal profession, 146–159

Rule of law, traditional communist rejection of, 117–120
Rule of law, transition to, 130–135
Russia, 168–174
Rustow, D. A., 43, 67, 102
Rutland, P., 242

S

Sabbat-Swidlicka,, A., 150
Sachs, J., 229, 234, 242
Saivetz, C., 254
Sajó, A., 115, 133, 134, 150
Sakwa, R., 20, 219
Sanford, G., 250
Sartori, G., 16, 29, 84, 86
Saunders, H. H., 254
Savitsky, V., 149, 150, 162, 178, 179, 182
Schattschneider, E. E., 31, 44
Scheinin, M., 168
Schmitter, P. C., 24, 32, 46, 53, 69, 74, 82
Schnably, S. J., 133
Schultz, D., 5
Schultz, F. M., 127
Schumpeter, J., 31, 83, 84
Schwartz, H., 161, 163, 164, 165, 166, 168, 169, 178, 183
Scott, J. C., 90
Sedaitis, J. B., 9
Seligman, A. B., 60
Sergeyev, V., 20
Sestanovich, S., 255, 261
Shamir, M., 89
Shapiro, R. Y., 103
Sharlet, R., 138, 169, 171, 173, 183
Shelley, L. I., 115, 118
Shleifer, A., 242, 243
Shock therapy, 220–223
Shugart, M. S., 36, 47, 72
Shvetsova, O. V., 72
Siegelbaum, L. H., 3
Simon, J., 95, 97, 98, 104
Skach, C., 74
Skinner, Q., 27
Skocpol, T., 46, 59, 64
Slater, W., 171, 172
Slaton, C. D., 31
Slider, D., 211, 214
Smith, A. D., 191
Smith, G. B., 94
Smith, M. G., 194
Sniderman, P. M., 99, 103
Sobchak, A. A., 111, 119
Social modernization as a precondition for democratization, theoretical cluster 1, 54–58
Socioeconomic classes, 61–62
Solé Tura, J., 131
Solomon, P. H. Jr., 118, 120, 148, 160
Somers, M., 64
Sorenson, E., 85
Stabilization policy, 223–233
- exports, 225–226
- foreign aid, 227–228
- foreign investment, 226–227
- imports, 225
- inflation, 224–225
- International Monetary Fund and conditionality, 228–233

Stalin, Josif, 4
Starr, F., 105
Starr, H., 249
State, the, 59
Steele, J., 20
Stepan, A., 60, 61, 74, 209
Stephens, E. H., 61, 63, 64
Stephens, J. D., 61, 63, 64
Stern, K., 137
Stouffer, S., 103

Structural adjustment and economic policy, 233–243
decontrolling prices and production, 234–235
privatizing state assets, 239–243
removing controls on international trade, 235–239
Sullivan, J., 89, 103
Summers, L., 227
Sunstein, C. R., 128
Sysyn, F., 205

T

Taagepera, R., 36, 47
Taylor, M., 68
Tedin, K., 95, 96, 98, 104
Tetlock, P. E., 103
Thorson, C., 150, 151
Ticktin, H., 9
Tilly, C., 64
Timmerman, H., 250
Toharia, J. J., 139
Truman, D., 32
Tsarist regime, 2
Tucker, R. C., 104, 192
Tyler, A., 94, 104

U

Urabe, N., 114, 180
United Nations, 237, 239

V

Value of individual liberty/rights orientation, 89–90
Van Dyke, V., 29
Vanhanen, T., 14, 15, 217, 250
Venclova, T., 200
Verba, S., 41, 56, 81, 92, 101, 102
Vishny, R., 242, 243

W

Wade, E. C. S., 113, 143
Walker, G. deQ., 112, 116, 136
Wallich, C., 230
Walsh, P., 89
Ware, A., 60
Weaver, R. K., 47
Weber, M., 59
Weiner, M., 194
Weintraub, J., 60
White, S., 5, 7, 8, 9, 14, 57, 94, 102, 104
Whitehead, L., 248, 249, 250, 251, 252
Wiersbowski, M., 160, 181
Wilson, J. Q., 183
Wishnevsky, J., 171, 172
Wolchik, S., 95, 97, 98, 99, 105
Wolf, N., 103
World Bank, 227, 237
Wyman, M., 14

Y

Yeltsin, Boris, 11–14
Young, J. N., 165, 183
Young Communist League, see Komsomol
Young Pioneers, 7

Z

Zelikov, P., 254, 261